JAGIRDARS IN THE MUGHAL EMPIRE DURING THE REIGN OF AKBAR

Jagirdars in the Mughal Empire During the Reign of Akbar

BALKRISHAN SHIVRAM

MANOHAR
2008

First published 2008

ISBN 81-7304-766-9

Published by
Ajay Kumar Jain *for*
Manohar Publishers & Distributors
4753/23 Ansari Road, Daryaganj
New Delhi 110 002

Printed at
Lordson Publishers Pvt Ltd
Delhi 110 007

To
Amma and Pitaji

Contents

Tables

Abbreviations

AA	*Ain-i-Akbari*
AMU	Aligarh Muslim University
AN	*Akbarnama*
Arif	*Tarikh-i-Akbari*
Bayazid	*Tazkira-i-Humayun wa Akbar*
Bib.Ind.	*Bibliotheca Indica, Calcutta*
Elliot	*History of India as Told by Its Own Historians*
Farishta	*Rise of Mohammadan Power in India*
IESHR	*The Indian Economic and Social History Review*
IHR	*The Indian Historical Review*
IIAS	Indian Institute of Advanced Study, Shimla
Iqbalnama	*Iqbalnama-i-Jahangiri*
JRAS	*Journal of the Royal Asiatic Society*
Khyat	*Munhot Nainsi ri Khyat*
Manucci	*Storia Do Mogor*, 1653-1708
MAS	*Modern Asian Studies*
MD	*Mughal Darbar* (Hindi tr. of *Maasir-ul-Umara*)
Medieval Gujarat	Based on Mohammad Ali Khan's *Mirat-i-Ahmadi* transcribed in 1822 by Narsain Dass of Kait Tribe at Ahmedabad, tr. James Bird
Mirat	*Mirat-i-Ahmadi*
MR	*Maasir-i-Rahimi*
MS	Manuscript
MT	*Muntakhab-ut-Tawarikh*
MU	*Maasir-ul-Umara*
OUP	Oxford University Press
PIHR	*Proceedings of the Indian History Congress*
Refaqat Ali	*Kachhwahas Under Akbar and Jahangir*
Stewart	*The History of Bengal* by Charles Stewart
TA	*Tabaqat-i-Akbari*
TM	*Tarikh-i-Masumi*

tr.	English translation
TT	*Tarikh-i-Tahari*
TU	*Tazkirat-ul-Umara*
Tuzuk	*Tuzuk-i-Jahangiri*
Vigat	*Marwar ra Pargana ri Vigat* by Munhot Nainsi
Vir Vinod	*Vir Vinod* by Kaviraj Shyamal Das
Z and *S*	*Zat* and *Sawar* (ranks)
ZK	*Zakhirat-ul-Khawanin*

Preface

The majority of historians working on medieval India classify the pre-colonial political system under one or more of the following three theoretical concepts: feudalism, segmentary state and patrimonialism. The models of the segmentary state and the patrimonial state are both applied to late medieval India. In the context of the Mughal state, even one and a half centuries after the exile of its last ruler Bahadur Shah II to Rangoon, it remains an active field of research in pre-colonial Indian history. More recently, Muzaffar Alam and Sanjay Subrahmanyam have raised pertinent questions: what after all was 'the Mughal state'? Leviathan or paper tiger? An inexorable instrument of political and fiscal centralization or a mere carapace? A conquest state or a proto-national entity?

Since its establishment in the sixteenth century the Mughal Empire in India has produced a rich historiography. The value judgements of historians on personalities, as on periods of history, are carried over as axioms in historiography. The writings on Mughal rulers give an insight into the mind of monarchs, and rev eal the different pressures they had to face in building up the imperial system. Clerics discussed the role Islam should play in the policies of rulers, and chronicles recorded the working of the imperial administration. European travellers reflected on the system through the eyes of the other.

The Mughal Empire was one of the largest centralized states known in pre-modern world history. It was founded in the early 1500s and by the end of the following century the Mughal emperor ruled almost the entire Indian subcontinent with a population varying between 100 and 150 millions (five times that of the Ottoman Empire, almost twenty that of the Safavid) and lands covering most of the Indian subcontinent (3.2 million sq. km.). Mughal or Timurid India far outstripped in sheer size and resources its two rival early modern Islamic Empires—Safavid Persia and Ottoman Turkey. The Mughal emperor's land and subjects were comparable only to those ruled by his contemporary, the Ming Emperor in early modern China.

The study of social and economic history of India is one of the dominant trends of recent historiography. In the past few decades a number of interpretations have been offered on the nature of the Mughal Empire. These interpretations are based principally on the *mansabdari* and *jagirdari* systems introduced during the reign of Akbar. It was these systems which generated the centripetal tendencies in linking the remote areas with the heart of the empire, the emperor. The present work shows how the focus has shifted over the years from the centre to the periphery, from the court to the locality, from the nitty-gritty of administration to the cultural rituals of kingship.

A large volume of work has been produced by scholars on *mansab* and *mansabdari* ever since the pioneer work of W.H. Moreland. However, the *jagirdari* system still remains an inadequately researched subject, even though scholars have for long realized the importance of its study. Satish Chandra's *Parties and Politics at the Mughal Court* (1959), for instance, has considered the *jagirdari* crisis as the basic cause of the downfall of the Mughal Empire. Irfan Habib, in his seminal work *The Agrarian System of Mughal India* (1963), has also sought to explain the fall of the Mughal Empire as an effect of the working of the *jagirdari* system. Francois Bernier's famous statement that the transfer of *jagirs* led to the ever-increasing oppression and ruining of the peasantry has found support amongst scholars and it certainly needs to be examined more closely. The Mughal officers received their salary either in cash (*naqd*) or in terms of the revenues of various territories, known as *jagirs*. Like the *iqta* of the Delhi sultanate, a *jagir* was the right to the revenue from a specified parcel of land, although it did not carry with it the administrative rights to the tract that were normally conferred on recipients of *iqtas*. The analysis of the structure and functioning of the *jagirdari* system is an extremely important theme of research because of the centrality of the institution to the Mughal political edifice. The organization of *jagirs* and their distribution played a key role in the political evolution of the Mughal Empire as it defined the relationship between the emperor and the nobles, determined the latter's fortune and had a close bearing on economic production. Indeed, the *jagir* has been an important element in discussion on the rise and fall of the Mughal Empire. The *jagirdari* system which evolved during the reign of Akbar actually served as a solid foundation for the Mughal government system. The problems which the *jagirdars* (holders of *jagirs*) faced in the work of revenue collection and government in its evolutionary phase under Akbar, when the system was evolving and not yet been standardized, stand in need of detailed critical analyses. At the same time the way the emperor sought to restrain the authority of the *jagirdars*—and the extent to which he succeeded in it—have to be carefully examined. No serious attention has been devoted by scholars to its evolutionary phase which presented a different picture from the fully evolved Mughal revenue assignment system. Iqtidar Alam Khan in his seminal article 'The Mughal Assignment System During Akbar's Early Years, 1556-1575', has revealed some new and interesting direction of research and inquiry. Even Iqtidar Alam Khan deals only with the early years of Akbar's reign and omits some important aspects of the *jagirdari* system, as it existed during the reign of Akbar. Here, it would be worthwhile to refer to the works of some scholars whose observations about the *jagirdari* system in the sixteenth–seventeenth century are significantly contradictory to mine: W.H. Moreland's *The Agrarian System of Moslem India* (1929); Satish Chandra's *Parties and Politics at the Mughal Court* (1959); Irfan Habib's *The Agrarian System of Mughal India* (1963); M. Athar Ali's *The Mughal Nobility Under Aurangzeb* (1966) and Noman Ahmad Siddiqi's *Mughal Land Revenue Administration Under the Mughals* (1970). As a matter of fact, their work has significantly contributed to a critical reconsideration of my own conclusions.

The Mughal Empire had once rested upon a firm base of military power, sustained by the loyalty of men of talent to the central figure of authority, the emperor. The emperor's authority, effected in the first instance by military conquest, was then perpetuated by an elaborate structure of symbols and rituals. Mughal emperors fashioned a system of symbols and rituals necessary for a pervasive network of authoritative and hierarchical relationship. The rituals that symbolized imperial authority took various forms, all of them designed to confirm the personal ties of loyalty among the emperor and his officers at the apex of the Mughal administrative hierarchy. An example of the ritual that best symbolized the personal loyalty of the subordinate to the emperor and the exchange of the patronage for service was the exchange of gifts. The subordinate would present the emperor two categories of gifts, *nazr* and *peshkash;* and the emperor would reciprocate by presenting his servant with a *khilat* or robe of honour, a horse or an elephant, jewelled weapons, money or other artefacts. An imperative ingredient in this exchange was its personal and incorporative nature (Chapter 4).

This book is the revised version of my doctoral thesis submitted to the Himachal Pradesh University, Shimla in 1996. In the course of revision I have been able to unearth a great deal of new evidence which has been incorporated in various chapters of this book. This evidence has helped me look at certain features of the *jagirdari* system from an altogether different perspective. This book, as the title reveals, does not pretend to cover the entire Mughal period, but concerns itself mainly with the reign of Akbar.

I am grateful to many scholars for shaping my ideas over the years. Professor Chetan Singh encouraged my initial forays and nurtured my attempts in this direction when he supervised my doctoral thesis. I will ever remain beholden to him for many insights he shared with me, for his mastery over the records pertaining to this period and for his personal warmth and affection. I am greatly indebted to Iqtidar Hussain Siddiqi, Iqtidar Alam Khan and Ahsan Raza Khan for their insightful comments which helped me in making substantial modifications to bridge certain gaps in my analyses.

My deep gratitude to Professor Laxman Thakur, who was always willing to advise me on many issues directly or indirectly relevant to this study.

I am grateful to Muzaffar Alam, Professor in the Department of South Asian Language and Civilization, University of Chicago and Refaqat Ali Khan, former Professor of History, Jamia Millia Islamia, New Delhi, for their critical evaluation of my thesis and valuable suggestions for revising it. In writing this book I have become deeply conscious of my debt to other scholars in this field. Among these I would like to mention Irfan Habib, Satish Chandra, M. Athar Ali, Noman Ahmad Siddiqi and Shireen Moosvi whose pioneering works enlightened me and provided me with various critical perspectives to build on in the present study. My intellectual debt to the authors of recent writings on the sixteenth century is evident from the endnotes, and calls for no special mention.

In order to clarify and substantiate the various aspects of the present study, I have considered appropriate to add a few tables and appendices which claim no perfection but which may prove useful in understanding various postulations and observations made by me. At the end of the book a classified select bibliography has been appended for necessary references.

I have aimed at simplicity in my translations, omitting diacritical marks as irrelevant for most readers and superfluous for skilled linguists. Persian and Indian terms not in common use in English language have been italicized and their plurals have been indicated by adding the letter 's'. For spellings and transliterations of Perso–Arabic and Turkish words, I have generally followed the system adopted by F. Steingass in his *Comprehensive Persian-English Dictionary.* For geographical names I have followed Irfan Habib's *Atlas of the Mughal Empire,* I have dispensed with diacritical marks in place names, since these are provided in the index of the *Atlas.*

This study is, in fact, based on original sources. The translations of the Mughal chronicles have been verified by the original texts. For the sake of conciseness, notes are given only wherever necessary. I have used abbreviations generally in tables. For a few important sources, when a published translation of a Persian text is available, I have cited both together except in tables, with the volume number, if different, and page number of the Persian text in square brackets. The spellings of place names given by Irfan Habib in his *Atlas* are generally used.

I am extremely grateful to the authorities of the Indian Institute of Advanced Study (IIAS) and Himachal Pradesh University Libraries, Shimla who extended all possible co-operation and went out of their way to make my work easy. A major part of research material for this book was collected from the IIAS. My thanks are also due to the authorities of the Department of History Library and the Maulana Azad Library, Aligarh Muslim University (Aligarh), Indian National Archives, National Museum, Central Secretariat Library, Jawaharlal Nehru University Library, Jamia Islamia University Library, University of Delhi Library, Indian Council of Historical Research (Delhi), Central Library BHU, Allahabad University Library, Rajasthan University Central Library and Himachal Pradesh Archives, Shimla.

Finally, I shall be failing if I do not thank Manohar Publishers for careful editing and meticulous production. All shortcomings and mistakes in this book, can only be due to my own shortcomings, for which I look forward to concrete suggestions from keen researchers, general readers and reviewers.

Shimla BALKRISHAN SHIVRAM

CHAPTER 1

Introduction

The Mughal[1] Empire was one of the largest centralized states of the pre-modern world history. By the late 1600s the Mughal emperor held supreme political authority over lands covering most of the Indian subcontinent (3.2 million sq km). Continuing in the tradition of Ibn Hasan, Paramatma Saran, Satish Chandra and Irfan Habib, John F. Richards argued that for nearly 170 years (1556-1719)[2] the Mughal Empire remained a dynamic, centralized, complex organization.[3] The emperor commanded cadres of officials and soldiers of proven loyalty who carried out his orders in every province. Men, money, information and resources moved regularly and routinely throughout the empire as official needs dictated. Mughal success was the outcome of hard-driving, active rulership exercised by extremely capable rulers who acted as their own chief executives. Military victory, territorial expansion and centralized control rested upon strategic vision and the management skills of the emperors and their advisors.

The empire was more than a superficial canopy stretched over the substantial social life of each region. It was an intrusive, centralizing system, which unified the subcontinent. Imperial military power imposed an unprecedented level of public order. The scale and level of organized violence diminished perceptibly in the lands within its borders. Imperial demands for revenue and tribute stimulated production and encouraged market growth. The uniform practices and ubiquitous presence of the Mughals left an imprint upon society in every locality and region of the subcontinent. Few persons and communities, if any, were left untouched by this massive edifice. If so, what was then the basis upon which the entire administrative structure of the Mughal Empire was founded?

The development of firearms has been regarded by some authorities as the underlying cause of the formation of great Asian empires of the sixteenth and seventeenth centuries.[4] The adequacy of this explanation in the case of the Indian Mughals may, however, be questioned. Artillery was not the decisive element of the army and the Mughals were never able to employ it very successfully against strong fortifications. The real strength of the Mughal forces lay in the cavalry. Not surprisingly, therefore, the principal obligation of the *mansabdars* (officers holding specified numerical ranks)[5] was the maintenance of cavalry contingents with horses of standard breeds. For this purpose they were given *jagirs* or territorial assignments of revenue in lieu of salary (*dar wajh-i alufa*). There was an intimate connection between the military powers of the Mughals and the *jagirdari* or assignment system. It was because of this system that the *mansabdars* became completely dependent upon the will of the emperor. The imperial government was, therefore, able to assemble and dispatch *mansabdars* along with their contingents to any place at any time, where and when the need arose.

Under the Mughals the officers could be employed either on military duty or in civil administration. Mughal officers at any particular time could be divided into two groups: *tainat-i-rakab*, or those who were stationed at the court; and the *tainat-i-subajat*, or those who were posted in the provinces. This division was based solely on the posting of individual officers who were frequently transferred from one group to the other. The monarch determined the physical location of his officers even when they were stationed elsewhere. Most of the *mansabdars* spent their careers either in a court post or in attendance at court, in a post in the provinces, or in transit between the court and a post. Officers were rarely given permission to be anywhere else—their *watans* or *jagirs* most frequently—and leaving their posts without permission, even to go to court, was an offence. Flight from the court constituted rebellion, as in the case of Mirza Sharafuddin Husain Ahrari.[6] The chronicles do not refer to departures from court, only to receiving permission to leave. There were no set rules regarding the posting of nobles at the court or outside it. However, their natural talents were kept in view while allocating a position to them. The officers engaged in service were entitled to receive an income in money, corresponding to their rank. The actual payment could be made either in cash (*naqd*) from the treasury, or by assignment of revenues of a specific area of land from which they were entitled to collect the land revenue and all other taxes (*mal-i wajib o huquq-i diwani*)[7] imposed or sanctioned by the emperor. The partial payment of both these methods was another means by which a *mansabdar* could receive his dues.[8] The emperor decided whether a *mansabdar* would receive his pay in cash or in *jagir* or in both.

DIVISION OF LAND REVENUE

During the Mughal period the land revenue was distributed among persons from different socio-political backgrounds. Persons from a religious background and the needy were assigned revenue free lands known as *milk*, *aimma*, *madad-i-maash* and *suyurghal*. The land revenue of some areas was earmarked as *khalisa-sharifa* and the income from them was remitted to the imperial treasury. The emperor assigned the revenue of a particular area to a noble in lieu of his salary. Such a revenue assignment was known in the Ottoman Empire as *timar*, in the Safavid Empire as *tuyul*, and in the Mughal Empire as *jagir* (less often as *iqta* or *tuyul*) and the assignee was known as *jagirdar*.

Suyurghal Lands

The Muslim rulers of India granted rent-free lands to men of piety and learning, and to persons belonging to noble families who had no other means of earning their livelihood. The Mughals continued the practice of granting subsistence allowance to the pious, the learned, the poor and the needy and to the Shaikhs, the Sayyids and Irani and Turani women.[9] Such a subsistence allowance could be granted in cash or in the form of a grant of land. The subsistence allowance in land was known as *madad-i-maash* or *milk*.[10] However, the term *suyurghal* was also used in the documents of Akbar's reign in particular.[11] Under Akbar, the conditions of the assignment of *madad-i-maash* lands were liberalized so as to help a larger number of people. According to Abul Fazl, persons belonging to four classes were eligible for the grant of *madad-i-maash* lands. First, those who were seekers after the truth and who had renounced the world; second, persons who strove to suppress sensual and carnal desires and had chosen a life of self-abnegation and self-effacement; third, the weak and the poor who could not earn their livelihood on account of physical disability; fourth, honourable men of gentle birth, who foolishly deemed it below their dignity or social status to follow any trade or profession.[12] Here, it is worth mentioning that this categorization applied to men of all religions. The recipients of such grant included the *ulema* and the *makhadim*. It was from amongst these classes that *sadrs*, *qazis* and *hafizs*, *maulavis* and *muazzins* were appointed. The recipients of the *madad-i-maash* grants included destitute women and institution like *khanqas*, shrines, temples and *maths*. The recipients of the *madad-i-maash* grants generally belonged to the orthodox class and as such constituted a bastion of conservatism to a large extent. The grantees were expected to engage themselves in praying for the perpetuity of the empire. The *madad-i-maash* grantees penetrated deep into the countryside and served as unofficial apologists and propagandists of the Mughal Empire. They, thus, constituted pockets of influence in rural areas.[13] Jahangir appropriately described them as an 'Army of the Prayers'.

In the early period of the Delhi Sultanate the terms used for subsistence allowance were *milk*, *wazifa*, *inam* and *auqaf*.[14] Subsequently, they were referred to as *wajh-i-maash*, *wajh-i-milk*, *idrarat* and *waqf* endowments.[15] Under the Mughals, the term *madad-i-maash* was commonly used except in the documents belonging to Akbar's reign for revenue-free land grant as compared with *milk*, *wajh-i-maash*, *inam* and *aimma*. Indeed, one *farman* of Babur (1526-30) on revenue-free land grants mentions the word *suyurghal*,[16] but in two other *farmans* of the same period the term *madad-i-maash* has been used.[17] In the documents of Akbar's reign in particular the term *suyurghal* was commonly used. There is a separate chapter in the *Ain-i-Akbari* entitled 'Suyurghal'.[18] The documents from Akbar's reign onwards that pertain to the grant generally bear the word *madad-i-maash*. Akbar took a keen interest in the system of revenue-free assignments as is evident from the fact that in the *Ain-i-Akbari*, '*pargana*-wise' assignment of these grants is recorded.[19] Some scholars are of the opinion that there was a difference between *suyurghal* and *madad-i-maash* grants.[20] However, the terms *suyurghal* and *madad-i-maash* in Mughal documents seem to be synonyms. Shireen Moosvi clearly explained that both *suyurghal* and *madad-i-maash* were granted in terms of land.[21] It seems that initially the Mughals used the term *suyurghal* for grants, but as they consolidated their empire, they preferred to use the commonly understood term *madad-i-maash* instead of *suyurghal*.[22]

Khalisa Lands

Khalisa or *khalisa-sharifa* was land from which the revenues were earmarked for imperial use and establishment. The *khalisa-sharifa* lands were under the direct administration of the imperial finance minister (*diwan-i-kul*) and generated funds that flowed directly to the central treasury (*khizanan-i-amira*). The revenues from *khalisa* were not meant only for the personal use of the emperor and his household. The *parganas* or the *mahals* reserved for the personal expenses of the emperor were instead known as *sarf-i-khas* (*khasa-i-sharifa*).[23] Revenue from these *khalisa* lands, as well as from a pool of temporarily unassigned *jagir* lands referred to as *paibaqi*, were the mainstay of the centre.[24] Cadres of salaried revenue officers directly employed by the minister of *khalisa-sharifa* collected *khalisa* revenues. It is difficult to agree with Stephen P. Blake's contention that the Mughal emperors' policy of dividing the realm into *khalisa* and *jagirs* (the household lands and the assignable lands) was a means of controlling a large part of the state revenue personally, which according to him was a typical characteristic of a patrimonial-bureaucratic empire[25] or even 'sultanistic'.[26] From the revenues of the *khalisa* land, the emperor defrayed the costs of his central household, military, diplomacy and the cash salaries of the *naqdi mansabdars*, which in no way can be termed as belonging to the 'household'. The cost of maintaining large numbers of *karkhanas* (workshops) including stables for various species of animals was also paid from this income.[27]

No specific lands adjacent to the capital were demarcated for the *khalisa*. The Mughal *khalisa* was instead a fiscal mechanism, a pool of sequestered revenues that set aside tax collections from designated villages or *parganas* scattered throughout the empire. It seems, however, to have been an accepted policy to demarcate the most fertile and conveniently located untroubled areas and well administered lands for the *khalisa*.[28] The extent of *khalisa* varied from time to time.[29] In Akbar's 31st regnal year (AD 1586), the *jama* of the *khalisa* in the provinces of Delhi, Awadh and Allahabad amounted to about one-fourth of their total *jama*.[30] A recent estimate for the latter years of Akbar's reign puts *khalisa* revenues as between 24 and 33 per cent of the total assessed revenues.[31] During the reign of Jahangir, there were substantial reductions in the *khalisa* till its *jama* fell to below 5 per cent of that of the whole empire.[32] The total *jama* of the empire was calculated at 6,30,00,00,000 *dams*, of which the *jama* of the assigned area was 5,98,50,00,000 *dams* and that of the *khalisa* 31,50,00,000 *dams* approximately.[33] During the reign of Shahjahan, steps were taken to increase the revenue of the *khalisa*, and by his 20th regnal year it increased to one-seventh of the total *jama* of the empire which stood at 8,80,00,00,000 *dams*.[34] Thus, revenue assignments totalled 7,54,28,57,000 *dams* and the *khalisa* was valued at 1,25,72,43,000 *dams* approximately. During the 10th regnal year of Aurangzeb, out of the total *jama* of the empire standing at 9,24,00,00,000 *dams*, one-fifth, i.e. 1,99,00,00,000 *dams* were earmarked for the *khalisa* and 7,25,00,00,000 *dams* were alienated in assignments.[35] The figures given here are only approximate, but they indicate the extent to which the emperor alienated the state revenue in granting the *jagirs*. No detailed information is available on the size of the *khalisa* under Akbar. It is likely that during Akbar's reign there was pressure for *jagir* assignment that is why the *khalisa* lost some ground in order to release lands for assignment as *jagirs*.

Jagir Lands

The revenues of the *khalisa* also indicate the extent of the *jagirs* held by the *mansabdars*. By far the larger part of the empire was assigned in *jagirs*. Under Akbar the bulk of the imperial territory was also assigned as *jagirs* to nobles in lieu of their services. The officers often preferred to get their dues in the form of *jagirs*, because they tried to collect more than the amount that was actually sanctioned to them. 'The whole country' wrote Badauni, 'with the exception of those lands held immediately from the *khalisa* land, were held by the *amirs* as *jagirs*'.[36] According to Moreland, nearly seven-eighth of the entire territory was in the hands of the assignees.[37] Shireen Moosvi has argued that during Akbar's reign between 67 to 76 per cent of the area was given out as *jagirs*.[38] This gives a floor of 2,65,34,192 *dams* for the payment of salaries, and a ceiling of 1,30,69,079 *dams* for expenses on the imperial establishment out of the total effective *jama* of 3,96,03,27,106 *dams* in 1595-6 (see Table 1.1). Stephen P. Blake opined that at least 75 per cent revenues of the empire under Akbar were as-signed to *mansabdars*.[39] Jesuit accounts, provide another estimate:

> For all the kingdoms and provinces which he (Akbar) conquers he holds as his own, appointing his captains over them. From these he takes a third portion of the revenues, the remainder being for their personal needs, and the maintenance of the soldiers, horses, and elephants which each of them is bound to keep.[40]

The only meaning this passage will bear is that *jagirs* normally accounted for two-thirds of the *dams*, and the *khalisa* for one-third. But it appears that the percentage of *jagirs* was higher than that mentioned here.

The sole claimant to the land revenues and other taxes was theoretically the emperor, but through a system of temporary alienations of the claim in specific areas (*jagirs*), members of a small ruling class of the Mughal Empire shared the revenue among themselves (see Table 1.1). According to Irfan Habib, the assignment of the larger portion of the empire in *jagirs*, meant giving control over much of the GNP of the country to a numerically very small class.[41] Toward the end of Akbar's reign *mansabdars* (*jagirdar* and *naqdi*) and their followers cornered 82 per cent of the total budget (80.95 million

TABLE 1.1: IMPERIAL REVENUE AND EXPENDITURE, 1595-6[42]

Income	*Million dams*	*Million rupees*
Effective *jama* 1595-6	3960.3	99.01
Expenditure: Salary bill of *mansabdars*		
Zat salaries	827.5	20.69
Animal allowance	371.4	9.29
Sawar payment	2,038.9	50.97
Total	3,237.8	80.95
Central military establishment		
Cavalry and foot	142.9	3.57
Animals/stables	194.0	4.85
Arsenal and armour	22.1	.55
Total	359.0	8.97
Imperial household (including harem/building construction)		
Total	187.4	4.69
Total expenditure	3,784.2	94.60
Balance	176.1	4.41
Grand total	3,960.3	99.01

from a total budget of Rs. 99.01 million) of the empire for their pay and allowances.

The ruling class consisted of persons who held *mansabs* or ranks granted by the emperor. Each rank (numerically expressed) entitled its holder (*mansabdar*) to a particular amount of pay (*talab*). This could be in terms of a salary paid in cash from the treasury, though it was common instead to assign an area that was officially estimated to yield an equivalent amount of revenue. Such standing estimates of the average annual income from taxes, known as *jama* or *jama-dami*, were prepared for administrative divisions down to villages so as to ensure accuracy in assigning *jagirs*.

Jagir accorded financial stability as well as political stature to nobles. The Mughal nobles attempted to extract a larger income from the *jagirs* than was their official worth. Sometimes they secured through their influential friends a larger *jagir* than the normal entitlement. In 1560, Bairam Khan Khan-i-Khanan gave his nephew Husain Quli Khan[43] (who according to Abul Fazl, 'did not have the spirit to face barn-door chicken') cultivated lands as *jagir*, while he satisfied the great Khans like Iskandar Khan (Sikander Khan), Abdullah Khan and Bahadur Khan with wastelands.[44] In 1558, Ali Quli Khan, *hakim* of Jaunpur, assigned the important *jagir* of Sandila (in Awadh) to one of his relatives Ismail Khan.[45] In 1560, he assigned the important *sarkar* of Banaras to his younger brother Bahadur Khan.[46] The extent of a *mansabdar's jagir* also determined his political status, as the possession of a *jagir* carried with it much prestige.[47] In return for the *jagir*, the noble was expected to devote all his time and effort to the service of the emperor.

MANSABDARI SYSTEM

The only powerful mechanism available to the Mughals to organize the nobility was the *mansab* (numerical rank) system.[48] The emperor assigned a rank to every noble or *mansabdar*,[49] but reserved for himself the right to create, promote, or demote as he saw fit. In return, each *mansabdar* was to maintain a standing body of troops, trained and equipped to imperial standards. The remuneration and expenditure necessitated by this were mostly made through the alienation of state revenue from the assigned territory to individuals. Thus, the *mansab* was critical for regulating the Mughal assignment system. The Mughal *jagirdars* were as a rule *mansabdars* holding ranks (*mansabs*) granted to them by the emperor. However, every *mansabdar* was not necessarily a *jagirdar*. He could receive his pay in cash. During Akbar's reign, the majority of nobles received their salary in the form of *jagirs*. The overlapping of these administrative categories was inevitable. A discussion of certain aspects of a *mansabdar's* life also includes to a great extent a study of a noble's role as a *jagirdar*.

Islamic rulers appear to have adopted early on the system of organizing their armies on the decimal basis; the system used by the Mongols was similar. Genghis Khan organized his troops into tens, hundreds and thousands. The larger units were combinations of thousands, a *tuman* consisted of 10,000. With the decline of Timurid power, many proverbial terms lost their original meaning and were used primarily for prestige. This affected military organization as well.[50] Under Babur, a *tuman* consisted of 500 to 1,000 persons.[51] This is an excellent instance of the difference between the nominal strength of a force and its actual numbers. The discrepancy continued at least in the earlier years of Akbar's reign. The arrangement appears to have been very flexible. During this period, land revenue assignment to a noble was announced first and thereon he spent a proportion of the income on the maintenance of his contingent. From all accounts, it appears that each noble or commander was free to fix the size of his contingent as well as rates of payment for his soldiers.

In all probability, the number of troops to be maintained by officers was fixed for the first time in the 11th regnal year (1566). According to Abul Fazl, 'As the branding department . . . has not been emerged into being, at this time the number of attendants for all the officers and servants of the threshold was fixed, so that everyone should keep some persons in readiness for service'.[52] A step which took cognizance of the revised yet highly inflated *jama* was the standardization of rates for troopers in the 11th regnal year. Predictably, the remuneration or allowances of individual nobles remained unchanged so as to avoid general discontentment among sections that had provided strength and military support to the state.

Obviously these preliminary regulations were considered insufficient, and Akbar contemplated a drastic reform of the army. In 1573-4, an innovative scheme was introduced that strengthened the position of the nobles in the state hierarchy. This ground-breaking scheme was known as the *mansab* or *mansabdari* system. Since its inception, the *mansabdari* system took the form of a decimal ranking system that was reminiscent of, but not identical to, that of the Mongols' *tumans.* The latter referred, at least in principle, to units of 10,000 men to be further broken up into smaller units of 1,000, 100 and 10. Further, the *mansab* also aimed to end the arbitrariness of past recruitment. Henceforth, *mansabdars* were to receive ranks and salaries in accordance with the real number of mounted retainers they provided for imperial service. Of course, this required a sophisticated system of inspection, monitoring and auditing. For this purpose, Akbar concomitantly promulgated the *dagh* or branding system. According to Abul Fazl, in the 18th regnal year (1573-4) the *dagh* system was introduced, and the ranks of the imperial officials were fixed.[53] Akbar initially faced considerable difficulties in establishing and enforcing the *mansabdari* system. There was stiff opposition from high officials including Prime Minister Muzaffar Khan, former Prime Minister Munim Khan and Akbar's foster brother Mirza Aziz Koka. It had the support of Todar Mal and other loyal officials. When the regulations were worked out in detail they were duly enforced the following year (1574-5).[54] Muzaffar Khan was dismissed from service because of his reluctance to enforce the regulations. Mirza Aziz Koka, who made negative comments about the new administrative regulations, was banished from court to Agra, deprived of his rank, and confined to lodgings in the garden of his own house there.[55]

Mutamad Khan offers the details of the new measures:

> The *mansabs* were fixed according to the capacity for maintaining and organizing a contingent. . . . *Mansabs* from *dahbashi* (10) to *panjhazari* (5,000) were established and the salary for each was fixed. A regulation to the effect that the *mansabdars* would separately bring their personal horses and elephants for branding (*daghs*) was imposed. A trooper, if capable of being a *sih-aspa* (horseman 'with three horses'), would bring three horses; if capable of being a *do-aspa* ('with two horses'), two horses; and if capable of a *yak-aspa* contingent ('with one horse'), he should bring one horse for the *dagh*. In this way the pay (*alufa*) for every one was fixed.[56]

It has been surmised that from Akbar's 18th regnal year (1573-4), Mughal nobles were assigned numerical ranks (*mansabs*), consisting of a pair of numbers, the first designating *zat* (setting personal rank and salary) and the second *sawar* (setting size of the cavalry contingent and payment thereof). A.J. Qaisar added: 'From the *Akbarnama* it becomes clear that in the [18th R.Y.] 'Fixing of the grades' for the officers was carried out.... The fixing of the grades means the fixing of the *mansab* and refers to the two ranks, i.e. the *zat* and the *sawar*. Thus both the ranks were introduced simultaneously in the 18th regnal year (1573-4)'.[57] However, prior to 1595, there were no actual references to paired ranks, and the two lists of nobles, prepared until 1595, mention only a single rank.[58] The existence of two ranks before the 40th regnal year (1595-6) thus becomes suspect. This impression is reinforced by the fact that the text of the *Ain-i-Akbari* mentions only a single rank, and neither the term *zat* nor *sawar* is employed in the sense of either of the two ranks. Since the *Ain-i-Akbari's* text mainly pertains to the 40th regnal year, the existence of paired ranks prior to this date cannot legitimately be taken for granted (the interpretation owes much to Shireen Moosvi).[59] Moreland's view[60] that Akbar introduced the 'double rank', i.e. the *sawar* rank in the 11th regnal year and acceptance of the existence of the *zat* rank prior to this date is indefensible, and has been the subject of cogent criticism.[61]

The *mansab* not only created a hierarchy of *amirs*, but their *mansabs* also indicated the degree to which the holders stood in the emperor's favour. As such, the *mansab* was an accurately standardized kind of honour, to be conveniently raised and reduced by the emperor pending the almost permanent assessment of the *mansabdar's* performance. As the degree of the *mansabdar's* honour could vary with his military stature, one single rank could hardly meet both criteria at the same time. This was even more so because the *mansabdari* organization included all government services, without any official subdivisions into military, financial and executive branches. Therefore, after two decades of working with a single rank, Akbar introduced in 1595-6 the system of double ranking, i.e. *zat and sawar.*[62] *Zat* indicated the holder's position in the hierarchy of imperial honour, whereas *sawar* represented the number of mounted retainers the *mansabdar* was supposed to maintain. This configuration is considered the classic form of the *mansab* system. It involved more than the compulsory branding of horses and mustering of men; it also fixed financial penalties for failing to maintain enough troops, including salary reduction and repayment of excess funds collected. The important purpose of the *mansabdari* system was to promote the size as well as the optimal composition of a *mansabdar's* contingent. Depending on the strength of the contingent *mansabdars* were placed in three categories. In the first, *zat* and *sawar* ranks were equal; in the second, *sawar* rank was less than *zat* but not less than half or 50 per cent of the *zat* rank; and in the third, *sawar* rank was below 50 per cent of the *zat* rank.[63] The salary for the *mansabdars* was calculated on the basis of both ranks, each requiring different tables of conversion.The schedule of pay for the *mansabdars* given in the *Ain-i-Akbari* was obviously redrawn after these changes were introduced. The schedule of pay in the *Ain-i-Akbari* also lists the size of stables, the species and number of war and transport animals to be maintained by the *mansabdars.*[64] Probably during the reign of Akbar the average annual pay of a trooper was Rs.240 or 9,600 *dams* as calculated by Abdul Aziz, which according to him continued during the reign of Jahangir.[65] The salary paid to the *mansabdars* on the basis of *tabinan* (trooper) was reduced from 9,600 *dams* during the reign of Akbar to 8,000 *dams* during the reign of Shahjahan which continued till the end of Aurangzeb's rule. [66]

Scholars have focused attention on the subsequent changes in the *mansab* system after Akbar's reign which are beyond the purview of the present study. William Irvine, Abdul Aziz, Moreland, Irfan Habib, Athar Ali and Shireen Moosvi are among those who have already made valuable contributions in this connection; it will therefore be only repetitive to go into minute niceties once again.

It has already been noted that the rudiments of the *mansab* system existed in the Mongol and Timurid military organization. However, it is equally important to remember that the *mansabdari* system, as instituted by Akbar, was different in vital respects from the earlier system. It was both more complex and manageable. The organization of the *mansab* was divided into sixty-six grades, though in practice only thirty-three grades were utilized. Beginning with a number of 10 they continued till the rank of 12000, though ranks above 5000 were the privilege of the royal princes.[67] It was only towards the end of Akbar's reign that a few officers were promoted to the rank of 7000. They were either the emperor's close relatives or men with a particularly distinguished record. The highest ranks reached by princes or distinguished noblemen are as follows:

Shahzada Sultan Salim (son)	12000/10000	*MT*, 2:353; *AN*, 3:998
Shahzada Sultan Murad (son)	9000	*MT*, 2:353
Shahzada Sultan Daniyal (son)	7000/7000	*MT*, 2:335; *AN*, 3:1077

Prince Sultan Khusrau (grandson)	10000	*AN*, 3:1257(n. 1); *AA*, 1: 323-4
Raja Man Singh (His sister was married to Salim)	7000/6000	*AN*, 3: 1257; *Iqbalnama*, 510
Khan Azam Mirza Aziz Koka (Akbar's foster brother)	7000/6000	*AN*, 3:1211; *Iqbalnama*, 510

The *mansab* system as it evolved reflected transparency both in relation to upward movement on the professional front as well as reward for services without any kind of racial or parochial considerations. The most imperative achievement of the *mansab* system was that it cut the nobility to size and the ruler emerged as the sole arbiter. Besides assuring the loyalty of the nobility, the *mansab* system encouraged efficiency and discipline. 'The very insecurity of wealth and rank', Abdul Aziz observed, 'acted as a powerful incentive for individual distinction'.[68] The *mansab* system also defined relations between the crown and the nobility. Since civil and military services were jointly governed through this mechanism, it revealed the crown's dependence upon the nobility. Imperial orders and policies were executed by the *mansabdars*. This dependence is also implied in the award of the *sawar mansab*, which determined the military obligations of its holder. Since the beginning the majority of the Mughal nobility was not attached to land and the *jagir* was not their personal property.[69] The position of the nobles, Nurul Hasan noted, 'did not depend on their being in control of a particular territory, but on their military capacity'.[70] This military capacity was determined by the *sawar* rank, which became an important factor in regulating the crown–nobility relationship. On the one hand, the military strength of the empire depended upon the contingents of the nobles, while on the other, this strength determined the power and position of the *mansabdars*. The greater the share of a group in the total awarded *sawar mansab*, the more the faith and dependence of the crown upon that group. Thus, *mansabdari* as an institution implied elements of interdependence as well as contradiction between the crown and the nobility.

TERMINOLOGY AND THEMES

The system of granting land or revenues of land to officers had been in vogue for centuries in European as well as Asian countries. According to K.M. Ashraf, 'The system of assignment in the form in which it came to India was first designed by the *Caliph* Muqtadir'.[71] Muslim rulers from the Abbasids to the Mughals and their contemporaries conceded land revenue from specified areas and the burden of collecting it to their servants directly as their salaries. Before the sixteenth century, the concessions were commonly referred to as *iqta*; the Ottomans used the term *timar* or military fief, the Safavids *tuyul*, and the Mughals *jagir*. Apart from being referred to as *jagirs*,[72] the areas from which revenues were thus assigned by the Mughal emperors were also called *tuyuls*.[73] Sometimes the term *iqta*,[74] used in the Delhi Sultanate, was employed. The assignees were known as *jaygirdars/jagirdars*, and occasionally *tuyuldars* and *iqtadars*.

The term *jagir*, which by the end of the sixteenth century came to be accepted as the standard term for revenue assignments, is actually a shortened form of the Persian *jaygir* meaning 'possessing, occupying a place, fixing a habitation, making a settlement'.[75] Commenting on the term *jagir*, Iqtidar Husain Siddiqi rightly observed that 'the terms such as *jagir* and *jagirdar* were adopted only during Akbar's early reign'. He noted its absence from any document or work written even in India before Akbar's accession.[76] The word *jagir* as it appears in the *Tarikh-i-Firuzshahi* is an obvious misreading of *chakar* (retainer), and correspondingly the word *jagir* employed in the sense of *iqta* during the Afghan period is fallacious.[77] The revenue assignments made by Babur to his nobles were generally referred to as *wajh* and casually as *wajh-wa-alufa* and *istiqamat-wa-wajib* (*wajh-wa-istiqamat*).[78] The holders of such assignments were called *wajhdars*. The term *jagir* was a substitute for the terms *wajh, wajhdar* and *wajh-i-alufa*. Indeed, the term *jagirdar* itself was a substitute for the term *wajhdar*.[79]

Although the Mughal *jagir* traces its institutional lineage back to the Islamic *iqta* of the Delhi Sultanate, it diverges in nature from the *iqta*. In essence, the Mughal *jagir* was closer to an uncontaminated revenue assignment than to an administrative-cum-fiscal charge like the *iqta* of the Delhi Sultanate period. The Mughal *jagir* was by no means a fixed territorial unit, and had no connection, except for convenience in assignment, with the administrative units, such as *sarkars* and *parganas*.[80] Under Muslim rulers in India, the troops drawing salaries from provincial land revenues greatly outnumbered those paid directly from the central treasury. It was a widespread practice of the Turkish sultans to assign different regions as *iqta* to commanders, who were required to maintain themselves and their troops out of the revenues of the *iqtas*.[81] These *iqtadars* were responsible for maintaining order and collecting taxes within their domains. After meeting the necessary expenses, the surplus funds were to be remitted to the central treasury.[82] In theory, the *iqtadars* held their *iqtas* at the pleasure of the ruler, and were not allowed to acquire hereditary rights over the regions falling under their jurisdiction. In practice, however, the dynastic shifts and political turmoil permitted the *iqtas* to remain with their holders over generations. As Irfan Habib noted, Firuz Tughlaq's 'policy of letting son succeed father to official posts' amounted 'to a complete capitulation to the sentiment in favour of permanent and semi-hereditary rights in the assignments'.[83] Under the Lodis, and to a lesser extent, the Surs, this process went a step further when the Afghan nobility held *iqtas* that permitted them local residence, local resources and local identities.[84]

More or less similar centrifugal tendencies of the Afghan period gained strength during the early years of Akbar's reign. Before this could assume serious dimensions, Akbar slowly but firmly adopted innovative schemes to exercise greater state control over the resources of the empire.[85] According to Moreland, 'we may fairly treat the accession of Akbar as the opening of a new period'.[86] With the passage of time, the system changed in various ways, often affecting or defining political centralization. Unlike the *iqta*, the *jagir* of the Mughals separated political and administrative responsibility from the task of tax collection. A *mansabdar* receiving lands in a salary assignment only had the right to collect the taxes assessed on that stipulated area. A *jagir* could consist of fields in a part of a village, the entire lands of one or more named villages or even one or more sub-districts (*parganas*). The *diwan-i-tan* (minister for salaries) matched assessed taxes with the specified salary and allowances of the *mansabdar* and issued multiple copies of an official *jagir* document.[87] At the same time, the emperor took precautions to maintain a distance from sectarian alignment of forces, and simultaneously gave greater weightage to merit in appointments and promotions.[88] This new ideology of the state is explicitly manifested in the evolution of the *mansab* system, the complete revamping of the revenue department with well defined rates of assessment applicable across all the Mughal territories, and the unambiguous linkage of revenue assignments (*jagirs*) to the prescribed salary entitlements of officials.

The assignment system was primarily evolved to secure the efficient and disciplined service of a body of men. At the same time it freed the emperor from the task of revenue collection along with the maintenance of law and order, which enabled him to extend the boundaries of his empire. There is some strength in the view that such a policy may have served to bring more area under actual cultivation,[89] for which *mansabdars* were given incentive. One of the recommendations made by Mir Fattullah Shirazi to Akbar was obviously inspired by the desire to offer some incentive to the *jagirdar* to improve the condition of his charge. 'It was laid down that if any assignee made his *iqta* (*jagir*) populous (*abad*) and increased its revenue, his rank was to be raised, so that by getting additional pay he might enjoy the fruits of his efforts'.[90]

In spite of this, scholars have not focused their attention on this popular system of Mughal India. In the initial years of Akbar's reign, the system was still evolving and had not yet been standardized, it presented a different picture from the fully developed Mughal system that has been studied in some detail by scholars.[91] They fail to analyse the way in which the *jagirdari* system was integrated with the central administration and how the prevalence of this institution created problems for which various devices had to be adopted from time to time. However, in his recent writings, Iqtidar Alam Khan, has thrown open new and interesting directions of research and enquiry.[92]

Under Akbar the system was an arrangement which fulfilled the special requirements of the Mughal polity in India as it evolved during the period of study. During this period the Mughals struggled for survival in the face of persisting local and regional hostility. The proposed research addresses this issue as an independent question and treats it in a comprehensive manner. It focuses on a period of fifty years of Akbar's reign and on an area covering twelve divisions, each of which was labelled *suba* by Akbar and distinguished by the appellation of the tract of country or its capital city. These were Agra, Ajmer, Allahabad, Awadh, Bengal, Bihar, Delhi, Gujarat, Kabul, Lahore, Malwa and Multan.

SOURCES

Fortunately, there is a rich treasure of sources. There is a vast body of literature covering official and non-official histories, biographical dictionaries, administrative manuals, official records, other documents, letters and accounts by foreigners. Most of the Persian sources have been published, though a few materials are available only in manuscript. Travellers' accounts provide useful raw data and different perspectives on the Mughal polity and society. Even such astute observers as Antonio Monserrate, Francois Bernier and Thomas Roe did not fully understand what they saw and experienced. They were outsiders, with access to common knowledge—rumour and gossip—and not to inside information. Travellers' accounts can only supplement the Mughal sources, they cannot provide an authentic research framework.[93]

Three chronicles dominate the literature of this period: the *Akbarnama* of Abul Fazl, the *Muntakhab-ut-Tawarikh* of Abdul Qadir Badauni and the *Tabaqat-i-Akbari* of Nizamuddin Ahmad Bakhshi. The *Akbarnama* covers not only Akbar's reign, but also the entire human history as portrayed in the mature Akbari political programme. It contains mostly facts about the reign, but they must be read with the utmost care, not merely because of the complexity and difficulty of Abul Fazl's Persian style. All official histories were written to persuade, but the *Akbarnama* is a masterpiece of historiographical propaganda. The entire presentation serves to glorify, justify and explain the status of Akbar in accord with his view of himself. K.A. Nizami and Iqtidar Alam Khan, from their very different perspectives, have demonstrated that this fact makes the *Akbarnama* difficult to use.[94] Akbar did not begin his reign with a complete political agenda, which he gradually revealed and actualized. He groped, improvized and evolved. Because this study concentrates on the period of groping, improvization and evolution, Abul Fazl's assertions have frequently come under critical scrutiny.[95]

Badauni's *Muntakhab-ut-Tawarikh* is the antithesis of the *Akbarnama*. Compiled secretly without official sponsorship, it presents the viewpoint of an intellectual and official who perceived himself and his colleagues who held similar views as disenfranchised by a regime for which he had high expectations. Though jealous and bitter, it supplements Abul Fazl's account, filling vital gaps. Badauni's complete freedom from fear or the desire for favour gave him a unique and valuable perspective. Except when he was personally involved, he offers an interpretation, not just information. His facts are frequently drawn from the *Tabaqat-i-Akbari*.[96] Compared to the other two chronicles, the *Tabaqat* is a mundane description of events. As *bakhshi* of Gujarat, and later as *mir bakhshi,* Nizamuddin Ahmad had an intimate knowledge of the workings of the Mughal government and had witnessed many important events.[97] The text, however, leads to just the opposite feeling. Even when he describes his own participation in events, he does so in an impersonal manner, without focusing on his own feelings or giving a sense of immediacy.[98] In addition, the *Tabaqat-i-Akbari* is more brief than the other two works.

For the early part of Akbar's reign, two other chronicles are also vital: the *Tarikh-i-Akbari,* generally known as the *Tarikh-i-Qandhari,* of Hajji Muhammad Arif Qandhari, and the *Tazkira-i-Humayun wa Akbar* of Bayazid Bayat. Both these men served in the establishment as high officers. Qandhari was the *mir-i-saman* (chief of the household) of Bairam Khan, Akbar's regent, and later served under Muzaffar Khan Turbati, one of the leading administrators. Bayazid Bayat served in the household of Munim Khan who became chief officer with the title Khan-i-Khanan after the death of Bairam Khan. He dictated his memoirs in his old age in accord with an imperial order for the collection of recollections of Humayun—an early instance of oral history. These works contain crucial information drawn from the personal experience of the authors, but even for the early periods the major chronicles are more valuable.[99]

As far as the *jagirdari* system is concerned, numerous references from the above-mentioned contemporary sources and other near contemporary sources are available. They have been cross-checked with secondary works and revealed some of the changes that took place in the system during Akbar's reign. For tabulations of the *jagirs* of different nobles, Abul Fazl's *Ain-i-Akbari* and Irfan Habib's *Atlas of the Mughal Empire* are particularly useful. The *mansabdars/jagirdars* were given titles, gifts and ranks by Akbar and these also find mention in these contemporary works. This has been systematically tabulated in a comprehensive manner. Further, an attempt has been made to portray the emperor's relations with *jagirdars* in terms of his sympathy, personal attitude and ideas to show how the different groups, which were constituted on the basis of family, race, clan and religious background, affected him.

In addition to these sources, it would be pertinent to mention some of the other important sources. The *Ain-i-Akbari* remains an unrivalled source of information for understanding political institutions, geographical and administrative divisions of the Mughal Empire. Abul Fazl's 'Account of Twelve *Subas*' as given in the *Ain-i-Akbari* is particularly useful in identifying the *parganas* and *sarkars* along with the approximate value of the *jagirs* that were allotted to *jagirdars*. However, it fails to throw sufficient light on the actual working of the *jagirdari* system. On certain topics, the *Ain-i-Akbari* mentions the theory and ideal, not the actual facts, while on many others it furnishes actual facts and details.

The *Tarikh-i-Farishta,*[100] the *Tuzuk-i-Jahangiri*[101] and the *Iqbalnama-i-Jahangiri*[102] supplement the information contained in the main sources cited earlier. In addition to these standard sources, biographical accounts also provide useful information. The biographies of nobles found in works like the *Zakhirat-ul-Khawanin,*[103] the *Maasir-ul-Umara,*[104] Blochmann's biographies in the *Ain-i-Akbari*[105] and the *Tazkirat-ul-Umara*[106] are valuable in constructing the life story of various leading nobles. They also throw light on the political, economic and social conditions of the period under study. Biographies are useful for tracing the successive promotions of officers and the various duties entrusted to them at different times.

Regional histories, including those of some provincial dynasties, supplement the information on the *jagirdars* in the region as given in the general chronicles. To begin with Kashmir, the *Baharistan-i-Shahi* (anonymous), written by a contemporary of Akbar and completed in 1614, provides an exhaustive account of the Mughal conquest of Kashmir. The histories of the provincial dynasties are particularly useful for the regions under the Akbari *suba* of Multan. The major authorities for this region are the *Tarikh-i-Masumi*[107] of Masum Bhakkari, the *Tarikh-i-Tahiri* of Mir Tahir Muhammad Nisyani, the *Maasir-i-Rahimi* of Abdul Baqi Nihawandi and the *Mazhar-i-Shahjahani* of Yusuf Mirak. The first one, a well-known work, was compiled during Akbar's lifetime by a person who had a personal knowledge of the region. The *Mazhar-i-Shahjahani,* written in 1634, offers an account of the administrative history of Sindh from the reign of Akbar to the time it was written. It provides a fairly good account of the region-wise distribution of various clans in Sindh.

For the *suba* of Gujarat, the *Mirat-i-Sikandari* of Sikandar Ibn Muhammad and the *Mirat-i-Ahmadi* of Ali Muhammad Khan are very useful. The former was compiled in AD 1611 and its author was a contemporary of Akbar and had served Mirza Aziz Koka in his campaign against the last Muzzaffarid Sultan of Gujarat in AD 1591-2. In addition to other useful information, it makes specific mention of *mansabdars* who held administrative posts in Gujarat. It also provides certain additives with regard to the information of the *Akbarnama*. The *Mirat-i-Ahmadi* of Ali Muhammad Khan although written around the mid-eighteenth century elaborates more on the subject than the *Mirat-i-Sikandari*. Its author was the last Mughal *diwan* of *suba* Gujarat and had personal knowledge of Gujarat. He wrote this work, a major portion of which deals with the administration of Gujarat under the Mughals, after painstaking research into the administration of Gujarat prior to his times and occasionally appended the document he has utilized.

Among other regional works mention may be made of the *Dalpat Vilas* and the works of Munhot Nainsi, which have greatly added to the information on the *mansabdars* of *suba* Ajmer. The author of the *Dalpat Vilas* belonged to the period under study and dedicated his work to his patron Dalpat, the son of Rai Rai Singh of Bikaner. The works of Munhot Nainsi, although they were written more than half a century after Akbar's death, are far more useful than any other Rajasthani work for the precision and minuteness of their detail. Munhot Nainsi (d. 1670) was the *diwan* of Jodhpur during the reign of Maharaja Jaswant Singh and authored *Munhot Nainsi ri Khayat* and the *Marwar ra Pargana ri Vigat*. The former was compiled on the basis of *khyats* and the existing *vamshavalis* procured by the author from the bards of Rajasthan. The latter work provides an exhaustive account of the various *parganas* of Marwar and, from the nature of evidence it contains, it may be favourably compared with the *Ain-i-Akbari*. Being personally involved in the revenue administration, the author offers a vivid account of the administration of Marwar during his time. Besides, he provides glimpses of Marwar and its administration prior to his times. In addition to this, he presents historical sketches of the various *parganas* of Marwar, which help in determining the area of the *parganas*, which were assigned to *jagirdars* during the period under review.

Some modern works of regional history, which have considerably supplemented the information of the contemporary works, are the two-volume *History of the Panjab Hill States* by J. Hutchison and J. Ph. Vogel. In addition to the Persian chronicles, which the authors have extensively used, they have carefully examined the dynastic *vamshavalis* of the various hill states of the Panjab and have exhaustively utilized the epigraphical records. Among the modern works, the nineteenth-century histories of Rajasthan cannot be overlooked. *The Annals and Antiquities of Rajasthan* of James Tod and the *Vir Vinod* of Kaviraj Shyamaldas, in spite of the romanticism of the former and the prejudices of the latter, are immensely valuable in working out the extent of the principalities of various dynasties of *suba* Ajmer. Malcolm's *Memoir of Central India Including Malwa* is a useful work for the region, which constituted the Akbari *suba* of Malwa.

A very important source on the eastern regions of the Mughal Empire is the *Baharistan-i-Ghayabi* of Alauddin Isfahani, popularly known as Mirza Nathan. Compiled during the early years of Shahjahan's reign, it primarily records the history of Bihar and Orissa in the 1608-24 period. Mirza Nathan himself actively participated in various Mughal campaigns in *suba* Bengal. He occasionally refers to the reign of Akbar and thereby helps to fill the gaps of the contemporary chronicles.

Among the modern works, W.H. Moreland's *The Agrarian System of Moslem India*, Irfan Habib's *The Agrarian System of Mughal India*, Athar Ali's *Mughal Nobility Under Aurangzeb* and Noman Ahmad Siddiqi's *Land Revenue Administration Under the Mughals* offer valuable insights into the *jagirdari* systems, even though their treatment of *jagirdars* and the *jagirdari* system during the reign of Akbar has been inadequate. Irfan Habib provides detailed information in *The Agrarian System of Mughal India* and dispels many doubts and misunderstandings.

NOTES

1. The members of the Mughal dynasty described themselves as Timurids and were not Mongols, the meaning of Mughal in Persian. Marshall G.S. Hodgson in his quest to refine scholarly terminology refers to the Mughals as Indo-Timurids. *The Venture of Islam*, 3 vols, Chicago: University of Chicago Press, 1974, 3: 62n. Though desirable, his usage has not become standard. I also call them Mughals in accord with standard usage. For a detailed exposition of the word 'Mughal', see Harbans Mukhia, *The Mughals of India*, Oxford and Delhi: Blackwell Publishing, 2004-5, pp. 2-5.

2. After AD 1720 (reigns of Muhammad Shah, AD 1719-48 and his successors) the essential structure of the centralized empire had disintegrated beyond repair. See J.F. Richards, *The Mughal Empire* (*vol. 1.5 of the New Cambridge History of India*), Cambridge: Cambridge University Press, 1993, p. XV; 'The Formulation of Imperial Authority Under Akbar and Jahangir', in *The Mughal State, 1526-1750*, ed. Muzaffar Alam and Sanjay Subrahmanyam, Delhi: Oxford University Press, 1998, p. 127.
3. The demarcation line is often drawn between Hindu states, which are regarded as less centralized, less successful and therefore more segmented than the centrally organized Muslim states. See Georg Berkemer, 'Political System and Political Structure of Medieval South India', in *Exploration in the History of South Asia*, ed. Georg Berkemer, et al., Delhi: Manohar, 2003, pp. 121-37; see also Burton Stein, 'The Segmentary State: Interim Reflections', in *The State in India, 1000-1700*, ed. Hermann Kulke, Delhi: Oxford University Press, 1995, pp. 134-61.
4. The renowned Russian orientalist V.V. Barthold first asserted that the Mughal, Ottoman and Safavid empires exceeded their predecessors in size, centralization and duration because of the development and diffusion of firearms. See V.V. Barthold, *Socheneniya* (Collected Works), tr. Shahib Suhrawardy, *Mussulman Culture*, Calcutta: Calcutta University Press, 1934; rpt, Philadelphia: Porcupine, 1977, pp. 99-102. See also Douglas E. Streusand, *The Formation of the Mughal Empire*, Delhi: Oxford University Press, 1989, pp. 10-11; M. Athar Ali, 'Toward an Interpretation of the Mughal Empire', in *The State in India*, ed. Kulke, p. 264. For the firearms empire hypothesis, see Marshall G.S. Hodgson, *The Venture of Islam*, 3: 17-18; William H. McNeill, *The Pursuit of Power*, Chicago: University of Chicago Press, 1982, pp. 95-8; Christopher Duffy, *Siege Warfare*, London: Routledge and Kegan Paul, 1979, pp. 9-13; Iqtidar Alam Khan, *Gunpowder and Firearms: Warfare in Medieval India*, Delhi: Oxford University Press, 2004.
5. As described in the text, the *mansabdari* system developed over time in the first half of Akbar's reign. For convenience, I have used the terms *mansabdar* and *mansab* for a post in Akbar's government before the definitive establishment of the system. Similarly, the terms *jagir* and *jagirdar* were used earlier than its tangible occurrence.
6. Mirza Sharafuddin Husain Ahrari was the great-grandson of Khwaja Ubaydullah Ahrar and, therefore, a member of a Sufi family which enjoyed high prestige among the Chaghatays. His maternal grandmother was a Timurid princess and in 1560 (AH 967) he had married Akbar's half-sister, Bakhshi Banu Begum. He held *jagirs* near Ajmer and Nagaur and the exalted title of *Amir-ul-Umara*. In October 1562 (AH 970), he fled from court to his *jagirs*. Flight from court meant revolt. Akbar sent Bairam Khan's nephew, Husain Quli Khan, who was later conferred the title Khan-i-Jahan, against the rebel. See Abul Fazl, *Akbarnama* (including its *takmila* by Inayatullah),

Persian text, ed. Maulvi Agha Ahmad Ali and Maulvi Abdur Rahim, 3 vols, Calcutta: Asiatic Society of Bengal, 1873-87; rpt, Delhi: Kitab Publishing House, 1977, in English tr. Henry Beveridge, 3 vols, rpt, Delhi: Low Price Publications, 1998, 2: 308-11 [198-200], 314 [202], 316-21 [204-7]; Abdul Qadir Badauni, *Muntakhab-ut-Tawarikh*, Persian text, ed. Maulvi Ahmad Ali, Kabiruddin Ahmad and W.N. Lees, 3 vols, Calcutta: Asiatic Society of Bengal, 1868, in English, vol. I, tr. E.S.A. Ranking; vol. II, tr. W.H. Lowe; vol. III, tr. T.W. Haig, rpt, Delhi: Idarah-i-Adabiyat-i Delhi, 1973, 2: 57-9 [59-60]; Nizamuddin Ahmad, *Tabaqat-i-Akbari*, Persian text, ed. Brajendranath De and Muhammad Hidayat Husain, 3 vols, Calcutta: Asiatic Society of Bengal, 1935, in English tr. Brajendranath De, 3 vols, Calcutta: Asiatic Society of Bengal, 1936, 2: 258 [164-5]; A.L. Srivastava, *Akbar the Great*, 2nd edn, 3 vols, Agra: Shiva Lal Agarwala, 1972, 1: 70-3.

On this family, see J. Spencer Trimingham, *The Sufi Order in Islam*, New York: Oxford University Press, 1971, pp. 92-5; Annemarie Schimmel, *Mystical Dimension of Islam*, Chapel Hill, NC: University of Carolina Press, 1975, p. 365.

7. These taxes were classified under the heads—*mal, jihat* and *sair-jihat*. The earliest definitions of these terms are available in the *Ain-i-Akbari*. In short, says Abul Fazl, 'whatever was assessed on the cultivated land in accordance with the *rai*' or crop-rates was known as *mal*. Whatever was collected from various kinds of arts and crafts was termed as *jihat*, and the rest of the taxes came to be known as *sair-jihat*'. Abul Fazl, *Ain-i-Akbari*, Persian text, ed. Sir Sayed Ahmad Khan, Lucknow: Munshi Newal Kishore Press, 1882, 1: 205, 294, 300-1; see also Yusuf Husain, ed., *Selected Documents of Shahjahan's Reign*, Hyderabad: Daftar-i-Diwani, 1950, p. 13; Irfan Habib, *The Agrarian System of Mughal India, 1556-1707*, 2nd revd edn, Delhi: Oxford University Press, 1999, pp. 283-4, n. 2; Noman Ahmad Siddiqi, 'Nature of the *Sair Jihat* Taxes', in *Essays in Medieval Indian Economic History*, ed. Satish Chandra, Delhi: Munshiram Manoharlal, 1987, pp. 36-42.
8. For one such example see Abul Fazl, *Akbarnama*, 3: 998-9 [649-50].
9. Abul Fazl, *Ain-i-Akbari*, 3 vols, in English, vol. 1, tr. H. Blochmann, vols. II and III, tr. H.S. Jarrett, rpt, Delhi: Low Price Publications, 1994, 1: 278-81.
10. Ibid., 1: 278.
11. Ibid. 'The word *suyurghal* which is of Mongol origin literally means a favour of a grant. Originally it denoted the documents under which *tuyul* was granted'. *Encyclopedia of Islam*, vol. IV, p. 800. In medieval Iran, the term *suyurghal* was used in general for revenue-free land grants. According to Roger Savory, a modern scholar of Iranian history, during the Safavid period religious persons were granted beneficiaries and immunities from taxation of the type known as *suyurghal*. *Iran Under the Safavids*, Cambridge: Cambridge University Press, 1980, p. 186.

12. Abul Fazl, *Ain-i-Akbari*, 1: 278. See also Muzaffar Alam, 'Some Aspects of the Changes in the Position of the *Madad-i-Maash* Holders in Awadh, 1676-1722', in *Essays in Medieval Indian Economic History*, ed. Satish Chandra, p. 72.
13. S.A.I. Tirmizi, *Mughal Documents, 1628-1659*, Delhi: Manohar, 1995, vol. 2, p. 20.
14. Jigar Mohammed, *Revenue Free Land Grants in Mughal India*, Delhi: Manohar, 2002, pp. 22-3.
15. R.P. Tripathi, *Some Aspects of Muslim Administration*, rpt, Allahabad: Central Book Depot, 1974, p. 255.
16. Moinuddin Momin, 'A *Suyurghal* of Babur', *Proceedings of the Indian Historical Records Commission*, pt. II, 1961, pp. 49-52.
17. Habib, *The Agrarian System*, p. 298.
18. Abul Fazl, *Ain-i-Akbari*, 1: 278-85.
19. Ibid., 2: 167-336.
20. According to Moreland, the *suyurghal* was an allowance paid in cash or granted in land. *The Agrarian System of Moslem India: A Historical Essay with Appendices*, rpt, Delhi: Oriental Books, 1968, p. 277. Noman Ahmad Siddiqi observes that the subsistence allowance in land was known as *madad-i-maash* or *milk*. The two types of grant were covered by the general term *suyurghal*. *Land Revenue Administration Under the Mughals, 1700-1750*, Bombay: Asia Publishing House, 1970, p. 123.
21. Shireen Moosvi, '*Suyurghal* Statistics in the *Ain-i-Akbari*', *Indian Historical Review*, vol. II, no. 2, 1967, p. 28.
22. This hypothesis can be examined from the fact that the word *suyurghal* was hardly ever used in the seventeenth-century grant documents. Habib, *The Agrarian System*, pp. 242-63. Apart from the works of Irfan Habib, Shireen Moosvi, Jigar Mohammed and Moinuddin, the other important works on *suyurghal* or *madad-i-maash* are S.Z.H. Jafari, 'Two *Madad-i-maash Farmans* from Awadh', *Proceedings of the Indian History Congress*, 40th Session, Waltair, 1979; Rafat Bilgrami, 'Some Mughal Revenue Grants to the Family and *Khanqah* of Sayyid Ashraf Jahangir', *Medieval India: A Miscellany II*, 4 vols, Bombay: Asia Publishing House, 1969-75; Iqbal Husain, '*Madad-i-Maash* Regulation in the Mughal Empire', *Proceedings of the Indian History Congress*, 38th Session, Bhubaneswar, 1977; Shaikh Abdur Rashid, '*Suyurghal* Lands Under the Mughals', in *Essay Presented to Sir J.N. Sarkar*, ed. H.R. Gupta, Hoshiarpur: Punjab University, 1958; Iqtidar Husain Siddiqi, '*Wajh-i-Maash* Grant Under the Afghan Kings, 1451-1555', *Medieval India: A Miscellany II*, pp.19-44; Muzaffar Alam, 'Changes in the Position of *Madad-i-Maash* Holders in Awadh'; Shireen Moosvi, *The Economy of the Mughal Empire c. 1595*, Delhi: Oxford University Press, 1987, pp. 153-73; Noman Ahmad Siddiqi, *Land Revenue Administration*, pp. 123-34; Jigar Mohammed, '*Madad-i-Maash* Grants in Punjab Under the Mughals', *Proceedings of the Punjab History Conference*, 35th Session, Patiala, 2003, pp. 214-19.

23. See Anand Ram Mukhlis, *Mirat-ul-Istilah*, tr. Tasneem Ahmad, *Encyclopedia Dictionary of Medieval India*, Delhi: Sundeep Publications, 1993, f.15a, f. 26a for the definitions of the terms *sarf-i-khas* and *khalisa*.
24. Noman Ahmad Siddiqi seems to be a pioneer historian who made a distinction between the sources of income for the personal expenses of the emperor and the sources of income claimed for the public treasury out of the *khalisa* lands. The *parganas* or the *mahals*, which were reserved for the personal expenses of the emperor, were known as *sarf-i-khas*. Such *parganas* were put in charge of separate officials and the income from them was deposited in a separate treasury. *Land Revenue Administration*, p. 103; see *Mirat-ul-Istilah*, f. 15a for a definition of this term.
25. The majority of Western historians classify the pre-colonial political system under the following theoretical concepts: Feudalism, Segmentary state, Patrimonialism or even Sultanistic. For a detailed discussion see Berkemer, 'Political System and Political Structure', pp. 122-37; Burton Stein, 'The Segmentary State', pp. 134-61; Ronald Inden, 'Ritual, Authority, and Cyclic Time in Hindu Kingship', in *Kingship and Authority in South Asia*, ed. J.F. Richards, Delhi: Oxford University Press, 1998, pp. 41-2. Stephen P. Blake, 'The Patrimonial–Bureaucratic Empire of the Mughal', in *The State in India*, ed. Kulke, pp. 278-303. According to Blake, in 1594 the income of Akbar's household (i.e. the monies from the emperor's private lands) was about 25 per cent of the total state revenue. See also Habib, *The Agrarian System*, pp. 313-16; Moosvi, *The Economy of the Mughal Empire*, pp. 196-201, 270.
26. Max Weber defines 'sultanism' as an extreme form of the patrimonial regime where rulership is a near complete personal monopoly of the absolute ruler. For a complete discussion of the patrimonial state, see Max Weber, *Economy and Society: An Outline of Interpretative Sociology*, ed. Guenther Roth and Claus Wittich, 3 vols, New York: Bedminister Press, 1968, 1: 229-64; 3: 966-72, 1006-69,1086-92.
27. See for a rebuttal of Blake's view, M. Athar Ali, 'The Mughal Polity—A Critique of "Revisionist" Approaches', *Proceedings of the Indian History Congress*, 52nd Session, Delhi, 1991-2, pt. II, pp. 302-12; also Sayed Ali Nadeem Rezavi, 'The Empire and Bureaucracy: The Case of Mughal Empire', *Proceedings of the Indian History Congress*, 59th Session, Patiala, 1998, pp. 361-76.
28. When deputed to manage the revenue administration of *sarkar* Sarangpur in Malwa in 1576, Bayazid reported that it was not 'suitable' for inclusion in the *khalisa* and it was accordingly assigned in *jagir*. Bayazid Bayat, *Tazkira-i Humayun wa Akbar*, ed. M. Hidayat Husain, Calcutta: Asiatic Society of Bengal, 1941, p. 353. The main criterion for the suitability or fitness of an area for inclusion in the *khalisa* may be judged from Hawkins' statement that 'the king taketh' any land 'for himself' (in it be rich ground and likely to yield much). William Foster, ed., *Early Travels in India, 1583-1619*, London: Humphery Milford, 1921, rpt, Delhi: Munshiram Manoharlal, 1985, p. 114.

29. See Irfan Habib, 'The Social Distribution of Landed Property in Pre-British India', in *Essays in Indian History: Towards a Marxist Perception*, ed. Irfan Habib, Delhi: Tulika, 1995, p. 95; U.N. Day, *The Mughal Government, 1556-1707*, Delhi: Munshiram Manoharlal, 1994, pp. 185-6.
30. Akbar is said to have remitted one-sixth of the *jama* in these provinces in 1586 and the remission in the *khalisa* amounted to 4,05,60,596 *dams*, so that the total *jama* of the *khalisa* in these provinces exceeded 243 million *dams*. Abul Fazl, *Akbarnama*, 3: 749 [494]. In the provincial statistics given in the *Ain-i-Akbari* the total *jama* of the three provinces amounts to nearly 1,014 million *dams*. The other cases of revenue remission mentioned in the *Akbarnama* do not offer such a straightforward opportunity for comparison. See also Habib, *The Agrarian System*, p. 314 (read 1586 for 1596-7).
31. Out of the total effective *jama* (3,96,03,27,106 *dams*) of the empire in 1595-6, a ceiling of 1,30,69,079 *dams* was under the *khalisa* for expenses on the imperial establishment. See Moosvi, *The Economy of the Mughal Empire*, pp. 197, 271; Habib, *The Agrarian System*, p. 314; Richards, *The Mughal Empire*, p. 76; Blake, 'The Patrimonial-Bureaucratic Empire', pp. 288, 294.
32. Habib, *The Agrarian System*, p. 314, n. 74; Blake, 'The Patrimonial-Bureaucratic Empire', p. 295.
33. Habib, *The Agrarian System*, p. 314; Day, *The Mughal Government*, p.186.
34. Abdul Hamid Lahori, *Padshahnama,* 2 vols, ed. Maulvi Kabiruddin and Maulvi Abdul Rahim, Calcutta: Asiatic Society of Bengal, 1867-8, 2: 709-12.
35. Shaikh Muhammad Baqa, *Mirat-al-Alam*, MS. Abdus Salam, Aligarh: Azad Library, f. 214b; Habib, *The Agrarian System*, pp. 314-15.
36. Badauni, *Muntakhab-ut-Tawarikh*, 2:193 [190].
37. Moreland, *The Agrarian System*, p. 75. See also Habib, 'The Social Distribution of Landed Property', pp. 95-8.
38. Moosvi, *The Economy of the Mughal Empire*, p. 197.
39. Blake, 'The Patrimonial–Bureaucratic Empire', p. 295.
40. Pierre Du Jarric's *Account of the Jesuit Mission at the Court of Akbar*, tr. C.H. Payne, *Akbar and the Jesuits*, New York: Harper & Brothers, 1926, pp. 5-6.
41. Tapan Raychaudhuri and Irfan Habib, eds., *The Cambridge Economic History of India*, vol. I, *c.1200-c.1750*, Cambridge: Cambridge University Press, 1982, p. 241.
42. Adapted from Moosvi, *The Economy of the Mughal Empire*, p. 270, Table 11.5.
43. Apparently this officer later became popular and was given the title Khan-i-Jahan. For details of his life and career, see Shah Nawaz Khan and Abdul Hayy, *Maasir-ul-Umara*, ed. Maulvi Abdur Rahim and Ashraf Ali, 3 vols, Calcutta: Asiatic Society of Bengal, 1887-96, in English tr. Henry Beveridge, completed by Beni Prasad, 3 vols, rpt, Patna: Janaki Prakashan, 1979, 1: 645-9; *Ain-i-Akbari*, 1: 348-51.
44. Abul Fazl, *Akbarnama*, 2: 163 [107].

45. Ibid., 2: 106 [68].
46. Bayazid Bayat, *Tazkira-i-Humayun wa Akbar*, p. 244.
47. William Irvine, *The Army of the Indian Moghuls*, Delhi: Eurasia Publishing, 1962, p. 95.
48. In Arabic, *mansab* was pronounced as *mansib*. In.Persia and India, however, the word was pronounced as *mansab*. It means a post, an office, and hence the term *mansabdar* signifies an officer. The word is generally restricted to high officials, cited in *Ain-i-Akbari*, 1: 247, n. 1; F. Steingass, *Persian-English Dictionary*, rpt, Delhi: Munshiram Manoharlal, 1973, p. 1328, *mansab* means post, dignity, office, ministry, magistracy, a high office.
49. It is generally held [W.H. Moreland's, 'Rank (*mansab*) in the State Service', *Journal of the Royal Asiatic Society*, 1936; reproduced in *The Mughal State*, ed. Muzaffar Alam and Sanjay Subrahmanyam, p. 221; Abdul Aziz, *Mansabdari System and the Mughal Army*, Delhi: Idarah-i-Adabiyat-i Delhi, 1972, pp. 147-9] that the recipient of high rank—500 under Akbar and 1,000 under Shahjahan—was designated *umara* while the word *mansabdar* was used for those holding lower rank, i.e. below 500 or 1000. However, Abul Fazl, *Akbarnama*, 3:1031[671]; *Ain-i-Akbari*, 1: 247-51; Mutamad Khan, *Iqbalnama-i-Jahangiri*, ed. Maulavi Abdul-Hayy and Maulavi Ahmad Ali Sahun, Calcutta: Asiatic Society of Bengal, 1865, vol. 2, p. 288, use the term *mansabdar* for all rank-holders without any distinction. According to the *Tabaqat-i-Akbari*, 2: 653[456], the word *umara* was reserved during Akbar's reign to those holding *mansabs* exceeding 500.
50. B.Y. Vladimirtsov, *The Life of Genghis Khan*, tr. D.S. Mirsky, London: Benjamin Blom, 1935, pp. 58, 69. For rudiments of *mansab*, see also Father A. Monserrate, *The Commentary of Father Monserrate, On His Journey to the Court of Akbar*, tr. J.S. Hoyland and annotated by S.N. Banerjee, Delhi: Oxford University Press, 1922; rpt, Jalandhar: Asian Publisher, 1993, pp. 68-9; Abdul Aziz, *The Mansabdari System and the Mughal Army*, pp. 16-25; M. Athar Ali, *The Mughal Nobility Under Aurangzeb*, revd edn, Delhi: Oxford University Press, 1997, p. 38.
51. Zahiruddin Muhammad Babur, *Baburnama*, tr. A.S. Beveridge, 2 vols, bound as I, Delhi: Oriental Books, 1979, pp. 170, 277.
52. Abul Fazl, *Akbarnama*, 2: 402-3[270].
53. Ibid., 3: [69].
54. Ibid., 3: [117].
55. Ibid., 3: 208-9 [147]; *Muntakhab-ut-Tawarikh*, 2: 218 [214-15].
56. Mutamad Khan, *Iqbalnama-i-Jahangiri*, 2: 288; see also Abul Fazl, *Ain-i-Akbari*, 1: 265-6.
57. A.J. Qaisar, 'Note on the Date of Institution of *Mansab* under Akbar', *Proceedings of the Indian History Congress*, 24th Session, Delhi, 1961, pp. 155-7.
58. Abul Fazl, *Ain-i-Akbari*, 1: 321-596; *Tabaqat-i-Akbari*, 1: 653-712 [425-56].

59. See Shireen Moosvi, 'Evolution of *Mansab* System Under Akbar Until 1596-97', *Journal of the Royal Asiatic Society*, 1981, pp. 173-85; idem, *The Economy of the Mughal Empire*, pp. 202-4.
60. Moreland, 'Rank (*Mansab*) in the State Service', pp. 213-33.
61. Cf. M. Athar Ali, *The Mughal Nobility Under Aurangzeb*, p. 39; Qaisar, 'Note on the Date of Institution of *Mansab*', pp. 155-7.
62. For an elaboration see Moosvi, 'Evolution of *Mansab* System', pp. 173-85; Irfan Habib, 'The *Mansab* System, 1596-1637', *Proceedings of the Indian History Congress*, 29th Session, Patiala, 1967, pp. 221-42.
63. Abul Fazl, *Akbarnama*, 3: 1031[671]; *Ain-i-Akbari*, 1:248-9.
64. Abul Fazl, *Ain-i-Akbari*, 1: 257-8.
65. Abdul Aziz, *The Mansabdari System and the Mughal Army*, pp. 96-8.
66. Cf. Irvine, *The Army of the Indian Moghuls*, p.10; Moreland, 'Rank (*mansab*) in the State Service', pp.213-33.The average pay calculated by earlier scholars has been re-examined by Irfan Habib and his conclusions throw more light on the pay and the composition of the troopers of a *mansabdar.* See 'The *Mansab* System, 1596-1637', pp. 221-42; also see his '*Mansab* Salary Scales Under Jahangir and Shahjahan', *Islamic Culture,* 1985, pp. 203-27.
67. Abul Fazl, *Ain-i-Akbari*, 1: 249-50. The principle for sub-classification of each *zat* rank is also given in *Mirat-ul-Istilah*, 15a-15b.
68. Abdul Aziz, *The Mansabdari System and the Mughal Army*, p. 171.
69. Athar Ali, *Mughal Nobility Under Aurangzeb*, Chaps. 2 and 3.
70. S. Nurul Hasan, 'New Light on the Relationships of the Early Mughal Rulers with Their Nobility', *Proceedings of the Indian History Congress*, 7th Session, Madras, 1944, pp. 389-97.
71. Kanwar Muhammad Ashraf, *Life and Conditions of the People of Hindustan*, Delhi: Munshiram Manoharlal, 1970, p. 58.
72. *Jagir* is a compound of two Persian words and should strictly be, though was not, spelt *jai-gir*. Literally, it means 'one holding or occupying a place'. *Bahar-i-Ajam,* the Persian dictionary, defines it as a 'tract of land, which kings, confer upon nobles and *mansabdars*'. See Munshi Tek Chand, 'Bahar', *Bahar-i-Azam, 1739-40 A.D.*, lithograph, Lucknow: Newal Kishore Press, 1916.
73. The author of the *Mirat-ul-Istilah* seeks to make a distinction between the meanings of *tuyul* and *jagir*. According to him, the former was used for assignments held by princes of royal blood and the latter for those held by *mansabdars*. Anand Ram Mukhlis, *Mirat-ul-Istilah*, f. 26a. There is no evidence of the existence of such a refinement in the literature of sixteenth and seventeenth centuries and both terms are used indiscriminately for all assignments, at least during the reign of Akbar.
74. *Iqta* is an Arabic word, almost as old as Islam. It initially denoted a piece of landed property received from the state, but gradually came to signify revenue assignments 'in which the state has the real right of property',

F. Lokkegaard, *Islamic Taxation in the Classic Period*, Copenhagen: Branner Og Korch, 1950, pp. 14ff. It was purely in the latter sense that the word was used in the literature of the Delhi Sultanate. By the Mughal period, it was used largely when a formal style was affected and to deliberately avoid the more mundane word *jagir*. In Mughal India, the word *jagir* was more common than the term *iqta*, but remained a secondary synonym of *jagir*. See Ali Muhammad Khan, *Mirat-i-Ahmadi*, tr. M.F. Lokhandawala, Baroda: Oriental Institute, 1965, 1: 355.

75. Cf. Steingass, *Persian–English Dictionary*.
76. Iqtidar Husain Siddiqi is the first scholar who noticed a dissimilarity between the revenue assignment terms used in the sense of *iqta*, *wajh* and *jagir*. See his '*Iqta* System Under the Lodi's', *Proceedings of the Indian History Congress*, 24th Session, Delhi, 1961, pp. 145-9; *Some Aspects of Afghan Despotism in India*, Aligarh: Three Men Publication, 1969, pp. 146-55; *History of Shershah Sur*, Aligarh: P.C. Dwadash Shreni, 1971, pp. 12-18.
77. For a more extensive discussion, see Iqtidar Husain Siddiqi, '*Iqta* System', pp.145-9; idem, *History of Shershah Sur*, pp. 12-18; idem, *Sher Shah Sur and His Dynasty*, Jaipur: Publication Scheme, 1995, Chap. 1. See also Habib, *The Agrarian System*, p. 298, n. 1; idem, 'The Social Distribution of Landed Property', p. 95: Iqtidar Alam Khan, 'The Mughal Assignment System During Akbar's Early Years, 1556-1575', in *Medieval India I: Researches in the History of India, 1200-1750*, ed. Irfan Habib, Delhi: Oxford University Press, 1992, pp. 66-7.
78. The expression *wajh-wa-istiqamat* was misread as *wajh-i-istiqamat* by Ahsan Raza Khan and Yog Raj Malhotra, which can lead to erroneous interpretations. Cf. Ahsan Raza Khan, 'Babur's Settlement of His Conquest in Hindustan', *Proceedings of the Indian History Congress*, 29th Session, Patiala, 1967, p. 218; Yog Raj Malhotra, *Babur's Nobility and Administration in Hindustan*, Jalandhar: ABS Publication, 1996, pp. 11-15. Compare with Iqtidar Alam Khan, 'Mughal Assignment System', pp. 67-8, n. 14.
79. The absence of the term *jagir* for assignments in the royal orders of Akbar's early years deserves further study. The suppositions drawn by Irfan Habib and S.Z.H. Jafari from their reading of *farmans* of Akbar's early years call for a careful examination. See the *farmans* translated and reproduced by S.Z.H. Jafari, 'A *Farman* of Akbar (1558) from the Period of the Regency', pp. 266-8; Irfan Habib, 'Three Early *Farmans* of Akbar, in Favour of Ramdas, the Master Dyer', pp. 270-87; both in *Akbar and His India*, ed. Irfan Habib, Delhi: Oxford University Press, 1997. See also Irfan Habib, 'Aspects of Agrarian Relations and Economy in a Region of Uttar Pradesh during the 16th Century', *The Indian Economic and Social History Review*, vol. IV, no. 3, 1967, pp. 205-32; Irfan Habib and Tarapada Mukherjee, 'Akbar and the Temples of Mathura and its Environs', *Proceedings of the Indian History Congress*, 48th Session, Bambolium, 1987, pp. 245-6. Their assumptions can

be compared with Iqtidar Alam Khan, who has cited not less than thirteen instances up to 1559 from the *Akbarnama* and the *Tabaqat-i-Akbari*, where the term *jagir* was in vogue for assignments. See 'Mughal Assignment System', pp. 66-7, 83-6, 120.

80. Iqtidar Alam Khan, 'Mughal Assignment System', pp. 62-3.
81. Genghis Khan and Timur also allotted substantial *jagirs* to their nobles, see Sharfuddin Ali Yezdi, *Political and Military Institution of Tamarlane,* tr. Major Davy, Delhi: Idarah-i-Adabiyat-i Delhi, 1972, pp. 85-6.
82. Richards, *The Mughal Empire,* p. 66.
83. Habib, 'The Social Distribution of Landed Property', pp. 84-6.
84. Ibid.; Iqtidar Husain Siddiqi, '*Iqta* System', pp. 145-9. For other important works on the assignment systems before Akbar see Iqtidar Husain Siddiqi, 'The Agrarian System of Afghans', *Studies in Islam, II*, January, 1965, pp. 229-53; see also his '*Wajh-i-Maash* Grants Under the Afghan Kings (1451-1555)', pp. 19-44; Ahsan Raza Khan, 'Babur's Settlement', pp. 207-20; W.H. Moreland, 'Shershah's Revenue System', *Journal of the Royal Asiatic Society*, pt. I, 1926, pp. 447-59; S. Nurul Hasan, 'Revenue Administration of the *Jagir* of Sahasram by Farid (Shershah)', *Proceedings of the Indian History Congress* 26th Session, Ranchi, 1964, pt. II, pp. 102-7.
85. K.K. Trivedi, *Agra: Economic and Political Profile of a Mughal Suba, 1580-1707*, Pune: Ravish Publishers, 1998, pp. 2-3.
86. Moreland, *Agrarian System*, p. 80.
87. Richards, *The Mughal Empire*, p. 66.
88. For a different viewpoint, see Iqtidar Alam Khan, 'The Nobility under Akbar and the Development of His Religious Policy', *Journal of the Royal Asiatic Society,* 1968, pp. 29-36. Akbar had maintained a discreet distance during the struggle for supremacy at the court between different factions of the nobility after the dismissal of Bairam Khan as *vakil-ul-sultanate.* Soon he appointed competent persons to manage in particular the revenue department.
89. Three historians of Akbar's reign agree that the entire land in Akbar's empire was fit for cultivation. Muhammad Arif Qandhari, *Tarikh-i-Akbari*, Persian text, ed. Sayyid Moinuddin Nadwi, Sayyid Azhar Ali and Imtiaz Ali Arshi, Rampur: Raza Library, 1962, p. 131, in English, tr. Tasneem Ahmad, Delhi: Pragati Publications, 1993; Khwaja Nizamuddin Ahmad, *Tabaqat-i-Akbari*, 2: 456. As for the area actually cultivated, Nizamuddin Ahmad explains the object of Akbar's administrative measures in 1574-5, and says that 'most of the vast, inhabited area of Hindustan was lying uncultivated'. See also Abul Fazl, *Ain-i-Akbari*, 2: [5-6].

    There are indications that the entire cultivable land within a village or a *mahal* was not brought under cultivation and a considerable part of it was left fallow. It has been recognized that under the Mughals there was not enough capital and manpower to bring all the cultivable land under cultivation. Compare with Moreland, *The Agrarian System*, Introduction,

p. xii; Irfan Habib, *The Agrarian System*, p. 1, n. 1. Noman Ahmad Siddiqi, *Land Revenue Administration*, p. 105. Describing the condition of land and cultivation Bernier says, 'that even of those that would be fertile, there is much that is not used for want of workmen', Francois Bernier, *Travels in the Mughal Empire, 1656-68*, tr. Archibald Constable, revd Vincent A. Smith, New Delhi: Oriental Books, 1983, pt. II, p. 5.

90. Abul Fazl, *Akbarnama*, 3: 692, n. 4 [459]; see also Arif Qandhari, *Tarikh-i-Akbari*, p. 231 [197]. The said argument is also supported in the *Tabaqat-i-Akbari*, 2: 456, 560-1, n. 3. According to him the appointment of a large number of men as *jagirdars* was Akbar's object to bring more parts of the empire which were still uncultivated under cultivation.
91. For pioneering work on the *jagirdari* system under the Mughals, see Moreland, *The Agrarian System*; Habib, *The Agrarian System*; M. Athar Ali, *The Mughal Nobility Under Aurangzeb*; Noman Ahmad Siddiqi, *Land Revenue Administration*.
92. Iqtidar Alam Khan, 'Mughal Assignment System', pp. 62-127.
93. Monserrate, *The Commentary of Father Monserrate*; William, ed., *Early Travels in India*; Jean-Baptiste Tavernier, *Travels in India, 1640-47*, tr. V. Ball, revd William Crook, 2 vols, London: Humphery Milford, 1925; rpt, Delhi: Oriental Books, 1977; Francois Bernier, *Travels in the Mughal Empire*; Sir Thomas Roe, *The Embassy of Sir Thomas Roe to India*, ed. William Foster, London: Humphrey Milford, 1926; rpt, Delhi: Munshiram Manoharlal, 1990.
94. Khaliq Ahmad Nizami, *On History and Historians in Medieval India*, Delhi: Munshiram Manoharlal, 1983, pp. 141-60, 224-44.
95. Ibid., pp. 141-60; see also Harbans Mukhia, *Historians and Historiography During the Reign of Akbar*, Delhi: Vikas Publishing House, 1976, pp. 41-89.
96. Nizami, *On History and Historians*, pp. 240-2; Mukhia, *Historians and Historiography*, pp. 89-132.
97. *Bakshi* were officials responsible for the administration of the *mansabdari* and *jagirdari* systems at the central and provincial levels. See Ishtiaq Husain Qureshi, *The Administration of the Mughal Empire*, rpt, Delhi: Low Price Publications, 1990, pp. 77-9; Ibn Hasan, *The Central Structure of the Mughal Empire*, Delhi: Munshiram Manoharlal, 1980, pp. 210-33; Paramatma Saran, *The Provincial Government of the Mughals*, Bombay: Asia Publishing House, 1973, pp. 182-3.
98. Nizamuddin Ahmad, *Tabaqat-i-Akbari*, 2: 370-1.
99. Nizami, *On History and Historians*, pp. 230-2, 238-9; Mukhia, *Historians and Historiography*, pp. 155-60.
100. Muhammad Qasim Hindu Shah Farishta, *Tarikh-i-Farishta*, Persian text, ed. J. Briggs, 2 vols, Lucknow: Newal Kishore Press, 1905, in English tr. J. Briggs, *History of the Rise of Mohammadan Power in India*, 4 vols, Calcutta: Asiatic Society of Bengal, 1908.

101. Nuruddin Muhammad Jahangir, *Tuzuk-i-Jahangiri*, ed. Sir Sayed Ahmad Khan, in English tr. Alexander Rogers, ed. Henry. Beveridge, *The Memoirs of Jahangir*, Delhi: Munshiram Manoharlal, 1978.
102. Mutamad Khan, *Iqbal Nama-i-Jahangiri*.
103. Shaikh Farid Bhakkari, *Zakhirat-ul-Khawanin*, ed. Syed Moin-ul-Haq, 3 vols, Karachi: Pakistan Historical Society, 1961-75, in English, vol. I, tr. Z.A. Desai, Delhi: Idarah-i-Adabiyat-i Delhi, 1993. I am grateful to Ahsan Raza Khan for lending the Persian text to me from his personal library.
104. Shah Nawaz Khan and Abdul Hayy, *Maasir-ul-Umara*.
105. H. Blochmann, 'Biographies', in *Ain-i-Akbari*, vol. I, rpt, Delhi: Low Price Publications, 1994.
106. Kewal Ram, *Tazkirat-ul-Umara*, tr. S.M. Azizuddin Husain, Delhi: Munshiram Manoharlal, 1985.
107. See Bibliography for sources mentioned hereafter in this chapter.

CHAPTER 2

General Features of the *Jagirdari* System

The Mughal emperor commanded the services of a body of warrior–aristocrats comprising the mature royal princes and several hundred *amirs* (nobles) and high ranking *mansabdars*. These officers served as provincial governors or occupied other higher administrative positions throughout the empire. Alternatively, they were employed as military commanders of armies in the field or as part of the central military. In their military capacity these *amirs* or *mansabdars* also served as commanders of strategic fortresses and reported directly to the emperor. Paid lavishly, these grandees headed households and troop contingents varying in size from several hundred to several thousand persons. When transferred from one administrative position to another, their establishments moved with them. The imperial system depended heavily on the martial qualities, administrative skills and political and entrepreneurial strengths of this body.

Members of this cadre and their privately employed officers and servants performed the major administrative tasks. Acting as military commanders, the nobles recruited, trained and equipped the bulk of the heavy cavalry, which formed the main striking arm of the Mughal armies. They employed bodies of skilled musketeers both mounted and on foot. At its core each military contingent relied on a body of closely related kinsmen and more distantly related lineage mates. Additional manpower was readily recruited from the vast military labour market of India and the Central Asia. Well-trained, professional cavalrymen, infantry and gunners were readily available for those who offered to pay cash.

As recipients of *jagirs* or salary assignments on the land revenue the nobles played a crucial role in tax collection from the countryside. *Amirs* and higher ranking *mansabdars* employed their own staff to collect the greater part of the land tax. Some of this was used to pay their own generous salaries, but the greater share was spent on the cash salaries of their troopers. The organization of that considerable effort was left to the nobles themselves. The role of the central administration was confined to inspection, monitoring and auditing.

GENERAL PATTERNS

The *jagirdari* system under the Mughals developed as a distinct institution and was governed by elaborate rules and regulations. The foundation of this unique institution was laid during the reign of Akbar. The system was mainly evolved to secure the efficient and disciplined service of a body of men and at the same time to relieve the government of the enormous burden of land revenue administration and the maintenance of law and order in the rural areas. By the end of the seventeenth century, however, this very system is believed to have threatened the administrative and economic stability of the empire. It is, therefore, important to consider once again the essentials of the system and investigate its nature and working in greater detail.

The *jagirdar* was entitled to collect the revenue from the area assigned to him as *jagir*. This enabled him to meet not only his personal expenses, but also those of the cavalry contingent that he was expected to maintain because of his service to the emperor. The *chaudhuris* or *deshmukhs*, *qanungos* and *muqaddams* and peasants and cultivators were answerable to the assignee for the whole of the *mal-i-wajib* (revenue) and *huquq-i-diwani*[1] (fiscal demands). Though this consisted mainly of land revenue, it could also include the numerous additional cesses[2] which were probably exacted by officials even in the fairly distant rural areas.[3] Generally speaking, the markets of large towns and ports were constituted into separate *mahals* (as distinct from *parganas*, or territorial *mahals*), but these again were as frequently assigned in *jagir* as others.[4] Theoretically, the sole claimant of the land revenue and other taxes was the emperor. A *jagirdar* had therefore no permanent rights in his assignment. His claim was confined to the authorized land revenue and taxes, and he could demand no more than the authorized taxes assessed according to the imperial regulations.[5]

The *jagir* was usually assigned in lieu of the *mansabdar's* service to the state. The principal assumption was that when an officer was sanctioned a salary and was assigned a *jagir*, his pay claim (*talab*) as determined by the pay schedules was exactly the same as the *jama* or *jamadami*[6] entered in the imperial register against the territorial units comprising his *jagir*. A standing assessment or *jama* was prepared for each unit of territory, the village and particularly the *paragana* or *mahal.*[7] To serve best, this *jama* was supposed to approximate as closely as possible to the actual collection or *hasil.*[8] According to Abul Fazl, the working of such a *jama* was one of the chief objectives of Akbar's revenue policy.[9]

The most common form of land revenue assessment in the Mughal Empire reflected this situation. Procedures and methods varied greatly in time and space, but the most common system was *nasaq* (method, arrangement). *Nasaq* entailed negotiations between the tax assessor/ collector (*amin* in *parganas* who paid their revenue to the central treasury, *amil* in *jagirs*) and the local officials and *zamindars*. The collector made an assessment of the production of the area on the basis of local records and calculated the revenue demand in accordance with the local prices.[10] His assessment stood unless the local officials challenged it. If they did, the assessor negotiated with them. Normally, they reached a compromise; if not, the assessor had to resort to threat or force to collect the revenue. The two local officials involved in this were the *qanungo* and the *chaudhuri*. Men were appointed to these positions by imperial diploma, but the appointment recognized rather than bestowed local status. The *qanungo* collected and maintained records of the cultivated area, crop production, revenue demand, tax rates and prices in his *pargana.*[11] The revenue records of the central government depended on those of the *qanungos*, most of whom belonged to the Hindu accounting castes. The *chaudhuri* was usually a leading *zamindar* of the *pargana* and he collected the revenue of the *pargana* from the other *zamindars* and handed it over to the imperial recipient. His signature on the revenue assessment guaranteed payment.[12]

The imperial representative and the *chaudhuri* confronted each other annually or biennially to decide the share of the revenue of the *zamindars* and the imperial treasury or assignee. The collector had the upper hand because the Mughals could, if the need arose, defeat any *zamindar.*[13] For this reason, they normally received 90 per cent of the land revenue.[14] If the collector pushed the *chaudhuri* so far that a military expedition became imminent, he reduced his profit drastically.

The *chaudhuri*, on the other hand, risked ruin if his inflexibility forced the imperial authorities to take action against him. For this reason, bargaining normally led to a settlement acceptable to both sides. *Zamindar* revolts, revenue wars were nonetheless common place in the Mughal Empire. H.K. Naqvi has found evidence of 144 such uprisings during Akbar's reign.[15] In some areas, fighting broke out every time the Mughals attempted to collect taxes.[16] Routine administration in such areas required the use of force.

The Mughal regime in the provinces thus did not touch the individual peasant or even many villages. It consisted of a series of relationships between the Mughal officials and the *zamindars*. After the defeat of the regional dynasty, the Mughal conquest concentrated on the development of these connections, which constituted a revenue settlement (*band o bast*). The settlements included recognition of the *zamindars, chaudhuris* and *qanungos*, fixing of the amount of revenue which the conquered area would yield, and assignment of the revenue to the Mughals for the first time.[17] This explains the unusual fluidity of Mughal expansion. The Mughal government had no roots; the elimination of the governor and his army ended the Mughal rule in the province. The Mughals had to conquer Malwa and most of Bengal twice for this reason.

As a rule *jagirs* were conditional on rendering military service, but there are references to *jagirs* to which no military service was attached.[18] This was known as *bedagh-o-mahalli*, i.e. the holder had neither to provide any military contingent nor to collect taxes.[19] Badauni had such a *jagir* of 1,000 *bighas* and he often described himself in jest as a *hazari* or commander of one thousand.[20] A similar *jagir* was held by Fattullah Shirazi of Baswar.[21]

As stated earlier, nobles who received their salary in *jagir* were known as *jagirdars* and those who received their salary in cash were known as *naqdi*. During the earlier years of Akbar's reign, salaries of nobles were paid by either of these means. In the later period many nobles received their salary partly in cash and partly in *jagir*.[22]

The system of granting land and land revenues to nobles had been in vogue for centuries in European as well as Asian countries. It was an essential feature of the monarchical system. In view of the status of barons, the monarchs assigned them vast estates which not only enabled them to maintain their troops, but also offered them an opportunity to demonstrate their military prowess and display their wealth and pelf. Besides, the extent of a *jagir* determined the political status of a noble. In lieu of the *jagirs*, the nobles supported their patron through thick and thin and even laid down their lives in their effort to extend the boundaries of the empire of their masters.

In medieval India, the appropriation of agricultural surplus and its systematic distribution amongst different segments of the ruling class was done mainly through the ingrained revenue assignment system. Each holder of a revenue assignment had the right to collect the revenue of an assigned piece of land in exchange of certain military or administrative services to the emperor. Through the assignment system, the emperors also exercised control over exploitation and redistribution of agrarian resources. As a result, the Turko–Persian armies were organized to match the assignment system. Each military unit, be it the great nobles or the individual horseman, received the proceeds from the earmarked territory.

Since the establishment of Mughal rule in India, officers were paid their salaries in terms of land revenue. There is no reference in the available literature to indicate that either Babur or Humayun introduced any significant changes in the prevalent assignment system. They accepted what they found.[23] Babur gave assignments to his nobles soon after the battle of Panipat.[24] It has been generally argued that Babur, after his victory over Sultan Ibrahim Lodi and occupation of Agra, parcelled out the land and cities of the more settled regions amongst his officers, who levied land tax from the peasant cultivators, duties from the merchants and shopkeepers, and pool tax from non-Muslims.[25] Humayun not only confirmed the assignments which had been given to nobles by his father,[26] but he also granted new assignments in Bengal and elsewhere. Jahangir wrote, 'Our ancestors and forefathers were in the habit of granting *jagirs* to everyone under proprietary title'.[27] During the early years of Akbar's reign the assignment of *jagirs* to nobles was similar in many ways to that which was followed by his ancestors: cities, towns and villages were allotted to officers according to their ranks. 'The whole country', wrote Badauni, 'with the exception of those lands held immediately for the *khalisa* lands were held by the *amirs* as *jagirs*'.[28] Akbar sought to improve the functioning of the system. That is why according to Moreland, 'we may fairly treat the accession of Akbar as the opening of a new period'.[29]

JAGIR AND *JAGIRDAR'S* OFFICIAL POSTING

A *jagir* holder possessed only fiscal rights and had no rights of land-ownership, occupancy, or residence. This was not a fief. It was purely a fiscal instrument designed to meet a narrowly defined end. Only Rajput *mansabdars* were given more extensive rights of residence and local power within their homelands. By special dispensation they received patrimonial (termed *watan*) lands as a part of the *jagirs* assigned to them.

The grant of *jagirs* inevitably involved political considerations. Since the emperor alone could confer, increase, diminish or resume the *jagir*, the *jagirdars* were essentially his creation.[30] The standard procedure of the distribution of *jagirs* within a region appears to be that at the time of the appointment of a high noble as the *hakim* of a certain region, an official of the central *diwan* would be deputed for supervising the distribution of *jagirs* among the nobles stationed there. Abul Fazl reported this procedure in connection with the assignment of *jagirs* in Malwa in 1562.[31] It may be assumed that the locale and value of the *jagirs* of even the highest nobles was expected to be properly defined through *sanads* issued by the central *diwan*. Refusal by the commandants of the regions to abide by this procedure was not condoned. One of the reasons for the breach between the Uzbek nobles and the court in 1565 was the refusal of Ali Quli Khan and other Uzbek nobles to accept such control.[32] However, there were occasional instances of the emperor virtually delegating his authority of assigning *jagirs* in different regions to the local commanders.[33]

There were, however, times when the provincial officers allotted *jagirs* to nobles without the approval of the concerned authority. Such allotments had later to be ratified by the emperor or the central *diwan*. In 1560, Ali Quli who was then the *hakim* of Jaunpur and the adjoining *sarkars*, assigned *sarkar* Banaras to his younger brother, Bahadur Khan, on the presumption that he was doing it on behalf of the emperor (*az qibl-i-padshahi*).[34] In the spring of 1581, Akbar went to the Panjab and Kabul to deal with Mirza Muhammad Hakim who had invaded Hindustan in response to the invitation of the rebel Masum Khan.[35] Akbar left Shahbaz Khan at Agra, effectively as a regent. In Akbar's absence, Shahbaz Khan had 'turned the whole of the imperial dominion right away from [Garhi] to the Panjab into people's *jagir*'. Upon Akbar's return he chastized Shahbaz for this unauthorized largesse. Shahbaz

Khan replied: 'If I had not thus won over the soldiery, they would have revolted *with one consent*. Now the empire is yours and the army is yours. You may give what you like to whom you will and take away appointment and *jagir* from whom you please. . . .'[36]

Hakim Abul Fath's letter also confirms that Shahbaz Khan was exchanging land revenue assignment for cash salaries and a harsh *farman* was despatched to him expressing the emperor's disapproval.[37] There are other instances where the emperor or the central *diwan* cancelled such a assignment. Ali Quli Khan had allotted the *jagir* of Sandila to one of his relatives, Ismail Quli Khan. But this assignment was superseded by the central *diwan*, who assigned it in *jagir* to Husain Khan Jalair. Ali Quli Khan, who initially encouraged Ismail Quli Khan in his resistance, subsequently, appears to have relented.[38] During the governorship of Shahabuddin Ahmad Khan in Gujarat, he assigned *jagirs* to many people without having the power to do so. After his transfer from Gujarat, Itimad Khan became governor of Gujarat, and refused to confirm these *jagirs* without the emperor's orders.[39] In 1581, Shaikh Ibrahim successfully maintained law and order at Fathpur. Shahbaz Khan Kambu offered the Shaikh a *jagir* in Mahaban (Mathura) so that he would put an end to the depredation of robbers there, but Shaikh Ibrahim rejected it on the ground that he could not accept any *jagir* without the emperor's consent.[40] Prince Daniyal appropriated the *jagir* of Mirza Shahrukh when he was serving in the Deccan. When the news of this incident reached the emperor, an order was issued to the prince stating that his resumption of the *jagir* was exceedingly disapproved of, and that he must restore it.[41]

There has been a general assumption that the location of a *jagir* bore little relationship to the official posting or service of the holder. From subsequent arguments, however, it would appear that there was a standard procedure to assign *jagirs* to officials either within or adjacent to the province of their postings.[42] Commenting on the working of the assignment system during the early years of Akbar's reign, Iqtidar Alam Khan says,

> At the time of Humayun's death, the Mughal Empire appeared to be divided into . . . [ideal *military-adminstrative-fiscal units, i.e. Vilayets*] commanded by leading nobles. Within these . . . [vast-*Vilayets*], there existed smaller charges held [*separately for adminstration*] by nobles placed in a subordinate position to the commanders (*hakims*) of larger territories [*Vilayets*]. Side by side with

military commands and charges there also existed revenue assignments (*jagirs*) of the individual nobles. The *jagir* (revenue assignment as distinct from military-administrative charge) of a high noble covering a number of contiguous *parganas*, sometimes even *sarkars*, would be mostly located within the territory controlled by him. But it would not always be concomitant with his military administrative charge. Speaking in terms of the territory covered by the two kinds of assignments, one might say that the military administrative charge of a high noble would always extend much beyond that of his revenue assignment. On the other hand, in the case of an ordinary noble holding charge of a *sarkar* or *pargana* in a subordinate position to a high noble, the meagre evidence we have suggests that the confines of his *jagirs* often conformed to the territory of his charge[43] (emphasis added).

There were numerous such instances. At the time of Humayun's death Tardi Beg administered the territory from Delhi which extended over a number of surrounding *sarkars* including Mewat and Narnaul. Tardi Beg's own revenue assignment in lieu of his salary was located in Mewat,[44] in the region of his posting. The *sarkar* of Narnaul apparently comprised the military charge as well as revenue assignment of one of Tardi Beg's subordinates, Majnun Khan Qaqshal.[45] In the same year Sambhal was not only under the military charge of Ali Quli Khan (Khan-i-Zaman), but he also held his salary assignment within the territory of Sambhal.[46] At the end of 1556, Sikandar Khan Uzbek (Khan-i-Aalam) was ordered to assist Khizr Khwaja Khan against Sikandar Sur in the Panjab while simultaneously the *jagir* of Sialkot within the region of his posting was allotted to him.[47] In March 1557, Bahadur Khan was appointed *hakim* of Multan and was ordered to quell the rebellion of the Baluchis in the neighbourhood of Multan. The *jagir* of Multan (which was held by Muhammad Quli Khan Barlas) was assigned to Bahadur Khan and Barlas was transferred to Nagaur.[48] In 1557, the *hukumat* of Lahore was entrusted to Husain Khan Tukriah and his *jagir* was also transferred to the place of his new posting. His personal *jagir* comprised part of the total estimated revenues of Lahore.[49]

During the initial period of Akbar's reign, the overall military administrative charge of *sarkar* Kabul rested with Munim Khan (Khan-i-Khanan), who also had the power to appoint or dismiss commanders of different places within that *sarkar*.[50] His personal *jagir* comprised part of the total estimated revenues of *sarkar* Kabul itself.[51] His subordinates' *jagirs* were also in *sarkar* Kabul. In this connection, mention may be made of Mir Hashim's *jagir* comprising Kahmard, Ghorband and Zuhak,[52] or of Khwaja Jalaluddin Muhammad Bujaq holding the *hukumat* of Ghaznin.[53] In 1567, Munim Khan was also appointed *hakim* of the territory of Jaunpur. After the defeat of Ali Quli Khan, Bahadur Khan and Ibrahim Khan, their *jagirs* in the Jaunpur region such as Jaunpur, Ghazipur and the forts of Chunar and Zamania were assigned to Munim Khan and his subordinates.[54] In August 1574, Munim Khan was appointed commander of the campaign against the Afghans in Bihar.[55] According to Abul Fazl, 'in order to soothe him and to assist him in his work he was given a *jagir* in Bihar'.[56] His former *jagir* of Jaunpur was included in the *khalisa-i-sharifa*.[57] On Munim Khan's behalf his subordinates, Muhasan Khan, Afaq and Arab Bahadur, looked after his *jagir* in Patna, which extended up to the frontier of Gaur-Bengal.[58] Hajipur in the territory of Bihar was assigned in *jagir* to Muhammad Quli Khan Barlas who served as Munim Khan's subordinate.[59] Later Muzaffar Khan was appointed as deputy to Munim Khan in Bihar and the *sarkar* of Hajipur which had been assigned in *jagir* to Muhammad Quli Khan Barlas, was conferred upon him.[60] Munim Khan was succeeded by Muzaffar Khan as governor of Bihar in 1575.[61] In June 1572, the charge of Lucknow was given to Sikandar Khan Uzbek along with his revenue assignment, the *jagir*.[62] For such arrangements in *sarkar* Qandahar, a very convincing argument is given by Iqtidar Alam Khan,

> Bairam Khan's *jagir* of *sarkar* Qandahar was administered by his deputy, Shah Muhmmad Qalati. Zamindawar described in the *Ain-i-Akbari* as one of the '*vilayats*' constituting Gharbi-i-Qandahar was held by Bahadur Khan as his military and revenue assignment. From this one might infer that the revenue assignment of Bairam Khan was actually confined to only a part of *sarkar* Qandahar, viz., the town (*balda*) of Qandahar and its environs (*muzafat*).[63]

In order to avoid any confusion, it may be stated at the outset that the introduction of *mansabs* in 1575 and regular *subas* in 1580 would not have affected the policy of assigning *jagirs* or transferring *jagirs* along with the official's posting, contrary to Moreland, Irfan Habib and Iqtidar Alam Khan. According to Iqtidar Alam Khan, the distinctive features associated with the seventeenth-century Mughal assignment system came into existence only after the introduction of the *mansab* (office, position, rank) in 1575.[64] Both Moreland and Irfan Habib proceed on the same assumption that prior to 1575 the assignments in the Mughal Empire were not substantially different from the permanent administrative-cum-revenue charges of the Lodi period.

In June-July 1577, Dastam Khan was posted to Ajmer and the *sarkar* of Ranthambor in the same province was assigned to him as *jagir*.[65] Shamsuddin Muhammad Khan Atka (Azam Khan) was appointed governor of Lahore in 1560 and was assigned a *jagir* in Lahore along with his brothers, Mir Muhammad (Khan-i-Kalan), Qutbuddin Muhammad Khan, Sharif Khan and son Mirza Aziz Koka (Khan-i-Azam). They stayed there till 1568. In September 1568, Akbar transferred the Atka Khail's (clan) *jagirs* except Mirza Aziz Koka's from Lahore and offered them new assignments: *sarkar* Sambhal to Mir Muhammad, *sarkar* Malwa to Qutbuddin Khan and Kanauj to Sharif Khan.[66] Akbar considered their transfer from the Panjab as one of his greatest achievements. Bayazid mentions that one day the emperor asked Munim Khan what the people thought of him as a ruler. When the Khan said that the people greatly admired his bold action against Adham Khan, Akbar replied: 'No; I have done something better, which it is strange that people don't mention. You know, but out of consideration for some people, you don't tell me . . . I have expelled the Atkas from the Panjab and have dispersed them all over the country, assigning them *jagirs* at different places'.[67]

Commenting on this, Abul Fazl says that 'whenever a large body is gathered together of one mind and speech, and show much push and energy, it is proper to disperse them firstly for their own good, and secondly, for the welfare of the community'.[68] It seems that the policy of transfer was in principle directed towards preventing any particular section of the Mughal nobility becoming too powerful in a region. Later, however, in order to seek close cooperation among his commanders in a recently conquered territory and to choose a member of the family closest to him personally as its head, Akbar reversed this policy of not posting officers of one family in the same province.

In 1568, Mir Muhammad Khan was succeeded by Husain Quli Khan (Khan-i-Jahan) as governor of Lahore. Husain Quli and his brother Ismail Quli Khan's *jagirs* in Nagaur were transferred to the place of their new posting in Lahore province.[69] They held *jagirs* in this area for at least seven years from 1568 to 1575. It was during Husain Quli Khan's tenure that a campaign was launched against Jai Chand of Nagarkot and the latter's territory was granted by Akbar as *jagir* to

Birbar.[70] Later, it led to vehement opposition from the local ruler. Akbar restored Nagarkot to the chief and a treaty was entered into between the imperial court and the Raja.[71] After the death of Munim Khan in 1575, Husain Quli Khan's *jagir* in Lahore was transferred to Bengal, the area of his official posting.[72] His former assignment in the Panjab was given to Shah Quli Khan Mahram. Subsequent to the conquest of Gujarat in 1572, Mirza Aziz Koka was appointed *hakim* of Gujarat, and the city of Ahmedabad and the *parganas* of Petlad and Haveli along with the other *parganas* (within the province of Gujarat) were assigned to him as *jagir*.[73] Following the appointment of Raja Bhagwan Das as governor of Lahore, a large number of the Kachhwahas' *jagirs* in addition to those of Bhagwan Das and his son Man Singh were also assigned in the region of Panjab.[74] Before he was assigned a *jagir* in the Panjab, Man Singh also held the *jagir* of Kachiwara.[75] In 1580, Itimad Khan Gujarati became in charge of the *khalisa-i-sharifa* lands in Gujarat and the *sarkar* of Patan (within Gujarat) was given to him as *jagir*.[76] In the same year Abdur Rahim Mirza Khan (Khan-i-Khanan) was appointed governor of Ajmer and was assigned Ranthambor as *jagir* which was in the same province.[77] Mirza Aziz Koka was appointed governor of Malwa in 1584, and the revenues of Garaha and Raisin in this province were assigned to him as *jagir*.[78] In 1587, Man Singh, the governor of Kabul, was transferred to Bihar and Zain Khan Koka was appointed in his place. At the same time Akbar ordered that the *jagirs* of the Kachhwahas in the Panjab be resumed and new *jagirs* be allotted to them in Bihar.[79] The *jagirdar* of Bihar, Muhibb Ali Khan Rohtasi was summoned to court and informed about his new assignment in Multan.[80] In October-November 1586, Muhammad Sadiq Khan was appointed governor of Multan and was assigned the *jagir* of Bhakkar and was entrusted with the task of reducing the Tarkhan principality in Thatta.[81] Abdur Rahim Mirza Khan was appointed governor of Multan in place of Muhammad Sadiq Khan in 1590. A part of the revenues of Multan and Bhakkar was given to him as *jagir*.[82] During his tenure, the annexation of Sindh entered its last phase.The evidence on Mirza Shahrukh's *jagir* is even more revealing. In 1594, he was assigned a *jagir* in the province of his posting in Malwa. In 1597, his rank was increased to 5000 of second class and a *jagir* in the province equivalent to his enhanced rank was assigned to him.[83] Following the appointment of Sultan Murad as governor of Gujarat in 1594, the revenues of *sarkars* like Surat, Baroda and Broach were assigned to him as *jagir*.[84] In 1597, Zain Khan Koka's *jagir* was transferred to Kabul when he took over from Qulij Muhammad Khan as governor of Kabul.[85] Nevertheless, there are scant references to *jagir* transfer, avoidance of transfer of official posts of the assignees. There is little evidence to suggest that these transfers were aimed at uprooting nobles from their *jagirs* in accordance with an explicit transfer policy. Rather, it was due to administrative and military exigencies that the concerned noble was posted to a particular place. The transfer of the *jagir* was incidental to the change in the administrative charge of the noble. Even the administrative transfers were not systematic and the uneven tenures suggest that there may not have been a policy in this regard either.

This process continued till the end of Akbar's reign, if not later—quite contrary to the argument that it was in vogue only in the early years of Akbar's reign. References to *jagirs* being assigned either within or adjacent to the provinces of *jagirdars'* postings are too voluminous to be cited here. It is interesting to note here that when the need arose to send expeditions in different directions, the nearest posted officers were generally given command. For example, in 1569, Akbar ordered Majnun Khan Qaqshal, Shaham Khan Jalair and other officers with *jagirs* near Kalinjar to seize the fort of Kalinjar from Raja Ram Chand.[86] Similarly, in 1583, officers posted or holding *jagirs* in the provinces of Ajmer and Malwa were ordered to quell the disturbances caused by Muzaffar Khan Gujarati in Gujarat.[87] The officers posted in Gujarat and Malwa were generally appointed to lead campaigns against the Deccan states. To check external invasions from the north-west, the command was generally given to officers posted in the Panjab.[88] In a few important expeditions, when officers had to lead an expedition for longer periods outside the region of their posting, they were allotted *jagirs* near the area of their operations. For instance, Akbar launched operations against Chittor in the autumn of 1567, with the appointment of Asaf Khan Harvi as *jagirdar* of Bayana, the territory nearest to Chittor.[89] In 1585, Mirza Aziz Koka was ordered to punish the rulers of the Deccan, and Garaha and Raisin of Malwa were assigned to him as *jagir*.[90] In 1595, Abdur Rahim Mirza Khan was ordered to assist Prince Murad in the conquest of the Deccan, and Bhilsa (in *suba* Malwa) was assigned to him as *jagir*.[91]

This is not to deny, however, that the policy of assigning *jagirs* adjacent to the postings of the officials (*mansabdars*) did not change in the later period. This change is evident from the fact that during Shahjahan's reign *mansabdars* posted outside the province of their *jagirs* were not required to muster the same number of horsemen as those posted in the province of their *jagirs.*[92]

In the evolution of the *jagir* system under Akbar, the revenue assignments covered a compact territory of contiguous *parganas* or *sarkars*. This is suggested by references to the assignment of *jagirs* and the appointment of *hakims*. Before 1560, one does not come across any case where a part of the salary of a noble was assigned against a fraction of the revenues of one *pargana* and another part against a fraction of the revenues of some other *pargana*. Till 1560, the salaries of nobles were arbitrarily settled in terms of the *jama* of the *pargana* against which it was assigned.[93] Under this practice, a noble could hold as his *jagir* part of a *pargana*, an entire *paragana*, or several contiguous *parganas* and a fraction of another adjacent *pargana*, but not in parts against the partial *jama* of two or more *parganas*. In *circa* 1560, when an attempt was made by the officials of the central *diwan* to fragment the *jagir* of a senior noble by assigning it against the partial *jama* of two different *parganas*, the nobles accused the officials of vindictiveness. In his letter to Akbar,[94] dated *circa* December 1560, Shamsuddin Muhammad Khan Atka bitterly complained that of the one crore copper *tankas* sanctioned as his *juldu* the authorities had assigned 40 lakh (80 lakh *dams*) against Firuzpur. When the *Ain-i-Akbari* was compiled, the *jama* of Firuzpur amounted to 1,14,76,404 *dams.*[95] This indicates that the remaining revenues of the *pargana* were either assigned to some other noble or were reserved for the *khalisa*. The remaining 60 lakh copper *tankas* (120 lakh *dams*) of Shamsuddin Muhammad Atka's assignment were given to him elsewhere. He regarded this as a deviation from the established practice.[96] There is other evidence to suggest that earlier the *parganas* assigned to nobles were always contiguous ones. For instance, after the capture of Jaunpur from Ibrahim Sur in 1559, Ali Quli Khan remained there till his insurgence. All his clansmen and relatives were granted contiguous *jagirs* in that region, where, except for Abdullah Khan, all the other Uzbeks were posted.[97] According to Bayazid Bayat and Arif Qandhari, in December 1560, 'Ali Quli Khan was assigned (*jagir*) contiguous *vilayets* and *parganas* such as the *sarkars* of Jaunpur, Banaras, Ghazipur and some of the *parganas* of *sarkars* Manikpur and Awadh'.[98] Apparently, part of Ali Quli Khan's (and his subordinates) salary that exceeded the total *jama* of Jaunpur, Banaras and Ghazipur *sarkars*, was assigned against the *parganas* of the two neighbouring *sarkars*. This strongly suggests that these *parganas* were contiguous to the rest of the territory of Ali Quli Khan's *jagir* of which *sarkar* Jaunpur was a part.

KHALISA LAND AND ITS RELATION WITH *JAGIRS*

The extent of area of the *khalisa* lands under the Mughals varied from time to time and from reign to reign. During Akbar's early years the *mahals* of the *khalisa* were not clearly demarcated. The centre's share in the revenues of the different regions was undoubtedly fixed, but its collection and remittance to the central treasury was the responsibility of the *hakim*.

It seems, however, to have been an accepted policy to reserve the most fertile and conveniently administered land for the *khalisa*. Bayazid, who was deputed to manage the revenue administration of the *sarkar* of Sarangpur in Malwa in 1576, reported that it was not 'suitable' for inclusion in the *khalisa* and it was accordingly assigned in *jagir*.[99] It was not necessary that an area once assigned as *jagir* would be permanently classified as *jagir* land. In principle, the revenue claim on the entire land belonged to the emperor. Any *jagir* could be classified as *khalisa* land by the emperor for whatever reason he wished. It was on grounds of political, economic or administrative expediency that these changes were usually made. In 1561, *sarkar* Hisar Firuza which constituted the *jagir* of Munim Khan was declared *khalisa* land,[100] and placed under the charge of a *hakim* appointed from the central *diwan*. In the 39th regnal year (1593) Bandar Lahari was declared *khalisa* property, and Siwistan, which had been a present (*peshkash*) in the first instance, was given in *jagir* to Bakhtiyar Beg and others.[101] The available sources do not provide the veritable *jama* figures for the *khalisa* land under Akbar but it appears that after the 15th regnal year the administration of the *khalisa* lands was put on a sound footing and the *parganas* and *mahals* constituting the *khalisa* provided enough income to maintain a rich imperial treasury.[102] In 1574, the *jagirs* of Jaunpur, Banaras, Chunar, Multan and Lahore up to the Indus were declared *khalisa* lands.[103] There is also the case of Narnaul being changed from *khalisa* to *jagir* land in 1563.[104] In 1575, the province of Ahmedabad was included in the *khalisa sharifa* from *jagir* land.[105] Multan which was the *jagir* of Mirza Rustam was included in the *khalisa sharifa* in 1595.[106] From an incidental reference it may be deduced that in 1596-7 the *jama* of the *khalisa* in the provinces of Delhi, Awadh and Allahabad amounted to nearly one-fourth of their total *jama*.[107]

However, area which was declared *khalisa* land at a given point of time could later be allotted as *jagir*. Later, it could be reconverted into *khalisa* land. For example, Jaunpur was converted into *khalisa* and *jagir* lands alternatively. Similarly, Kashmir was converted into *khalisa* land so that order could be restored there before it was parcelled out as a *jagir*. In 1592, it was assigned as a *jagir* to Mirza Yusuf Khan while in Bihar the *jagir* of Mirza Yusuf Khan was declared *khalisa* land.[108] If a noble failed to administer his *jagir* efficiently, the emperor could resume it and offer him a cash salary status. The Mirza brothers, Muzaffar Husain and Rustam, suffered because their agents had oppressed the tenants. Muzaffar Husain's tenants repeatedly complained about the atrocious attitude of Muzaffar Husain and, consequently, his *jagir* was declared as *khalisa* land and he was given a cash salary.[109] Mirza Rustam was transferred to Patan for a similar reason and his Multan *jagir* was converted into *khalisa* land. Badauni wrote, 'Multan which had been completely desolate by the tyranny of Mirza Rustam, was converted into *khalisa* land'.[110]

THE DEGREE AND NATURE OF IMPERIAL CONTROL

John F. Richards rightly observed that under the Mughals, written rules and procedures applied to all parts of the empire and to all servants—unless exempted for some special reason.[111] The land assigned to nobles in the form of *jagirs* were for all practical purposes subjected to the dual control of the central administration and the *jagirdars*. While the income of a *jagir* was estimated by the revenue ministry, the actual collections were made by the *jagirdar* or his agents (*gumashtas*).[112] The local officials and 'the headmen and peasants and cultivators' were informed that 'they must answer to the agents (*gumashtas*) of the person named (i.e. the *jagirdar*) for the authorized revenue (*mal-i-wajibi*) and all claims of the state (*huquq-i-diwani*), properly and honestly'.[113] No other right other than that of collecting the land revenue and authorized taxes was delegated to the *jagirdar* in his *jagirs*. He was expected to exercise this right in conformity with imperial regulations. Even in matters of assessing individual holdings the *jagirdar* was not permitted a free hand.[114] He was required to conform to the revenue rates sanctioned by the revenue ministry.[115] The financial ministry exercised strict control over methods and levels of tax collection. The main pillars of government kept abreast of the news of the kingdom. Officers of the provincial *diwan* obtained information from the local intelligence writer who sent reports almost daily to the provincial capital. They also relied upon complaints and petitions from aggrieved subjects to identify brutal or excessive collection of the revenues. Obviously flawed, nonetheless this system did prevent abuse and ensured a generally uniform standard for revenue collection in the areas under the regulation sytem.[116] It is obvious, therefore, that a *jagirdar* was required to collect the revenue (*mal-o-jihat*) and taxes in accordance with the established code (*dastur-al-amal*).[117] Even in matters of collection he had to forgo a part of his own claim in case a remission was granted by the emperor on account of damage to the crops.[118] Imperial regulations concerning matters other than land revenue were equally applicable to the *jagir* lands. In 1581, the *jagirdars* along with other government officials were directed to maintain records of names and profession of the inhabitants of the villages within their jurisdiction. They were further instructed to ensure that all inhabitants engaged in some profession or the other.[119] Abul Fazl also mentions that the *jagirdars* were required to report about their *jagirs*.[120]

The internal administration of the *jagir* land was supervised and controlled in more ways than one. The governor (*subadar*) was the overall incharge of a province. The *amirs* and *jagirdars* in the province were normally subservient to his authority and had to appear before him whenever they were summoned. The governor also ensured that the servants received their due from the *amirs* and *jagirdars* as fixed by the central authority. The *sawanih nigars* (news writers) posted in the different areas were required to report the activities of the *jagirdars* and the conditions that prevailed in their *jagirs*. If a *jagirdar* was reported to be oppressive or if he failed to conform to the imperial regulations, he was liable to punishment. The punishment involved the transfer or resumption of the *jagir* or the imposition of a fine.

When Muzaffar Khan was appointed governor of Bengal in 1579, he instituted severe punishment to enforce the imperial regulations. Khaldin Khan's *jagir* was resumed and Roshan Beg was executed in public for embezzlement. He also forced the *jagirdars* to return the excess funds to the treasury which they had collected from the peasantry.[121] Again in 1587, when it came to the notice of the emperor that the Rajput clan headed by Man Singh was doing injustice to the peasantry of Kabul, he was transferred from Kabul to Bihar.[122] Besides this, the local administration also served as a check in the working of the land revenue administration in a *jagir*. Whereas the right to collect the land revenue was vested in the *jagirdars*, the executive authority was entrusted with the *faujdar* (area commandant) who was also responsible for the maintenance of law and order and exercised general supervision over several matters related to the *jagir*.[123] It is said that the *faujdar* and the *amin* had to ensure that none of the cesses remitted by the court were collected by any person entrusted with the work of collection. The *faujdars* had to keep in check the rebellious attitude of the *jagirdars*. Whenever the *jagirdars* became rebellious, their job was to advise them and if that failed they collected the written evidence of the principal officers and punished such *jagirdars*.[124] There were some other local officers (*ahl-i-khidmat*)[125] who were appointed by the court and they were expected to report those activities of the agents of the *jagirdars* which interfered with their authority.[126] Among these officers were the *chaudhari*, the *qanungo* and the *qazi*.

It should also be noted that dishonesty among *jagirdars* was fairly widespread. This compelled Akbar to adopt other measures to check it. The system of a double rank (*zat* and *sawar*) which was established during the second half of Akbar's reign was probably instituted with the purpose of compelling every *mansabdar* to maintain a definite number of horses and cavalrymen for use in the imperial service. To check all such evasions Akbar also introduced *dagh* (branding) for horses and *chehra* (descriptive rolls) for men.[127] Father Monserrate observed:

> In order to prevent fraud, every man should be required to be present with his horse; the horses should be branded: and if a horse had died, its tail should be brought. No borrowing or substituting of horses should be permitted; and no horses should be sold without the King's sanction. Failing, the pay of the cavalry and its officers should be reduced.[128]

According to Abul Fazl, it was important that the servants (*mansabdars*) of His Majesty had their horses branded every year so as to maintain the efficiency of the army and also their actions would encourage unprincipled people to choose the path of honesty. The strict enforcement of the regulation caused major discontent among the officers.[129] Nizamuddin Ahmad asserts that Masum Khan Kabuli, the *jagirdar* of Patna, Said Beg Badakshi, Arab Bahadur, the *jagirdars* of Sahasram and other officers of Bihar were deprived of their *jagirs*.[130] As mentioned earlier, Mirza Aziz Koka also refused to abide by this regulation. Stern action was taken against him and his *jagir* of Ahmedabad was forfeited.[131] Until a *mansabdar* brought the required number of troops and horses for branding, he received only a proportion of his pay known as *bar-awardi*[132] (estimated). He received full pay only on presenting his full contingent for inspection.[133] Formerly, when the mark was repeated, the number of the muster was branded on the horse, for example, a horse was branded with '2' when it was mustered the second time, but under this regulation each class of soldiers had a particular mark, the mark was only repeated at the subsequent musters. In the case of the *ahadis* (4000-5000 high status cavalrymen employed directly by the emperor, having no following of mounted retainers, therefore not awarded a *mansab*), the former custom was followed.[134] Apart from the *ahadis*, the close servants of the emperor including a large number of *ahsham* (all categories of ragtag foot retainers [*piyadagan*] comprising clerks, runners, gate keepers, palace guards, couriers, swordsmen, musketeers, wrestlers, slaves and palanquin bearers, etc.), who had no time to look after *jagirs*, received their monthly salaries in cash and mustered their horses every eighteen months. Grandees, whose *jagirs* were in remote areas, brought their horses to the muster not before twelve years, but at the end of the six-year period after the last muster, one-tenth of their income would be retrenched. If a *mansabdar* had been promoted to a higher *mansab* and three years had elapsed since he last presented his horses at a muster, he received a *zat* (personal) increase of salary but was given allowances for the increased number of his men only after the first muster. His men both old and new then got their assignments. If at the renewal of the mark at subsequent musters, soldier brought a superior horse in place of his old one, the animal would be brought before the emperor, who inspected and accepted it.[135]

According to Shireen Moosvi, the continuing discrepancies between *mansab* requirement and the actual contingent led to the separation of *zat* and *sawar* rank in 1595-6.[136] The system involved more than the compulsory branding of horses and mustering of men, it also imposed financial penalties for failing to maintain enough troops, including salary reduction and repayment of the excess funds collected.[137] The account given by Abul Fazl reveals that during the reign of Akbar a *mansabdar* was expected to bring for muster the number of men indicated by his *sawar* rank and was penalized in case of default. An interesting point to consider is whether the number which the *mansabdars* were required to present in accordance with their *sawar* ranks, was that of horsemen or horses. According to the rule prescribed by Akbar after 1595-6, a unit of *dahbashi* or 10 men (*do-aspa-si-aspa* rank) had 3 *si-aspa* (9 horses), 4 *do-aspa* (8 horses) and 3 *yak-aspa* (3 horses) which adds up to 10 men and 20 horses; in other words, the number of horses in a contingent had to be twice the number of horsemen. Thus, a *mansabdar* holding a 100 *sawar* rank had to maintain either 100 men and 200 horses or 50 men and 100 horses.[138] During Shahjahan's reign under the 'rule of one-third', he was expected to bring 33 men and 66 horses; the gap between 100 and 33 is substantial; it seems likely that in Akbar's time no more than 50 men and 100 horses were required for a 100 *sawar* rank.[139] This is largely a matter of conjecture.

Jagirdars were also required to attend the court from time to time. In the case of a transfer or promotion the noble presented himself to the court for an audience before proceeding to his new posting. If, however, an officer was transferred because he had erred, he was not permitted to have an audience. If a noble appeared in the court after achieving outstanding feats, the emperor ordered his court nobles to go out and embrace him. The emperor made it obligatory for officers serving in the frontier to periodically appear in the court. The purpose of this was to keep the *jagirdars* under as close supervision as possible. Father Antonio Monserrate observed, 'In order to prevent the great nobles becoming insolent through the unchallenged enjoyment of power, the king summons (them) to court . . . and gives them many imperious commands, as though they were his slaves—commands, moreover, obedience to which ill suits their exalted rank and dignity'.

There is the instance of a *farman* being issued in AH 1001/AD 1593 to Azam Khan who had absented himself from court for six years. He was ordered to repair to the court.[140] In 1589, a similar *farman* had been issued to Muhibb Ali Khan Rohtasi, *jagirdar* of Rohtas.[141] The nobles were not allowed to attend the court without the permission of the emperor or authorized officials and any violation was regarded as a serious offence. Khan Alam Sikandar Khan Uzbek appeared in the court without permission in 1574 and he was rebuked by the emperor.[142] Similarly, in 1590, Shahbaz Khan attended the court without an order from the Sawad and he was censured.[143] In some genuine cases *jagirdars* were entertained in the court even if they came without permission. When Hakim-Ain-ul-Mulk appeared in the court without permission in 1590, he was not allowed in the court. But when it became known that Khan Azam Mirza Aziz Koka had seized his *jagir*, and he had come to complain about it, he was permitted to have an audience with the emperor.[144] Flight from the court also constituted rebellion, as in the case of Mirza Sharafuddin Husain Ahrari. He had a *jagir* near Ajmer and Nagaur and in October 1562, he fled from the court to his *jagir*. Akbar despatched Husain Quli Khan in the pursuit of the rebel and resumed his *jagir*.[145]

THE POSITION OF POWERFUL *JAGIRDARS*

During the reign of Akbar the *mansabdars* were entirely his creation. The resumption and allotment of *jagirs* was the prerogative of the emperor. 'For the ancient usage and custom', wrote Father Monserrate, 'still obtain, the territories acquired by conquest can be given by the king to anyone he likes, not on perpetual tenure but to be held at his pleasure. Anybody acting in contravention to this principle would earn the displeasure of the emperor'.[146] There was no hereditary claim on the *jagir*. An individual holding an assignment could not acquire a hereditary right over it. The Mughal nobility too, therefore, at least in theory was not hereditary. In actual practice, however, heredity or family prestige played an important role in the allotment of *jagirs*. The sons and relatives of a nobleman found it easier to enter the services of the emperor than an outsider. When Bairam Khan served as the regent of Akbar, he allotted *jagirs* to his own kin and ignored the Akbari nobles.[147] He promoted his brother-in-law Wali Beg Zulqadar and his sons Husain Quli and Ismail Quli who had in no way distinguished themselves in the service of the emperor to an equal position with Sikandar Khan, Abdullah Khan and Bahadur Khan, and gave them cultivated *jagirs* while he allotted wastelands (*jagirs*) to the great Khans.[148] When Maham Anaga and her party decided to win over Bairam Khan's companions, they were promised *jagirs* commensurate with their status.[149] After the death of Bairam Khan, the emperor expressed his sympathy to his son Mirza Khan and assigned him Patan as *jagir.* As at that time he was not able to look after it, Sayyid Ahmad Khan was appointed to manage it.[150] In 1593, the sons of Khan Azam Mirza Aziz Koka obtained *jagirs* for themselves.[151] Sometimes in the event of the death of an influential *jagirdar*, due sympathy was expressed to his servants as well. Shahabuddin Ahmad Khan died in Ujjain in 1590. He had rendered outstanding service to the empire and was one of the most distinguished men of his time who had done much to develop cultivation in the country. In sympathy with his relics, Shahabuddin's *jagirs* of Ujjain were entrusted to his servants.[152]

As expected in a centralized monarchial system based on a small ruling class, some selected and influential nobles and those belonging to the royal families were allotted the best *jagirs*. Mirza Muzaffar Husain, an Irani related to the ruling Safavid dynasty, was granted Sambhal in *suba* Delhi as *jagir.*[153] Mirza Rustam, another noble of the same dynasty, received Multan.[154] In both these cases the value of their *jagirs* was worth more than Qandahar, their earlier domain. In 1560, Shamsuddin Atka Khan and his brethren were allotted some of the richest parts of the Panjab as *jagir.*[155] After the defeat of rebels in Bengal in 1574, Munim Khan despatched Khwaja Shah Mansur of Shiraz to court with a request for a *jagir* in Bengal. His request was granted by the emperor.[156] In 1583, Mirza Aziz Koka was appointed to Bengal. As he disliked the climate of that *suba* he pleaded for a transfer to some other part of the empire. Akbar agreed to this request and an order was issued, transferring his *jagir* to Bihar.[157] Later in 1594, on his promotion as Khan-i-Azam, Mirza Aziz Koka was given a *mansab* rank of *panjhazari* (5000) and was given a choice to select his *jagirs* in Gujarat, in the Panjab or in Bihar, etc., he chose Bihar.[158] In 1597, when he wanted to make amends for his misconduct (going to Mecca) he requested for a *jagir* near the court in Lahore. His request was granted and Multan was alloted to him.[159] He was also given a *jagir* of his choice in Malwa, when he was sent on an expedition against the rulers of the Deccan (Khandesh and Berar).[160] There are substantial references to prove that on many occasions Akbar did allot *jagirs* to nobles according to their preference. Akbar even helped the influential *jagirdars* in their old age. In 1567, an ageing Muhammad Sultan Mirza was relieved from military service and given the *pargana* of Azimpur in *sarkar* Sambhal for his maintenance, so that he could spend the remaining days in tranquillity and in offering prayer (for Akbar's success). He sired several children in his old age and they all received *jagirs* in accordance with their status.[161]

Though Akbar accorded immense importance to high birth, due consideration was also given to ability, learning and merit of a person. After the conquest of Gujarat[162] in 1573, the government was entrusted to Mirza Aziz Koka and the city of Ahmedabad and the *parganas* of Petlad and Haveli along with several other *parganas* were assigned to him in *jagir*. The other members of the family were also assigned *jagirs* in the province. Patan was assigned to Mir Muhammad and his sons, Fazil Khan and Farrukh Khan. Qutbuddin Khan received the *sarkar* of Broach and its neighbouring regions; Naurang Khan was given Baroda, Sharif Khan and his sons, Arif and Zahid, were also assigned *jagirs* in Gujarat.[163]

In the presence of senior members of the family (Mir Muhammad and Qutbuddin Khan) Mirza Aziz Koka was appointed governor of Gujarat and his uncles were posted to serve under him. Reacting to the obvious supersession of seniority, Abul fazl argued that 'the foundation of appointment is talent and virtue and the quality of ancestors is not required'.

> Though Mir Muhammad Khan Kalan and Qutbuddin Muhammad Khan were the uncles of the Khan Azam and were old, yet the far-sightedness of the Shahinshah put them in a subordinate position, for the code of just sovereignty weight is given to wisdom and not to years, and reliance is placed upon abundance of loyalty, and not upon age. Farsightedness is the pillar, not bodily bulk. Intellect was the substantive thing, not the largeness of the visible body. The foundation of appointment is talents and virtues and the qualities of ancestor are not regarded.[164]

As a result of this policy a person of humble origin could rise to a high position and become a member of the Mughal *mansabdari* and *jagirdari* system. Mughal India was permeable to foreign adventurers.

Because of the recognition of ability and merit many foreigner adventurers were attracted to seek imperial services. They knew that if entry was difficult promotion was not, provided they were able to show their ability in the discharge of their duties. This had one great advantage, the adventurers in the employment of the Mughal emperor depended entirely on him. Improving their fortunes depended upon their loyalty at least so long as they were hopeful of receiving something more.

TRANSFER OF *JAGIRS*

The European visitor, Francois Bernier, considered the transferability of *jagirs* as the source of all evil in the Mughal Empire, including oppression and downfall of the peasantry and artisans. The absence of private property, according to Bernier, affected the oriental states: the king, being the owner of the soil, distributed the right to collect taxes over particular territories to assignees who had temporary tenures, as holders of *jagir* or *timar,* unlike the hereditary European lords. *Jagirs* were constantly transferred, the period of assignment on an average barely exceeded two to three years. There are appreciable references to the transfer of *jagirs* in contemporary chronicles. This policy has been recognized by historians as one that was most regularly practised by the Mughal emperors.[165] The transfer of *jagirs* was also noted by seventeenth-century European travellers such as Hawkins and Bernier.[166] Bernier's famous statement that the frequent transfer of *jagirs* led to the ever increasing oppression and ruination of the peasantry[167] has attracted the attention of historians of the Mughal Empire and needs to be closely examined. Abul Fazl linked the transfer of assignments to the way a gardener transplants plants,[168] and this also calls for further scrutiny. Hawkins complained bitterly of the frequent transfer of *jagirs.*[169] Commenting on the last years of Aurangzeb, Bhim Sen observed, 'the agents of the *jagirdar*' never had 'any hope of the confirmation (*bahali*) of the *jagirs* for the following year'.[170]

To generalize these views to all assignments in the Mughal period would be at risk of ignoring many other facts. It is important to realize that most of the modern scholars' hypotheses on frequent *jagir* transfers have been largely based on these famous observations. These, however, can be disapproved after a detailed examination of individual instances of *jagir* transfer and the tenure for which it was held. Moreover, no convincing reference has been made to the cause of a single *jagir* transfer/tenure case particularly during Akbar's reign. One is at a loss to understand the crucial question: Was it a transfer of the *jagir* or a transfer of the official (political–administrative–military) post? There seems to be no convincing reason to believe that the principle underlying the policy of frequent transfer of *jagirs* was to prevent officials from developing strong local roots in a manner that was likely to pose a threat to the empire's stability and integrity.

Abul Fazl elaborates this principle by means of an interesting analogy:

> It is not hidden from the hearts of the far-seeing and the clear-sighted that the spiritual garland-twiners of sovereignty [i.e. kings] resemble gardeners. As gardeners adorn gardens with trees and move them from one place to another, and reject many, and irrigate others, and labour to rear them to a proper size, and extirpate bad trees and lop off evil branches and remove trees that are too large, and graft some upon others, and gather their various fruits and flowers and enjoy their shade when necessary, and do things which are established in the science of horticulture. . . .[171]

The context in which this was written was the removal of the Atka Khail (family) from *suba* Lahore.[172] Keeping in view Abul Fazl's tendency of providing an ideological justification for the political actions of Akbar, it seems likely that the policy of transfer was in principle directed towards preventing any particular section of the Mughal nobility from becoming too powerful in a region, not for individual *jagirdars* as misapprehended by the majority of historians. Bayazid Bayat reports that Akbar told Munim Khan that he considered the removal of the Atka Khail from Lahore and their dispersal to *jagirs* in different regions his greatest accomplishment.[173] Iqtidar Alam Khan avers, 'the concentration in particular regions of *jagirs* of nobles belonging to the same clan in Akbar's early years also developed the process of transfer of *jagirs*'.[174] In the wake of the Uzbek rebellion, it was held that a strong clan holding *jagirs* at one place was not in the interest of the empire.[175]

An attempt has been made to trace the cases of individual *jagir* transfer and the length of tenure of *jagirdars* in a particular place during Akbar's reign (Tables 3.1–3.12). It appears that a *jagir* was not always transferred because of a highly emphasized principle, and the tenure of all assignments was not as short as believed by earlier scholars. Suffice it is to say that references to assignments (with various designations) given to, or held by officers, and the causes of their transfer at different points of time are very voluminous. If arranged and sifted properly, they could illuminate many important aspects of the working of the Mughal assignment system during Akbar's reign.

Judging from the duration for which *jagirdars* held theirs *jagirs*, it does not seem that the assigned areas changed hands frequently as a precaution against the assignee developing local roots in his *jagir*. During Akbar's reign there are hardly any references to indicate that officials (*jagirdars*) were transferred specifically on the basis of this policy. Drawing primarily on the observations of Abul Fazl, Hawkins, Bernier, Bhimsen and a few others, scholars have argued that *jagirdars* were not allowed to remain in one place for long periods and were transferred on an average every three or four years. Surprisingly, not a single specific reference to *jagir* transfer and its tenure has been cited for Akbar's reign. Of the few references of this nature cited by Irfan Habib, only one pertains to Akbar's reign.[176] This referred to *sarkar* Bhakkar where the average term of the *jagir* was one year and seven months as revealed by the assignment accounts in the *Tarikh-i-Masumi*. It is, however, not clear as to what is being discussed: the *jagir* tenure or the tenure of the official post held by the *jagirdar*. The account in the *Tarikh-i-Masumi* creates the impression that these assignments deal with the officers appointed to administer the *sarkar* of Bhakkar,[177] not to the *jagirs*. Sources reveal that Bhakkar was not always assigned in *jagir* to *mansabdars* posted only in *sarkar* Bhakkar; it was sometimes assigned as *jagir* to the governors of Multan, for example, Muhammad Sadiq Khan, Abdur Rahim Mirza Khan and Said Khan Chaghta.[178] During their governorship of Multan, they also held Bhakkar as their *jagir* which was generally viewed as their administrative post by scholars.

From the foregoing account it is interesting to note that during Akbar's reign *mansabdars* were generally assigned *jagirs* in the province of their postings. Scholars have, therefore, confounded the assignment of a particular *jagir* with the holding of a specific official position by a *mansabdar*. Even the assignment tenure of Bhakkar mentioned by Irfan Habib has not made this clear. It, in fact, appears that the change that occurred in Bhakkar was part of an administrative reshuffle.[179]

One might reiterate here that the principle for periodic transfers of *jagirs* as a means of preventing officers from developing roots in a particular area and connections with the local people is not discernible under Akbar. The *jagirs* were often transferred from the viewpoint of administrative convenience, because when an official was sent to serve in a province, he had to be assigned a *jagir* there. Similarly, those recalled would require *jagirs* elsewhere. Deaths, transfers, promotions and demotions in the imperial cadres also necessitated the transfer of assignments from one serving officer to another. An important consideration was that the holder should be competent to manage the area that was assigned to him. There are instances where officials were not transferred even after holding their assignments for long periods. This would have been contrary to any policy of systematic transfer—if such a policy existed—so as to prevent nobles from becoming local autonomous rulers/potentates.

The evidence gleaned from contemporary sources suggests that there were various reasons underlying the assignments but a deliberate policy of transfer was not one of them. After serving for twenty-one years in and around Rohtas, Muhibb Ali Khan was transferred from Rohtas *on his own request.*[180] He was appointed governor of Multan. But he had not been there, contrary to what Athar Ali alleged.[181] In fact, after his transfer from Rohtas he accompanied the emperor to Kashmir, where he fell ill and died.[182] His previous *jagir* in Bihar was allotted to the Kachhwahas, who had been transferred from the Panjab to Bihar. In 1587, Said Khan, the governor of Bihar, was transferred to Bengal after the death of its governor Wazir Khan.[183] In 1595, he was succeeded by Man Singh as governor of Bengal. After a few months at court he was again appointed governor of Bihar for the third time. In 1579-80, Muzaffar Khan was transferred to Bengal because its governor, Husain Quli Khan, had died.[184] Similarly, in 1580, Sharif Khan was appointed governor of Malwa because its governor, Shujaat Khan had been killed.[185] With the appointment and promotion of Mirza Shahrukh, governor of Malwa, the *jagir* of Shahbaz Khan in Ujjain area (in *suba* Malwa) was assigned to him.[186] Shahbaz Khan's *jagir* was transferred in accordance with the policy of assigning *jagirs* near the place of the *mansabdar's* posting.

Sometimes the *jagirs* of privileged and influential officers were transferred because they desired assignments in the place of their choice. For instance, when Munim Khan conquered Bengal, he sent Shah Mansur Shirazi to court with the request to transfer his *jagir* from Bihar to Bengal. His request was granted.[187] Mirza Aziz Koka was unhappy with his position in Bengal, he requested the emperor to send him to some other territory on the plea that the climate of Bengal did not suit him. Akbar accordingly appointed Shahbaz Khan as governor of Bengal and Mirza Aziz Koka was transferred to Bihar.[188] In 1594, Sharif Khan was shifted to Ghaznin on the grounds that he desired to serve in Ghaznin.[189] In 1596, the assignment of Multan was also conferred upon Mirza Aziz Koka on his request for it.[190]

Obvious misconduct or disloyalty by an assignee also led to the transfer of assignments. For instance, in 1577 when Wazir Khan failed to administer his charge of Gujarat efficiently, he was transferred and Shahabuddin Ahmad Khan was appointed in his place. The latter was distinguished for his knowledge of state of affairs, industry, justice and benevolence towards the subjects.[191] In 1586, the Rajputs oppressed the subjects of Kabul but the governor Man Singh failed to look closely into the case of the oppressed. When this matter came to the emperor's notice, Man Singh was transferred to Bihar and Zain Khan Koka was appointed in his place.[192] In 1597, Qulij Muhammad Khan was transferred from Kabul for failing to manage Afghanistan efficiently.[193]

To carry the argument further, it may be suggested that the policy of transferring officials from one place to another was not deliberately aimed at preventing the Mughal bureaucracy from developing regional moorings. It is very likely that the transfer of officials did not always involve the shifting of an official from one end of the empire to the other.[194] An examination of transfers during Akbar's reign reveals numerous such instances when officials held assignments for long periods in one region only. For example, the Kachhwaha clan including Raja Bhagwan Das and Man Singh remained in charge of Lahore and Kabul for nine years. Said Khan Chaghta was appointed to *suba* Bihar thrice. In 1587, he was transferred to neighbouring Bengal,[195] where he remained until 1595. Again in 1595, he was reappointed as governor of Bihar.[196] Another example is the case of Man Singh. After completing a seven-year tenure (1587-94) in *suba* Bihar, Man Singh's next assignment was in *suba* Bengal,[197] and he remained there for the next ten years. In 1589, Mirza Aziz Koka, governor of Malwa was transferred to the nearby *suba* of Gujarat.[198] Administrative requirements as well as pressures of a local and regional nature were important factors in influencing transfers. Such factors could prompt deviations from what have widely come to be regarded as some of the fundamental principles of Mughal administration. Among these principles were procedures supposedly related to the transfer of officials so as to avoid the emergence of powerful local interests.

By way of conclusion it may be argued that the *jagirdari* system of the Mughals in general, and particularly under Akbar, needs to be understood in the context of official posts (political–administrative–military) held by *jagirdars*. The *jagirdari* system involved the inextricable overlapping of *jagirs* and official posts. The officers under Akbar held their assignment as long as they remained competent and loyal, treated the inhabitants of their *jagirs* fairly, and met their military obligations, and if their services were not required elsewhere.

NOTES

1. Tapan Raychaudhuri and Irfan Habib, eds., *The Cambridge Economic History of India*, vol. I (*c. 1200-1757*), Cambridge: Cambridge University Press, 1982, p. 241.
2. S.A.A. Tirmizi, *Mughal Documents* (*1628-1659*), vol. II, Delhi: Manohar, 1995, p. 23.
3. For the renovation of the Agra citadel, Akbar imposed an additional tax of the value of 3 *sers* of corn on every *jarib* (measuring rope, unit of length) in the districts of Agra in 1565. The officers who held *jagirs* in this area were ordered to collect it. See Badauni, *Muntakhab-ut-Tawarikh*, 2: 74 [74, read year 972 instead of 982]; *Tabaqat-i-Akbari*, 2: 292.
4. Irfan Habib, *The Agrarian System of Mughal India*, pp. 300-1, n. 9.
5. As early as Akbar's 27th regnal year it was laid down that *jagirdars* should collect land revenue and other taxes in accordance with *dastur-i-amal* (administrative or fiscal regulations). Abul Fazl, *Akbarnama*, 3: 561-2 [381].
6. *Jama*, broadly speaking, included the estimated revenue from all the sources of income of a *mahal*, which were generally classified under the heads—*mal-o-jihat*, *sair-jihat* and *sair-ul-wajuh*. However, in calculating the *jama* of a *mahal* all cultivable land within it was taken into account and an assessment was made of it. See Noman Ahmad Siddiqi, *Land Revenue Administration*, p. 105.
7. The village-wise *jama* was known as *deh-ba-dehi* and a record of it was kept in the court. Habib, *The Agrarian System*, p. 303, n. 19.
8. This *jama* represented the revenue income of the territory as estimated or fixed by the Mughal administration, and did not by any means correspond to the actual income (*hasil*). The difference between the two figures, namely

jama and *hasil*, led to the introduction of the so-called month scale. See A. J. Qaisar, 'Distribution of the Revenue Resources of the Mughal Empire among the Nobility', in *The Mughal State*, ed. Muzaffar Alam and Sanjay Subrahamanyam, pp. 252-7. For more details, see Habib, *The Agrarian System*, pp. 303-6; Athar Ali, *The Mughal Nobility Under Aurangzeb*, pp. 46-53.

9. Abul Fazl, *Akbarnama*, 2: 402-3 [270]. See also Habib, *The Agrarian System*, p. 303.
10. For more discussion on *nasq*, see Moreland, *The Agrarian System*, pp. 234-47; Habib, *The Agrarian System*, pp. 257-65, 334-40.
11. Habib, *The Agrarian System*, pp. 329-36.
12. Ibid., pp. 336-8.
13. Raychaudhuri and Habib, eds., *The Cambridge Economic History of India*, p. 243. So great was a *jagirdar's* power that it was said that 'the *hakim* (*jagirdar*) of a day can in a moment remove a *zamindar* of five hundred years, and put in his stead a man who has been without a place for a lifetime'.
14. Habib, *The Agrarian System*, pp. 190-6.
15. H.K. Naqvi, *Urbanization and Urban Centres Under the Great Mughals*, Shimla: Indian Institute of Advanced Study, 1972, pp. 160-86.
16. Villages and areas which rebelled or refused to pay taxes, were known as *mawas* and *zor-talab*, as opposed to the *raiyati*, i.e. revenue-paying village. See Habib, *The Agrarian System*, p. 379, n. 5.
17. For examples of making of a revenue settlement after a conquest, see Abul Fazl, *Akbarnama*, 2: 259-60 [168], 3: 91 [65], 830-2 [548-9].
18. Abul Fazl, *Ain-i-Akbari*, 1: 271.
19. Ibid. In the words of Blochmann,

    jagirs, to which no military service attaches appear to be called *bedagh-o-mahalli*, i.e., the holder had nothing to do with the army and the muster of their contingents, nor with the collection of the taxes of the several *mahals* or *parganas*.

    According to Shireen Moosvi, it was assignments of *jagirs* without prior branding and descriptive role (*be-dagh o mahalli*). Cf. 'Evolution of the *Mansab*-System under Akbar', *Journal of the Royal Asiatic Society*, no. 2, 1981, pp. 180-3.

    Such kind of *jagir* in Rajasthan is known as *ghar baithan ki jagir* (*jagir* that enables one to sit at home; *jagir* without any service obligations). In Rajasthan a *jagir* of this kind was assigned in recognition of exceptionally meritorious outstanding services rendered by the holder or to the dependents of deceased officials. See Dilbagh Singh, *The State, Landlords and Peasants: Rajasthan in the 18th Century*, Delhi: Manohar, 1990, pp. 144-5.
20. Badauni, *Muntakhab-ut-Tawarikh*, 2: 353 [342].
21. Ibid., 2: 379-80 [368].
22. Abul Fazl, *Akbarnama*, 3: 998-9 [649-50].

23. Moreland, *The Agrarian System*, p. 79.
24. Gulbadan Begam, *Humayunnama*, tr. A.S. Beveridge, Delhi: Oriental Books, 1983, pp. 96-7[11b].
25. Babur, *Baburnama*, pp. 480-534; *Humayunnama*, pp. 96-7[11b].
26. Gulbadan Begam, *Humayunnama*, pp.109-10 [20b].
27. Jahangir, *Tuzuk-i-Jahangiri*, p.23.
28. Badauni, *Muntakhab-ut-Tawarikh*, 2:193 [190].
29. Moreland, *The Agrarian System*, p. 80.
30. In a system of despotic monarchy, such as that of the Mughals, the fortunes of all officials depended directly or indirectly upon the approbation of the emperor. The court, therefore, was the centre on which the nobles constantly focused their attention.
31. At the time of Abdullah Khan Uzbek's appointment to Malwa in the 7th regnal year (1562-3), Khwaja Muinuddin Ahmad Farankhudi, then a *wazir* in the *diwan-i-buyutat*, was deputed to supervise the distribution of *jagirs* there. He was under instructions to return to Agra upon completion of this task. Abul Fazl, *Akbarnama*, 2: 260-1 [168-9]. A large number of persons accompanied Muinuddin Ahmad Farankhudi in order that he may regulate the province and supervise the distribution of *jagirs* and also define the exchequer land. He was to allot the *jagirs* according to the rules of the central *diwan*. Cities, towns and villages of Malwa were distributed among the officers according to their ranks.
32. It is noteworthy that while agreeing to suspend military operations against Ali Quli Khan in 1565 without insisting on his surrender, Akbar was nevertheless determined that he would only be allowed to reoccupy his *jagir* after obtaining a formal *sanad* from the central *diwan*. Again, during a brief period of peace in 1566, Ali Quli Khan was persuaded to send his agent to Agra to obtain formal papers of his *jagir* from the court. Cf. Abul Fazl, *Akbarnama*, 2: 388 [260], 421 [285]; *Tabaqat-i-Akabri*, 2: [181]; *Muntakhab-ut-Tawarikh*, 2: 84 [82]; See also *Tazkira-i-Humayun wa Akbar*, pp. 339-40.
33. One such case pertains to 1574; Munim Khan was authorized by Akbar to recommend the assignment of *jagirs* in the eastern *sarkars*. Akbar told Munim Khan: 'I recognize your handwriting. [A noble] will be assigned a *jagir* [only] after receiving a recommendation in your handwriting.' It may be assumed that the practice had existed earlier as well. Cf. Iqtidar Alam Khan, 'The Mughal Assignment System', in *Medieval India*, ed. Irfan Habib, p. 72, n. 34.
34. Bayazid Bayat, *Tazkira-i-Humayun wa Akbar*, p. 244.
35. Abul Fazl, *Akbarnama*, 3: 492-5 [335-7]; *Muntakhab-ut-Tawarikh*, 2: 299 [291]; *Tabaqat-i-Akbari*, 2: 357; Abdul Baqi Nihawandi, *Maasir-i-Rahimi*, ed. M. Hidayat Husain, 3 vols, Calcutta: Asiatic Society of Bengal, 1940, 1: 877.

36. Badauni, *Muntakhab-ut-Tawarikh*, 2: 304-5 [296]. See also A. J. Qaisar, 'Shahbaz Khan Kambu', in *Medieval India: A Miscellany I*, pp. 63-4; Streusand, *The Formation of the Mughal Empire*, p. 164.
37. Hakim Abul-Fath Gilani, *Ruqqat-i-Hakim Abul-Fath*, ed. Mohammad Bashir Ahmad, Lahore: Idarah-i-Tahqiqat-i-Pakistan, 1968, pp. 26-7, 34, 37-8; Afzal Husain, 'The Letters of Hakim Abul Fath Gilani—An Unexplored Source of Akbar's Reign', *Proceedings of the Indian History Congress*, 44th Session, Burdwan, 1983, pp. 189-93.
38. Abul Fazl, *Akbarnama*, 2: 106, 126 [68, 82].
39. *Medieval Gujarat: Its Political and Statistical History*, based on Muhammad Ali Khan's *Mirat-i-Ahmadi* transcribed in 1822 by Narsain Dass of the Kait tribe at Ahmedabad, Delhi: Indian Bibliographies Bureau, 1985, pp. 335-6. Itimad Khan replied that though he could not, contrary to the emperor's order's, assign them a *jagir*, he would do so much as he personally had the power to do.
40. Abul Fath Gilani, *Ruqqat-i-Hakim Abul Fath Gilani*, pp. 37-8; Afzal Husain, 'The letters of Hakim Abul Fath Gilani', pp. 189-93. See also S.A.A. Rizvi, *Religious and Intellectual History of the Muslim in Akbar's Reign, 1556-1605*, New Delhi: Munshiram Manoharlal, 1975, p. 338.
41. Abul Fazl, *Akbarnama*, 3: 1216 [810].
42. For a recent example of such an argument see my article, '*Padshah, Jagir, and Jagirdar*—A Re-examination of the Mughal Assignment System During the Reign of Akbar', *Proceedings of the Indian History Congress, 65th Session*, Bareilly, 2004, pp. 380-99.
43. Iqtidar Alam Khan, 'Mughal Assignment System', p. 68.
44. Abul Fazl, *Akbarnama*, 2: 25 [14] (here and further in the endnotes, references to the sources refer not only to *jagir* assignments concomitant to *jagirdars'* postings, but also to holding assignments and indicating *jagirdars'* official postings/services in the provinces of their *jagirs*).
45. Ibid., 2: 36 [20]. After Majnun Khan Qaqshal, who is described as the *jagirdar* of Narnaul, was expelled by the Sur noble, Haji Khan, Tardi Beg went there to re-establish Mughal authority. This suggests that at that time the protection of *sarkar* Narnaul was his responsibility.
46. Ibid., 2: 25[14], 46-7[27-8], 71[45]; *Tabaqat-i-Akbari*, 2: 213; *Tarikh-i-Akbari*, p. 75[52]: Muhammad Qasim Hindu Shah Farishta, *Rise of Mohammadan Power in India*, 2: 111.
47. Abul Fazl, *Akbarnama*, 2: 74 [47].
48. Ibid., 2: 83-4[54], 94[62]; *Muntakhab-ut-Tawarikh*, 2: 4[11]; Farishta, *Rise of Mohammadan Power in India*, 2: 111.
49. Abul Fazl, *Akbarnama*, 2: 96-7[64].
50. For Munim Khan's position as the *hakim* of Kabul, see Iqtidar Alam Khan, *The Political Biography of a Mughal Noble: Munim Khan Khan-i-Khanan, 1497-1575*, New Delhi: Orient Longman, 1973, pp. 33-51.
51. Abul Fazl, *Akbarnama*, 2: 25[14], 30[17], 56[34-5]; *Tabaqat-i-Akbari*, 2: 211,

271; *Tazkira-i-Humayun wa Akbar*, p. 221; Farishta, *Rise of Mohammadan Power in India*, 2: 123.

52. Abul Fazl, *Akbarnama*, 2: 30[17].
53. Ibid., 2: 85[53].
54. Ibid., 2: 436-7[298-9], 478[325]; *Muntakhab-ut-Tawarikh*, 2:104[101]; *Tabaqat-i-Akbari*, 2: 338; *Tazkira-i-Humayun wa Akbar*, pp. 299, 307; *Tarikh-i-Akbari*, pp. 143[107], 189[155].
55. For interesting details of this campaign, see Shaikh Farid Bhakkari, *Zakhirat-ul-Khawanin*, I: 24-5.
56. Abul Fazl, *Akbarnama*, 3: 144[103], 164[116]; *Tazkira-i-Humayun wa Akbar*, pp. 312, 341-2; *Tarikh-i-Akbari*, p. 224[193]; Farishta, *Rise of Mohammadan Power in India*, 2: 151.
57. Abul Fazl, *Akbarnama*, 3: 144[103]; *Tarikh-i-Akbari*, pp. 224-5[193-4].
58. Abul Fazl, *Akbarnama*, 3: 189[133]; *Tarikh-i-Akbari*, p. 224[193].
59. Abul Fazl, *Akbarnama*, 3: 192[136]; *Tazkira-i-Humayun wa Akbar*, p. 341; *Tarikh-i-Akbari*, p. 224[193].
60. Abul Fazl, *Akbarnama*, 3: 192[136]; *Tabaqat-i-Akbari*, 2: 486; *Tazkira-i-Humayun wa Akbar*, p. 348; *Tarikh-i-Akbari*, pp. 246-7[210].
61. For details about Bihar governors under Akbar, see Imtiaz Ahmad, 'Mughal Governors of Bihar Under Akbar', in *Professor Nurul Hasan Commemoration Volume*, ed. W.H. Siddiqi, Rampur: Raza Library, 2003; idem, 'Mughal Governors of Bihar Under Akbar and Jahangir', *Proceedings of the Indian History Congress*, 63rd Session, Kolkata, 2003, pp. 281-7.
62. Arif Qandhari, *Tarikh-i-Akbari*, p. 189[155]; *Akbarnama*, 2: 534[368]; *Muntakhab-ut-Tawarikh*, 2: 135/138-9; *Tazkira-i-Humayun wa Akbar*, p. 307; *Tabaqat-i-Akbari*, 2: 368-9.
63. Iqtidar Alam Khan, 'Mughal Assignment System', p. 70.
64. Ibid., p. 64.
65. Abul Fazl, *Akbarnama*, 3: 295[210].
66. Ibid., 2: 177[115-16], 299[193], 486-7[332-3]; *Tazkira-i-Humayun wa Akbar*, p. 253; *Tabaqat-i-Akbari*, 2: 351-2. For a detailed discussion on the Atka Khail (clan), see Afzal Husain, *The Nobility Under Akbar and Jahangir*, Delhi: Manohar, 1999, pp. 45-69.
67. Bayazid Bayat, *Tazkira-i-Humayun wa Akbar*, p. 253.
68. Abul Fazl, *Akbarnama*, 2: 486-7[332-3]; *Tabaqat-i-Akbari*, 2: 351-2; *Muntakhab-ut-Tawarikh*, 2: 109[106].
69. Abul Fazl, *Akbarnama*, 2: 486-7[332-3]; 3: 56-62[37-43]; *Tabaqat-i-Akbari*, 2: 352, 366, 396, 407, 480; *Muntakhab-ut-Tawarikh*, 2: 109[106], 137[134], 164[161]; *Tarikh-i-Akbari*, p. 171 [133].
70. For a detailed description of the Kangra campaign, see Abul Fazl, *Akbarnama*, 2: 538 [370]; *Muntakhab-ut-Tawarikh*, 2: 164-5 [160-1]; *Tabaqat-i-Akbari*, 2: 398-401.
71. Abul Fazl, *Akbarnama*, 3: 52 [37]. See also Ahsan Raza Khan, *Chieftains in*

the Mughal Empire During the Reign of Akbar, Shimla: Indian Institute of Advanced Study, 1977, pp. 57, 114; S. Inayat A. Zaidi, 'Akbar and the Rajput Principalities: Integration into Empire', in *Akbar and His India*, ed. Irfan Habib, p. 18.

72. Abul Fazl, *Akbarnama*, 3: 230[162], 431[292]; *Tabaqat-i-Akbari*, 2: 480, 517; *Muntakhab-ut-Tawarikh*, 2: 222[218]; *Tarikh-i-Akbari*, pp. 250[212], 281-2[246]; Farishta, *Rise of Mohammadan Power in India*, 2: 154.
73. Abul Fazl, *Akbarnama*, 3: 13-5[8-11], 46[33]; *Tabaqat-i-Akbari*, 2: 376, 393, 454, 476; *Muntakhab-ut-Tawarikh*, 2: 167[164]; *Tarikh-i-Akbari*, pp. 193-5[161-4], 200[173], 239[205]. For details of the Atka clan's appointments in *suba* Gujarat, see Ali Muhammad Khan, *Mirat-i-Ahmadi*, ed. Sayyid Nawab Ali, Baroda: Gaekward's Oriental Research Institute, 1927-35, pp. 102-3.
74. Abul Fazl, *Akbarnama*, 3: 358[248-9], 380[262], 423-4[288], 478[326], 493-4[336]; *Tabaqat-i-Akbari*, 2: 552; *Muntakhab-ut-Tawarikh*, 2: 218[214]. For more details about the Kachhwahas under Akbar, see Afzal Husain, *The Nobility Under Akbar and Jahangir*, pp. 86-103.
75. Cf. Iqtidar Alam Khan, 'Mughal Assignment System', p. 108. Alam Khan perhaps failed to trace the location of Kachiwara. That explains why the Kachiwara *jagir* was not placed under any *sarkar* or *suba* like the other *jagirs*. It has in *suba* Malwa. See Abul Fazl, *Akbarnama*, 2: 62 [43]. See also Munhot Nainsi, *Munhot Nainsi ri Khyat*, ed. Badri Prasad Sakaria, Jodhpur: Rajasthan Oriental Research Institute, 1960, 1: 342.
76. Abul Fazl, *Akbarnama*, 3: 465[317-18].
77. Ibid., 480[327]; *Tabaqat-i-Akbari*, 2: 567, 651.
78. Abul Fazl, *Akbarnama*, 3: 629[422-3], 655[436-7], 701[464], 739[489], 865[571], 886[584], 891[587]; *Tabaqat-i-Akbari*, 2: 585, 629; *Muntakhab-ut-Tawarikh*, 2: 372/383-4.
79. Abul Fazl, *Akbarnama*, 3: 790[517-18], 801[525], 816[536], 872[576]; *Tabaqat-i-Akbari*, 2: 622-3; *Muntakhab-ut-Tawarikh*, 2: 375[364]; Farishta, *Rise of Mohammadan Power in India*, 2: 161.
80. Abul Fazl, *Akbarnama*, 3: 816-17[536-7]; see also Iqtidar Alam Khan, 'Mughal Assignment System', p. 119. In 1580, Khan erroneously described Muhibb Ali Khan Rohtasi as the *jagirdar* of Bhera (Chinhat Doab) and Rohtas (Sindh Sagar Doab) in the Panjab. Iqtidar Alam Khan may have confounded with *Sahar-Bahira* and Rohtas. Instead of Bhera the place assigned to Muhibb Ali Khan was some city in Bihar called *Sahara* of Bahira and instead of Rohtas in Sindhi Sagar Doab the area assigned was *sarkar* Rohtas in *suba* Bihar. For details see Abul Fazl, *Akbarnama*, 3: 472, n. 3, [322], 475 [324], 816-17 [536]; *Muntakhab-ut-Tawarikh*, 2: 290 [282]; *Tarikh-i-Akbari*, p. 258. He is clearly mentioned as the governor of Rohtas (Bihar). As he was governor of Rohtas for a long period, he is generally known as Rohtasi (see serial no. 2 of Table 3.6).
81. Abul Fazl, *Akbarnama*, 3: 708[470], 750[495], 792[519], *Tabaqat i Akbari*,

2: 605, 621; *Muntakhab-ut-Tawarikh*, 2: 359[347-8], 369-70[358]; Mir Muhammad Masum, *Tarikh-i-Masumi*, ed. Daud Pota, Pune: Bhandarkar Oriental Research Institute, 1938, pp. 248-9.

82. Abul Fazl, *Akbarnama*, 3: 917-18[601-2]; *Tabaqat-i-Akbari*, 2: 632; *Muntakhab-ut-Tawarikh*, 2: 386[374]; *Tarikh-i-Masumi*, pp. 249-52; Abdul Baqi Nihawandi, *Maasir-i-Rahimi*, 2: 345, 358-9.
83. Abul Fazl, *Akbarnama*, 3: 991[644], 1069[717], 1120[749]; *Tabaqat-i-Akbari*, 2: 649; *Muntakhab-ut-Tawarikh*, 2: 401[388].
84. Badauni, *Muntakhab-ut-Tawarikh*, 2: 401[387]; *Tabaqat-i-Akbari*, 2: 648-9.
85. Abul Fazl, *Akbarnama*, 3: 1073[720].
86. Ibid., 3: 498-9[340-1]; *Muntakhab-ut-Tawarikh*, 2: 124[120]; *Tabaqat-i-Akbari*, 2: 357[225-6]; *Tarikh-i-Akbari*, pp. 223-5[192-4]. For secondary accounts, see Srivastava, *Akbar the Great*, I: 115.
87. Abul Fazl, *Akbarnama*, 3: 610-13[411-13], 628-9[422-3]; *Tabaqat-i-Akbari*, 2: 567-73; *Muntakhab-ut-Tawarikh*, 2: 346[336].
88. For further minutiae the assignment in the Panjab expanse, see my paper, 'Some Notes on Mughal Assignment System: A Case Study of *Jagirs* in Panjab During Akbar's Reign', *Proceedings of the Punjab History Conference*, 36th Session, Patiala, 2004, pp. 234-46.
89. Nizamuddin Ahmad, *Tabaqat-i-Akbari*, 2: 341[214-15].
90. Abul Fazl, *Akbarnama*, 3: 701[464-5], 739[489].
91. Ibid., 3: 1045[698-9].
92. Abdul Hamid Lahori, *Padshahnama*, 2: 505-7.
93. Iqtidar Alam Khan, 'Mughal Assignment System', p. 73.
94. Abul Fazl, *Akbarnama*, 2: 182 [120].
95. Abul Fazl, *Ain-i-Akbari*, 2: 335 [1: 554].
96. Abul Fazl, *Akbarnama*, 2: 182-5 [120-2].
97. Ibid., 2: 104-29[67-85]. For details about the family and relatives of Ali Quli Khan, see Afzal Husain, *The Nobility Under Akbar and Jahangir*, pp. 70-85.
98. Bayazid Bayat, *Tazkira-i-Humayun wa Akbar*, p. 239; *Tarikh-i-Akbari*, p. 134 [95].
99. Bayazid Bayat, *Tazkira-i-Humayun wa Akbar*, p. 353.
100. Abul Fazl, *Akbarnama*, 2: 293-4 [189-90].
101. Ibid., 3: 986 [642].
102. Ibid., 2: 487-8 [333].
103. Badauni, *Muntakhab-ut-Tawarikh*, 2: 185 [182]; *Akbarnama*, 3: 144 [103]; *Tarikh-i-Akbari*, pp. 225-32 [194-8]; *Tabaqat-i-Akbari*, 2: 451.
104. Abul Fazl, *Akbarnama*, 2: 309 [199].
105. Nizamuddin Ahmad, *Tabaqat-i-Akbari*, 239 [205].
106. Abul Fazl, *Akbarnama*, 3: 1041 [696].
107. Ibid., 3: 749 [494]; Habib, *The Agrarian System*, p. 314, n. 73.
108. Abul Fazl, *Akbarnama*, 3: 986 [642].

109. Ibid., 3: 1110-11 [743-4].
110. Badauni, *Muntakhab-ut-Tawarikh*, 2: 417 [403]; *Akbarnama*, 3: 1041 [696].
111. Richards, *The Mughal Empire*, p. 65.
112. Abul Fazl, *Akbarnama*, 3: 561 [381-2].
113. *Selected Documents of Shahjahan's Reign*, pp. 5ff.
114. Moreland, *The Agrarian System*, pp. 91-2.
115. Habib, *The Agrarian System*, p. 303-4.
116. However, the mature system of tax collection and salary payments was one of flexibility and efficiency. Some of the mammoth functions of the imperial administration were thereby placed in the hands of the *jagirdars* themselves who were forced to become capable managers on their own behalf.
117. It was laid down that the *jagirdars* should collect the land revenue and other taxes in accordance with the *dastur*. Abul Fazl, *Akbarnama*, 3: 561 [381].
118. In 1585, Akbar granted remissions in the provinces of Allahabad, Awadh and Delhi, the remissions in the *khalisa* lands amounted to 7 crore, 7 lakh, 47,062 *dams*. Abul Fazl adds that the 'remissions granted in *iqtas* (*jagirs*) can be calculated accordingly'. The remission was also applicable to *jagir* lands. Abul Fazl, *Akbarnama*, 3: 749 [494], 699 [463], 812-13 [533-4].
119. Abul Fazl, *Akbarnama*, 3: 509 [346-7]. This also means that the entire cultivable land within a village or *mahal* was not brought under cultivation and a considerable part of it was left fallow. It has been recognized that during Akbar's reign not enough capital and manpower were available to bring all the cultivable land under cultivation. Cf. Moreland, *The Agrarian System*, Introduction, p. XII; Noman Ahmad Siddiqi, *Land Revenue Administration*, p.105.
120. Abul Fazl, *Akbarnama*, 3: 561-5 [381-3].
121. Ibid., 3: 426-33 [289-93]; *Muntakhab-ut-Tawarikh*, 2: 288-9 [280-1]; *Tabaqat-i-Akbari*, 2: 348-9; Srivastava, *Akbar the Great*, 1: 251-2.
122. Abul Fazl, *Akbarnama*, 3: 790 [517-18].
123. See Noman Ahmad Siddiqi, '*Faujdar* and *Faujdari* Under the Mughals', in *Medieval India Quarterly IV*, Bombay: Asia Publishing House, 1961, pp. 22-35; reproduced in *The Mughal State*, ed. Muzaffar Alam and Sanjay Subrahmanyam, pp. 234-51; Noman Ahmad Siddiqi, *Land Revenue Administration*, p. 113; Richards, *The Mughal Empire*, p. 67.
124. Abul Fazl, *Ain-i-Akbari*, 2:42. For details about the position of *faujdars*, see *Ain-i-Akbari*, 2: 41-2.
125. Noman Ahmad Siddiqi, *Land Revenue Administration*, p.113.
126. Abul Fazl, *Ain-i-Akbari*, 2:50. For details about the position of collectors, *bitikchis* and *khazandars*, see *Ain-i-Akbari*, 2: 46-63.
127. Ibid., 1: 265-6; *Muntakhab-ut-Tawarikh*, 2: 193-4 [190-1], 209 [206], 289 [281].
128. Monserrate, *Commentary of Father Monserrate*, p. 69.
129. Abul Fazl, *Akbarnama*, 3: 209[147]; *Ain-i-Akbari*, 1:266-7[135]. See also Mutamad Khan, *Iqbalnama-i-Jahangiri*, 2: 298; *Mirat-i-Ahmadi*, p. 113.

130. Nizamuddin Ahmad, *Tabaqat-i-Akbari*, 2: 531-2 [349-50]; *Tabaqat-i-Timuri*, f. 144r, in *The Formation of the Mughal Empire*, Streusand, p. 156, n. 10.
131. Arif Qandhari, *Tarikh-i-Akbari*, 239 [205]. For details about this officer, see Shaikh Farid Bhakkari, *Zakhirat-ul-Khawanin*, 2: 200-1; *Maasir-ul-Umara*, 3: 215-19 [1: 174-80].
132. The translation of *bar-awardi* is based on the definition of *bar-award* given in *A Dictionary of Urdu, Classical Hindi and English*, John Platts, Delhi: Oriental Books, 1984. None of the Persian definitions fit the usage.
133. The inflexible *dagh* regulations made the *mansabdars* too insecure and vulnerable to humiliation and punishment at the hands of imperial bureaucrats. The *jagirdars* of the provinces found it difficult to meet the *dagh* requirement and bribed the officials to satisfy them. Streusand, *The Formation of the Mughal Empire*, pp. 156-7, 171.
134. For *ahadis*, see Abul Fazl, *Ain-i-Akbari*, 1: 259-60[187]. See also Moosvi, *The Economy of the Mughal Empire*, pp. 224-33; Richards, *The Mughal Empire*, pp. 68-9; Blake, 'The Patrimonial-Bureaucratic Empire', p. 295.
135. Abul Fazl, *Ain-i-Akbari*, 1: 266-7.
136. Moosvi, 'Evolution of the *Mansab* System Under Akbar', pp. 171-83; Abdul Aziz, *The Mansabdari System and the Mughal Army*, p. 69.
137. Streusand, *The Formation of the Mughal Empire*, p.110.
138. Abul Fazl, *Ain-i-Akbari*, 1: 254-6 [123-4]. See also Irfan Habib, 'The *Mansab* System, 1596-1637', *Proceedings of the Indian History Congress*, 29th Session, Patiala, 1967, pp. 221-42.
139. Abul Fath, *Ruqqat-i-Abul Fath Gilani*, p. 45.
140. Badauni, *Muntakhab-ut-Tawarikh*, 3: 391, 400 [386-7]. According to Shaikh Farid Bhakkari, he had not visited the court for the previous ten years. *Zakhirat-ul-Khawanin*, 1: 96, but it appears to me that he had not attended court for two years. See also *Mukatabat-i-Allami* (*Insha-i-Abul Fazl*), tr. Mansura Haidar, Delhi: Munshiram Manoharlal, 1998, pp. 72-8.
141. Abul Fazl, *Akbarnama*, 3: 816 [536]. This man was Muhibb Ali Khan Rohtasi, not Muhibb Ali Khan, the son of Mir Khalifa (Babur's *vakil*). See Shah Nawaz Khan and Abdul Hayy, *Maasir-ul-Umara*, 3: 226-9.
142. Abul Fazl, *Akbarnama*, 3: 147-8 [106].
143. Ibid., 3: 885-6 [584].
144. Ibid.
145. Ibid., 2: 197 [128], 308-11 [198-200], 314 [202], 316-21 [204-7]; *Muntakhab-ut-Tawarikh*, 2: 46 [50], 57-9 [59-60]; *Maasir-ul-Umara*, 3: 808-12; Streusand, *The Formation of the Mughal Empire*, pp. 91-2.
146. Monserrate, *The Commentary of Father Monserrate*, pp. 88-9.
147. Badauni, *Muntakhab-ut-Tawarikh*, 2: 30 [35-6]. See also *Ain-i-Akbari*, 1: 331.
148. Abul Fazl, *Akbarnama*, 2: 163 [107]. The *farman* addressed to Bairam Khan, as given in the *Akbarnama* states,

    He himself knows what was the position and rank of Wali Beg among

Qizilbashes, without considering his service, his lineage or his position, and mainly on account of relationship, viz., his being his (Bairam Khan's) brother-in-law, he brought him and put him over the great officers. . . . He gave Husain Quli who has not even fought with a chicken, equal position with Sikandar Khan, Abdualla Khan and Bahadur Khan and gave them cultivated *jagirs*, while he satisfied the great Khans with wasteland.

149. Badauni, *Muntakhab-ut-Tawarikh*, 2: 30-1 [35-6].
150. Abul Fazl, *Akbarnama*, 3: 9 [6].
151. Ibid., 3: 982 [639].
152. Ibid., 3: 885 [584].
153. Ibid., 3:1031 [671]; *Muntakhab-ut-Tawarikh*, 2: 416-17 [403].
154. Abul Fazl, *Akbarnama*, 3: 993-4 [646]; *Muntakhab-ut-Tawarikh*, 2: 399 [386].
155. Abul Fazl, *Akbarnama*, 2: 177 [115-16].
156. Ibid., 3: 164 [116].
157. Ibid., 3: 594 [401-2].
158. Ibid., 3: 1006 [655].
159. Ibid., 3: 1068 [717].
160. Ibid., 3: 739 [489].
161. Ibid., 2: 413-14 [279].
162. For details of the conquest of Gujarat, see Abul Fazl, *Akbarnama*, 2: [372], 3: [8-9, 17-18, and 24-7]; *Mirat-i-Ahmadi*, pp. 102-3.
163. Abul Fazl, *Akbarnama*, 3: 46-7 [33]; *Mirat-i-Ahmadi*, pp. 102-3, provide details of appointments. See also *Muntakhab-ut-Tawarikh*, 2:[142]; *Tabaqat-i-Akbari*, 2: [253].
164. Abul Fazl, *Akbarnama*, 3: 46-7 [33].
165. Compare the treatment of the transfer policy of *jagirs* in Moreland, *The Agrarian System*; Habib, *The Agrarian System*, p. 301; Athar Ali, *The Mughal Nobility Under Aurangzeb*, p. 78; Chandra, *Medieval India*, pp. 72-4; Noman Ahmad Siddiqi, *Land Revenue Administration*, pp. 110-11.
166. See William Foster, ed., *Early Travels of India*, p. 114; Joannes De Laet, *Description of India and Fragment of Indian History*, tr. J.S. Hoyland and annotated by S.N. Banerjee, *The Empire of the Great Mogol*, Bombay: Kitab Mahal, 1928, pp. 94-5; Francois Bernier, *Travels in the Mughal Empire*, p. 227; Peter Mundy, *The Travels of Peter Mundy in Europe and Asia*, ed. R.C. Temple, London: Hakluyat Society, 1914-24, 2: 85.
167. Bernier, *Travels in the Mughal Empire*, p. 227.
168. Abul Fazl, *Akbarnama*, 2: 486-7 [332].
169. Hawkins, in *Early Travels of India*, p. 114.
170. Bhimsen, *Nuksha-i-Dilkusha*, MS, BM, Or. 23, 139a.
171. Abul Fazl, *Akbarnama*, 2: 486-7 [332-3]. For a full discussion see pp. 486-8 [332-3]; see also *Tabaqat-i-Akbari*, 2: 223; *Muntakhab-ut-Tawarikh*, 2: 109 [106].
172. Abul Fazl, *Akbarnama*, 2: 486-7 [331-2]; *Muntakhab-ut-Tawarikh*, 2: 109 [106].

173. Bayazid Bayat, *Tazkira-i-Humayun wa Akbar*, p. 253.
174. Iqtidar Alam Khan, 'Mughal Assignment System', pp. 74-5.
175. Badauni, *Muntakhab-ut-Tawarikh*, 2: 85 [83-4].
176. Habib, *The Agrarian System*, p. 301.
177. After the death of Sultan Mahmmud, the ruler of Bhakkar, in 1574, the areas of Bhakkar were annexed to the Mughal Empire, and from 1574 imperial governors were successively appointed to administer it. After the establishment of regular *subas* in 1580, the area was consolidated as *sarkar* Bhakkar under *suba* Multan, see *Maasir-i-Rahimi*, 2: 340-2; Muhammad Tahir Nisyani, *Tarikh-i-Tahiri*, ed. Nabi Bakhsh Khan Biloch, Hyderabad: Sindhi Adabi Board, 1964, p. 147; Abul Fazl, *Ain-i-Akbari*, I: 554. For details of assignments conferred, transfers and dismissals in *sarkar* Bhakkar, see *Tarikh-i-Masumi*, pp. 235-6, 242-51.
178. For details of their *jagirs* in Bhakkar, see *Tarikh-i-Masumi*, pp. 248-9; *Tarikh-i-Tahiri*, p. 169; *Muntakhab-ut-Tawarikh*, 2: 359[348], 386[374]; *Tabaqat-i-Akbari*, 2: 605, 632; *Akbarnama*, 3: 917[600], 918-19[602], 1216[810]; *Maasir-i-Rahimi*, 2: 345. For more information on these *mansabdars* see their biographies, for Sadiq Muhammad Khan, *Zakhirat-ul-Khawanin*, I: 176; *Maasir-ul-Umara*, 2: 659-61; for Abdur Rahim Mirza Khan, *Zakhirat-ul-Khawanin*, I: 31-63; *Maasir-ul-Umara*, 1: 50-65; for Said Khan, *Zakhirat-ul-Khawanin*, I: 190-3; *Maasir-ul-Umara*, 2: 679-80.
179. Habib, *The Agrarian System*, p. 301, n. 13.
180. Abul Fazl, *Akbarnama*, 3: 816[536].
181. M. Athar Ali, *The Apparatus of Empire: Awards of Ranks, Offices and Titles to the Mughal Nobility, 1574-1658*, Delhi: Oxford University Press, 1985, the tabulation on p. 13 shows that Muhibb Ali Khan Rohtasi held *suba* of Multan for some time.
182. Abul Fazl, *Akbarnama*, 3: 840[553].
183. Ibid., 3: 801[525].
184. Nizamuddin Ahmad, *Tabaqat-i-Akbari*, 2: 517; *Tarikh-i-Akbari*, pp. 281-2[246].
185. Nizamuddin Ahmad, *Tabaqat-i-Akbari*, 2: 537-8.
186. Abul Fazl, *Akbarnama*, 3: 1069[717].
187. Ibid., 3: 164[116].
188. Ibid., 3: 594[401-2].
189. Ibid., 3: 993[645].
190. Ibid., 3: 1086[717].
191. Ibid., 3: 306[217-18].
192. Ibid., 3: 790[518]; *Tabaqat-i-Akbari*, 2: 622-3.
193. Abul Fazl, *Akbarnama*, 3: 1073[720].
194. See Chetan Singh, 'Center and Periphery in the Mughal State: The Case of the Seventeenth-Century Panjab', *Modern Asian Studies*, vol. XXII, no. 2, 1988, pp. 304-5. For some nuances of this debate, see M. Athar Ali, 'The

Mughal Polity', p. 309; Sayed Ali Nadeem Rezavi, 'The Empire and Bureaucracy', p. 363; Irfan Habib, 'The Eighteenth Century in Indian Economic History', in *The Eighteenth Century in India*, ed. Seema Alvi, Delhi: Oxford University Press, 2002, p. 59.

195. Abul Fazl, *Akbarnama*, 3: 801[525].
196. Ibid., 3: 711[1060].
197. Ibid., 3: 999 [650-1].
198. Ibid., 3: 877[578-9].

CHAPTER 3

Jagirdars and their *Jagirs*

It is fairly evident that the Mughal nobility depended practically for all its income on the pay it received from the state, irrespective of whether it was in the form of cash or *jagir*. It was for the emperor to decide whether a *mansabdar* would receive his pay in cash or in the form of a *jagir*.

MAGNITUDE OF *JAGIRS*

During Akbar's reign, nobles mostly preferred to receive their salaries in the form of *jagir*. There is good reason to believe that the system of granting *jagirs* was highly popular amongst the nobles, and that there was an intense struggle for *jagirs*. As Abdul-Jalil of Bilgram wrote to his son, 'Service has its foundation on a *jagir;* an employee without a *jagir*, might just as well be out of employ'.[1] Ensigns of royalty did not have much significance for the nobles who considered the award of a *jagir* to be the best form of recognition. On his appointment as governor of Qandahar, Shah Beg Khan received the *alam* and *naqara* from Akbar,[2] which led him to remark, 'what is all this trash for? Would that His Majesty gave me an order regarding my *mansab* and a *jagir* to enable me to get better troopers for his service'.[3] On the other hand, a chance of dealing with land and handling the income from it held enormous attraction all over the world. Under the Mughals, nobles and officers by securing an assignment of revenue hoped to ensure some regular income instead of depending helplessly for payment on the whims of the court. In negotiating a *jagir* there were all sorts of possibilities. In 1560, Bairam Khan allotted highly paying *jagirs* to his kith and kin and as a result earned the displeasure of the emperor for bypassing the other deserving nobles.[4] Many of his personal servants were promoted to high positions.[5] Bairam Khan accorded Wali Beg Zulqadar and his sons, Husain Quli and Ismail Quli Khan, along with some other nobles equal position with Sikandar Khan, Abdullah Khan and Bahadur Khan, and gave them cultivated fiefs, while he satisfied the great Khans with wastelands.[6] A judicious bribe could often obtain for a noble a larger *jagir* than was his due, and if he was shrewd, he could even make it yield somewhat more than its nominal return.

JAGIRDARS AND *MUQARRARA TALAB*

Under the integrated administrative system established by Akbar, the pay that each noble received was determined by the *mansab* or rank he held. A *mansabdar* of 5000 rank of the first[7] category was paid Rs. 30,000 per month, one of the second category received Rs. 29,000 and of the third category Rs. 28,000. Nobles of 4000 rank of the first category were paid Rs. 22,000, etc.[8]

Whenever a person was assigned a *jagir*, the *pargana* or village assigned to him was such that the *jama*[9] mentioned in the imperial register was exactly equal to his pay.[10] This is substantiated by some of the actual assignment orders which have survived. These orders state the rank of the assignee, followed by the statement of pay, which he was entitled to according to the sanctioned schedules and was known as *muqarrara talab* or sanctioned claim. To meet this claim, the orders describe the *parganas* with their *jama* figure, the total of the *jama* figure being equal to the amount of the pay claim. In case the sanctioned amount of the pay claim could be met by assigning only a fraction of the *jama* of a *pargana*, this fraction was stated.[11] In that case, the central *diwan* had to order a division (*qismat*) of the villages of the *paragana* among the assignees, who had obtained claims on its *jama*. However, the assignment of a whole *pargana* (*dar o bast*) in one *jagir* was always preferred by the administration to dividing it among two or more *jagirdars*.[12] Since the *jagir* that was assigned to a noble was expected to yield revenue equivalent to his salary, an adjustment was sometimes made. If the collection from the *jagir* was far below expectations, the *jagirdar* was compensated either by a cash payment from the treasury or the assignment of an additional *jagir* of an equivalent amount. On the other hand, if the actual collection by the *jagirdar* exceeded the *jama* of the sanctioned amount, the difference could be recovered from him or added to the *mutalba*, i.e. the state financial claims from him.[13] Akbar had, however, approved the suggestion that any increase in revenue brought about by the good administration of the *jagirdar* (assignee) was to remain with him through a corresponding increase in his rank.[14] A periodical correction of the revenue papers concerning the assignment was also made and the paper value of the *jagir* was often compared with the actual collection.[15] To serve best it was essential that the *jama* should closely approximate to the actual collection or *hasil.* Abul Fazl clearly states that the working of such a *jama* was one of the chief objectives of Akbar's revenue policy.[16] However, a study of the documents reveals that the criterion of matching the *jama* with the pay of the *jagirdar* was not adopted in all cases of revenue assignments. For instance, the *jama* of a *jagir* Sunam in the Delhi province was the subject of bargaining between the administration and the prospective assignee in 1584.[17]

JAGIRDARS AND IMPORTANT *JAGIRS*

The emperor and the central *diwan* had to consider many factors besides the *mansab* and the *jama* in the allotment of *jagirs.* Generally, the allocation of a *jagir* was the responsibility of the revenue ministry. A few assignments which carried with them a special administrative charge or jurisdiction were allocated by the emperor's personal order.[18] Thus, a district surrounding a fort such as Ranthambor or Kalinjar usually went with the command of the fortress, and so was the case with some historic areas such as Kanauj and Jaunpur and many rich and fertile *jagirs* in Lahore, Multan, Sambhal and Hisar-Firuza. Moreover, these places were generally assigned to important nobles. In addition, when a *jagir* was assigned to a noble, it had to be assessed whether he would be able to manage the assigned area effectively and also bring more land under cultivation. The *jagirdar* was also expected to expand the boundaries of the empire, subdue rebellious nobles and *zamindars* and protect the empire from external threats. If a noble was unable to manage his *jagir* efficiently he was liable to be transferred sooner or later.

During Akbar's reign external invasion from the north-western provinces was the pressing concern of the emperor. For this reason *subas* like Kabul, Lahore and Multan were always assigned to high ranking nobles. They were better equipped to check external invasions and control internal disorder. The *suba* of Kabul (see Table 3.9) was assigned to eminent nobles like Bairam Khan, Munim Khan, Man

Singh, Sharif Khan, Qulij Khan and Zain Khan Koka. The *sarkars* of *suba* Kabul which were frequently assigned as *jagirs* to nobles were those of Kabul, Ghaznin and Kashmir. Other *sarkars* like Qandahar and Pakli which were incorporated into the Mughal Empire during the later years of Akbar's reign, were held by nobles like Shah Beg Khan[19] and Husain Beg Shaikh Umari.[20]

In *suba* Lahore, a fertile area, the situation was slightly different. It appears that all the *sarkars* of this *suba* were somewhat equally assigned to nobles as *jagirs* (see Table 3.10). *Parganas* such as those of Sialkot (Rechna Doab), Bhera (Chinhat Doab), Birka and Jalandhar (Bet Jalandhar Doab) were important places and were frequently assigned to nobles. *Sarkars* like Multan, Dipalpur and Bhakkar in *suba* Multan had political importance for the Mughal Empire and were therefore frequently assigned to influential nobles (see Table 3.12). In the earlier years of Akbar's reign the *sarkar* of Multan was held by Muhammad Quli Khan Barlas (1555-7), Bahadur Khan Uzbek (1557-9), Muhammad Qasim Nishapuri (1560-4) (see serial nos. 1, 2 and 5 of Table 3.12) and again in 1563-7 Muhammad Quli Khan Barlas became the *jagirdar* of Multan (see serial no. 7 of Table 3.12). In 1571–4/5, it was held by Muhibb Ali, a son of Mir Khalifa and by Said Khan Chaghta (see serial nos. 8, 9 of Table 3. 12). It was held by Muhammad Sadiq Khan in 1585-7 and by Abdur Rahim Khan-i-Khanan in 1590-3 (see serial nos. 18, 20 of Table 3.12). During the last years of Akbar's reign Multan was under Mirza Rustam (1594-5) and thereafter under Said Khan Chaghta again (see serial nos. 25, 30 of Table 3.12). It is interesting to note that all of them held a rank of more than 4000.[21] The *sarkars* of Dipalpur and Bhakkar[22] were held by high ranking nobles like Bahadur Khan Uzbek, Shamsuddin Muhammad Atka, Mirza Aziz Koka, Mir Sayyid Muhammad, Sharif Khan, Abdur Rahim and Abdul Qasim Namkin (see Table 3.12). Mirza Aziz Koka held Pakpattan (Ajodhan) and Dipalpur for twelve years (see serial no. 6 of Table 3.12). In 1568, after the transfer of the Atka Khail from the Panjab,[23] he was not transferred from his *jagir*, even though he also belonged to the Atka family. The *sarkar* of Thatta[24] was divided into five parts—Thatta, Hajkan, Siwistan, Nasirpur and Chakarhalah. These divisions were largely under their chiefs as *watan jagir*. There are very few references to these areas being assigned as *tankhwah jagirs* to other nobles.

The annexation of Sindh (Thatta) to the Mughal Empire had

considerable strategic significance as it secured access to the Arabian Sea for the Panjab. Mughal interference in Sindh began in 1567-8, with the arrival of imperial troops at Bhakkar under the command of Mujahid Khan and Muhibbullah Khan. The campaign against Sindh entered its last phase when Akbar appointed Abdur Rahim Khan-i-Khanan as commander-in-chief to lead an expedition against its ruler Mirza Jani Beg in 1590.[25] After a fierce struggle, Mirza Jani Beg was forced to accept Mughal terms as a *banda-i dargah* (servant of the court) and appear in court in person. Akbar made him realize that he was no longer the ruler of Sindh in his own right, but only a noble of the imperial court. He was granted a *mansab* of 3000[26] and Multan as *jagir* for a couple of months.[27] Sindh was assigned to Mirza Shahrukh[28] (see serial no. 23 of Table 3. 12). Before this order could be implemented, news reached Akbar that members of the Arghun clan, numbering around 10,000 men, women and children, had moved up the river, following Mirza Jani Beg to his new *jagir* and as a result great distress had been caused both to the emigrants and those who had been left behind. Akbar felt that under such circumstances the policy needed to be altered. Mirza Jani Beg was, therefore, appointed as govenor of Sindh and Sindh was assigned to him as his *watan jagir.* Lahari Bandar, became the *khalisa* and the *sarkar* of Siwistan which had formerly paid *peshkash* was parcelled out amongst several grandees.[29] After Mirza Jani Beg's death in 1601,[30] his son Mirza Ghazi Beg, who had a brief tussle with Akbar, was assigned Sindh as his *watan jagir* with a *mansab* of 5000.[31] The continuance of Mirza Jani Beg and later Ghazi Beg as the *jagirdar* and governor of the *suba* should not be perceived as an argument against the centralizing tendencies of the Mughal state.[32] After the dismissal of Ghazi Beg from the governorship of the *suba* in 1611, none of his family members were given charge of the *suba*, contrary to the contentions of Sanjay Subrahmanyam.[33]

The largest numbers of references to the grant of *jagirs* are from areas which were under effective Mughal supervision and administrative control—Malwa, Allahabad, Awadh, and Gujarat *subas. Suba* Malwa, had a total of twelve *sarkars*. The most frequent references to *jagirs* in the available sources are to Mandu, Ujjain and Sarangpur *sarkars*. The other *sarkars* in order of frequency in which they were assigned were Handia, Garaha and Chanderi. An important *sarkar* was

Sarangpur and a large number of *jagir* references pertain to it. In 1561-2, it was held by Adham Khan (see serial no. 1 of Table 3.11); in 1564, it was allotted as *jagir* to Muhammad Qasim Khan Nishapuri (see serial no. 9 of Table 3.11) and in 1567 to Shah Budagh Khan and it remained with him till 1577[34] (see serial no. 20 of Table 3.11). In 1573, it was held by Muzaffar Khan and in 1576-7 it was under Shahabuddin Ahmad Khan, Bayazid Bayat, Sujaat Khan, etc. (see serial nos. 29, 32, 33, 34 of Table 3.11). Nobles who led military expeditions to the Deccan were also assigned *jagirs* in *suba* Malwa which lay on the route to the Deccan.[35] This was because the entire Deccan had not been brought under Mughal control during Akbar's reign. In 1584, Mirza Aziz Koka was sent on an expedition to the south and at the same time Garaha and Raisin[36] were assigned to him as *jagirs* (see serial no. 44 of Table 3.11). In 1599, Mirza Rustam was assigned the territory of Raisin as *jagir* and sent on an expedition to the Deccan[37] (see serial no. 65 of Table 3.11).

The *suba* of Allahabad had ten *sarkars*, of which Jaunpur, Kara-Manikpur, Banaras, Ghazipur and Kalinjar were often assigned to nobles as *jagirs* (see Table 3.3). The *sarkars* of Jaunpur and Kara-Manikpur were most frequently allotted to nobles as *jagirs*. In 1559-60, Jaunpur was assigned as *jagir* to Ali Quli Khan and he remained there until the Uzbek rebellion in 1565 (see serial no. 5 of Table 3.3). In 1561, the *pargana* of Surharpur in Jaunpur was held by Ibrahim Khan Uzbek (see serial no. 7 of Table 3.3). The *sarkars* of Jaunpur, Banaras, Ghazipur and fort Chunar were held by Munim Khan from 1567 till 1574 (see serial no. 13 of Table 3.3). In 1574, Jaunpur and Banaras were included in the *khalisa-i-sharifa*.[38] It was held by Masum Khan Farankhudi as *jagir* in 1579 (see serial no. 31 of Table 3.3). In the following year *sarkar* Jaunpur was assigned to Tarsun Khan (see serial no. 32 of Table 3.3) and in 1589 it was allotted to Abdur Rahim (see serial no. 41 of Table 3.3). In 1592, it was held by Qulij Khan and in 1594 by Yusuf Khan (see serial nos. 42, 43 of Table 3.3). In July 1597, *sarkar* Jaunpur was assigned as *jagir* to Prince Sultan Daniyal (see serial no. 44 of Table 3.3). The *sarkar* of Kara-Manikpur was held as *jagir* by Kamal Khan Gakkhar in 1558 (see serial no. 4 of table 3.3). It was assigned to Ali Quli Khan along with Jaunpur and Banaras in 1560 (see serial no. 5 of Table 3.3) and in 1563 it was held as *jagir* by Khwaja Abdul Majid Asaf Khan (see serial no. 11 of Table 3.3). In

1561-9, it was held by Majnun Khan Qaqshal, Shaham Khan Jalair and Muhibb Ali Khan (see serial nos. 8, 9, 12 of Table 3.3). *Pargana* Chekur in *sarkar* Manikpur was allotted as *jagir* to Baba Khan Qaqshal in 1574 (see serial no. 26 of Table 3.3) and in 1580 it was under Asad Khan Turkman, Ismail Quli Khan and Iliyas Khan Langa (see serial nos. 34, 35, 36 of Table 3.3). The other *sarkars* in order of frequency with which *jagirs* were assigned were Banaras, Ghazipur and Kalinjar.

In *suba* Awadh out of a total five *sarkars* Lucknow, Khairabad and Bahraich are more important from the point of view of this study than the other *sarkars*. Lucknow, Khairabad and Bahraich were frequently assigned as *jagirs* to nobles. In 1558-60, Sultan Husain Khan Jalair was the *jagirdar* of *pargana* Sandila in *sarkar* Lucknow (see serial no. 1 of Table 3.4). In 1559, *sarkar* Lucknow was held by Ali Quli Khan (see serial no. 2 of Table 3.4). It was under Husain Khan and Mahdi Qasim Khan in 1569 (see serial nos. 21, 22 of Table 3.4). For a few months in 1572, *Khitta-i*-Lucknow was held as *jagir* by Sikandar Khan Uzbek and in 1575 it was assigned to Khwaja Amina Khwaja Jahan (see serial nos. 23, 25 of Table 3.4). In 1585, it was under Mir Abdul Ghuyas (see serial no. 31 of Table 3.4). *Sarkar* Bahraich was held by nobles like Qaya Khan Gung in 1560, Wazir Khan and Mihtar Khan in 1581 and in 1604-5 it was held by Mir Sharif Amuli (see serial nos. 3, 28, 29, 35 of Table 3.4). A part of *sarkar* Khairabad was held as *jagir* by Munim Khan in 1563 (see serial no. 4 of Table 3.4), in 1565 *pargana* Nimkhar was allotted as *jagir* to Amir Khan, Shah Budagh Khan and Shaham Khan Jalair (see serial nos. 7, 8, 9 of Table 3.4). In 1567 and 1586-91, *pargana* Khairabad was held by Yarshahi, Asdullah and Qasim Ali Khan respectively (see serial nos. 18, 19, 32 of Table 3.4). In *suba* Gujarat comprising nine *sarkars*, Ahmedabad, Patan and Surat *sarkars* were frequently assigned to nobles. In 1572-5, Ahmedabad was held by Khan Azam Mirza Aziz Koka as *jagir*[39] (see serial no. 3 of Table 3.8). In 1573-7, Dholka, Dhandhuka and Idar *parganas* in *sarkar* Ahmedabad were held by Wazir Khan and in 1577-83 *sarkar* of Ahmedabad was held by Shahabuddin Ahmad Khan (see serial nos. 14, 16 of Table 3.8). It was under Abdur Rahim in 1589 (see serial no. 39 of Table 3.8) and under Prince Sultan Murad in 1593 (see serial no. 44 of Table 3.8). *Sarkar* Patan was assigned as *jagir* to Mirza Abdur Rahim in 1572 and Sayyid Ahmad Khan Baraha was appointed to take care of it[40] (see serial nos. 1, 2 of Table 3.8). Mir Muhammad Khan-i-

Kalan and his sons (1573-5) (see serial no. 7 of Table 3.8), Tarsun Khan (1576-9), Shah Fakhruddin Mashadi (1577) and Sayyid Qasim (1584) were *jagirdars* of *sarkar* Patan (see serial nos. 15, 17, 36 of Table 3.8). It was also assigned as *jagir* to Itimad Khan Gujarati, Sher Khan Fuladi, Qutbuddin Khan Atka, Shaikh Muhammad Bukhari, Shaikh Hamid Bukhari, Sharif Khan Atka, Qulij Khan, Ismail Quli Khan, Raja Rai Singh and Mirza Yusuf Khan at different points of time. The other *sarkars* in order of frequency with which *jagirs* were assigned are Surat, Broach and Baroda (see Table 3.8 for more details).

In *suba* Ajmer, the situation was different. In this *suba* there were many powerful Rajput chieftains towards whom Akbar followed a conciliatory policy. Since many of these chiefs had joined the imperial service and were assigned *mansabs,* they were paid through the assignment of revenues in the form of a *jagir* equivalent to their salary. In addition, a portion of the revenues was always assigned to the chiefs in their *watans.* Thus, the revenues assigned to the chiefs in their *watans* were a part of their salary and not an extra privilege.[41] In addition to their *watan* they were assigned handsome *jagirs* in different parts of the Mughal Empire.[42] Mota Raja Udai Singh was given Jodhpur as a hereditary dominion after his accession in 1583 and was allotted Siwana and Sojat as *jagirs* by the emperor (see serial no. 36 of Table 3.2). Similarly, Raja Jagmal, Ram Das Kachhwaha, Raja Lonkaran, Rao Kalyan Mal and Rai Rai Singh were also assigned *jagirs* by Akbar in addition to their *watan jagirs* (see Table 3.2 for details). Ahsan Raza Khan found sixty-one persons belonging to various ruling houses holding a *mansab* of 200 and above under Akbar at one time or the other. In his study forty of these *mansabdars* belonged to the ruling families of *suba* Ajmer while the remainder belonged to the other regions of the Mughal Empire.[43] In the present study, out of 51 references (see Table 3.2) to the *jagirs* assigned in *suba* Ajmer, 19 pertained to Hindu and Rajput nobles. Apart from Rajput and Hindu *jagirdars*, other notable *jagirdars* who held *jagirs* in *suba* Ajmer were Muhammad Quli Khan Barlas, Muhammad Qasim Khan Nishapuri, Tarsun Muhammad Khan, Khwaja Abdul Majid Asaf Khan, Sadiq Muhammad Khan, Payanda Muhammad Khan, Abdur Rahim Mirza Khan and Prince Sultan Daniyal (see Table 3.2 for more details). *Suba* Ajmer comprised seven *sarkars* and the *sarkars* which were directly under Mughal control were Ajmer, Nagaur and Ranthambor. In fact, the highest numbers of references to the assignment of *jagirs* pertain to these *sarkars*.

For a study of the political status of the principalities of *suba* Ajmer, the account given in the *Ain-i-Akbari* is extremely valuable and illuminating.[44] It should be remembered that in the case of the imperial territories proper, the *Ain-i-Akbari* gives the area, *suyurghal* and total revenue figures, but in the case of territories outside the jurisdiction of the imperial government these statistics are incomplete. In the case of Ajmer, Nagaur, Ranthambor and Chittor *sarkars* only a few *mahals* have *suyurghals*, several *mahals* of these *sarkars* are not measured, and their revenues are given in round figures.[45] This indicates that even in these *sarkars* (although some *jagir* references are available) most of the *mahals* were still held by petty tributary chiefs, and only a small number was administered by the imperial government. For the remaining three *sarkars*—Jodhpur, Sirohi and Bikaner—no area figures are available and for Bikaner only the totals of revenue and army are available. The imperial government's control over these *sarkars* was symbolic and most of the areas were under the chieftains.

The *subas* of Agra and Delhi, which were nearest to the imperial court, were largely under the direct control of the central authority. However, sizeable areas of these *subas* were also assigned as *jagirs* to eminent nobles[46] as can be seen from Tables 3.1 and 3.7. Some of the *parganas* in *suba* Agra which were assigned to nobles as *jagirs* were Bayana, Patiali, Etawah and Shamsabad. Agra *suba* included thirteen *sarkars*[47] of which the maximum references pertain to the *sarkars* of Kalpi, Agra, Etawah and Kanauj. Kalpi *sarkar* and Etawah *pargana* were frequently assigned to nobles as *jagir*. Abdullah Khan Uzbek was assigned Kalpi *sarkar* as *jagir* in 1556 which he held till 1562 (see serial no. 2 of Table 3.1). Again in 1572, it was held by Shaham Khan Jalair and in 1579 by Qasim Ali Khan Baqqal (see serial nos. 28, 30 of Table 3.1). It was assigned as *jagir* to Muttalib Khan in 1583 and to Qasim Ali Khan in 1590 (see serial nos. 35, 36 of Table 3.1). In 1594, Ismail Quli Khan was appointed *jagirdar* of Kalpi (see serial no. 38 of Table 3.1). The *pargana* of Etawah was held by nobles like Qaya Khan Gung, Bahadur Khan Uzbek, Munim Khan and Zain Khan Koka at different times (see serial nos. 4, 14, 17, 31 of Table 3.1). Other *sarkars* in order of frequency of *jagir* assignments were Agra, Narnaul and Kanauj.

Suba Delhi consisted of eight *sarkars*,[48] and areas in the *sarkars* of

Sambhal, Hisar-Firuza, Saharanpur, Sirhind and Badaun were assigned as *jagirs* to nobles. The *sarkars* of Sambhal, Hisar-Firuza and Sirhind were most frequently assigned to nobles. In 1556-8, Ali Quli Khan was the *jagirdar* of *sarkar* Sambhal (see serial no. 1 of Table 3.7). In 1566, *pargana* Azampur of Sambhal was the *jagir* of Ibrahim Husain Mirza, Hafiz Rakhna and Muhammad Sultan Mirza (see serial nos. 18, 19, 20 of Table 3.7). In 1568-70, Mir Muhammad Khan-i-Kalan held this *sarkar* as *jagir* (see serial no. 24 of Table 3.7). It was assigned to Muinuddin Ahmad Khan Farankhudi in 1573, in 1583-4 to Said Khan Chaghta and in 1589-93 to Qulij Khan (see serial nos. 25, 35, 36 of Table 3.7). In 1595, *sarkar* Sambhal was held by Muzaffar Husain Mirza (see serial no. 38 of Table 3.7). Hisar-Firuza and Sirhind were also allotted as *jagirs* to nobles like Beg Mirak, Sher Muhammad Diwana, Khwaja Muzaffar Ali, Munim Khan, Ibrahim Husain Mirza, Malik Ashraf, Abu Said and Raja Rai Rai Singh (see Table 3.7 for details).

Regarding the more distant *subas* of Bengal and Bihar, because of their distance from the imperial court, territories in those *subas* were always assigned to powerful nobles. The underlying reason for this was that these nobles were capable of suppressing internal revolts which frequently broke out in these *subas*. Due to these disturbances, imperial officers at times demanded that their salaries be paid in cash instead of *jagirs* in Bihar and Bengal.[49] The *suba* of Bengal consisted of twenty-four *sarkars* of which Ghoraghat, Jaleasar, Khalifabad, Tanda and Orissa were often referred to as *jagirs*. These *sarkars* were assigned as *jagirs* to nobles like Munim Khan, Majnun Khan Qaqshal, Khaldin Khan, Sher Khan, Shahbaz Khan, Khan Azam Aziz Koka and Wazir Khan. Regarding the other *sarkars*, there are very few references to *jagirs* being granted there (see Table 3.5 for details). In *suba* Bihar comprising seven *sarkars*, those of Rohtas, Hajipur, Chunar and Tirhut were generally assigned to nobles as *jagirs*. In 1568, Muhibb Ali Khan Rohtasi was assigned the *sarkar* of Rohtas and he held that for at least twenty-one years. In 1577, along with the other *parganas*, Rohtas fort was also assigned to him (see serial no. 2 of Table 3.6). Farhat Khan held the *pargana* of Arraha and fort Rohtas in 1574-6 (see serial no. 7 of Table 3.6). In 1575-7, the *pargana* of Sahasram in *sarkar* Rohtas was held as *jagir* by Muzaffar Khan (see serial no. 12 of Table 3.6). Again in 1577, *pargana* Ishar in this *sarkar* was assigned to Muhammad Masum

Kabuli and after 1580 the other *parganas* in this *sarkar* were held by Said Beg Badakshi, Mir Muizulmulk, Jamaluddin Husain Sistani and Saadat Ali (see serial nos. 20, 27, 31, 34, 37 of Table 3.6). Fort Rohtas was assigned to Mirza Yusuf Khan in 1581 and in 1587-9 members of the Kachhwaha family became the *jagirdars* of Rohtas (see serial nos. 42, 45, 46 of Table 3.6). The *sarkar* of Hajipur was held by Muhammad Quli Khan Barlas in 1574 and Muzaffar Khan in 1575 (see serial nos. 6, 12 of Table 3.6). In 1580, it was held by Shaham Khan Jalair and Khan Azam Aziz Koka. Again in 1585, it was given as *jagir* to Said Khan Chaghta and in 1587 to Man Singh. In 1594, Khan Azam Aziz Koka was again appointed *jagirdar* of this *sarkar* (see serial nos. 28, 41, 44, 46, 48 of Table 3.6). The other *sarkars* in order of the frequency of *jagir* assignments were Chunar, Tirhut and Saran (see Table 3.5 for details).

The system of assignment of *jagirs* enabled the states to lessen some of the difficulties associated with revenue collection. Through this system the arduous task of collecting the revenue from distant places was circumvented. The task was left to the *jagirdars* who appropriated it as salary. In the case of *mansabdars* who held lower ranks, and were not high in imperial favour, *jagirs* were allotted in less important areas which had no administrative and political significance for the Mughal Empire.

TENURE OF *JAGIRS*

Irfan Habib, Athar Ali, Noman Ahmad Siddiqi and many others have implicitly stressed that all *jagirs*, except for *watan* or *al-tamgha jagirs*, were subject to *taghaiyur* or transfer after every three or four years.[50] Surprisingly, no one has mentioned the case of any particular *jagir* transfer nor calculated the exact length of time for which a *jagir* was held. Judging from the duration for which *jagirdars* held their *jagirs*, it does not appear that the assigned areas frequently changed hands as a precaution against the assignee developing local roots in his *jagir*. For Akbar's reign there are hardly any references that indicate that officials *(jagirdars)* were transferred in accordance with this policy. Based primarily on the observations of European travellers such as Hawkins and Bernier, scholars have argued that *jagirdars* were not allowed to stay in one place for long and were transferred on an average every three or four years. Surprisingly, not a single specific reference to *jagir* transfer and its tenure has been cited for Akbar's reign.

As argued earlier, most of the information pertaining to the reign of Akbar shows that *jagirs* were generally transferred along with the post held by the *mansabdars*. Moreover, the transfer of assignments of large holders during the reign of Akbar was not as frequent as was previously believed.[51] There are numerous cases where Mughal (Akbar's) notables with high *mansabs* remained undisturbed in their place of assignment for exceptionally long periods. For instance, Muhibb Ali Khan Rohtasi remained the *jagirdar* of the Rohtas area in Bihar for nearly twenty-one years (1568-89). In 1576, fort Rohtas was also assigned to him.[52] In 1586, he was appointed co-governor of Bengal. Iqtidar Alam Khan erroneously described him as the *jagirdar* of Bhera (Chinhat Doab) and Rohtas (Sind Sagar Doab) in November-December 1580.[53] Hasan Ali Khan remained the *qiladar* of fort Chunar for not less than twelve years (1561-73).[54] Said Khan Chaghta held assignments in the *subas* of Lahore and Multan for ten years (1573-83)[55] and in the *subas* of Bengal and Bihar for eleven years (1587-98).[56] Raja Bhagwan Das Kachhwaha and his family, including Man Singh, remained in the *subas* of Lahore and Kabul for nine years (1578-87).[57] Again, Man Singh held the assignments of Bihar (1587-94) and Bengal (1594-1604) for seven and ten years respectively.[58] Sharif Khan Atka's assignments in *suba* Malwa (1579-94) and Ghaznin (1594-1603) were for fifteen and eight years respectively.[59] Shah Budagh Khan remained in Sarangpur and Mandu for not less than ten years (1567-77).[60] Qulij Muhammad Khan also held assignments in the areas of Gujarat including Surat fort for at least sixteen years (1573-89).[61] Mirza Shahrukh remained in *suba* Malwa for almost ten years (1594–1604/5).[62]

In addition to these cases, there are other references to high ranking *mansabdars* holding their assignments for twelve years or more before being transferred. (For details see the *suba*-wise tabulations of *jagirs* in Tables 3.1-3.12). Moreover, it should be remembered that the *jagirdar* supervised and generally collected the land revenue from a hereditary class holding superior rights in land, viz., the *zamindars*. The arguments of Bernier and other European travellers can also be refuted on the ground that the frequent transfer of smaller *jagirdars* would not have affected the cultivator of the area, as long as the *zamindars* as a class remained strong and the *jagirdars* would hardly have been in a position to extract more than their sanctioned dues.[63]

Shireen Moosvi's study reveals that toward the end of Akbar's reign, *mansabdars* and their followers cornered 82 per cent of the total budget of the empire for their pay and allowances.[64] By far, the larger part of the revenue of the empire was assigned in *jagirs*. According to Moreland, Irfan Habib, Shireen Moosvi and Stephen P. Blake between 75 and 88 per cent of the territories under Akbar were in the hands of assignees as their *jagirs*.[65] On the basis of the present study, however, it may be argued that a still higher percentage of territories was assigned as *jagirs* under Akbar. There were hardly any occasions when high ranking *mansabdars* were not paid in the form of *jagirs*. Therefore, if high ranking *mansabdars* were generally paid in the form of *jagirs*, they certainly had a bigger share of the land assigned in *jagirs*. Since the transfer of *jagirs* held by these *mansabdars* was not frequent, the impact of frequent transfers of smaller *jagirdars* on the peasantry and on the agrarian system should not be overestimated. It is quite likely that without holding important official posts (political–administrative–military) the lower ranking *jagirdars* may not have been in a position to oppress and ruin the peasantry on a very large scale or to pose a serious threat to the empire. There are hardly any references to a *jagirdar* of a lower or even higher rank posing a serious threat to the stability and integrity of the empire after developing roots in the *jagirs*. Out of 144 rebellions during the reign of Akbar, H.K. Naqvi did not find any uprising that was specifically raised by a *jagirdar*.[66] Moreover, the Mughal administrative machinery was, in some ways, designed to check the abuse of power by individual *jagirdars*. Under Akbar, there is little evidence of abuse of the kind that Bernier's mentions.

INFLUENTIAL *JAGIRDARS*

In so far as the important nobles were concerned, the *jagirs* they were assinged carried special administrative jurisdiction and were far more valuable.[67] Great caution was exercised at the time of their assignment. During Akbar's reign, many nobles were assigned rich and fertile *jagirs*. Munim Khan, who was the *ataliq* of Prince Akbar and was given the title of Khan-i-Khanan and appointed *vakil*, was assigned *jagirs* which were established, fertile and administratively important. From the beginning of Akbar's reign to 1560, he held 'Kabul-wa-Ghaznin' as his *jagir.*[68] In 1560, he held a *jagir* in Hisar-Firuza.[69] In 1563, he requested a *jagir* in the Panjab, and his compact *jagir* of Hisar-Firuza was reduced by half and for this he was compensated by being assigned *jagirs* in *sarkar* Etawah and Khairabad and in the *pargana* of Shahpur (in *sarkar* Bari Doab), Jalandhar (in *sarkar* Bet Jalandhar Doab) and Indri (in *sarkar* Saharanpur).[70] After the defeat of Ali Quli and Bahadur Khan in 1567, their *jagirs* in Jaunpur, Banaras and Ghazipur up to the banks of the Chausa river were assigned to Munim Khan.[71] In 1574, Munim Khan's *jagir* was included in the imperial exchequer (*khalisa-i-sharifa*) and he was assigned Patna as *jagir* and ordered to assist the royal army against Daud (son of Sultan Sulaiman Kararani, the ruler of Bengal).[72] Following the death of Sulaiman Kararani in October 1572, Daud became a source of annoyance in Bengal. Munim Khan held a *jagir* in Bengal in 1575. When Akbar visited the eastern provinces, Munim Khan's estates were also transferred to Bihar in accordance with his request. When the rebels of Bengal were finally defeated and the province was brought under greater imperial revenue supervision, Munim Khan sent Khwaja Shah Mansur of Shiraz to court with a request for a *jagir* in Bengal. The emperor granted his request.[73] The same was true of other eminent nobles who were assigned important *jagirs* at different points of time. Noteworthy among them were Ali Quli Khan, Sikandar Khan Uzbek, Khan Azam Mirza Aziz Koka, Man Singh, Abdullah Khan Uzbek, Qaya Khan Gung, Haider Muhammad Khan, Majnun Khan Qaqshal, Mahdi Qasim Khan, Muhammad Quli Khan Barlas, Bahadur Khan Uzbek, Shahabuddin Ahmad Khan, Husain Quli Khan, Muhibb Ali Khan Rohtasi, Abdur Rahim Khan, Qutbuddin Muhammad Khan, Ismail Quli Khan, Qulij Khan and Muhammad Sadiq Khan. References to the granting of *jagirs* frequently appear in the sources and it is clear that the powerful nobles always held important *jagirs* in different parts of the empire like Kalpi, Multan, Sambhal, Lucknow, Sialkot, Bayana, Lahore, Manikpur, Etawah, Ghoraghat and Nagaur.

Ali Quli Khan distinguished himself in Kabul and in the conquest of Hindustan under Humayun. He also played a significant role at the time of Akbar's accession. He was posthumously described by Abul Fazl as a *mansabdar* of 5000 rank. Ali Quli Khan and his brother

Bahadur Khan held *jagirs* in Sambhal, Multan, Dipalpur, Lucknow, Jaunpur, Banaras and Ghazipur. Sikandar Khan Uzbek was assigned important *jagirs* such as Agra, Sialkot, Awadh and Lucknow. Khan Azam Mirza Aziz Koka and Man Singh who had reached the high rank of 7000 *zat*/6000 *sawar* held important *jagirs*. They were often assigned *jagirs* of their own choice. When the Atka clan was removed from the Panjab in 1568, Khan Azam retained Dipalpur.[74] He was given the title of Khan Azam and in Akbar's words, 'between me and Aziz is a river of milk (*juy-i-shir*) which I cannot cross'. In 1572, after the conquest of Gujarat he was assigned Ahmedabad as *jagir*.[75] In 1580, he was sent to Bihar to suppress the rebellion, and Hajipur was assigned to him. He also held Multan in 1596[76] and in 1605 the *jagir* of Bihar was allotted to him.[77] Man Singh who was given the title of Farzand (son) by Akbar and who also played an important role in many battles was assigned rich and fertile *jagirs* in Lahore, Bihar, Bengal, Kabul and Multan.

After the murder of Bairam Khan at Patan (in Gujarat), his son Abdur Rahim Khan was graciously treated by Akbar. Akbar gave him the title of Mirza Khan and married him to Mahbanu, a sister of Mirza Aziz Koka. In 1572, he held a *jagir* in Patan. In the 25th regnal year, he was appointed *Mir Arz* and three years later *ataliq* of Prince Salim. For his outstanding efforts against Muzaffar Khan Gujarati, he was appointed the commander of 5000 and given the coveted title of Khan-i-Khanan. He was appointed *vakil* in 1589 and received Jaunpur as *tuyul*; in 1590-1 his *jagir* was transferred to Multan and he received orders to take Thatta. In 1595, Bhilsa was given to him as *jagir* and he was sent on an expedition to the Deccan with Sultan Murad.[78] Khan-Jahan Husain Quli Khan was also a commander of 5000 rank and in the 8th regnal year, he was proclaimed a Khan and was assigned *parganas* in Ajmer and Nagaur as *jagirs*. In the 13th regnal year, his *jagirs* were transferred to the Panjab where he remained till 1573. He led an expedition against Sharafuddin Husain and Jai Chand of Nagarkot. He was given the title of Khan-Jahan, which was next to that of Khan-i-Khanan. In 1575-6, he was sent against Isa Khan, the chief of Bhati in Bengal, and was assigned *jagirs* in Bengal and Ghazipur.

Mir Muhammad Atka Khan-i-Kalan also served under Kamran and Humayun and rose to a high position during the reign of Akbar. He belonged to the Atka clan that held *jagirs* in the Panjab up to 1568. In 1568, when the Atka clan was ousted from the Panjab, Mir Muhammad

Atka received Sambhal as *jagir.*[79] In 1572-3, he held *jagirs* in *suba* Ajmer and Gujarat. He was given the title of Khan-i-Kalan and a rank of 5000. Shahabuddin Ahmad Khan was another important noble during Akbar's reign. He was a relative and a friend of Maham Anaga (Akbar's nurse). At the beginning of Akbar's reign he was commandant of Delhi and in 1566, he held a *jagir* in *suba* Malwa. In the 21st regnal year he was promoted to the rank of 5000. He distinguished himself in the conquest of Broach in 1584 and received that district as *jagir.*[80] In addition to these he held Saraonj, Sarangpur, Ujjain and Raisin as *jagirs.* Muhammad Quli Khan Barlas was also given important *jagirs* under Akbar and was a commander of 5000. He served under Humayun and held Multan as *jagir*. During the early years of Akbar's reign his *jagir* was transferred to Nagaur. For a short time he was governor of Malwa. In 1563-7, he was assigned Multan as *jagir* and in 1567 Awadh. (For these details see Tables 3.1-3.12.)

RACIAL AND RELIGIOUS GROUPS

For the complex task of establishing an effective administrative system and maintaining law and order in a large empire, Akbar had successfully developed a centralized government structure. He had brought together a group of nobles or a ruling class which was entirely dependent upon him. Among the reasons for Akbar's success in developing a strong class of nobles around him was that he chose the right men for the right job. Praising Akbar as a good physiognomist, Abul Fazl notes that the emperor could, by a simple glance, ascertain whether or not a candidate merited selection.[81]

The credit of evolving an administratively homogeneous nobility out of multiracial and religiously heterogeneous elements goes to Akbar. But this heterogeneous character of the Mughal nobility should not be interpreted in terms of universal generosity or open-hearted welcome to all meritorious candidates to this class. It was 'a closed aristocracy and entrance into this class was not easily available to ordinary subjects, whatever their merits'.[82] *Khanazads*[83] (the descendants and relatives of *mansabdars*) and Turanis were usually accommodated in the nobility. Unusual favour was extended to these groups as revealed by the available sources.

Even during the early years of Akbar's reign, the Mughal nobility had taken a composite shape; it included Turanis, Iranis, Afghans, Indian Muslims, Rajputs, etc.[84] These labels should not be considered as rigid, ascriptive categories indicating inbred loyalty or cohesion. The inclusion of diverse elements into Mughal service was the result of historical circumstances. Partly, however, especially in the case of Rajputs it was the result of planned imperial policy. In spite of this clear-cut division, there was a sense of unity among the nobility. In crisis, this ethnically divided nobility stood united, irrespective of its racial and religious bonds and ties.

As is evident from Tables 3.1-3.12 and Appendix A, in terms of *jagir* assignments the Turanis were the chief components of Akbar's nobility. The Turanis were perceived as men of the sword, experts in military operations such as making charges, raids, night attacks and arrests, and well trained horsemen and archers. Most significantly, in view of the fact that the ruling family was of Turani origin, they formed the bulk of the nobility in spite of various fluctuations in their fortunes. It is clear from the tables that the share of the Turanis in *jagirs* was slightly less than half (41.27 per cent) of the total number of *jagir* assignments. Out of the 550 total available *jagir* references, 227 pertained to the Turanis. These observations can be verified from Appendix A, which is an abridged version of Tables 3.1-3.12. It emerges that the share of the Turanis in the total assignments remained unsurpassed from the beginning till the end of Akbar's reign. In contrast to the disciplined Turanis, the Iranis were considered to be more civilized men of the pen, who served as excellent administrators and accountants, and were far more 'cunning' and 'ease-loving' than the Turanis. Hence, the Iranis were far from being unfit for military service as this required military talent as well as a great deal of administrative acumen. It appears that Iranis were hardly less involved in purely military functions.[85] However, after the dismissal of Akbar's Irani regent Bairam Khan in 1560, and the promulgation of the so-called infallibility decree (*mahzar*) in 1579, the emperor began to rid himself of the Iranis. Henceforth, the Iranis were less trusted and the emperor preferred the Turanis in comparison to them.[86] As far as the share of the Iranis in *jagirs* is concerned, out of 550 *jagir* references, 145 pertained to the Iranis.

The Afghans were known to be rather uncivilized but ferocious fighters. They were notorious for their unfaithfulness and their proclivity to defeat. Abdur Rahim rightly observed that the relationship between the Afghans and the Mughals under Akbar may be summed up as one of hostility.[87] There were not very many Afghan nobles who were allotted *jagirs* of any significance, only 25 out of 550 references pertained to them. Popularly known as *Shaikhzadas*, Indian Muslims are described by Manucci as those 'who are descended from the family of Mohammedan but very remote from the Sayyids'.[88] Before they settled down as Mughal nobles, many of them had lived as itinerant dervishes, such as the prominent Akbari noble Shahbaz Khan Kambu, who claimed to be a descendant of the famous Makhdum Bahauddin Zakaria of Multan. When Akbar took over the reigns of government and had to deal with hostile elements in the old Turani dominated nobility, he turned to Indian Muslims and Rajputs. The most important section of the *Shaikhzadas* that was inducted into the Mughal nobility was the Sayyids of Baraha. Mahmud Baraha of Kundliwal was the first Baraha Sayyid to have joined the Mughal service in 1556-7. After the overthrow of Bairam Khan a large number of Baraha Sayyids and other *Shaikhzada* families were admitted into the nobility.[89] Henceforth, special favour was shown to them and they carved out a place of distinction for themselves. Among this group of nobles, the Sayyids of Baraha and the Kambus held leading positions under Akbar; 45 out of 550 references pertained to them.

According to Farid Bhakkari, Humayun's advice to Akbar was that the Rajputs should be treated with kindness and love because they were obedient and faithful; rebellion and disobedience were alien to them. Farid Bhakkari adds that for this reason Akbar favoured the Rajputs so much that it became a subject of comment.[90] This favourable attitude towards the Rajputs helped Akbar in balancing his nobility and in creating a new faction, which largely remained loyal to him. The recruitment of Rajputs in the Mughal service began soon after Akbar's assumption of power.[91] The presence of important clans of Kachhwaha Rajputs in the Mughal service can be detected after 1562. Rajput nobles, who had over a long period acquired a reputation for courage and bravery, were usually sent to the battlefield. That the emperor trusted Rajput nobles is evident from the fact that he did not hesitate to send military expeditions under them against other Rajput chiefs. Besides the Rajputs, there were a few other Hindu nobles who were inducted into the royal service because of Akbar's liberal and religious outlook. There are 60 (including *watan*) *jagir* references pertaining to noteworthy Rajput and Hindu nobles, who received their pay in the form of *jagirs*. Statistical evidence reveals that the Rajputs, as a racial group, accounted for a higher share than the Afghans. They held 10.90 per cent of *jagir* revenues under Akbar. (For details see Tables 3.1-3.12. For clan-wise break-up see Appendices A and B.)

TABLES

It is not possible to draw a map showing the territories of individual *jagirs* held in the empire or any of the provinces in a particular year. An attempt has been made to tabulate all the available information pertaining to the assignments conferred upon or held by individual nobles at different points of time during the reign of Akbar. Though it is difficult to discern any definite policy regarding the transfer of *jagirs*, the evidence in the tables indicates that the transfer of *jagirs* of large holders was not as frequent as has been previously believed by many scholars. There are several references to show that *jagirdars* with very high *mansabs* remained in their place of assignment for exceptionally long periods. Sources for the tables are the chronicles of Akbar's reign—the *Akbarnama* by Abul Fazl, the *Muntakhab-ut-Tawarikh* by Abdul Qadir Badauni, the *Tabaqat-i-Akbari* by Nizamuddin Ahmad, the *Tarikh-i-Akbari* by Arif Qandhari and the *Tazkira-i-Humayun wa Akbar* by Bayazid Bayat. In addition, some valuable data have been drawn from biographical works like the *Zakhirat-ul-Khawanin*, the *Maasir-ul-Umara*, Blochmann's biographies in the *Ain-i-Akbari*, and the *Tazkirat-ul-Umara*. They provide insights into the antecedents of these officials, which help in formulating some plausible suggestions in this regard. The available information is presented under nine heads. The date is established either on the basis of specific dates furnished by the chronicles or by the sequence of reporting in Abul Fazl's chapters arranged by regnal years. In a few cases where the exact year of *jagir* allotment is not known, the available information about the *jagir* held by the noble is given within parentheses.

Where the place assigned is identified with the *pargana* headquarters or a small town (*qasba*) located in the *sarkar*, its name is entered under column *jagir*. The name of the *sarkar* which the *pargana/qasba* under reference transpired, is mentioned under the column *sarkar*. (The *Ain-i-Akbari* offers a complete list of *parganas* in each *sarkar*.) The location of places other than *pargana* or *sarkar* headquarters has been determined on the basis of Irfan Habib's *Atlas of the Mughal Empire* (in view of the fact that down to 1580, regular *subas* did not exist). In a few cases, where the information is vague and alludes only to the assignment of unspecified *parganas* in a particular *sarkar* or *suba*, it is entered as *parganas* in the column *jagirs* with the name of the *sarkar* under the column *sarkar*. In these cases if the *sarkar* is not known, the name of the *suba* is given within parentheses under the column *sarkar*. If the place assigned is identified by the sources with the name of a *sarkar* headquarters or the territory of a *sarkar* it is also placed under the column *jagirs*. The spellings of place names used by Irfan Habib in his *Atlas* have generally been adopted. References to the sources (in column no. 9) not only indicate *jagirs* assignments concomitant to *jagirdars'* postings, but also holding assignments, biographies of the *jagirdars*, and *jagirdars'* official postings/services in the province of their *jagirs*.

References

The following abbreviations are used: *AN* (Abul Fazl, *Akbar-nama*); *MT* (Abdul Qadir Badauni, *Muntakhab-ut-Tawarikh*); *TA* (Nizamuddin Ahmad, *Tabaqat-i-Akbari*); Arif (Arif Qandhari, *Tarikh-i-Akbari*); Bayazid (Bayazid Bayat, *Tazkira-i-Humayun wa Akbar*); *MR* (Abul Baqi Nihawandi, *Maasir-i-Rahmi*); *TM* (Mir Masum, *Tarikh-i-Masumi*); *ZK* (Shaikh Farid Bhakkari, *Zakhirat-ul-Khawanin*, cited only for biographies of *jagirdars*); *MU* (Shah Nawaz Khan and Abdul Hayy, *Maasir-ul-Umara*, translated by H. Beveridge, cited mostly for biographies); *AA* (Blochmann's Biographies in the *Ain-i-Akbari*, cited mostly for biographies); *TU* (Kewal Ram, *Tazkirat-ul-Umara*, translated by M. Azizuddin Husain, cited only for biographies); *Mirat-i-Ahmadi* (Ali Muhammad Khan, *Mirat-i-Ahmadi*); Farishta (Muhammad Qasim Hindushah Farishta, translated by J. Briggs as *History of the Rise of Mohammadan Power in India*); *Khyat* (Munhot Nainsi, *Munhot Nainsi ri Khyat*); *Vigat* (Munhot Nainsi, *Marwar ra Pargana ri Vigat*); *Vir Vinod* (Kaviraj Shayamal Das, *Vir Vinod*); *Dalpat Vilas* (Dalpat Singh, *Dalpat Vilas*); *Medieval Gujarat* (Based on Muhammad Ali Khan's *Mirat-i-Ahmadi*, translated by James Bird); Stewart (Charles Stewart, *The History of Bengal*).

TABLE 3.1: ASSIGNMENT OF *JAGIRS* IN *SUBA* AGRA

S. No.	*Name of Assignee*	*Racial Group*	*Period*		*Approximate Tenure*	*Jagirs*	*Sarkar*	*Sources*
			From *Year(s) of Assignment Conferred/ Held*	*To* *Year(s) of Transfer (T), Revolt by Jagirdars (R), Flight (F), Death (D), etc.*		*Sarkar (S), Pargana (P), Qasba (Q), Fort (F), etc.*		
1	*2*	*3*	*4*	*5*	*6*	*7*	*8*	*9*
1.	Sikandar Khan Uzbek (Khan-i-Alam)	Turani	Mar. 1556	Nov.-Dec. 1556 (T)	Few mths.	Agra (S)	Agra	*AN*, II, 25, 74; *TA*, II, 214; Farishta, II, 111; *MU*, I, 691; *AA*, I, 394-5; *ZK*, I, 213
2.	Abdullah Khan Uzbek (Shujaat Khan)	Turani	Mar. 1556	Aug. 1562 (T)	6 yrs. 6 mths.	Kalpi (S)	Kalpi	*AN*, II, 25, 71, 214, 260-1; *MT*, II, 6, 44; *TA*, II, 256; Arif, 97; *MU*, I, 82; *AA*, I, 337; *ZK*, I, 210
3.	Tardi Beg Khan	Turani	Mar. 1556	Oct. 1556 (killed)	Few mths.	Mewat (P)	Alwar	*AN*, II, 25; *MU*, II, 940-3; *AA*, I, 334-5

4.	Qaya Khan Gung	Irani	Mar. 1556 1560 (T)	Apr.-May	4 yrs.	Kol-wa-Jalali (P), Etawah (P)	Kol Agra	*AN*, II, 25, 71, 150; *MT*, II, 6; *MU*, II, 530; *AA*, I, 366; *ZK*, I, 210
5.	Haider Muhammad Khan	Turani	Mar. 1556	–	–	Bayana (P)	Agra	*AN*, II, 25; *MT*, II, 6; *MU*, I, 599-600; *AA*, I, 418; *TU*, 47
6.	Majnun Khan Qaqshal	Turani	Mar. 1556	–	–	Narnaul (S)	Narnaul	*AN*, II, 36; *MU*, II, 38-41; *AA*, I, 399; *ZK*, I, 218
7.	Shaikh Jamal Khan Bakhtiyar	Indian Muslim	(1557)	–	–	Chandwar (P), Jaleasar (P)	Agra	*MU*, I, 741; *AA*, I, 469-70
8.	Adham Khan	Turani	1558-9 (T)	Mar. 1561	2-3 yrs.	Hat Kant (P)	Agra	*AN*, II, 119-20; *MU*, I, 145; *AA*, I, 341; *ZK*, I, 125-6
9.	Habib Ali Khan	Irani	1558	1559 (T)	Few mths.	Bayana (P)	Agra	*MT*, II, 25; *AA*, I, 482
10.	Chaghtai Khan	Turani	1558	–	–	Bhasawar (P), Toda Bhim (P)	Agra	*MT*, II, 25
11.	Muhammad Baqi Baqlani	Turani	Mar. 1560	–	–	Sikandra Rao (P)	Kol	*AN*, II, 141-2
12.	Bairam Khan (Khan-i-Khanan)	Irani	(1560)	1560 (F)	–	Alwar (S)	Alwar	*AN*, II, 148; *MU*, I, 368-78; *AA*, I, 330-2; *ZK*, I, 11-20

(contd.)

1	2	3	4	5	6	7	8	9
13.	Husain Khan	Irani	Nov.-Dec. 1560	1573 (T)	13 yrs.	Patiali (P)	Kanauj	*MT*, II, 38, 88; *AN*, III, 51; *AA*, I, 402; *MU*, I, 645-9; *ZK*, I, 219
14.	Bahadur Khan	Irani	Mar.-Apr. 1560[92]	1563 (T)	3 yrs.	Etawah (P)	Agra	*AN*, II, 151, 175; Bayazid, 244; *MU*, I, 348; *AA*, I, 347; *ZK*, I, 26-31
15.	Ibrahim Badakshi	Turani	(Mar.-Apr. 1562)	–	–	Sakit (Q)	Kanauj	*AN*, II, 252; *AA*, I, 481-2; *MU*, I, 660
16.	Mirza Sharafuddin Husain	Turani	(Jan. 1562)	–	–	Mewat (P)	Alwar	*AN*, II, 240-1; *MU*, II, 808-12; *AA*, I, 339-40; *ZK*, I, 79-80
17.	Munim Khan (Khan-i-Khanan)	Turani	(1563)	–	–	Etawah (P)	Agra	*AN*, II, 294; *AA*, I, 333-4; *MU*, II, 284-5; *ZK*, I, 24-5
18.	Gesu Khan Khurasani	Turani	–	1563 (T)	–	Narnaul (F)	Narnaul	*TA*, II, 274; *MT*, II, 58; Arif, 106
19.	Khanzada Muhammad (Shah-i-Laudan)	Turani	(1563)	–	–	*Parganas*	Narnaul	*TA*, II, 274

20. Muqim-i-Arab (Shujaat Khan)	Turani	Nov.-Dec. 1563	Jun. 1567	3 yrs. 7 mths.	Narnaul (S), Etawah (Q)	Narnaul Agra	*AN*, II, 309, 437; *MU*, II, 851; *TU*, 92; *AA*, I, 401; *ZK*, I, 210
21. Junaid Kararani	Afghan	–	1567 (F)	–	Hindaun (P)	Agra	*AN*, II, 420
22. Husain Quli Khan (Khan-i-Jahan)	Irani	1566-7	1573 (T)	6-7 yrs.	Shamsabad (P)	Kanauj	*MT*, II, 88; *MU*, I, 645-9; *ZK*, I, 209
23. Mirza Yusuf Khan	Irani	(Mar. 1567)	–	–	Shergarh (F), Kanauj (S)	Kanauj	*AN*, II, 42-6; *MT*, II, 96; Arif, 136; *ZK*, I, 170-2
24. Shahabuddin Ahmad Khan Nishapuri	Turani	(Mar. 1567)	1574	7 yrs.	Bhojpur (Q)	Kanauj	*AN*, II, 424; *MT*, II, 178; *TA*, II, 434
25. Haji Muhammad Khan Sistani	Irani	–	Sept. 1567 (T)	–	Bayana (P)	Agra	*TA*, II, 341; *MT*, II, 105; *MU*, II, 162-3; *AA*, I, 405-6; *ZK*, I, 231
26. Khwaja Abdul Majid (Asaf Khan)	Irani	Sept. 1567	–	–	Bayana (P), Bhasawar (P), Wazirpur (P), Mandalgarh (P)	Agra Agra Agra Chittor (Ajmer)	*TA*, II, 341, *MT*, II, 105; *MU*, I, 36-40; *AA*, I, 396-8; *TU*, 7; *ZK*, I, 122-3

(contd.)

1	*2*	*3*	*4*	*5*	*6*	*7*	*8*	*9*
27.	Sharif Khan Atka	Turani	Aug. 1568	1572 (T)	4 yrs.	Kanauj (S)	Kanauj	*AN*, II, 487, 538-9; *MU*, II, 820-1; *AA*, I, 415-16; *TU*, 95; *ZK*, I, 213
28.	Shaham Khan Jalair	Turani	(Dec. 1572)	–	–	Kalpi (S)	Kalpi	*AN*, III, 27; *ZK*, I, 213
29.	Sayyid Abdullah Khan (Chugan Begi)	Turani	(Aug. 1574)	–	–	Bayana (P)	Agra	*MT*, II, 183
30.	Qasim Ali Khan Baqqal	Turani	Oct. 1579	–	–	Kalpi (S)	Kalpi	*MT*, II, 290; *AA*, I, 518
31.	Zain Khan Koka	Irani	(Nov.-Dec. 1579)	Oct. 1583	4 yrs.	Etawah (P)	Agra	*AN*, III, 407, 617; *MU*, II, 1022-8; *AA*, I, 367-9; *ZK*, I, 123-4
32.	Muhammad Ghaznavi	Afghan	Mar. 1581	–	–	Shamsabad (P)	Kanauj	*AN*, III, 512
33.	Shahbaz Khan Kambu	Indian Muslim	–	Dec.1590(F)	–	Kalpi (S)	Kalpi	*AN*, III, 885; *AA*, I, 438-9; *ZK*, I, 148-60
34.	Birbar	Hindu	(Oct. 1583)	–	–	Akbarabad (P)	Kol	*AN*, III, 617

35. Muttalib Khan	Turani	(Oct. 1583)	–	–	Kalpi (S)	Kalpi	*AN*, III, 617; *ZK*, I, 248
36. Qasim Ali Khan	Turani	(Jan.-Feb. 1591)	–	–	Kalpi (S)	Kalpi	*AN*, III, 888; *AA*, I, 518
37. Mirza Nizamuddin Ahmad	Turani	(Mar. 1591)	–	–	Shamsabad (P)	Kanauj	*MT*, II, 389; *ZK*, I, 208-9
38. Ismail Quli Khan	Irani	May 1594	–	–	Kalpi (S)	Kalpi	*AN*, III, 1001; *MU*, I, 704; *AA*, I, 388-9; *TU*, 8; *ZK*, I, 213
39. Raja Rai Rai Singh	Rajput	–	–	–	Shamsabad (P), Nurpur (P), Niryad (P)	Kanauj	*Dalpat Vilas*, 30, 41-2; *MU*, II, 567-9; *ZK*, I, 215
40. Khwaja Abdullah (Safdar Khan, Firoj Jung)	Turani	1604	1606	2 yrs.	Kalpi (S)	Kalpi	*AN*, III, 1249; *Maasir-i-Jahangiri* 18a, 39a-40a; *ZK*, II, 172-85; *TU*, 112
41. Raja Jagman	Rajput	Nov.-Dec. 1604	–	–	Bhangaon (P)	Kanauj	*AN*, III, 1247

TABLE 3.2: ASSIGNMENT OF *JAGIRS* IN *SUBA* AJMER

S. No.	*Name of Assignee*	*Racial Group*	*Period*		*Approximate Tenure*	*Jagirs*	*Sarkar*	*Sources*
			From	*To*		*Sarkar (S), Pargana (P), Qasba (Q), Fort (F), etc.*		
			Year(s) of Assignment Conferred/ Held	*Year(s) of Transfer (T), Revolt by Jagirdars (R), Flight (F), Death (D), etc.*				
1	*2*	*3*	*4*	*5*	*6*	*7*	*8*	*9*
1.	Muhammad Quli Khan Barlas	Turani	Mar. 1557	Apr.-May 1560(T)	3 yrs. 2 mths.	Nagaur (S)	Nagaur	*AN*, II, 84, 157; *MU*, II, 184; *AA*, I, 364; *TU*, 150; *ZK*, I, 209
2.	Muhammad Qasim Khan Nishapuri	Irani	Mar. 1558	Sept. 1560 (T)	2 yrs. 7 mths.	*Parganas*	(Ajmer)	*AN*, II, 103; *MU*, II, 516; *AA*, I, 379; *ZK*, I, 211-12
3.	Mirza Sharafuddin Husain (Amir-ul-Umara)	Turani	Apr.-May 1560	Oct. 1562 (F)	2 yrs. 6 mths.	Nagaur and its territory	Nagaur	*AN*, II, 157, 197, 303; *TA*, II, 258, 272, 273; *MT*, II, 46; Farishta, II, 127; *MU*, II, 809; *AA*, I,

							339-40; *TU*, 222; *ZK*, I, 79-80
4. Tarsun Muhammad Khan	Irani	(Jan.-Feb. 1562)	–	–	*Parganas*	(Ajmer)	*AN*, II, 243
5. Shah Budagh Khan	Turani	(Jan.-Feb. 1562)	–	–	*Parganas*	(Ajmer)	*AN*, II, 243
6. Abdul Muttalib Khan (s/o Budagh Khan)	Turani	(Jan.-Feb. 1562)	–	–	*Parganas*	(Ajmer)	*AN*, II, 243
7. Khurram Khan	Turani	(Jan.-Feb. 1562)	–	–	*Parganas*	(Ajmer)	*AN*, II, 243
8. Muhammad Husain Shaikh	Indian Muslim	(Jan.-Feb. 1562)	–	–	*Parganas*	(Ajmer)	*AN*, II, 243
9. Husain Quli Khan (Khan-i-Jahan)	Irani	Oct. 1562	Aug.-Sept. 1568 (T)	6 yrs.	*Parganas*, Hajipur (P), Dandauna (P)	Ajmer Jodhpur Nagaur	*AN*, II, 304; *MT*, II, 58; *TA*, II, 273, 352; Arif, 106; *MU*, I, 646; *AA*, I, 349; *ZK*, I, 209
10. Ismail Quli Khan	Irani	–	Aug.-Sept. 1568(T)	–	*Parganas*	Nagaur	*TA*, II, 352; *MU*, 1, 703-4; *AA*, I, 388-9; *ZK*, I, 213-4
11. Jagmal	Rajput	Oct. 1562	–	–	Merta (F)	Nagaur	*AN*, II, 305; *MU*, I, 727; *AA*, I, 483; Ziegler,[93] 206-7

(contd.)

1	2	3	4	5	6	7	8	9
12.	Jagmal	Rajput	– Oct. 1583	– –	– –	Jahazpur Sirohi[94] and its territory	Sirohi	*AN*, III, 614; *Khyat*, I, 131-2; *MT*, II, 337; *TA*, II, 564; *Vir Vinod*, 146
13.	Mir Gesu Khurasani	Turani	–	Oct. 1583 (D)	–	Merta (F)	Nagaur	*AN*, III, 615; *MU*, I, 575
14.	Raisal Darbari (Chief of Shaikhawat)	Rajput	1565 –	– –	– –	Rewasa (P), Kausli (P), Khandela (P), Udaipur (P)	Nagaur Nagaur Nagaur Chittor	Refaqat Ali,[95] 168; *MU*, II, 564-5
15.	Nazar Bahadur	Turani	Sept.-Oct. 1567	–	–	Siwi Super (F)	Ranth-ambor	*AN*, II, 443-4; *TA*, II, 342; *MT*, II, 105
16.	Shah Muhammad Khan Qalati	Irani	Sept.-Oct. 1567	–	–	Kota (P)	Ranth-ambor	*TA*, II, 342; *AN*, II, 443-4; *MT*, II, 105; *MU*, II, 758-9; *AA*, I, 448-9
17.	Khwaja Abdul Majid (Asaf Khan)	Irani	Feb. 1568	1573-4	5-6 yrs.	Mandalgarh (P)	Chittor	*AN*, II, 476; *TA*, II, 341, 348; Farishta, II, 142; *MU*, I, 39-40; *AA*, I, 398; *ZK*, I, 122-3

18. Mihtar Khan (Anisuddin)	Turani	Mar. 1569	–	–	Ranthambor (F)	Ranth-ambor	*AN*, II, 495; *TA*, II, 355; *MU*, II, 72; *AA*, I, 459
19. Rao Kalyanmal (Chief of Bikaner)	Rajput	1570	1574	–	*(watan jagir)*[96] Bikaner, Nagaur, Jodhpur, Hisar	 Bikaner Nagaur Jodhpur Hisar (*suba* Delhi)	G.S.L. Devra, 78-9
					(tankhwah jagir) Nagaur (P), Sirsa (P), Jodhpur (P), Harot (P),	 Nagaur Hisar (Delhi) Jodhpur Multan	
20. Mir Muhammad Khan (Khan-i-Kalan)	Turani	Nov.1570	Mar.-Apr. 1573 (T)	2 yrs. 5 mths.	Ajmer (S), Nagaur (S), Jodhpur up to the Gujarat frontier	Ajmer Nagaur Jodhpur	*AN*, II, 517; Arif, 170, 191; *MU*, II, 154-5; *AA*, I, 339; *ZK*, I, 248
21. Farrukh Khan (s/o Khan-i-Kalan)	Turani	Apr. 1573	–	–	Merta (F)	Nagaur	*AN*, III, 49; *TA*, II, 395; *MT*, II, 153
22. Rai Ram (s/o Maldeo)	Rajput	(Mar.-Apr. 1573)	–	–	Sojat (P)	Jodhpur	*AN*, III, 49

(contd.)

1	2	3	4	5	6	7	8	9
23.	Sadiq Muhammad Khan	Irani	Sept. 1573	–	–	Sirohi (S)	Sirohi	*AN*, III, 90-1; *MU*, II, 658-9; *AA*, I, 382-4
24.	Ram Das Kachhwaha (Kachhwaha Chief of Neota)	Rajput	(Oct.-Nov. 1573)	–	–	Luni[97] or Harba or Sanganir (*Mahal*)	Ajmer	*AN*, III, 91; *TA*, II, 422; *MR*, I, 804; *Khayat*, I, 331; *MU*, II, 587; *AA*, I, 539-40; *ZK*, I, 238-41
25.	Raja Rai Rai Singh (s/o Kalyanmal)	Rajput	1574	1605	–	(*watan jagir*)[98] Bikaner, Nagaur, Jodhpur, Hisar	Bikaner Nagaur Jodhpur Hisar (*suba* Delhi)	*AN*, III, 8, 632; *TA*, II, 651; *Dalpat Vilas*, 22-3, 30, 41-2; *MT*, II, 144; G.S.L. Devra, 78-9; *MU*, II, 568-9; *AA*, I, 384-6; *TU*, 260; *ZK*, I, 215
						(*tankhwah jagir*)		
				Jodhpur(P), Phalodi (P), Nagaur (P), Sirsa (P), Hisar (P), Bahlod (P), Dariwal (P), Varva (P), Agarva (P), Atagarh (P), Bhatner (P), Punia (P), Toson (P), Veniwal (P), Shivran (P), Bhatinda (P), Tahroh (P), Marot (P),			Jodhpur, Jodhpur, Nagaur Hisar (*suba* Delhi) Hisar (*suba* Delhi) Hisar (*suba* Delhi) Hisar (*suba* Delhi) Sirhind (*suba* Delhi) Multan (*suba* Multan)	

			Dipalpur Lakhi (P), Qasur (P), Karhar, Nadiyad Junagarh and 47 other *parganas*			Jalandhar Doab Thatta (*suba* Multan) Ahmedabad (*suba* Gujarat) Junagarh and Surat (*suba* Gujarat)	
26. Kala (s/o Ram Rai)	Rajput	(Jul. 1575)	–	–	Merta (P)	Nagaur	*AN*, III, 224-5
27. Raja Lonkaran (Chief of Sambhar)	Rajput	1576	1584 (D)	–	Sambhar[99]	Ajmer	*MT*, II, 236; *TA*, II, 571; *MU*, I, 836-7; *AA*, I, 554; *ZK*, I, 219-21
28. Ghazi Khan	Turani	Jan. 1577	–	–	Islampur Mohi (P)	Chittor	*MT*, II, 249
29. Abdur Rahman Beg	Indian Muslim	Jan. 1577	–	–	Madaria (P)	Chittor	*MT*, II, 249
30. Dastam Khan	Turani	Jun.-Jul. 1577	1580(D)	3 yrs.	Ranthambor (S)	Ranth-ambor	*AN*, III, 295; *MU*, I, 458; *AA*, I, 435
31. Majahid Beg	Irani	Sept. 1577	–	–	Islampur Mohi (P)	Chittor	*AN*, III, 304-5
32. Payand Muhammad Khan	Turani	(Aug.-Sept. 1580)	–	–	Parganas	(Ajmer)	*AN*, III, 466; *TA*, II, 571; *MU*, II, 494-5; *ZK*, I, 221

(contd.)

1	2	3	4	5	6	7	8	9
33.	Saiyed Hashim	Indian Muslim	(Aug.-Sept. 1580)	1584 (T)	–	*Parganas*	(Ajmer)	*AN*, III, 466; *TA*, II, 571; *MU*, II, 494-5; *ZK*, I, 221
34.	Saiyed Qasim	Indian Muslim	(Aug.-Sept. 1580)	1584 (T)	–	*Parganas*	(Ajmer)	*AN*, III, 466; *TA*, II, 571; *MU*, II, 494-5; *ZK*, I, 221
35.	Abdur Rahim Mirza Khan (Khan-i-Khanan)	Irani	Oct.-Nov. 1580	Dec. 1584 (T)	4 yrs.	Ranthambor (S)	Ranth-ambor	*AN*, III, 480; *TA*, II, 567, 651; *MU*, I, 50-1; *AA*, I, 355; *TU*, 54; *ZK*, I, 31-63
36.	Udai Singh (Mota Raja) (Chief of Jodhpur)	Rajput	1583	Jul. 1595(D)	–	Jodhpur,[100] Jodhpur (F), Siwana (P), Sojat (P), Satalmer (P),[101] Pokhran (P), (half of Jaitran)[102]	Jodhpur Jodhpur Jodhpur Jodhpur Bikaner Bikaner Bikaner	*Vir Vinod*, III, 815-17; *Vigat*, I, 76, 83; *TA*, II, 571; *MU*, II, 915; *AA*, I, 474-5
37.	Rai Durga	Rajput	(Dec. 1583)	–	–	*Parganas*	(Ajmer)	*AN*, III, 632; *TA*, II, 571; *ZK*, I, 226

38. Chander Sain	Hindu	(Dec. 1583)	–	–	*Parganas*	(Ajmer)	*TA*, II, 571n; *AN*, III, 632
39. Raja Ram Chand (Chief of Bhatta)	Rajput	(Dec. 1583)	–	–	*Parganas*	(Ajmer)	*TA*, II, 571n; *AN*, III, 632
40. Sharmodi Turkman	–	(Dec. 1583)	–	–	*Parganas*	(Ajmer)	*TA*, II, 571n; *AN*, III, 632
41. Sangu Rajput	Rajput	(Dec. 1583)	–	–	*Parganas*	(Ajmer)	*TA*, II, 571n; *AN*, III, 632
42. Shartan Rathore	Rajput	(Dec. 1583)	–	–	*Parganas*	(Ajmer)	*TA*, II, 571n; *AN*, III, 632
43. Shiroda	Rajput	(Dec. 1583)	–	–	*Parganas*	(Ajmer)	*TA*, II, 571n; *AN*, III, 632
44. Tulsi Das Jadun	Rajput	(Dec. 1583)	–	–	*Parganas*	(Ajmer)	*TA*, II, 571n; *AN*, III, 632
45. Ali Murad	–	Nov.-Dec. 1586	–	–	Baroda (P)	Ranth-ambor	*AN*, III, 780
46. Ghaznin Khan	Indian Muslim	May 1590	–	–	Jalaur (P)	Sirohi	*AN*, III, 875; *TU*, 124
47. Bikramjit	Rajput	1593	–	–	Bhatta[103] (Bandu)	–	*AN*, III, 985, 997; *MU*, II, 582-3; *TU*, 249

(contd.)

1	2	3	4	5	6	7	8	9
48.	Suraj Singh Rathore (s/o Udai Singh)	Rajput	1595	–	–	Jodhpur,[104] Jaitran (P), Sojat (P), Merta	Jodhpur Jodhpur Jodhpur Nagaur	*Jodhpur ri Khyat*, I, 124-5; *AN*, III, 1027; *MU*, II, 916: *TU*, 264
49.	Mir Sharif Amuli	Irani	Nov. 1598	–	–	Islampur (Mohan), etc. (P)	Chittor	*AN*, III, 1112; *MU*, II, 815; *AA*, I, 502
50.	Prince Sultan Daniyal	Prince	1598-9	1601 (shifted)[105]	–	Bhatta	–	*AN*, III, 1068-9, 1089, 1104
51.	Raja Duryodhan (grandson of Raja Ramchand)	Rajput	Mar. 1601	–	–	Bandu (F)[106]	–	*AN*, III, 1180; *MU*, II, 582-3; *TU*, 258; *Khyat*, I, 313

TABLE 3.3: ASSIGNMENT OF *JAGIRS* IN *SUBA* ALLAHABAD

S. No.	*Name of Assignee*	*Racial Group*	*Period*		*Approximate Tenure*	*Jagirs*	*Sarkar*	*Sources*
			From *Year(s) of Assignment Conferred/ Held*	*To* *Year(s) of Transfer (T), Revolt by Jagirdars (R), Flight (F), Death (D), etc.*		*Sarkar (S), Pargana (P), Qasba (Q), Fort (F), etc.*		
1	2	3	4	5	6	7	8	9
1.	Sikandar Khan Afghan	Afghan	Jul. 1557	1559	2 yrs.	Kharid (P)	Jaunpur	*AN*, II, 91; *AA*, 1, 394-5n
2.	Jamal Khan (*Gulam* of Adili)	Afghan	Sept.-Oct. 1558	–	–	Five *parganas* in exchange of fort Chunar	Jaunpur	*MT*, II, 27; Elliot, V, 494
3.	Abdur-Rahman Beg (s/o of Sikandar Afghan)	Afghan	Mar.-Oct. 1558	–	–	Surharpur (P)	Jaunpur	*AN*, II, 127; *MT*, II, 16; *TA*, II, 227
4.	Kamal Khan Gakkhar	Afghan	1558	1563 (T)	5 yrs.	Fathpur (P),	Kara-	*AN*, II, 119, 297; *TA*,

(contd.)

1	2	3	4	5	6	7	8	9
	(Chief of Gakkhar) and his son Mubarak Khan					Hanswa (P), Kara (Q)	Manikpur	II, 267; Elliot, V, 279; *MU*, I, 759-60; *AA*, I, 507; *TU*, 141-2; *ZK*, I, 216-17
5.	Ali Quli Khan (Khan-i-Zaman)	Irani	1559-60	1565 (R)	5-6 yrs.	Jaunpur (S), Banaras (S), Ghazipur (S), *Parganas*	Jaunpur Banaras Ghazipur Manikpur	*AN*, II, 126; *TA*, II, 257, 295, 309; Arif, 97; Bayazid, 239; Farishta, II, 117; *MU*, I, 197-207; *AA*, I, 335-6; *TU*, 55; *ZK*, I, 26-31
6.	Bahadur Khan	Irani	1560	1565 (R)	5 yrs.	Banaras (S)	Banaras	*TA*, II, 257; Bayazid, 244, 339-40; *MU*, I, 348; *AA*, I, 347; *TU*, 28; *ZK*, I, 26-31
7.	Ibrahim Khan Uzbek	Turani	Jul. 1561	1567 (R)	6 yrs.	Surharpur(P)	Jaunpur	*TA*, II, 256, 295; *AN*, II, 376, 425; *MT*, II, 76; *AA*, I, 416; *TU*, 2
8.	Majnun Khan Qaqshal	Turani	Jul. 1561	Aug. 1569 (T)	8 yrs.	Manikpur (S)	Manikpur	*AN*, II, 376, 419, 499; *TA*, II, 256, 296, 329, 357; *MT*, II, 76; Arif, 138; *MU*, II, 38; *AA*, I, 399; *ZK*, I, 218

9. Shaham Khan Jalair	Turani	Jul. 1561	1569	8 yrs.	*Jagir* in eastern Sarkar	Jaunpur	*AN*, II, 376, 499; *TA*, II, 256, 296; *MT*, II, 76; *MU*, II, 728-9; *AA*, I, 450-1
10. Hasan Ali Khan Turkman	Turani	Nov. 1561	Jul.-Aug. 1573	12 yrs.	Chunar (F)	Chunar	*AN*, II, 232; *MT*, II, 62; Arif, 142; Bayazid, 310; *TU*, 49
11. Khwaja Abdul Majid (Asaf Khan)	Irani	Mar. 1563	1566 (F)	3 yrs.	Kara (S)	Kara	*AN*, II, 282, 324, 404, 418-19; Bayazid, 287; *TA*, II, 317, 329; Farishta, II, 132; *AA*, I, 397; *ZK*, I, 122-3
		1567-8	1568 (T)	Few mths.	Prayag (P)	Allahabad	*AA*, I, 397
12. Muhibb Ali Khan (s/o Mir Khalifa)	Turani	(Apr.-May 1567)	– (Left service)	–	Manikpur	Manikpur	*AN*, II, 428; *AA*, 1, 463
13. Munim Khan (Khan-i-Khanan)	Turani	Jun. 1567	Aug. 1574 (T)[107]	7 yrs.	Jaunpur (S), Banaras (S), Ghazipur (S), Chunar (F)	Jaunpur Banaras Ghazipur Chunar	Arif, 143, 189; Bayazid, 299, 307, 312, 341; *AN*, II, 436, 478; *MT*, II, 104; *TA*, II, 338; *AN*, III, 144; Stewart, 162; *ZK*, I, 24-5

(contd.)

1	2	3	4	5	6	7	8	9
14.	Qasim Mushki (Gumashta-i-Munim Khan)	Turani	Jun. 1567	Aug. 1574 (T)	7 yrs.	Zamanya (F)	Ghazipur	*AN*, II, 478; Bayazid, 300, 318; *AN*, III, 30
15.	Bayazid Bayat	Turani	Jan. 1567	–	–	Banaras (S)	Banaras	Bayazid, 294-5, 310
16.	Farhat Khan	Turani	Jun. 1567	1574	7 yrs.	Kora (Q)	Kora	*AN*, II, 437; *AA*, I, 489
17.	Majnun Khan Qaqshal	Turani	Aug. 1569	1574 (T)	5 yrs.	Kalinjar (F)	Kalinjar	*TA*, II, 357; *TU* 151; *AA*, I, 399; *ZK*, I, 218
18.	Raja Ram Chand of Bhatta	Rajput	Aug. 1569	–	–	Arail (P)	Allahabad	*MT*, II, 124; *AA*, I, 381-2
19.	Qulij Khan	Turani	Jun. 1572	–	–	Saraon (P)	Allahabad	Bayazid, 307; *TU*, 136-7; *MU*, II, 536; *AA*, I, 381-2; *ZK*, I, 172-5
20.	Talib Sultan	Turani	Jan.-Feb. 1573	Jun. 1575	2 yrs. 5 mths.	Ghazipur (S)	Ghazipur	Bayazid, 314, 347
21.	Mirza Quli Sultan	–	Jan.-Feb. 1573	–	–	Badohi (P)	Allahabad	Bayazid, 314
22.	Nadim Sultan	–	Jan.-Feb. 1573	–	–	Dostpur (P)	Jaunpur	Bayazid, 314

23. Muhammad Khan	–	Feb. 1573	–	–	Zamanya (F)	Ghazipur	Bayazid, 318
24. Saadat Yar	Turani	1573	–	–	Sinjhauli (P)	Jaunpur	Bayazid, 318
25. Naraun Sultan Uzbek	Turani	Feb.-Mar. 1573	–	–	Rai Bareily (P)	Manikpur	Bayazid, 322
26. Baba Khan Qaqshal	Turani	(May.-Jun. 1574)	–	–	Chekur (Q)	Manikpur	*TA*, II, 437
27. Niyabat Khan (s/o Mir Hashim Nishapuri)	Irani	(1574)	Jan.-Feb. 1581	7 yrs.	Jhusi-Paryag(P)	Allahabad	*TA*, II, 542; *AN*, III, 481; *MT*, II, 297; *MU*, II, 392-4; *AA*, 1, 470
28. Bayazid Bayat	Turani	Mar. 1575	–	–	Parganas	Chunar	Bayazid, 250, 351-2
29. Rai Surjan Hada (Chief of Bundi) and his son Bhoj	Rajput	Oct. 1575	1579	4 yrs.	4 *parganas* of Chunar, 26 *parganas* near Banaras, Garli	Chunar Banaras	*AN*, III, 223, 422; *Khyat*, 1: 111; A.R. Khan, 106;[108] *ZK*, I, 228-9
30. Husain Quli Khan (Khan-i-Jahan)	Irani	(1576)	–	–	Ghazipur (S)	Ghazipur	*AN*, III, [170]; *ZK*, I, 209
31. Masum Khan Farankhudi	Turani	(1579)	Jan.-Feb. 1580(T)	Few mths.	*Khitta*-i-Jaunpur	Jaunpur	*MT*, II, 284, 290; *AN*, III, 410, 484; *TA*, II, 527, 534; *ZK*, I, 217

(contd.)

1	2	3	4	5	6	7	8	9
32.	Tarsun Muhammad Khan	Irani	Feb. 1580	1584 (D)	4 yrs.	*Khitta*-i-Jaunpur	Jaunpur	*AN*, III, 410, 422, 483; *MT*, II, 297; *TA*, II, 541; *MU*, II, 944-8; *AA*, 1, 365; *TU*, 37; *ZK*, I, 211
33.	Ghazi Khan Badakshi	Turani	(1580)	–	–	*Parganas*	Allahabad	*AN*, III, 422
34.	Asad Khan Turkman	Turani	(1580)	–	–	*Parganas*	Manikpur	*AN*, III, 455; *AA*, I, 415; *TU*, 11
35.	Ismail Quli Khan	Irani	(1580)	–	–	Kara (S)	Kara	*AN*, III, 480; *MT*, II, 297; *TA*, II, 542; *ZK*, I, 213-14
36.	Iliyas Khan Langa (Gumashta-i-Ismail Quli)	–	(1580)	–	–	*Parganas*	Kara	*AN*, III, 480; *TA*, II, 542
37.	Masum Khan Farankhudi	Turani	Feb. 1580	Jan. 1581 (T)	1 yr.	Ghazipur (S)	Ghazipur	*AN*, III, 410, 422; *TA*, II, 534
38.	Pahar Khan (Chief of Baloch)	Indian Muslim	(1581)	–	–	*Parganas*	Ghazipur	*AN*, II, 544; *AA*, I, 593-4
39.	Birbar	Hindu	(1582)	–	–	*Parganas*	Kara	*MT*, II, 312; *ZK*, I, 183-5

40. Birbar	Hindu	(1588)	–	–	*Parganas*	Kalinjar	*AN*, III, 805; *MT*, II, 369; *ZK*, I, 183-5
41. Abdur Rahim Mirza Khan (Khan-i-Khanan)	Irani	Dec. 1589	1590	Few mths.	Jaunpur (S)	Jaunpur	*AN*, III, 865; *MT*, II, 384, 386; *TA*, II, 629; *MU*, 1, 51-2; *AA*, I, 355-6; *ZK*, I, 31-63
42. Qulij Khan	Turani	(1592)	Aug. 1594 (T)	2 yrs.	Jaunpur (S)	Jaunpur	*AN*, III, 959-60, 1004; *MU*, II, 538; *AA*, I, 381-2; *ZK*, I, 172-5
43. Mirza Yusuf Khan	Irani	Aug. 1594	Jul. 1599 (T)	5 yrs.	Jaunpur (S)	Jaunpur	*AN*, III, 1004, 1133; *MU*, II, 1006; *AA*, I, 371; *TU*, 189-90; *ZK*, I, 170-2
44. Prince Daniyal	Prince	1597	1599 (T)	2 yrs.	Jaunpur (S)	Jaunpur	*AN*, III, 1077, 1133
45. Shaikh Bayazid	Indian Muslim	1604	–	–	Allahabad (F)	Allahabad	*AN*, III, 1249
46. Kalyan Das (s/o Todar Mal)	Hindu	1604-5	–	–	Kalinjar (F)	Kalinjar	*AN*, III, 1249; *TU*, 268
47. Nuran Qulij Khan	Turani	Aug. 1605	–	–	Jaunpur (S)	Jaunpur	*AN*, III, 1256; *MU*, II, 459-60

TABLE 3.4: ASSIGNMENT OF *JAGIRS* IN *SUBA* AWADH

S. No.	*Name of Assignee*	*Racial Group*	*Period*		*Approximate Tenure*	*Jagirs*	*Sarkar*	*Sources*
			From *Year(s) of Assignment Conferred/ Held*	*To* *Year(s) of Transfer (T), Revolt by Jagirdars (R), Flight (F), Death (D), etc.*		*Sarkar (S), Pargana (P), Qasba (Q), Fort (F), etc.*		
1	*2*	*3*	*4*	*5*	*6*	*7*	*8*	*9*
1.	Sultan Husain Khan Jalair	Turani	Apr. 1558	1560 (D)	2 yrs.	Sandila (P)	Lucknow	*AN*, II, 106, 126, *TA*, II, 226 (n. 1); *MT*, II, 39
2.	Ali Quli Khan (Khan-i-Zaman)	Irani	1559 Nov.-Dec. 1560	–	–	Lucknow (P), *Parganas*	Lucknow Awadh	*AN*, II, 125; *TA*, II, [141]; *MU*, I, 197-204; *AA*, I, 335-7; *TU*, 55; Bayazid, 239; *ZK*, I, 26-31
3.	Qaya Khan Gung	Irani	Apr.-May 1560	Mar. 1561 (T)	1 yr.	Bahraich (S)	Bahraich	*AN*, II, 150-1; *MU*, II, 530-1; *AA*, I, 366; *ZK*, I, 210

4.	Munim Khan (Khan-i-Khanan)	Turani	(Mar. 1563)	–	–	*Parganas*	Khairabad	*AN*, II, 188, 294; *MU*, II, 283-92; *AA*, I, 333-4; *ZK*, I, 24-5
5.	Sikander Khan Uzbek	Turani	(Mar. 1565)	Aug. 1567 (F)	2 yrs. 6 mths.	Awadh(S)	Awadh	*AN*, II, 376, 439; *TA*, II, 294, 340; *MT*, II, 75-6; Arif, 119; *MU*, I, 691-2; *AA*, I, 394-5; *ZK*, I, 213
6.	Muhammad Quli Khan Barlas	Turani	Aug. 1567	1574 (T)	7 yrs.	Awadh (S)	Awadh	*AN*, II, 440; *TA*, II, 340; Arif, 224; Bayazid, 341; *MU*, II, 183-5; *AA*, I, 364; *ZK*, I, 209
7.	Amir Khan	–	(Jun. 1565)	–	–	Nimkhar (P)	Khairabad	*AN*, II, 376; *TA*, II, 295; Bayazid, 286
8.	Shah Budagh Khan	Turani	(Jun. 1565)	–	–	Nimkhar (F)	Khairabad	*AN*, II, 376; Arif, 119; *MU*, II, 745-7; *AA*, I, 402; *ZK*, I, 210-11
9.	Shaham Khan Jalair	Turani	(Jun. 1565)	–	–	*Parganas*	Khairabad/ Awadh	*AN*, II, 376, *MU*, II, 728-9; *AA*, I, 450-1

(contd.)

1	2	3	4	5	6	7	8	9
10.	Muhammad Amin Diwana	Turani	(Jun. 1565)	–	–	*Parganas*	Awadh/ Khairabad, Kara/ Manikpur	*AN*, II, 376; *TA*, II, 295
11.	Sultan Quli Khaldar	–	(Jun. 1565)	–	–	*Parganas*	Awadh/ Khairabad, Kara/ Manikpur	*AN*, II, 376; *TA*, II, 295
12.	Chalma Tawachi	–	(Jun. 1565)	–	–	*Parganas*	Awadh/ Khairabad, Kara/ Manikpur	*AN*, II, 376; *TA*, II, 295
13.	Shah Tahir Badakshi	Turani	(Jun. 1565)	–	–	*Parganas*	Awadh/ Khairabad, Kara/ Manikpur	*AN*, II, 376; *TA*, II, 295
14.	Khalilullah	Turani	(Jun. 1565)	–	–	*Parganas*	Awadh/ Khairabad, Kara/ Manikpur	*AN*, II, 376; *TA*, II, 295

15. Gada Ali Tolkchi	–	(Jun. 1565)	–	–	*Parganas*	Awadh/ Khairabad, Kara/ Manikpur	*AN*, II, 376; *TA*, II, 295
16. Khan Quli Sarban	–	(Jun. 1565)	–	–	*Parganas*	Awadh/ Khairabad, Kara/ Manikpur	*AN*, II, 376; *TA*, II, 295
17. Yusuf Toqbai	–	(Jun. 1565)	–	–	*Parganas*	Awadh/ Khairabad, Kara/ Manikpur	*AN*, II, 376; *TA*, II, 295
18. Yarshahi	Irani	(Jan.-Mar. 1567)	–	–	Nimkhar (P)	Khairabad	*AN*, II, 414-15
19. Asdullah	Irani	Jan. 1567	–	–	Sultanpur and a few other *parganas* of Hasan Khan Bachgoti	Awadh	Bayazid, 300; *AA*, I, 471
20. Lal Khan Badakshi	Turani	Feb. 1568	–	–	Daryabad (P)	Awadh	Bayazid, 302
21. Husain Khan (not Khan-i-Jahan)	–	–	Feb.-Mar 1569(T)	–	Lucknow (P)	Lucknow	*MT*, II, 128; Bayazid, 302

(contd.)

1	*2*	*3*	*4*	*5*	*6*	*7*	*8*	*9*
22.	Mahdi Qasim Khan	Turani	Feb.-Mar. 1569	–	–	Lucknow (P)	Lucknow	*AN*, II, 491-2; *MT*, II, 128; *MU*, II, 503-5; *AA*, I, 373
23.	Sikandar Khan Uzbek	Turani	Jun.-Jul. 1572	Sept.1572 (D)	Few mths.	Khitta-i-Lucknow, Saran (P)	Lucknow	*AN*, II, 534; *MT*, II, 139; *TA*, II, 368-9; Arif, 188-9; Bayazid, 307; *MU*, I, 692; *AA*, I, 395; *ZK*, I, 213
24.	Payand Muhammad Khan	Turani	Feb. 1573	–	–	Gorakhpur (S)	Gorakhpur	Bayazid, 314, 317; *MU*, II, 473-4; *AA*, I, 421
25.	Khwaja Amina (Khwaja Jahan)	Irani	–	Jan. 1575(D)	-	Lucknow (P)	Lucknow	*MT*, II, 189; *MU*, I, 823-4; *AA*, I, 467-8
26.	Tarsun Muhammad Khan	Irani	1579-80	Nov.-Dec. 1580	1 yr.	*Parganas*	Awadh	*AN*, III, 422; *MT*, II, 297; *MU*, II, 944-8; *AA*, I, 364-6: *ZK*, I, 211
27.	Masum Khan Faran Khudi	Turani	Nov.-Dec. 1580	1582 (R)	2 yrs.	Awadh (P)	Awadh	*AN*, III, 484; *MT*, II, 297; *TA*, II, 541; *MU*, II, 64-6; *AA*, I, 491-2; *ZK*, I, 217

28. Mihtar Khan (Anisuddin)	Turani	(Oct. 1581)	–	–	Bahraich (Q)	Bahraich	*AN*, III, 543; *MU*, II, 72-3; *AA*, I, 459
29. Wazir Khan	Irani	(Oct. 1581)	–	–	Bahraich (Q)	Bahraich	*AN*, III, 480, 543; *MU*, II, 985; *AA*, I, 380; *ZK*, I, 211
30. Mirza Yusuf Khan	Irani	–	Jul. 1585 (T)	–	Awadh (S)	Awadh	*AN*, III, 701; *MU*, II, 1001; *AA*, I, 370; *TU*, 189-90; *ZK*, I, 170-2
31. Mir Abdul Ghuyas	Indian Muslim	Aug. 1585	–	–	*Parganas*	Lucknow	*MT*, II, 358
32. Qasim Ali Khan	Turani	Nov. 1586	Jan.-Feb. 1591(T)	4 yrs. 3 mths.	Khairabad (P)	Khairabad	*AN*, III, 878; *MU*, II, 496; *AA*, I, 518; *TU*, 138
33. Shamanji Khan Quraghuji	Turani	Apr. 1594	–	–	*Parganas*	Awadh	*AN*, III, 1000; *MU*, II, 704; *AA*, I, 489
34. Mir Sharif Amuli	Irani	1598	–	–	Mohan (F)	Lucknow	*MU*, II, 815; *AA*, I, 502; *ZK*, I, 193-4
35. Mir Sharif Amuli	Irani	1604-5	–	–	*Parganas*	Bahraich	*AN*, III, 1249; *MU*, II, 813-15; *AA*, I, 502; *TU*, 222; *ZK*, I, 193

TABLE 3.5: ASSIGNMENT OF *JAGIRS* IN *SUBA* BENGAL

S. No.	*Name of Assignee*	*Racial Group*	*Period*		*Approximate Tenure*	*Jagirs*	*Sarkar*	*Sources*
			From	*To*		*Sarkar (S), Pargana (P), Qasba (Q), Fort (F), etc.*		
			Year(s) of Assignment Conferred/ Held	*Year(s) of Transfer (T), Revolt by Jagirdars (R), Flight (F), Death (D), etc.*				
1	*2*	*3*	*4*	*5*	*6*	*7*	*8*	*9*
1.	Qaya Khan Gung	Irani	Aug. 1574	Feb. 1580 (T)	5yrs. 7 mths.	Burdwan (P)	Sharifabad	Bayazid, 341; *AN*, III, 386; *ZK*, I, 210
2.	Sayyid Khan Toghbai	Turani	Aug. 1574	–	–	Sonargaon (P)	Sonargaon	Bayazid, 341
3.	Takhta Alabam	Turani	Aug. 1574	–	–	*Parganas*	Satgaon	Bayazid, 341
4.	Munim Khan (Khan-i-Khanan)	Turani	Jan.-Mar. 1575	Oct. 1575 (D)	Few mths.	*Parganas*	(Bengal)	Bayazid, 342; *AN*, III, 164; *TA*, II, 448; *MU*, II, 289-90; *AA*, I, 333-4; *TU*, 54; *ZK*, I, 24-5.

5.	Majnun Khan Qaqshal	Turani	Mar. 1575	1578-9 (D)	3-4 yrs.	Ghoraghat (S)	Ghoraghat	Bayazid, 341; *TA*, II, 459; Arif, 239; *MU*, II, 39-40; *AA*, I, 400; *TU*, 151; *ZK*, I, 218
6.	Baba Khan Qaqshal	Turani	Mar. 1575	–	–	*Parganas*	Ghoraghat	Bayazid, 341; *AN*, III, 386; *TU*, 31
7.	Husain Quli Khan (Khan-i-Jahan)	Irani	Oct.-Nov. 1575	Dec. 1578 (D)	3 yrs.	*Parganas*	(Bengal)	*AN*, III, 231, 431; *MT*, II, 222; *TA*, II, 480, 517; Arif, 250, 282; Farishta, II, 154; *MU*, I, 648-9; *AA*, I, 350; Stewart[109], 162-3, 167; *ZK*, I, 209
8.	Ismail Quli Khan	Irani	Oct.-Nov. 1575	Mar. 1579 (T)	3 yrs. 5 mths.	*Parganas*	(Bengal)	*AN*, III, 386, 431; *TA*, II, 517; *MU*, I, 703; *AA*, I, 388; *TU*, 8; *ZK*, I, 213-14
9.	Daud Kararani	Afghan	Mar. 1575	–	–	*Parganas*	Orissa	*AN*, III, 185; *TA*, II, 469, 478

(contd.)

1	*2*	*3*	*4*	*5*	*6*	*7*	*8*	*9*
10.	Muzaffar Khan	Irani	Mar. 1579	Apr.-May 1580(D)	1 yr.	*Parganas*	(Bengal)	Arif, 282; *TA*, II, 517; *MU*, II, 362-3; *TU*, 155; *AA*, I, 373-5
11.	Khaldin Khan	–	–	1579 (T)	–	Jaleasar (P)	Jaleasar	*AN*, III, 430-1
12.	Mir Jamaluddin Husain Anju	Irani	1579	–	–	Jaleasar (P)	Jaleasar	*AN*, III, 430-1; *ZK*, I, 196-7
13.	Masum Kabuli	Turani	Feb. 1580	1583 (F)	3 yrs.	Orissa (S)	Orissa	*AN*, III, 410, 619-22; *MU*, II, 67-8
14.	Hafi Kolabi	Turani	(Feb.-Mar. 1580)	–	–	Dilwara (P)	Tajpur	*AN*, III, 418-19
15.	Mirza Aziz Koka (Khan-i-Azam)	Turani	Feb.-Mar. 1580	Aug. 1584 (T)	4 yrs. 6 mths.	*Parganas*	(Bengal)	*AN*, III, 454, 655; *MT*, II, 293; *MU*, I, 324-5; *AA*, I, 344-5; *ZK*, I, 80-99
16.	Murad Khan	Turani	Sept. 1580	1589 (D)	9 yrs.	Fatehabad (P)	Fatehabad	*AN*, III, 468-9; *AA*, I, 404-5; *TU*, 152; Stewart, 174-5
17.	Tarsun Muhammad Khan	Irani	(1583)	1584 (D)	1 yr.	Tajpur (F)	Tajpur	*AN*, III, 619, 625; *MU*, II, 946-8; *AA*, I, 365; *ZK*, I, 211
18.	Qutlu Khan Lohani	Afghan	1583	–	–	*Parganas*	Orissa	*AN*, III, 600-1

19. Wazir Khan	Irani	(Jun.-Jul. 1584)	Aug. 1587 (D)	3 yrs.	Tanda (S)	Tanda	*AN*, III, 654, 801; *MU*, II, 985-6; *AA*, I, 380; *TU*, 184; Stewart, 179; *ZK*, I, 211
20. Majahid Khan Kambu	Irani	(1584)	–	–	*Parganas*	(Bengal/ Bihar)	*AN*, III, 660
21. Peshrau Khan	Irani	(1584)	–	–	*Parganas*	(Bengal/ Bihar)	*AN*, III, 660
22. Khwajagi Fathullah	Irani	(1584)	–	–	*Parganas*	(Bengal/ Bihar)	*AN*, III, 660
23. Ram Das Kachhwaha	Rajput	(1584)	–	–	*Parganas*	(Bengal/ Bihar)	*AN*, III, 660; *ZK*, I, 238-41
24. Muhammad Sadiq Khan	Irani	(1585)	Jul.-Aug. 1585 (T)[110]	Few mths.	*Parganas*	(Bengal)	*AN*, III, 695; *MU*, II, 660-1; *AA*, I, 382-3; *ZK*, I, 176
25. Shahbaz Khan Kambu	Indian Muslim	Aug. 1585	1589 (T)	4 yrs.	*Parganas*	(Bengal)	*AN*, III, 594, 701; *TA*, II, 501; *MU*, II, 735-6; *AA*, I, 438-9; *TU*, 97; Stewart, 179; *ZK*, I, 148-60

(contd.)

1	*2*	*3*	*4*	*5*	*6*	*7*	*8*	*9*
26.	Said Khan Chaghta	Turani	Aug. 1587	1594 (T)	7 yrs.	*Parganas*	(Bengal)	*AN*, III, 801, 878, 935, 1060; *MU*, II, 679-80; *AA*, I, 351; Stewart, 187; *ZK*, I, 190-3
27.	Payanda Muhammad Khan	Turani	Aug. 1587	–	–	Ghoraghat (S)	Ghoraghat	*AN*, III, 801; *MU*, II, 473-4; *AA*, I, 421; *ZK*, I, 221
28.	Pahar Khan	–	(1592)	–	–	*Parganas*	(Bengal)	*AN*, III, 935; *TU*, 31, 110
29.	Tahir Khan	Irani	(1592)	–	–	*Parganas*	(Bengal)	*AN*, III, 935; *TU*, 31, 110
30.	Makhdum Zada (s/o Tarsun Khan)	Irani	(1592)	–	–	*Parganas*	(Bengal)	*AN*, III, 935; *TU*, 31, 110
31.	Maksus Khan	Irani	(1592)	–	–	*Parganas*	(Bengal)	*AN*, III, 935; *TU*, 31, 110
32.	Mir Muhammad Diwana	–	(1592)	–	–	*Parganas*	(Bengal)	*AN*, III, 935; *TU*, 31, 110

33. Khwaja Baqar Ansari	Afghan	(1592)	–	–	*Parganas*	(Bengal)	*AN*, III, 935; *TU*, 31, 110
34. Babul Mankil	Afghan	(1592)	–	–	*Parganas*	(Bengal)	*AN*, III, 935; *TU*, 31, 110
35. Khwaja Sulaiman	Afghan	(Jan. 1593)	–	–	*Parganas*	Khalifabad	*AN*, III, 968
36. Khwaja Usman Lohani (s/o Isa Khan Lohani)	Afghan	(Jan. 1593)	–	–	*Parganas*	Khalifabad	*AN*, III, 968
37. Sher Khan	Afghan	(Jan. 1593)	–	–	*Parganas*	Khalifabad	*AN*, III, 968
38. Haibat Khan	Afghan	(Jan. 1593)	–	–	*Parganas*	Khalifabad	*AN*, III, 968
39. Ram Chand	Hindu	Feb.-Mar. 1593	–	–	Manpur (F)	(Bengal)	*AN*, III, 969; *TU*, 261
40. Sakat Singh	Rajput	Mar. 1594	–	–	*Parganas*	(Bengal)	*AN*, III, 998
41. Darjan Singh	Rajput	Mar. 1594	–	–	*Parganas*	(Bengal)	*AN*, III, 998
42. Jagat Singh (s/o Man Singh)	Rajput	Mar. 1594	–	–	*Parganas*	(Bengal)	*AN*, III, 998
43. Baqir Ansari	Indian Muslim	Mar. 1594	–	–	*Parganas*	(Bengal)	*AN*, III, 998
44. Baqir Safarci	Turani	Mar. 1594	–	–	*Parganas*	(Bengal)	*AN*, III, 998

(contd.)

1	*2*	*3*	*4*	*5*	*6*	*7*	*8*	*9*
45.	Mir Qasim Badakshi	Turani	Mar. 1594	–	–	*Parganas*	(Bengal)	*AN*, III, 998
46.	Yuqub Kashmiri	Indian Muslim	Mar. 1594	–	–	*Parganas*	(Bengal)	*AN*, III, 998
47.	Sharif Sharmadi	Irani	Mar. 1594	–	–	*Parganas*	(Bengal)	*AN*, III, 998
48.	Sultan Khusrau	Prince	Mar. 1594	–	–	*Parganas*[111]	Orissa	*AN*, III, 999; *MU*, II, 53
49.	Man Singh	Rajput	Mar. 1594	1604-5 (recalled to Court)[112]	10 yrs.	*Parganas*	(Bengal)	*AN*, III, 999, 1256; *MU*, II, 53-4; *AA*, I, 362-3; *TU*, 271-2; Stewart, 186-7, 190; *ZK*, I, 103-11
50.	Khwaja Usman Lohani	Afghan	1601	–	–	*Parganas*	Orissa,[113] Satgaon	*AA*, I, 586-7

TABLE 3.6: ASSIGNMENT OF *JAGIRS* IN *SUBA* BIHAR

S. No.	*Name of Assignee*	*Racial Group*	*Period*		*Approximate Tenure*	*Jagirs*	*Sarkar*	*Sources*
			From	*To*		*Sarkar (S), Pargana (P), Qasba (Q), Fort (F), etc.*		
			Year(s) of Assignment Conferred/ Held	*Year(s) of Transfer (T), Revolt by Jagirdars (R), Flight (F), Death (D), etc.*				
1	*2*	*3*	*4*	*5*	*6*	*7*	*8*	*9*
1.	Sikandar Afghan	Afghan	Jul. 1557	1559 (D)	2 yrs.	Kharid (P), Bihar *wa an hudud*	Bihar Jaunpur	*AN*, II, 91; *MU*, I, 814; *AA*, I, 394-5n
2.	Muhibb Ali Khan Rohtasi	Turani	Jan./Feb. 1568	1588 (T)	21 yrs.	Rohtas (S)	Rohtas	Bayazid, 302; *AN*, III, 280, 672, 816-17; Arif, 258; *MT*, II, 290; *MU*, II, 226-8; *AA*, I, 466; *ZK*, I, 215
3.	Raja Gajpati	Hindu	Feb.-Mar. 1573	–	–	Bhojpur (P), Bahia-Jit (P)	Rohtas Rohtas	Bayazid, 319
4.	Hasan Khan Batani	Afghan	Mar. 1574	–	–	Saran (S)	Saran	*AN*, III, 115; *AA*, I, 532

(contd.)

1	2	3	4	5	6	7	8	9
5.	Munim Khan (Khan-i-Khanan)	Turani	Jul.-Aug. 1574	1575 (D)	1 yr.	Patna (S)	Bihar	*AN*, III, 144, 164, 189; Arif, 224; Bayazid, 312, 341-2; Farishta, II, 151; *MU*, II, 289-90; *AA*, I, 333-4; *TU*, 54; *ZK*, I, 24-5
6.	Muhammad Quli Khan Barlas	Turani	Jul.-Oct. 1574	Dec.1574-Jan.1575 (D)	Few mths.	Khitta-i-Hajipur	Hajipur	*AN*, III, 192; Arif, 224; Bayazid, 341; *MU*, II, 184-5; *AA*, 1, 364; *ZK*, I, 209.
7.	Farhat Khan	Turani	Jul.-Oct. 1574	1576 (D)	2 yrs.	Arraha (P), Rohtas (F)	Rohtas	*AN*, III, 240; *TA*, II, 490; *MT*, II, 185, 244; Arif, 225; *MU*, I, 519-20; *AA*, I, 488-9; *TU*, 127
8.	Mushin Khan	–	Aug. 1574	1576 (D)	2 yrs.	Parganas	(Patna)	Bayazid, 347; *AA*, I, 408
9.	Chalma Beg (Khan-i-Alam)	Turani	Aug. 1574	–	–	Tirhut (S)	Tirhut	Bayazid, 341; *MU*, I, 431-2; *AA*, I, 411
10.	Wazir Khan (Khan-i-Jamil)	Turani	Aug. 1574	1578-9 (F)	4-5 yrs.	Kahlgaon (P)	Monghyr	Bayazid, 341; *AN*, III, 429; *MU*, II, 980; *AA*, I, 527-8

11. Bayazid Bayat	Turani	Jan.-Mar. 1575	–	–	Chunar (F)	Chunar	Bayazid, 250, 352
12. Muzaffar Khan	Irani	Jun. 1575	1577 (T)	2 yrs.	Sahasram (P), Hajipur (S)	Rohtas Hajipur	Bayazid, 348; *AN*, III, 192; Arif, 247, 263; *MT*, II, 235; *TA*, II, 486; *MU*, II, 362-3; *AA*, I, 374; *ZK*, I, 212
13. Tangar Quli Sultan	–	Jun. 1575	–	–	*Parganas*	Bihar	Bayazid, 347; *TU*, 38
14. Khwaja Muhammad Zakariya	–	Oct. 1575	–	–	Tajpur (P)	Tirhut	Bayazid, 351
15. Mir Muhammad Shaukati (*Gumashta*-i-Muzaffar Khan)	–	Oct.-Nov. 1575	–	–	*Parganas*	Hajipur	*AN*, III, 193
16. Muhammad Sadiq Khan	Irani	–	1585 (T)	–	*Parganas*	Bihar	*AN*, III, 574, 654; *MU*, II, 660-1; *AA*, I, 382-3; *TU*, 105
17. Rai Surjan	Rajput	Nov. 1575	–	–	Chunar (P)	Chunar	*AN*, III, 223; *AA*, I, 450
18. Karamullah (brother of Shahbaz Khan)	Indian Muslim	Dec. 1576	Jan. 1577	2 mths.	Rohtas (F)	Rohtas	Arif, 258
19. Muhibb Ali Khan Rohtasi	Turani	Jan. 1577	1588 (T)	12 yrs.	Rohtas (F)	Rohtas	Arif, 258; *MT*, II, 290; *AN*, III, 816; *MU*, II, 228; *AA*, I, 466; *ZK*, I, 215-16

1	*2*	*3*	*4*	*5*	*6*	*7*	*8*	*9*
20.	Muhammad Masum Kabuli	Turani	(Jan. 1577)	Feb. 1580 (R)	3 yrs. 2 mths.	Ishhar (P)	Rohtas	Arif, 222-3; *AN*, III, 410, 418-19; *TA*, II, 515, 531; *MU*, II, 67-8
21.	Shujaat Khan	Turani	Nov. 1577	Mar. 1578 (T)	Few mths.	*Parganas*	Bihar	*AN*, III, 320; Arif, 257; *AA*, I, 401; *ZK*, I, 210
22.	Mir Muizzulmulk	Irani	Nov. 1577	–	–	*Parganas*	Bihar	*AN*, III, 320
23.	Shahbaz Khan Kambu	Indian Muslim	Jan. 1577	–	–	Bihar (S)	Bihar	*AN*, III, 280, 672, 701-5, 817; Arif, 257; *MU*, II, 733; *AA*, I, 438-9; *ZK*, I, 148-60
24.	Pahar Khan (*Khasa Khail*)	-	Sept.-Oct. 1579	–	–	Bihar (F)	Bihar	*MT*, II, 292; *ZK*, I, 226
25.	Saadat Ali	Turani	Sept.-Oct. 1579	–	–	Nahor (P), Qila-i-Kant (F)	Rohtas	*AN*, III, 418-19, 475
26.	Arab	Turani	Sept.-Oct. 1579	–	–	Sahasram (P)	Rohtas	*AN*, III, 418-19
27.	Said Beg Badakshi	Turani	Feb.-Mar. 1580	–	–	Sahasram (P), Tirhut (P)	Rohtas Tirhut	*AN*, III, 410, 418-19; *TA*, II, 531

28. Shaham Khan Jalair	Turani	Feb.-Mar. 1580[114]	1587-8 (T)	7-8 yrs.	Hajipur (S), Garaha	Hajipur	*AN*, III, 418-19, 544; *MU*, II, 729; *AA*, I, 450-1
29. Durvesh Ali Sanjar	Indian Muslim	Feb.-Mar. 1580	–	–	Tirhut (P)	Tirhut	*AN*, III, 418-19
30. Bahadur (s/o Said Beg Badakshi)	Turani	Feb.-Mar. 1580	1581 (F)	1 yr.	Tirhut (P)	Tirhut	*AN*, III, 418-19, 549
31. Mir Muizulmulk	Irani	Feb.-Mar. 1580	–	–	Arraha and its territory	Rohtas	*AN*, III, 419
32. Mir Akbar Ali	Irani	Feb.-Mar. 1580	–	–	Arraha and its territory	Rohtas	*AN*, III, 419
33. Samanji Khan	Turani	Feb.-Mar. 1580	–	–	Arraha and its territory	Rohtas	*AN*, III, 419
34. Jamaluddin Husain Sistani	Irani	Feb.-Mar. 1580	–	–	Khitta-i-Buxur (*mahal*)	Rohtas	*AN*, III, 421-2
35. Sayyid Hasan	Indian Muslim	Feb.-Mar. 1580	–	–	Khitta-i-Buxur (*mahal*)	Rohtas	*AN*, III, 421-2
36. Dudraj	Hindu	Feb.-Mar. 1580	–	–	Khitta-i-Buxur (*mahal*)	Rohtas	*AN*, III, 421-2
37. Saadat Ali	Turani	Sept.-Oct. 1580	–	–	Qila-i-Kant (F)	Rohtas	*AN*, III, 475

(contd.)

1	2	3	4	5	6	7	8	9
38.	Payanda	Turani	Sept.-Oct. 1580	–	–	Qila-i-Kant (F)	Rohtas	*AN*, III, 475
39.	Rustam	Irani	Sept.-Oct. 1580	–	–	Qila-i-Kant (F)	Rohtas	*AN*, III, 475
40.	Rup Narayan	Hindu	Sept.-Oct. 1580	–	–	Qila-i-Kant (F)	Rohtas	*AN*, III, 475
41.	Khan Azam Mirza Aziz Koka	Turani	Oct.-Nov. 1580	Mar.1584 (T)	3 yrs. 5 mths.	Hajipur (T)	Hajipur	*AN*, III, 476, 544, 549-50, 574, 594, 600, 625; *TA*, II, 538, 556; *MU*, I, 323-4; *AA*, I, 344; *ZK*, I, 80-99
42.	Mirza Yusuf Khan	Irani	(Jul. 1585)	1587 (T)	2 yrs.	Bihar	Bihar	*AN*, III, 701, 801; *MU*, II, 1000-1; *AA*, I, 535-6; *TU*, 189-90; *ZK*, I, 170-2
43.	Ghazi Khan Badakshi	Turani	(1581)	Jul. 1584(D)	3 yrs.	Tirhut (P) Awadh (P)	Tirhut Awadh	*AN*, III, 549; *MU*, I, 583-4; *AA*, I, 487-8
44.	Said Khan Chaghta	Turani	Jan. 1585	Aug. 1587 (T)	2 yrs. 8 mths.	Hajipur(S)	Hajipur	*AN*, III, 629, 660, 801; *MU*, II, 679-80; *AA*, I, 351; *ZK*, I, 190-3

		1594-5	1597-8	3-4 yrs.	Bihar	Bihar	*AN*, III, 999, 1060
45. Raja Bhagwan Das	Rajput	Aug. 1587	Nov. 1589 (D)	2 yrs. 4 mths.	Bihar (S)	Bihar	*AN*, III, 790, 801, 816; *MU*, I, 405; *AA*, I, 353; *TU*, 248; *ZK*, I, 103
46. Raja Man Singh	Rajput	Aug. 1587	1594 (T)	7 yrs.	Hajipur (S), Patna (S), Rohtas (S)	Hajipur Patna Rohtas	*AN*, III, 790, 801, 872; *MT*, II, 375; *TA*, II, 622; Farishta, II, 161; *MU*, II, 50-3; *AA*, I, 362-3; *TU*, 272; *ZK*, I, 103-11
47. Farrukh Khan (s/o Mir Muhammad)	Turani	(1590)	–	–	Dharbhanga (P)	Tirhut	*AN*, III, 872
48. Khan Azam Mirza Aziz Koka and his sons Sadman, Abdullah Khan)	Turani	1594	1595	1 yr.	Hajirpur (S), Ghazipur	Hajipur	*AN*, III, 1006, 1033, 1068; *MT*, II, 412; *AA*, I, 345; *ZK*, I, 80-99
49. Asaf Khan (Jafar Beg)	Irani	1604-5	1605	1 yr.	*Parganas*	(Bihar)	*AN*, III, 1249; *TU*, 7; *ZK*, I, 187-90
50. Khan Azam Mirza Aziz Koka	Turani	Aug. 1605	–	–	Bihar (S)	Bihar	*AN*, III, 1257; *ZK*, I, 80-99

TABLE 3.7: ASSIGNMENT OF *JAGIRS* IN *SUBA* DELHI

S. No.	*Name of Assignee*	*Racial Group*	*Period*		*Approximate Tenure*	*Jagirs*	*Sarkar*	*Sources*
			From	*To*		*Sarkar (S), Pargana (P), Qasba (Q), Fort (F), etc.*		
			Year(s) of Assignment Conferred/ Held	*Year(s) of Transfer (T), Revolt by Jagirdars (R), Flight (F), Death (D), etc.*				
1	*2*	*3*	*4*	*5*	*6*	*7*	*8*	*9*
1.	Ali Quli Khan (Khan i-Zaman)	Irani	Mar. 1556	1558 (confiscated)	3 yrs.	Sambhal and other *Pargarnas*	Sambhal	*AN*, II, 25, 46-7, 71; *TA*, II, 213; Farishta, II, 111; Arif, 75; *ZK*, I, 26-31; *MU*, I, 198-9; *TU*, 55; *AA*, I, 335-6
2.	Bairam Khan (Khan-i-Khanan)	Irani	1556	–	–	Sirhind (Q), Sambhal (S)	Sirhind Sambhal	*ZK*, I, 11-20; *MU*, I, 370-1; *AA*, I, 330
3.	Mahdi Qasim Khan	Turani	Dec. 1556	–	–	*Parganas*	Delhi	*AN*, II, 75; *MU*, II, 504-5; *AA*, I, 372-3

4.	Beg Mirak	–	Mar.-Sept. 1559	–	–	*Parganas*	Hisar-Firuza	Bayazid, 279
5.	Husain Khan Tukriya	Turani	Mar. 1560	Jun-Dec. 1568 (T)	8 yrs. 4 mths.	Inderi (P)	Saharan-pur	*MT*, II, 29, 130; *ZK*, I 221; *MU*, I, 644-5; *AA*, I, 402-3
6.	Sayyid Muhammad Baraha	Indian Muslim	1560	–	–	*Parganas*	(Delhi)	*MU*, II, 36; *ZK*, I, 181-2
7.	Shahabuddin Ahmad Khan	Turani	Mar. 1560	–	–	Delhi (S)	Delhi	*AN*, II, 141; *TA*, II, 236; Farishta, II, 119; *ZK*, I, 101; *MU*, II, 846-7; *AA*, I, 352; *TU*, 94-5
8.	Sher Muhammad Diwana	-	Mar.-Apr. 1560	1565 (killed)	5 yrs.	Bhatnair (P)[115]	Hisar-Firuza	*AN*, II, 166-7; *TA*, 243; Bayazid, 225; Arif, 86; *MT*, II, 34; Farishta, II, 123; *AA*, I, 332
9.	Khwaja Abdul Majid (Asaf Khan)	Irani	Jul.-Aug. 1560	Mar. 1563 (T)	2 yrs. 8 mths.	Delhi (S)	Delhi	*TA*, II, 246; *AN*, II, 168-9; *MU*, I, 37-8; *AA*, I, 396; Farishta, II, 123; *TU*, 7; *ZK*, I, 122-3

(contd.)

1	2	3	4	5	6	7	8	9
10.	Khwaja Muzaffar Ali	Irani	Oct.-Dec. 1560	–	–	Hisar-Firuza (S)	Hisar-Firuza	Bayazid, 240
11.	Munim Khan (Khan-i-Khanan)	Turani	Dec. 1560	1562 (F)	2 yrs.	Hisar-Firuza (S), Inder (P)	Hisar-Firuza Saharan-pur	Bayazid, 240, 249; *AN*, II, 272-3, 294; *MU*, II, 284-5; *AA*, I, 333; *ZK*, I, 24-5
12.	Mir Muhammad Munshi	Irani	Jul.-Aug. 1562	–	–	Sarut (P)	Saharan-pur	*AN*, II, 279; *TA*, II, 265; *MU*, II, 285; *ZK*, I, 211
13.	Qasim Ali Sistani (*Gumashta* of Mir Muhammad Munshi)	Irani	1562	–	–	Sarut (P)	Saharan-pur	*AN*, II, 279; *MT*, II, 52; *TA*, II, 265
14.	Shah Qurban	–	Sept. 1563	–	–	Ponian (P)	Hisar-Firuza	Bayazid, 278
15.	Qulich Chugan Begi	Turani	Sept. 1563	–	–	Shaswan (P)	Badaun	*MT*, III, [121]
16.	Tatar Khan	Irani	Jan. 1564	Mar. 1567	3 yrs. 3 mths.	Delhi (S)	Delhi	*AN*, II, 424; Bayazid, 284; *TA*, II, 331; *AA*, I, 468

17.	Nuruddin Muhammad Tarkhan	Irani	Jan. 1564	1580	16 yrs.	Safadaon (P) Samana (Q)	Delhi Sirhind	Bayazid, 284; *MT*, III [199]; *AN*, II, 392; *MU*, II, 461-2
18.	Ibrahim Husain Mirza	Turani	Mar.-Jul. 1566	1571 (R)	5 yrs.	Azampur (P)	Sambhal	*MT*, II, 87; *AN*, II, 413-14; *TA*, II, 326, 397
19.	Hafiz Rakhna	–	Nov.-Dec. 1566	–	–	Balda-i-Sirhind	Sirhind	*TA*, II, 323
20.	Muhammad Sultan Mirza	Turani	Jan.-Mar. 1567	1571 (R)	4-5 yrs.	Azampur (P)	Samhbal	*AN*, II, 414; *TA*, II, 327; *ZK*, I, 111-22
21.	Shah Mirza and Ulugh Mirza	Turani	Jan.-Mar. 1567	–	–	Nihtaur (P)	Sambhal	*AN*, II, 413; *MT*, II, 93; *TA*, II, 326
22.	Shahabuddin Ahmad Khan	Turani	–	Mar. 1567 (killed)	–	Bhojpur (Q)	Delhi	*AN*, II, 424; *TA*, II, 331-2
23	Husain Khan Tukriya	Turani	1568	Oct.-Nov. 1574(F)	6 yrs.	Kant-Gola (P), Patiali (P)	Badaun Kanauj	*AN*, III, 154, 182; *MT*, II, 130; *MU*, I, 644-5; *AA*, I, 402-3; *ZK*, I, 221

(contd.)

1	2	3	4	5	6	7	8	9
24.	Mir Muhammad (Khan-i-Kalan)	Turani	Aug.-Sept. 1568	1570 (T)	2 yrs.	Sambhal (S)	Sambhal	*AN*, II, 487, 517; *MT*, II, 109; *TA*, II, 352; *MU*, II, 154-5; *AA*, I, 339; *TU*, 149
25.	Muinuddin Ahmad Khan Faran Khudi	Turani	–	Mar.-Apr. 1573 (T)	–	Sambhal (S)	Sambhal	*MT*, II, 158; *MU*, II, 237; *AA*, I, 480
26.	Malik Ashraf	–	Jun.-Oct. 1575	–	–	Thanesar (P)	Sirhind	*AN*, III, 201
27.	Deep Chand Manjhula	Rajput	(Apr.-May 1577)	–	–	Bareilly (P)	Badaun	*MT*, II, 257
28.	Mehr Ali Sildoz	Turani	Jan. 1578	–	–	*Parganas*	Hisar-Firuza	Arif, [232]; *MU*, II, 72; *AA*, I, 481
29.	Muhibb Ali Khan (s/o Mir Khalifa)	Turani	May 1578	1581 (D)	3 yrs.	*Parganas*	(Delhi)	*AN*, III, 357; *TA*, II, 527; *MU*, II, 224-5; *AA*, I, 465; *ZK*, I, 166-70
30.	Bakhtiyar Beg	Irani	(1581)	–	–	Badaun (P)	Badaun	*AN*, III, 512
31.	Shaikh Muazam	Indian Muslim	(1581)	–	–	Amroh (P)	Sambhal	*AN*, III, 512

32. Mir Abul Hasan	Irani	(1581)	–	–	Amroh (P)	Sambhal	*AN*, III, 512
33. Maulana Mahmud	–	(1581)	–	–	Parganas	Sambhal	*AN*, III, 512
34. Abul Qasim	Irani	(1581)	–	–	Amroh (P)	Sambhal	*AN*, III, 512
35. Said Khan Chaghta	Turani	Jan. 1583	Dec. 1584 (T)	2 yrs.	Sambhal (S)	Sambhal	*AN*, III, 587, 625, 629; *MU*, II, 679; *ZK*, I, 190-3; *AA*, I, 351; *TU*, 83
36. Qulij Khan	Turani	Apr. 1589	1593-4 (T)	4-5 yrs.	Sambhal (S)	Sambhal	*AN*, III, 817; *MU*, II, 535; *ZK*, I, 172-5
37. Abul Fazl	Indian Muslim	–	1595 (T)	–	Sambhal	Sambhal	*MT*, II, 416
38. Muzaffar Husain Mirza	Irani	1595	1597 (resumed)	2 yrs.	Sambhal (S)	Sambhal	*MU*, II, 354; *AA*, I, 328; *MT*, II, 416; *AN*, III, 1030-1
39. Shaikh Sultan	Indian Muslim	–	Dec.1598 (killed)	–	Thaneshwar (P)	Delhi	*AN*, III, 1118
40. Abu Said	Turani	Oct.-Nov. 1598	–	–	Parganas	Sirhind	*AN*, III, 1116
41. Raja Rai Rai Singh	Rajput	–	–	–	Bhatnair (P)	Hisar-Firuza	*Dalpat Vilas*, 30, 41-2; *ZK*, I, 215

TABLE 3.8: ASSIGNMENT OF *JAGIRS* IN *SUBA* GUJARAT

S. No.	*Name of Assignee*	*Racial Group*	*Period*		*Approximate Tenure*	*Jagirs*	*Sarkar*	*Sources*
			From	*To*		*Sarkar (S), Pargana (P), Qasba (Q), Fort (F), etc.*		
			Year(s) of Assignment Conferred/ Held	*Year(s) of Transfer (T), Revolt by Jagirdars (R), Flight (F), Death (D), etc.*				
1	*2*	*3*	*4*	*5*	*6*	*7*	*8*	*9*
1.	Abdur Rahim Mirza Khan (s/o Bairam Khan)	Irani	Nov. 1572	–	–	Patan (S)	Patan	*AN*, III, 8-9; *MU* I, 50-2; *TU*, 54; *ZK*, I, 31-63; *AA*, I, 355-6
2.	Sayyid Ahmad Khan Baraha[116]	Indian Muslim	Nov. 1572	–	–	Patan (S)	Patan	*AN*, III, 8-9, 32; Medieval Gujarat, 319

3.	Khan Azam Mirza Aziz Koka	Turani	Dec. 1572	1575 (resumed)[117]	3 yrs.	City of Ahmedabad and *parganas* of Petlad and Haveli	Ahmeda-bad	*AN*, III, 13, 15, 46; *MT*, II, 167; *TA*, II, 376, 393, 454, 456, 476; Arif, 192-3, 195, 200, 239; Farishta, II, 151; *MU*, I, 320-1; *AA*, I, 343-4; *Mirat-i-Ahmadi*, 102-3; *Medieval Gujarat*,[118] 311, 324-5; *ZK*, I, 80-99; *TU*, 5
4.	Hasan Khan Khazanchi	Afghan	Dec. 1572	–	–	Bandar Khambayat	Ahmeda-bad	*AN*, III, 15, 59; *TA*, II, 404; *Medieval Gujarat*, 312
5.	Shaikh Muhammad Bukhari	Indian Muslim	(Jan. 1573)	1573 (killed)	Few mths.	Dholka (P)	Ahmeda-bad	*AN*, III, 16, 32; *Medieval Gujarat*, 319-20; *MU*, II, 128; *AA*, I, 433
6.	Shujaat Khan	Turani	–	Mar. 1573 (killed)	–	Surat (F)	Surat	Bayazid, 322; *Medieval Gujarat*, 324

(contd.)

1	*2*	*3*	*4*	*5*	*6*	*7*	*8*	*9*
7.	Mir Muhammad Atka (Khan-i-Kalan) and his sons Fazil Muhammad Khan, Farrukh Khan	Turani	Mar.-Apr. 1573	Dec. 1575[119] (D)	2 yrs. 9 mths.	Patan (S)	Patan	*AN*, III, 46, 89, 231; Bayazid, 334; Arif, 200, 240; *TA*, II, 392-3 (n. 1), 420; *Medieval Gujarat*, 339; *MU*, II, 155; *Mirat-i-Ahmadi*, 102-3; *Tarikh-i-Gujarat*, 92-3; *AA*, I, 339; *TU*, 149; *ZK*, I, 248
8.	Shaikh Hamid Bukhari	Indian Muslim	Mar.-Apr. 1573	1577 (T)	4 yrs.	Dholka(P), Dandhuka(P)	Ahmeda-bad	*AN*, III, 46-7; *Medieval Gujarat*, 325; *MU*, I, 608-9; *TA*, II, 394n; *Mirat-i-Ahmadi*, 102-3, 122-4, 127-9; *AA*, I, 434
9.	Qutbuddin Khan Atka and his son Naurang Khan	Turani	Mar.-Apr. 1573	Feb. 1583 (killed)	10 yrs.	Broach (S), Baroda (S), Champanir(S)	Broach Baroda Champanir	*AN*, III, 46-7, 410; Bayazid, 334; *MT*, II, 257; *TA*, II, 393n-4n; Arif, 268; *AN*, III, 583, 627-9;

							Mirat-i-Ahmadi, 102-3; *MU*, II, 546-7; *AA*, I, 354; *TU*, 136; *Medieval Gujarat*, 325-6
10. Sharif Khan Atka and his son Baz Bahadur Khan	Turani	Mar.-Apr. 1573	–	–	Dholka (P), Dandhuka (P)	Ahmeda-bad	*TA*, II, 394n; *MU*, II, 820-1; *Mirat-i-Ahmadi*, 102-3; *AA*, I, 416; *TU*, 95
11. Qulij Khan	Turani	Mar.-Apr. 1573	1589 (T)	16 yrs.	Surat (F),[120] *Parganas*	Surat Ahmeda-bad	Bayazid, 333; Arif, 199; *TA*, II, 388, 404, 480-2, 571; *AN*, III, 44, 59, 383, 681; *MU*, II, 535; Farishta, II, 161; *AA*, I, 380; *ZK*, I, 172-5; *TU*, 137
12. Mirza Muqim	Turani	Jul. 1573	–	–	Idar (P)	Ahmeda-bad	*AN*, III, 59
13. Shah Ali Langah	–	Oct.-Nov. 1573	–	–	Deesa (P)	Patan	*AN*, III, 89; *TA*, II, 411; *Medieval Gujarat*, 329

(contd.)

1	*2*	*3*	*4*	*5*	*6*	*7*	*8*	*9*
14.	Wazir Khan	Irani	Sept.-Oct. 1573	Oct.-Nov. 1577 (T)	4 yrs.	Dholka (P), Dandhka (P), Idar (P)	Ahmeda-bad	*AN*, III, 89, 306, 389; *TA*, II, 420, 501; *MT*, II, 173, 256; *Medieval Gujarat*, 339; *MU*, II, 984-5; *AA*, I, 380; *TU*, 184; *ZK*, I, 211
15.	Tarsun Khan	Irani	Sept.-Oct. 1576	Dec. 1579 (recalled to court)	3 yrs.	*Parganas*	Patan	*AN*, III, 267, 382; *MT*, II, 282; *TA*, II, 525; *Medieval Gujarat*, 343, 351; *TU*, 37
16.	Shahabuddin Ahmad Khan	Turani	Oct.-Nov. 1577	1583 (recalled to court)	6 yrs.	*Parganas*	(Gujarat)	*AN*, III, 306, 389, 596-7, 610, 657; *TA*, II, 566-7; *MU*, 847-9; *AA*, I, 352; *TU*, 95; *ZK*, I, 101
17.	Shah Fakhruddin Mashadi	Irani	Nov.-Dec. 1577	–	–	Patan (P)	Patan	*AN*, III, 382, *Medieval Gujarat*, 351
18.	Qulij Khan	Turani	–	1593 (recalled to	–	Surat (S), Baroda (S),	Surat Baroda	*MT*, II, 401; *TA*, II, 622-3, 648n; *AN*, III,

			court)		Broach (S)	Broach	995; *MU*, II, 535; *AA*, I, 380; *ZK*, I, 172-5; *TU*, 137
19. Itimad Khan Gujarati and other officers	Indian Muslim	1583	1587 (D)	4 yrs.	Baroda (S), Champanir(S), Surat (S)	Baroda Champanir Surat	*AN*, III, 485, 596, 632; *TA*, II, 561; *MT*, II, 332-3; *AA*, I, 420; *ZK*, I, 214-5; *MU*, I, 706-8
20. Shahabuddin Ahmad Khan	Turani	1584	1589 (T)	5 yrs.	Broach (S)	Broach	*TA*, II, 566-7; *AN*, III, 596-7, 610; *MU*, II, 847-9; *Medieval Gujarat*, 348, 355-6; *AA*, I, 352; *TU*, 95; *ZK*, I, 101
21. Mir Hashim	Turani	1584	1584-5 (D)	Few mths.	*Parganas*	(Gujarat)	*MT*, II, 332-3, 338-9; *AN*, II, 634; *TA*, II, 561, 567-8; *Medieval Gujarat*, 355
22. Mir Calih Dai	Afghan	1584	–	–	*Parganas*	(Gujarat)	*MT*, II, 332-3, 338-9; *AN*, II, 634; *TA*, II, 561, 567-8; *Medieval Gujarat*, 355
23. Sayyid Abul Ashaq	Indian Muslim	1584	–	–	*Parganas*	(Gujarat)	*MT*, II, 332-3, 338-9; *AN*, II, 634; *TA*, II,

(contd.)

1	2	3	4	5	6	7	8	9
								561, 567-8; *Medieval Gujarat*, 355
24.	Sher Khan (s/o Itimad Khan)	Indian Muslim	1584	–	–	*Parganas*	(Gujarat)	*MT*, II, 332-3, 338-9; *AN*, II, 634; *TA*, II, 561, 567-8; *Medieval Gujarat*, 355
25.	Mir Muhammad Masum	Turani	1584	–	–	*Parganas*	(Gujarat)	*MT*, II, 332-3, 338-9; *AN*, II, 634; *TA*, II, 561, 567-8; *Medieval Gujarat*, 355
26.	Sher Khan Fuladi	Afghan	1584	–	–	*Parganas*	(Gujarat)	*MT*, II, 332-3, 338-9; *AN*, II, 634; *TA*, II, 561, 567-8; *Medieval Gujarat*, 355
27.	Sayyid Julal Bukhari	Indian Muslim	1584	–	–	*Parganas*	(Gujarat)	*MT*, II, 332-3, 338-9; *AN*, II, 634; *TA*, II, 561, 567-8; *Medieval Gujarat*, 355

28. Beg Muhammad Toqbai	Turani	1584	–	–	*Parganas*	(Gujarat)	*MT*, II, 332-3, 338-9; *AN*, II, 634; *TA*, II, 561, 567-8; *Medieval Gujarat*, 355
29. Bumiyad Beg	Irani	1584	–	–	*Parganas*	(Gujarat)	*MT*, II, 332-3, 338-9; *AN*, II, 634; *TA*, II, 561, 567-8; *Medieval Gujarat*, 355
30. Mir Abul Muzaffar	Irani	1584	–	–	*Parganas*	(Gujarat)	*MT*, II, 332-3, 338-9; *AN*, II, 634; *TA*, II, 561, 567-8; *Medieval Gujarat*, 355
31. Mir Habibullah Ashaq	Indian	1584	–	–	*Parganas*	(Gujarat)	*MT*, II, 332-3, 338-9; *AN*, II, 634; *TA*, II, 561, 567-8; *Medieval Gujarat*, 355
32. Mir Sharafuddin (nephew of Mir Abul Turab)	Irani	1584	–	–	*Parganas*	(Gujarat)	*MT*, II, 332-3, 338-9; *AN*, II, 634; *TA*, II, 561, 567-8; *Medieval Gujarat*, 355

(contd.)

1	*2*	*3*	*4*	*5*	*6*	*7*	*8*	*9*
33.	Muhammad Husain Shaikh	Turani	1584	-	-	Parganas	(Gujarat)	*MT*, II, 332-3, 338-9; *AN*, II, 634; *TA*, II, 561, 567-8; *Medieval Gujarat*, 355
34.	Qabil Khan Gujarati	Indian Muslim	Sept.-Oct. 1584	–	–	Badhnagar (P)	Patan	*AN*, III, 656
35.	Radham Khan	Indian Muslim	Sept.-Oct. 1584	–	–	Badhnagar (P)	Patan	*AN*, III, 656
36.	Sayyid Qasim	Irani	1584	1599 (D)	15 yrs.	*Parganas*	Patan	*MT*, II, 356; *MU*, II, 494-5; *AN*, III, 1133; *ZK*, I, 43-5
37.	Amin Khan Ghori and his son Daulat Khan	Afghan	(1585)	–	–	Junagarh (S)	Junagarh	*MT*, II, 355, 392; *AN*, III, 902; *Medieval Gujarat*, 352-3, 378
38.	Khan Azam Mirza Aziz Koka	Turani	Dec. 1589[121]	1593[122] (recalled to court)	4 yrs.	Junagarh (S) and other *parganas* of Gujarat	Junagarh Ahmedabad	*TA*, II, 595, 628; *AN*, III, 865, 877, 902; *MT*, II, 383-4, 400; Farishta, II, 162; *Medieval Gujarat*, 405; *MU*, 1, 325; *ZK*, I, 95-96; *TU*, 5

39. Abdur Rahim Mirza Khan (Khan-i-Khanan)	Irani	–	Dec. 1589 (T)	–	Ahmedabad (S)	Ahmeda-bad	*AN*, III, 865, 877, 902; *TA*, II, 588, 629; *MT*, II, 384; *MU*, II, 52-3; *TU*, 54; *ZK*, I, 31-63
40. Khudawand Deccani	Irani	(1590)	–	–	Kari (P)	Ahmeda-bad	*MT*, II, 384; *ZK*, I, 226-7
41. Ismail Quli Khan	Irani	Mar. 1591	–	–	*Parganas*	(Ahmeda-bad)	*MT*, II, 376; *AN*, III, 888; *TA*, II, 622; *AA*, I, 388; *MU*, I, 704; *TU*, 8
42. Taj Khan and Miyan Khan (sons of Daulat Khan of Junagarh)	Afghan	1592	–	–	*Parganas*	(Gujarat)	MD (H), II, 20; *AN*, III, 948-9
43. Daulat Khan Lodi	Afghan	–	–	–	Half of Jhalawar	(Gujarat)	*Tarikh-i-Khanjahani*, II, 462-3; *ZK*, II, 69-70; *AN*, III, 1175
		1599	1602[123] (D)	3 yrs.	Six *paraganas* including Kavi Dawalgaon, Khalgaon and Nakalur (in Bhatta)	Ahmeda-bad	*Tarikh-i-Khanjahani*, II, 478-83; *ZK*, II, 69-73; *MU*, I, 465

(contd.)

1	*2*	*3*	*4*	*5*	*6*	*7*	*8*	*9*
44.	Sultan Murad	Prince	Apr. 1593	–	–	*Parganas*	(Gujarat)	*AN*, III, 982; *MT*, II, 401; *TA*, II, 648
45.	Raja Rai Rai Singh	Rajput	1594	–	–	Junagarh	Junagarh	*MT*, II, 400; *ZK*, I, 215
46.	Muhammad Sadiq Khan[124]	Irani	Jun.-Aug. 1594	1597 (D)	3 yrs.	Broach (S), Surat (S), Baroda (S)[125]	Broach Surat Baroda	*MT*, II, 401; *TA*, II, 648-9; *MU*, II, 660-2; *AA*, I, 383-4; *TU*, 105; *ZK*, I, 176
47.	Mirza Yusaf Khan	Irani	Apr. 1596-7[126]	–	–	*Parganas*	(Gujarat)	*AN*, III, 1064, 1081; *MU*, II, 1006-7; *AA*, I, 371
48.	Khan Azam Mirza Aziz Koka and his sons Samsuddin, Sadman, Khurram, Abdullah	Turani	1602	1605[127](T)	3 yrs.	*Parganas* of Gujarat including Junagarh	Gujarat	*AN*, III, 1184, 1236; *Medieval Gujarat*, 426-7; *ZK*, I, 95-6; *Mirat-i-Ahmadi*, 159; *TU*, 5

TABLE 3.9: ASSIGNMENT OF *JAGIRS* IN *SUBA* KABUL

S. No.	*Name of Assignee*	*Racial Group*	*Period*		*Approximate Tenure*	*Jagirs*	*Sarkar*	*Sources*
			From *Year(s) of Assignment Conferred/ Held*	*To* *Year(s) of Transfer (T), Revolt by Jagirdars (R), Flight (F), Death (D), etc.*		*Sarkar (S), Pargana (P), Qasba (Q), Fort (F), etc.*		
1	*2*	*3*	*4*	*5*	*6*	*7*	*8*	*9*
1.	Munim Khan (Khan-i-Khanan)	Turani	1555	Aug. 1560 (T)	5 yrs.	Kabul-wa-Ghaznin & other districts commonly known as Nilab	Kabul	*AN*, II, 25, 30, 56; *TA*, II, 211, 271; Farishta, II, 123; *MU*, II, 284-5; *AA*, I, 333; *ZK*, I, 24-5; *TU*, 150
			1562	Jun. 1567 (T)	5 yrs.	Kabul-wa-Ghaznin & other districts commonly known as Nilab	Kabul	*AN*, II, 25, 30, 56; *TA*, II, 211, 271; Farishta, II, 123; *MU*, II, 284-5; *AA*, I, 333; *ZK*, I, 24-5; *TU*, 150

1	*2*	*3*	*4*	*5*	*6*	*7*	*8*	*9*
2.	Bairam Khan (Khan-i-Khanan)	Irani	1555	1556 (T)	Few mths.	Qandahar (Q) and its *parganas*	Qandahar	*AN*, II, 25, 82; *TA*, II, 212; *MU*, I, 370-1; *AA*, I, 330-1; *ZK*, I, 11-20; *TU*, 30
3.	Mir Hashim	Turani	1555	1556 (impri-soned)	Few mths.	Kahmard (Q), Ghorband, Zuhak	Kabul	*AN*, II, 30
4.	Khwaja Jalaluddin Bujuq (cut nose)	Irani	Nov. 1556	1556-7 (F)	Few mths.	Ghaznin (S)	Ghaznin	*AN*, II, 85; *MU*, I, 740-1; *AA*, I, 417
5.	Haidar Muhammad Khan Akhata Begi	Turani	May 1560	1561 (removed)	1 yr.	Kabul	(Kabul)	*TA*, II, 269; *MU*, I, 599-600, *AA*, 1, 418
6.	Ghani Khan (s/o Munim Khan)	Turani	1560	–	–	Kabul	(Kabul)	*TA*, II, 269; *AA*, I, 333
7.	Tulak Khan Qulchin	Turani	(Jan. 1563)	– (F)	– (Q)	Mama-Khatun	Kabul	*AN*, II, 285; *MU*, II, 959-60; *AA*, I, 493
8.	Mirza Khizr Khan Hazara	Turani	Jan. 1563	–	–	Ghaznin (S)	Ghaznin	*AN*, II, 288
9.	Hamza Arab	–	Mar. 1563	–	–	Peshawar	Kabul	Bayazid, 255
10.	Mirza Faridun (s/o Muhammad Quli Khan Barlas)	Turani	Nov.-Dec. 1566	–	–	*Parganas*	(Kabul)	*AN*, II, 409

11. Yar Ali	Turani	Jul. 1581	–	–	Peshawar (F)	Kabul	*AN*, III, 528
12. Mirza Muhammad Hakim	Turani	1582	Jul. 1585	3 yrs.	Kabul	Kabul	*TA*, II, 551
13. Raja Bhagwan Das, Man Singh (s/o Bhagwan Das), Jagat Singh (s/o Man Singh)	Rajput	Jul. 1585	Mar. 1587	2 yrs.	Kabul	Kabul	*AN*, III, 713, 780, 790; *TA*, II, 584, 608, 614-15; *MT*, II, 361, 364, 370; Farishta, II, 161; *MU*, I, 404-5; *MU*, II, 49-50; *AA*, I, 353, 361-2; *ZK*, I, 103-11, 230
14. Khwaja Shamsuddin Khafi	Irani	1585	–	–	*Parganas*	(Kabul)	*AN*, III, 713, 780, 802; *ZK*, I, 195-6
15. Zain Khan Koka	Irani	Mar. 1587	1591	4 yrs.	Kabul	Kabul	*AN*, III, 790; *TA*, II, 622; *MT*, II, 370; Farishta, II, 161; *MU*, II, 1024-7; *AA*, I, 368-9; *TU*, 79; *ZK*, I, 123-4
16. Sayyid Hamid Bukhari	Indian Muslim	–	1585-6 (D)	–	Peshawar	Kabul	*AN*, III, 777; *MU*, I, 609
17. Muhammad Qasim Khan (Mir Bahr)	Irani	1587	Nov. 1589 (T)	2 yrs.	Kashmir (S)	Kashmir	*TA*, II, 622; *MT*, II, 376; *MU*, II, 513-14; *AA*, I, 412-13

1	*2*	*3*	*4*	*5*	*6*	*7*	*8*	*9*
18.	Husain Beg Shaikh Umari	Turani	Aug. 1589	May 1590 (T)	1 yr.	Pakli (S)	Pakli	*AN*, III, 855, 874; *MU*, I, 620; *AA*, I, 504.
19.	Shah Beg Khan	Turani	Sept. 1589	–	–	Begram (Peshawar)	Kabul	*AN*, III, 855-6, 993; *MU*, II, 740; *AA*, I, 409, 416
20.	Muhammad Qasim Khan (Mir Bahr)	Irani	Nov. 1589	1594 (D)	5 yrs.	Kabul	Kabul	*AN*, III, 861, 867; *TA*, II, 628; *MT*, II, 383, 393, 409; Farishta, II, 162; *MU*, II, 513-14; *AA*, I, 412-13; *TU*, 134
21.	Sultan Husain Khan Pakliwal	Turani	May 1590	–	–	Pakli	Pakli	*AN*, III, 855, 875; *AA*, I, 504, 563
22.	Takhta Beg	Turani	Jan. 1590	1594	4-5 yrs.	Ghaznin	Kabul	*AN*, III, 867; *MU*, II, 921; *AA*, I, 523
23.	Mirza Yusuf Khan	Irani	Oct.-Nov. 1592	Aug.-Sept. 1594	2 yrs.	Kashmir (S)	Kashmir	*TA*, II, 508, 622; *AN*, III, 959-60, 1004; *MT*, II, 376; *AA*, I, 370-1; *ZK*, I, 170-2
24.	Qulij Khan	Turani	1594	Mar. 1597 (T)	3 yrs.	Kabul	Kabul	*AN*, III, 1004, 1066, 1073; *MU*, II, 535-6; *AA*, I, 381; *ZK*, I, 172-5; *TU*, 137

25. Ahmad Beg Kabuli	Turani	Sept. 1594	–	–	*Parganas*	Kashmir	*AN*, III, 1004, 1235; *TA*, II, 508, 628; *MU*, II, 284; *AA*, I, 370, 452, 518; *TU*, 12
26. Muhammad Quli Beg	Turani	Sept. 1594	–	–	*Parganas*	Kashmir	*AN*, III, 1004, 1235; *TA*, II, 508, 628; *MU*, II, 284; *AA*, I, 370, 452, 518; *TU*, 12
27. Hamza Beg	Turani	Sept. 1594	–	–	*Parganas*	Kashmir	*AN*, III, 1004, 1235; *TA*, II, 508, 628; *MU*, II, 284; *AA*, I, 370, 452, 518; *TU*, 12
28. Hasan Beg Gurd	Turani	Sept. 1594	–	–	*Parganas*	Kashmir	*AN*, III, 1004, 1235; *TA*, II, 508, 628; *MU*, II, 284; *AA*, I, 370, 452, 518; *TU*, 12
29. Hasan Ali Arab	Turani	Sept. 1594	–	–	*Parganas*	Kashmir	*AN*, III, 1004, 1235; *TA*, II, 508, 628; *MU*, II, 284; *AA*, I, 370, 452, 518; *TU*, 12
30. Muhammad Beg Aimaq	Turani	Sept. 1594	–	–	*Parganas*	Kashmir	*AN*, III, 1004, 1235; *TA*, II, 508, 628; *MU*, II, 284; *AA*, I, 370, 452, 518; *TU*, 12

1	2	3	4	5	6	7	8	9
31.	Sharif Khan Atka	Turani	1594	Jan.-Feb. 1603 (T)	8 yrs.	Ghaznin	Kabul	*AN*, III, 993, 1223; *MU*, II, 820-1; *AA*, I, 415-6; *TU*, 95
32.	Asaf Khan (Mirza Qiwamuddin)	Irani	Jul. 1597	1599 (T)	2 yrs.	Kashmir	Kashmir	*AN*, III, 1092; *MU*, II, 284; *AA*, I, 452; *ZK*, I, 187-90; *TU*, 7
33.	Zain Khan Koka	Irani	Mar. 1597	Aug. 1601 (D)	4 yrs. 6 mths.	Kabul	Kabul	*AN*, III, 1073, 1192, 1194; *MU*, II, 1024-7; *AA*, I, 368-9; *ZK*, I, 123-4
34.	Qulij Khan	Turani	1601	– (T)	–	Kabul	Kabul	*AN*, III, 1196-7; *MU*, II, 535-6; *AA*, I, 381; *ZK*, I, 172-5
35.	Husain Beg Shaikh Umari	Turani	1602	1606 (recalled to court)	4 yrs.	Mozaffarwal, Bahlulpur, Rohtas (F)	Sindh Sagar Doab (*suba* Lahore)	*AN*, III, 1206-7; *MU*, I, 620; *AA*, I, 504; *TU*, 214
36.	Shah Beg Khan	Turani	Jan.-Feb. 1603	–	–	Ghaznin	Ghaznin	*AN*, III, 1223; *MU*, II, 740; *AA*, I, 409, 416

TABLE 3.10: ASSIGNMENT OF *JAGIRS* IN *SUBA* LAHORE

S. No.	*Name of Assignee*	*Racial Group*	*Period*		*Approximate Tenure*	*Jagirs*	*Sarkar*	*Sources*
			From	*To*				
			Year(s) of Assignment Conferred/ Held	*Year(s) of Transfer (T), Revolt by Jagirdars (R), Flight (F), Death (D), etc.*		*Sarkar (S), Pargana (P), Qasba (Q), Fort (F), etc.*		
1	*2*	*3*	*4*	*5*	*6*	*7*	*8*	*9*
1.	Khizar Khwaja Khan	Turani	Mar. 1556	–	–	Lahore (Q)	Bari Doab	*AN*, II, 50, 73; Elliot, V, 254; *TA*, II, 221; *MU*, I, 813-14; Farishta, II, 113: *AA*, I, 394 (n. I); *ZK*, I, 209; *TU*, 56
2.	Haji Muhammad Khan Sistani	Irani	Nov. 1556	1559 (recalled to court)[128]	3 yrs.	Lahore (Q)	Bari Doab	*AN*, II, 73-4; *MU*, II, 167-8; *AA*, I, 405; *ZK*, I, 231

1	*2*	*3*	*4*	*5*	*6*	*7*	*8*	*9*
3.	Sikandar Khan Uzbek (Khan-i-Aalam)	Turani	Dec. 1556	–	–	Sialkot (Q)	Rechna Doab	*AN*, II, 74, 376; *MU*, I, 691; *AA*, I, 394-5; Arif, 119; *ZK*, I, 213
4.	Abul Qasim (b/o Muhammad Qasim Khan Mauji)	Turani	Jul. 1557	–	–	Mankot (F)	Rechna Doab	*AN*, II, 91
5.	Husain Khan Tukriya	Turani	Dec. 1557	1559 (F)	2 yrs.	*Parganas*	(Lahore)	*AN*, II, 96-7; *MU*, I, 644-5; *AA*, I, 403; *ZK*, I, 221; *TU*, 47
6.	Shamsuddin Muhammad Khan Atka (Khan-i-Azam)	Turani	Mar. 1560	May 1562 (D)	2 yrs. 3 mths.	Bhera, Khushab	Chinhat Doab Sindh Sagar Doab	*AN*, II, 143; *ZK*, I, 80; *MU*, II, 158-9; *AA*, I, 337-8; Farishta, 127
			Sept. 1560	May 1562 (D)	1 yr. 9 mths.	Choicest part of Panjab	Bari Doab	*AN*, II, 177; *TA*, II, 257; Bayazid, 245
7.	Mir Muhammad Atka (Khan-i-Kalan)	Turani	Mar. 1560	Aug.1568 (T)	8 yrs. 6 mths.	*Parganas*	(Lahore)	*AN*, II, 143, 299, 361-2, 421-2; *TA*, II, 290, 322; Arif, 130; Bayazid, 270; *MU*, II, 152-4; *AA*, I, 338-9; *TU*, 149

8. Qutbuddin Khan Atka	Turani	Mar. 1560	Aug. 1568 (T)	8 yrs. 6 mths.	*Parganas*	(Lahore)	*AN*, II, 299, 362, 421-2; *TA*, II, 290; Bayazid, 270; *MU*, II, 545-6; *AA*, I, 353-4; *ZK*, I, 213; *TU*, 136
9. Sharif Khan Atka	Turani	Mar. 1560	Aug. 1568 (T)	8 yrs. 6 mths.	*Parganas*	(Lahore)	*AN*, II, 299, 362, 421-2; *TA*, II, 290; Bayazid, 270; *MU*, II, 820-1; *AA*, I, 415-16; *ZK*, I, 215; *TU*, 95
10. Mahdi Qasim Khan	Turani	Mar. 1560	1565-6 (T)	5-6 yrs.	Lahore (Q)	Bari Doab	*AN*, II, 143, 299, 362; *TA*, II, 316, 322; Bayazid, 270; *MU*, II, 503-5; *AA*, I, 372-3
11. Mirza Abdullah Mughal	Turani	Apr.-May 1560	–	–	Pathara/Thara	Bari Doab	*AN*, II, 167; Bayazid, 225; *AA*, I, 432
12. Jan Muhammad Bihsudi	–	Apr.-May 1562	1565	3 yrs.	Birka (P)	Bet Jalan-dhar Doab	*AN*, II, 261, 299, 362; Bayazid, 270
13. Raja Kapur Deo	Rajput	Aug. 1563	–	–	*Parganas*	Lahore	*AN*, II, 299; Bayazid, 270

(contd.)

1	2	3	4	5	6	7	8	9
14.	Raja Ram Chand	Rajput	Aug. 1563	–	–	*Parganas*	Lahore	*AN*, II, 299; Bayazid, 270
15.	Munim Khan (Khan-i-Khanan)	Turani	(1563)	1567 (T)	4 yrs.	Shahpur, Kalnaur, Jalandhar	Bari Doab Bari Doab Bari Doab	*AN*, II, 294; Bayazid, 240, 248-50, 299; *MU*, II, 284-6; *AA*, I, 333-4; *ZK*, I, 24-5
16.	Kamal Khan Gakkhar (Chief of Gakkhar)	Afghan	Sept.1563	–	–	*Parganas*	(Lahore)	*AN*, II, 362; *TA*, II, 267-8; Arif, 104, 130; *ZK*, I, 216-17; *MU*, I, 758-60; *TU*, 141; *ZK*, I, 216-17
17.	Hasan Sufi Sultan	–	(1565)	–	–	*Parganas*	(Lahore)	*AN*, II, 362
18.	Fazil Muhammad Khan	Turani	(1565)	–	–	*Parganas*	(Lahore)	*AN*, II, 362
19.	Sayyid Muhammad Khan Baraha	Indian Muslim	(1567)	–	–	*Parganas*	(Lahore)	Arif, 130; *AA*, I, 424; *ZK*, I, 181-2
20.	Khurram Khan	Turani	(1567)	–	–	*Parganas*	(Lahore)	Arif, 130.
21.	Husain Quli Khan (Khan-i-Jahan)	Irani	Aug.-Sept. 1568	Oct.-Nov. 1575 (T)	7 yrs.	*Parganas*	(Lahore)	*AN*, II, 486-7, 529; *AN*, III, 56; *MT*, II,

							109, 137, 164; *TA*, II, 218, 316, 352, 366, 396, 407, 480; Arif, 171, 194, 226; *MU*, I, 645-8; Farishta, II, 147-8, 151; *AA*, I, 349-50
22. Ismail Quli Khan	Irani	Aug.-Sept. 1568	Oct.-Nov. 1575 (T)	7 yrs.	*Parganas*	(Lahore)	*AN*, II, 529; *MT*, II, 109; *TA*, II, 351, 366, 615; *MU*, I, 703-4; *AA*, I, 384-8; *TU*, 8; *ZK*, I, 213
23. Said Khan Chaghta	Turani	Sept.-Oct. 1573	Jun. 1583 (T)	10 yrs.	*Parganas*	Lahore Multan	*AN*, III, 61-2, 356; *MT*, II, 138, 168, 261; *TA*, II, 367, 513; Arif, 194; *MU*, II, 679-80; *AA*, I, 351-2; *TU*, 83; *ZK*, I, 190-3
24. Raja Birbar	Hindu	Mar.-Apr. 1573	–	–	*Nagarkot*	Bari Doab	*AN*, III, 52; *TA*, II, 398-9; *MT*, II, 165; *MU*, I, 420-1; *AA*, I, 442-3; *ZK*, I, 183-5

(contd.)

1	*2*	*3*	*4*	*5*	*6*	*7*	*8*	*9*
25.	Mirza Yusuf Khan	Irani	Oct.-Nov. 1573	–	–	*Parganas*	(Lahore)	*AN*, III, 61-2; *MU*, II, 1001-7; *AA*, I, 369-72; *TU*, 189
26.	Raja Bhagwan Das	Rajput	Sept.-Oct. 1578	Oct.-Nov. 1587 (T)	9 yrs.	*Sarkars/ Parganas*	(Lahore)	*AN*, III, 358, 380, 801; *MT*, II, 218; *TA*, II, 552; *MU*, I, 404-5; *AA*, I, 353; *ZK*, I, 103
27.	Jagannath (s/o Raja Bahar Mal)	Rajput	Dec. 1578	1581 (T)	3 yrs.	*Parganas*	(Lahore)	*AN*, III, 380, 546; *MU*, I, 724; *AA*, I, 421-2
28.	Raja Gopal	Rajput	Dec. 1578	–	–	*Parganas*	(Lahore)	*AN*, III, 380; *TU*, 267
29.	Jagmal	Rajput	Dec. 1578	–	–	*Parganas*	(Lahore)	*AN*, III, 380; *MU*, I, 727; *AA*, I, 483
30.	Rahman Quli Qush Begi	–	Jan. 1578	–	–	Thara/Pathara (P)	Bari Doab	*AN*, III, 333; Arif, 271
31.	Man Singh	Rajput	Nov.-Dec. 1578	1587 (T)	9 yrs.	Sialkot Nilab	Rechna Doab Sindh Sagar Doab	*AN*, III, 493-4, 508; *MT*, II, 376; *ZK*, I, 103-11; *MU*, II, 48-57; *AA*, I, 361-3

32. Mirza Yusuf Khan	Irani	Nov.-Dec. 1580	–	–	Rohtas	Sindh Sagar Doab	*AN*, III, 493, 507
33. Rai Rai Singh	Rajput	Oct. 1581	1583 (T)	2 yrs.	*Parganas*	(Lahore)	*AN*, III, 546; *MU*, II, 567-8; *AA*, I, 384-5; *ZK*, I, 215
34. Birbar	Hindu	(Mar.-Apr. 1581)	–	–	Desuha (P)	Bet-Jalandhar Doab	*AN*, III, 511; *ZK*, I, 183-5
35. Khwaja Shamsuddin Khafi	Irani	Jun.-Jul. 1581	–	–	Katak–Benaras (F)	Sindh Sagar Doab	*AN*, III, 520-1; *AA*, I, 495; *MU*, II, 804-5; *ZK*, I, 195-6
36. Bayazid Bayat	Turani	(1584)	–	–	Sunam	Bet-Jalandhar Doab	Bayazid, 357-62
37. Muhammad Sadiq Khan	Irani	1588	1593 (T)	5 yrs.	Sialkot (Q)	Rechna Doab	*AN*, III, 806; *MT*, II, 376; *TA*, II, 622; *MU*, II, 660-1; *AA*, I, 382-4; *ZK*, I, 176
38. Zain Khan Koka	Irani	1588	1591	3 yrs.	Sialkot, Zainabad (Badalgarh)	Rechna Doab	*AN*, III, 790, 817, 916; *ZK*, I, 123-4; *MU*, II, 1022-8; *AA*, I, 367-9

(contd.)

1	2	3	4	5	6	7	8	9
39.	Hamza Arab	–	(Aug. 1591)	–	–	Bhimbar (P)	Chinhat Doab	*AN*, III, 908
40.	Shah Beg Khan	Turani	(Apr. 1594)	–	–	Khushab Bangash	Sindh Sagar Doab	*AN*, III, 1000; *MU*, II, 740-43; *AA*, I, 408-10
41.	Salahauddin Banga	–	Mar. 1594	–	–	*Parganas*	(Lahore)	*AN*, III, 998
42.	Rai Manohar	Rajput	Mar. 1594	–	–	*Parganas*	(Lahore)	*AN*, III, 998
43.	Takht Beg	Turani	Mar. 1594	–	–	*Parganas*	(Lahore)	*AN*, III, 998
44.	Bahadur Khan Qurdar	Turani	Mar. 1594	–	–	*Parganas*	(Lahore)	*AN*, III, 998
45.	Shaikh Khubu	Indian Muslim	Mar. 1594	–	–	*Parganas*	(Lahore)	*AN*, III, 998
46.	Muqim Khan	–	Mar. 1594	–	–	*Parganas*	(Lahore)	*AN*, III, 998
47.	Khwaja Muhibb Ali Khafi	Irani	Mar. 1594	–	–	*Parganas*	(Lahore)	*AN*, III, 998
48.	Shaikh Kabir	Indian Muslim	Mar. 1594	–	–	*Parganas*	(Lahore)	*AN*, III, 998
49.	Hakim Muzaffar	Irani	Mar. 1594	–	–	*Parganas*	(Lahore)	*AN*, III, 998

50. Mir Murad Sarmat	Turani	Mar. 1594	1597	3 yrs.	Bhimbar (P)	Chinhat Doab	*AN*, III, 998, 1082
51. Mir Abul Qasim Namkin	Irani	Jan.-Feb. 1595	1598	3 yrs.	Bhera (P)	Chinhat Doab	*AN*, III, 1021, 1117; *MU*, II, 508-9; *AA*, I, 525-6; *ZK*, I, 198-200
					Gujrat (P)	Chinhat Doab	
					Khushab (P)	Sindh Sagar Doab	
52. Mirza Rustam	Irani	Jun. 1596	1597-8	1-2 yrs.	Pathankot (P) (Paithan)	Bari Doab	*AN*, III, 1060; *MU*, II, 633-4; *AA*, I, 329
53. Hasan Beg Shaikh Umari	Turani	1602	–	–	Rohtas (F)	Sindh Sagar Doab	*AA*, I, 504
54. Qulij Khan	Turani	(1602-3)	–	–	*Parganas*	(Lahore)	*AN*, III, 1196, 1235, 1250; *MU*, II, 536; *TU*, 137

TABLE 3.11: ASSIGNMENT OF *JAGIRS* IN *SUBA* MALWA

S. No.	*Name of Assignee*	*Racial Group*	*Period*		*Approxi-mate Tenure*	*Jagirs*	*Sarkar*	*Sources*
			From	*To*		*Sarkar (S), Pargana (P), Qasba (Q), Fort (F), etc.*		
			Year(s) of Assignment Conferred/ Held	*Year(s) of Transfer (T), Revolt by Jagirdars (R), Flight (F), Death (D), etc.*				
1	*2*	*3*	*4*	*5*	*6*	*7*	*8*	*9*
1.	Adham Khan (s/o Maham Anga)	Turani	Mar. 1561	Jan. 1562 (T)	11 mths.	Sarangpur (S) and other selected *parganas*	Sarangpur	*AN*, II, 214, 235; *TA*, II, 260; Arif, 97; *MU*, I, 145-6; *AA*, I, 341-2; *TU*, 5; *ZK*, I, 124-6
2.	Pir Muhammad Khan	Turani	Mar. 1561	1562 (D)	1-2 yrs.	Mandu (S) Ujjain (S)	Mandu Ujjain	*AN*, II, 214, 235; *TA*, II, 255, 260; Farishta, II, 127; Arif, 97; *MU*, II, 480; *AA*, I, 442-3; *TU*, 31; *ZK*, I, 101-2

3.	Qaya Khan Gung	Irani	Mar. 1561	1562-3 (F)	1-2 yrs.	Handia (S)	Handia	*AN*, II, 214, 259; *TA*, II, 261 n; *MU*, II, 531; *AA*, I, 366; *TU*, 134; *ZK*, I, 210
4.	Sadiq Muhammad Khan	Irani	Mar. 1561	–	–	Mandasor *wa-an-hudud*	–	*AN*, II, 214
5.	Abdullah Khan Uzbek	Turani	Aug, 1562	Jul. 1564 (F)	2 yrs.	Mandu (S)	Mandu	*AN*, II, 260; Arif, 97, 113; Bayazid, 243; *TA*, II, 283; Farishta, II, 132; *MU*, I, 82; *AA*, I, 337; *TU*, 112; *ZK*, I, 209
6.	Shah Muhammad Qalati	Irani	(Aug. 1562)	–	–	*Parganas*	(Malwa)	*AN*, II, 259; *MU*, III, 758-9; *AA*, I, 449; *TU*, 96
7.	Habib Ali Khan	Irani	(Aug. 1562)	1562 (D)	Few mths.	*Parganas*	(Malwa)	*AN*, II, 259; *AA*, I, 483; *TU*, 50
8.	Abdul Majid Asaf Khan	Irani	Apr.-Jun. 1564	Sept. 1565 (F)	1 yr. 4 mths.	*Parganas*	Garaha-Katanga	*AN*, II, 324; *TA*, II, 296, 316; *MU*, I, 38-9; *AA*, I, 397; *TU*, 7; *ZK*, I, 122-3

(contd.)

1	2	3	4	5	6	7	8	9
9.	Muhammad Qasim Khan Nishapuri	Irani	Jun.-Jul. 1564	–	–	Sarangpur (S)	Sarangpur	*AN*, II, 345; *TA*, II, 283; Farishta, II, 132; *MU*, II, 516; *AA*, I, 379; *TU*, 134-5; *ZK*, I, 211-12
10.	Khan Quli (*Gumashta*-i-Abdullah Khan)	–	Jul.-Aug. 1564	–	–	Handia (P)	Handia	*AN*, II, 285, 351
11.	Muqarrab Khan	–	Jul.-Aug. 1564	–	–	Satwas (F)	Handia	*AN*, II, 351, 415; *TA*, II, 285; *AA*, I, 403
12.	Qara Bahadur Khan	Turani	Jul.-Aug. 1564	–	–	Mandu (S)	Mandu	*AN*, II, 252-3; *TA*, II, 285-6; *AA*, I, 513; *TU*, 134
13.	Mahdi Qasim Khan	Turani	1565-6	1566 (F)	1 yr.	Garaha (S)	Garaha	*AN*, II, 404-5, 491; *MU*, II, 504; *AA*, I, 372-3; *TU*, 150
14.	Shah Quli Khan Naranji	Irani	May 1566	–	–	*Parganas*	Garaha	*AN*, II, 406; *MU*, II, 777; *AA*, I, 537; *TU*, 96; *ZK*, I, 229
15.	Kakar Ali Khan	Turani	May. 1566	–	–	*Parganas*	Garaha	*AN*, II, 406; *MU*, I, 757; *AA*, I, 447; *TU*, 142

16. Shahabuddin Ahmad Khan	Turani	Jan.-Mar. 1566/7	Jul.-Aug. 1568	1–2 yrs.	Garaha (S), Sironj (P)	Garaha Chanderi	*AN*, II, 403, 462, 485; Farishta, II, 140; *TA*, II, 342, 351, 496, 498; *MT*, II, 110; *AA*, I, 352-3; *MU*, II, 847-8; *ZK*, I, 101
17. Khwaja Hadi (Khwaja Kilan)	Irani	Jan.-Mar. 1567	–	–	Ujjain (P)	Ujjain	*AN*, II, 415
18. Qadam Khan (b/o Muqarrab Khan)	–	Jan.-Feb. 1567	1567 (killed)	Few mths.	Handia (P)	Handia	*AN*, II, 415
19. Muhammad Quli Khan Barlas	Turani	Jan.-Mar. 1567	Aug.-Sept. 1567 (T)	Few mths.	*Parganas*	Malwa	*AN*, II, 415; *MU*, II, 184; *AA*, I, 364; *TU*, 150; *ZK*, I, 209
20. Shah Budagh Khan	Turani	Sept.-Oct. 1567	1577	10 yrs.	*Parganas*	Sarangpur	*AN*, II, 462, 485; *AN*, III, 32; *MT*, II, 105, 110; *TA*, II, 342, 351; Arif, 268; *MU*, II, 745; *AA*, I, 402; *TU*, 95; *ZK*, I, 210-11
21. Murad Khan	Turani	Sept.-Oct. 1567	1572-3 (T)	5-6 yrs.	*Parganas*	Ujjain	*AN*, II, 462, 485; *MT*, II, 105; *TA*, II, 342, 351, 390; *MU*, II, 170-1; *AA*, I, 404; *TU*, 152

1	2	3	4	5	6	7	8	9
22.	Hajji Muhammad Khan Sistani	Irani	Sept.-Oct. 1567	1575 (T)	8 yrs.	*Parganas*	Mandu	*AN*, II, 462; *MT*, II, 105; *TA*, II, 342; *MU*, II, 169; *AA*, I, 405-6; *ZK*, I, 231
23.	Abdul Majid Asaf Khan	Irani	Sept.-Oct. 1567	–	–	*Parganas* near Gagraun	Gagraun	*AN*, II, 464; *TU*, 7; *ZK*, I, 122-3
24.	Wazir Khan	Irani	Sept.-Oct. 1567	–	–	*Parganas* near Gagraun	Gagraun	*AN*, II, 464; *ZK*, I, 211
25.	Mirza Aziz Mashhadi (Mir Muizzulmulk)	Irani	Feb.-Mar. 1568	–	–	*Parganas*	Ujjain	*TA*, II, 351; *MT*, II, 110; *AA*, I, 414; *MU*, II, 238-9
26.	Qutbuddin Muhammad Khan	Turani	Dec. 1572	–	–	*Parganas*	(Malwa)	*AN*, III, 25, 32, 46-7; *TA*, II, 390, 498; *AA*, I, 353-4; *MU*, II, 546; *ZK*, I, 213
27.	Abdul Muttalab Khan (s/o Shah Budagh Khan)	Turani	(Jan. 1573)	–	–	*Parganas*	(Malwa)	*AN*, III, 32; *MU*, I, 40-1; *AA*, I, 441; *TU*, 114; *ZK*, I, 248
28.	Man Singh	Rajput	Aug. 1573	–	–	Kachiwara (P)	(Malwa)	*AN*, III, 62; Khyat, I, 342; *ZK*, I, 103
29.	Muzaffar Khan	Irani	(Nov. 1573)	–	–	*Parganas*,[129] *Parganas*, Sultanpur	Saragpur Ujjain Nandurbar	*TA*, II, 394-5; Bayazid, 334; Arif, 200, 215

30. Rai Surjan Hada	Rajput	–	Nov. 1575 (T)	–	Garaha (S)	Garaha	*AN*, III, 223; *AA*, I, 450; *ZK*, I, 228-9
31. Sadiq Khan	Irani	Nov. 1575	–	–	Garaha (S)	Garaha	*AN*, III, 223; *TU*, 105; *ZK*, I, 176
32. Shahabuddin Ahmad Khan	Turani	Sept.-Oct. 1576	Oct.-Nov 1577(T)	1 yr.	Sarangpur (S), Gargaun (F)	Sarangpur Mandu	*AN*, III, 306; Arif, 268; *MT*, II, 249, 251; *TU*, 94-5
33. Bayazid Bayat	Turani	Sept.-Oct. 1576	–	–	*Parganas*	Ujjain Sarangpur	Bayazid, 353
34. Muqim-i-Arab (Sujaat Khan)	Turani	Mar.-Apr. 1577	Jun.-Jul. 1580(killed)	3 yrs. 3 mths.	Sarangpur (S)	Sarangpur	Bayazid, 353; *MT*, II, 292; *TA*, II, 498, 537; Arif, 268; *MU*, II, 851-2; *AA*, I, 401; *TU*, 92; *ZK*, I, 210
35. Qasim Khan	Irani	(Oct.-Nov. 1577)	–	–	*Parganas*	(Malwa)	*AN*, III, 306
36. Tahir Khan	Irani	(Oct.-Nov. 1577)	–	–	*Parganas*	(Malwa)	*AN*, III, 306
37. Naqib Khan	Irani	(Oct.-Nov. 1577)	–	–	*Parganas*	(Malwa)	*AN*, III, 306; *ZK*, I, 237
38. Qamar Khan	Irani	(Oct.-Nov. 1577)	–	–	*Parganas*	(Malwa)	*AN*, III, 306; *ZK*, I, 216-17

1	2	3	4	5	6	7	8	9
39.	Firuz	–	(Oct.-Nov. 1577)	–	–	*Parganas*	(Malwa)	*AN*, III, 306; *ZK*, I, 216-17
40.	Shaikh Muazzam	Indian Muslim	(Oct.-Nov. 1577)	–	–	*Parganas*	(Malwa)	*AN*, III, 306; *ZK*, I, 216-17
41.	Shaikh Junaid	Indian Muslim	(Oct.-Nov. 1577)	–	–	*Parganas*	(Malwa)	*AN*, III, 306; *ZK*, I, 216-17
42.	Shah Fakhruddin Khan (Naqib Khan)	Irani	Dec. 1577	Dec. 1578 (T)	1 yr.	Ujjain (S)	Ujjain	*AN*, III, 382; *TA*, II, 496, 498; Arif, 268 (n. 7)
43.	Sharif Khan Atka and his son Baz Bahadur	Turani	Sept.-Oct. 1579	1594 (T)	15 yrs.	*Parganas*	(Malwa)	*AN*, III, 459, 657, 701, 878; *MT*, II, 293; *TA*, II, 501, 538, 571; *MU*, II, 820-1; *AA*, I, 416; *TU*, 95; *ZK*, I, 215
44.	Khan Azam Mirza Aziz Koka	Turani	Jul.-Dec. 1584	Dec. 1589[130] (T)	5 yrs.	Garaha (S), Raisin (S)	Garaha Raisin	*AN*, III, 629, 655, 701, 739, 865, 886, 891; *MT*, II, 383-4; *TA*, II, 585, 629; *MU*, I, 323-5; *AA*, I, 343-6; *ZK*, I, 80-99

45. Naurang Khan (s/o Qutbuddin Muhammad Khan)	Turani	(Oct. 1584)	1594 (D)	10 yrs.	*Parganas*	(Malwa)	*AN*, III, 642, 657; *TA*, II, 498, 571; *TU*, 177
46. Qulij Khan	Turani	(Oct. 1584)	1594 (D)	10 yrs.	*Parganas*	(Malwa)	*AN*, III, 642, 657; *TA*, II, 498, 571; *TU*, 177
47. Tulak Khan	Turani	(Oct. 1584)	1594 (D)	10 yrs.	*Parganas*	(Malwa)	*AN*, III, 642, 657; *TA*, II, 498, 571; *TU*, 177
48. Rai Durga	Rajput	(1585)	–	–	*Parganas*	(Malwa)	*TA*, II, 584-5; *ZK*, I, 226
49. Raja Askaran	Rajput	(1585)	–	–	*Parganas*	(Malwa)	*TA*, II, 584-5; *ZK*, I, 226
50. Burhan-ul-Mulk	Irani	(1585)	1591	6 yrs.	*Parganas*	(Malwa)	*TA*, II, 584-5; *AN*, III, 891
51. Shaikh Abdullah	Indian Muslim	(1585)	–	–	*Parganas*	(Malwa)	*TA*, II, 584-5; *AN*, III, 891
52. Subhan Quli Turk	–	(1585)	–	–	*Parganas*	(Malwa)	*TA*, II, 584-5; *AN*, III, 891
53. Shahabuddin Ahmad Khan	Turani	Apr. 1585	1591 (D)	6 yrs.	Raisin (S)	Raisin	*AN*, III, 687, 865, 877, 885; *MT*, II, 384; *TA*, II, 585-6, 629n; Farishta, II, 162; *MU*, II, 849

1	*2*	*3*	*4*	*5*	*6*	*7*	*8*	*9*
54.	Muhammad Baqi Khan (b/o Adham Khan)	Turani	–	1585 (D)	–	Garaha/Katanga (P)	Garaha	*MT*, II, 351; *AA*, I, 413; *MU*, I, 385
55.	Muhibb Ali Khwafi	Irani	Dec. 1590	–	–	*Parganas*	(Malwa)	*AN*, III, 885, 915
56.	Hakim Ain-ul-Mulk	Irani	(Dec. 1590)	1595 (D)	5 yrs.	Handia (D)	Handia	*AN*, III, 886; *MT*, II, 417; *AA*, I, 537; *TU*, 197
57.	Nazr Be Qambar Be (s/o Nazr Be)	Afghan	–	1591 (F & D)	–	Handia (S)	Handia	*AN*, III, 915
58.	Jamaluddin Husain	Irani	(1591)	–	–	*Parganas*	Handia	*AN*, III, 915; *ZK*, I, 196-7
59.	Ismail Quli Khan	Irani	Sept. 1591[131]	1593-4 (called to court)	2-3 yrs	*Parganas*	(Malwa)	*AN*, III, 914; *MT*, II, 401; *MU*, I, 704; *AA*, I, 388-9; *ZK*, I, 213-14
60.	Mukhtar Beg	–	Sept. 1591	–	–	*Parganas*	(Malwa)	*AN*, III, 914; *AA*, I, 558; *TU*, 8
61.	Sultan Murad	Prince	Sept. 1591	Apr.1593 (T)	1 yr. 8 mths.	*Parganas*	(Malwa)	*AN*, III, 911, 922; *TA*, II, 634, 648; *TU*, 165

62. Mirza Shahrukh (s/o Mirza Ibrahim)	Turani	Oct. 1594 Jan. 1597[132]	1604-5	10 yrs.	*Parganas* Ujjain and other choice *Parganas* of Malwa	(Malwa) Ujjain	*AN*, III, 991, 1069, 1120, 1216; *TA*, II, 649; *MT*, II, 401; *MU*, II, 781; *AA*, I, 326; *TU*, 222; *ZK*, I, 20-3
63. Shahbaz Khan Kambu	Indian Muslim	Oct. 1594[133]	Jan. 1597 (resumed)[134]	2 yrs. 4 mths.	*Parganas*	(Malwa)	*AN*, III, 1069, 1092; *TA*, II, 649; *MU*, II, 736-7; *AA*, I, 439; *TU*, 97
64. Abdur Rahim Mirza Khan (Khan-i-Khanan)	Irani	(Jun 1595)	–	–	Bhilsa and other *Parganas*	Raisin	*AN*, III, 1045, *MU*, I, 54-6; *AA*, I, 355-7; *TU*, 54; *ZK*, I, 31-63
65. Mirza Rustam	Irani	Jan.-Feb. 1599	1605	6 yrs.	Raisin (S) and its territories	Raisin	*AN*, III, 1120, 1144; *MU*, II, 634, *AA*, I, 329; *TU*, 218; *ZK*, I, 216
66. Rai Rayan (Rai Patar Das, Raja Bikramjit)	Hindu	(Mar.-Apr. 1602)	–	–	*Parganas*	Garaha	*AN*, III, 1208
67. Shaikh Abdar Rahman (s/o Abul Fazl)	Indian Muslim	1602	–	–	*Parganas*	(Malwa)	*AN*, III, 1223-4

TABLE 3.12: ASSIGNMENT OF *JAGIRS* IN *SUBA MULTAN*

S. No.	*Name of Assignee*	*Racial Group*	*Period*		*Approximate Tenure*	*Jagirs*	*Sarkar*	*Sources*
			From	*To*		*Sarkar (S), Pargana (P), Qasba (Q), Fort (F), etc.*		
			Year(s) of Assignment Conferred/ Held	*Year(s) of Transfer (T), Revolt by Jagirdars (R), Flight (F), Death (D), etc.*				
1	*2*	*3*	*4*	*5*	*6*	*7*	*8*	*9*
1.	Muhammad Quli Khan Barlas	Turani	1555	Mar. 1557	2 yrs.	*Parganas*	Multan	*AN*, II, 83-4; *MU*, II, 183-4; *ZK*, I, 209; *AA*, I, 364
2.	Bahadur Khan	Irani	Mar.1557	1559 (T)	2 yrs.	Dipalpur (S)	Dipalpur	*AN*, II, 83-4, 94, 155; *MT*, II, 4; Farishta, II, 111; *MU*, I, 348; *AA*, I, 34
3.	Darwesh Muhammad Uzbek	Irani	Mar.-Apr. 1560	–	–	Dipalpur (S)	Dipalpur	Arif, 86; Bayazid, 226; *TA*, II, 244; Farishta, II, 123; *AA*, I, 440-1

4.	Shamsuddin Mahhamad Khan Atka (Khan-i-Azam)	Turani	Oct. 1560	May 1562	1 yr. 8 mths.	Firuzpur	Dipalpur	*AN*, II, 177, 185; *TA*, II, 257; Bayazid, 245; *ZK*, I, 80; *MU*, II, 158-9; *AA*, I, 337-8
5.	Muhammad Qasim Nishapuri, Abul Qasim Akhund and others	Irani	Aug.-Sept. 1560	Jun.-Jul. 1564	4 yrs.	*Parganas*	Multan	*AN*, II, 175; *MU*, II, 516-8; *AA*, I, 379; *ZK*, I, 211-2; *MU*, II, 515-16
6.	Mirza Aziz Koka (Khan-i-Azam)	Turani	1560	1572	12 yrs.	Pakpattan, Dipalpur	Dipalpur	*AN*, II, 528; *MT*, II, 137; *TA*, II, 364; Arif, 171; *ZK*, I, 80-98; *MU* I, 319-20; *AA*, I, 343-7
7.	Muhammad Quli Khan Barlas	Turani	Mar. 1563	Jan.-Mar. 1567 (T)	4 yrs.	*Parganas*	Multan	*AN*, II, 175, 290, 362, 415; *TA*, II, 290; *ZK*, I, 209; *MU*, II, 183-4; *AA*, I, 364; *TU*, 150
8.	Muhibb Ali Khan (s/o Mir Khalifa) and Mujahid Khan (his grandson)	Turani	Mar.-Apr. 1571	1574-5 (T)	3-4 yrs.	*Parganas*[135]	Multan	*MR*, II, 340-2; *TM*, 235-6; *MT*, II, 138; *TA*, II, 367; Arif, 233-4; *MU*, II, 222-

(contd.)

1	2	3	4	5	6	7	8	9
								3; *AA*, I, 463-65; *ZK*, I, 166-70
9.	Said Khan Chaghta	Turani	Mar.-Apr. 1571	1578 (recalled to court)	7 yrs.	*Parganas*	Multan	*AN*, III, 53, 61-2, 356; *MT*, II, 138, 168, 261; *TA*, II, 367, 394, 513; Arif, 194; *MU*, II, 679-80; *AA*, I, 351-2; *TU*, 83; *ZK*, I, 190-3
10.	Makhsus Khan (s/o Said Khan Chaghta)	Turani	Oct.-Nov. 1573	–	–	*Parganas*	Multan	*AN*, III, 61-2; *MU*, II, 41-2; *AA*, I, 422; *ZK*, I, 230
11.	Mir Gesu Khan Khurasani	Turani	–	Oct. 1574 (D)	–	Bhakkar (F)	Bhakkar	*AN*, III, 615, *TA*, II, 457; Arif, 233-4; *MU*, I, 575
12.	Mir Saiyid Muhammad (Mir-i-Adl)	Indian Muslim	Oct.-Nov. 1575	Oct. 1576 (D)	1 yr.	Bhakkar	Bhakkar	*AN*, III, 224; *MT*, II, 252; *AA*, I, 485; Elliot, I, 243
13.	Mir Sayyid Abul Qasim, Mir Sayyid Abul Fazl (sons of Mir Sayyid Muhammad)	Indian Muslim	–	Feb.-Mar. 1577 (recalled to court)	–	Siwistan	Bhakkar	*MT*, II, 252; *AA*, I, 548

14. Itimad Khan Khwajasara	Indian Muslim	Oct. 1576	–	–	Bhakkar	Bhakkar	*AA*, I, 13n, 473; *MU*, I, 708-9; Elliot, I, 243; *ZK*, I, 216
15. Sayyid Hamid Bukhari	Indian Muslim	Aug.-Sept. 1577	1581	4 yrs.	*Parganas*	(Multan)	*AN*, III, 300, 508, 546; *MU*, I, 608-10; *AA*, I, 433-4; *TU*, 214
16. Khwaja Shah Mansur	Irani	(1581)	–	–	Firuzpur (P)	Dipalpur	*AN*, II, 503; *MT*, 300-1; *TA*, II, 546; *MU*, II, 750-5; *AA*, 475-7
17. Sharif Beg (Mansur's *shiqdar*)	–	(1581)	–	–	Firuzpur (P)	Dipalpur	*MT*, II, 300-1; *TA*, II, 546
18. Muhammad Sadiq Khan	Irani	Oct.-Nov. 1585	Jul. 1587 (T) (recalled to court)	1 yr. 9 mths.	Multan (S), Bhakkar (S)	Multan	*AN*, III, 708, 717, 792; *MT*, II, 359, 369-70; *TM*, 248-9; *TA*, II, 605, 621; *MU*, II, 659-61; *AA*, I, 382-4; *ZK*, I, 176
19. Muhibb Ali Khan Rohtasi	Turani	Mar.-Apr. 1589	1589 (D)	Few mths.	Multan (S)	Multan	*AN*, III, 816-17; *AA*, I, 466; *MU*, II, 228-9; *ZK*, I, 215

(contd.)

1	2	3	4	5	6	7	8	9
20.	Abdur Rahim Mirza Khan (Khan-i-Khanan)	Irani	1590	1593 (recalled to court)	3 yrs.	Multan (S), Bhakkar (S)	Multan	*AN*, III, 908, 917; *MT*, II, 386; *TA*, II, 632; *TM*, 249; *MR*, II, 345; *ZK*, I, 31-64; *MU*, I, 50-65; *AA*, I, 354-61
21.	Mir Masum (Historian)	–	1590	1595	5 yrs.	Darbela (P), Kakari (P), Chanduka(P)	Bhakkar Bhakkar Bhakkar	*AN*, III, 1021; *TA*, II, 632; *TM*, 252; *MR*, II, 359
22.	Bakhtiyar Beg and others	Irani	1593	1595	2 yrs.	Siwistan (Sehwan)	Thatta	*AN*, III, 986, 1021; *AA*, I, 529
23.	Mirza Shahrukh	Turani	1593	1593	Few mths.[136]	Thatta (S)	Thatta	*AN*, III, 979, 985-6; *MU*, I, 780-1; *AA*, I, 326-7
24.	Mirza Jani Beg	Turani	1593 1593	1593 Feb. 1601[137]	Few mths. 8 yrs.	Multan (S) Thatta[138]	Multan Thatta	*AN*, III, 979, 985-6; *MU*, I, 743-8; *AA*, I, 389-94; *ZK*, I, 176-81; *AN*, III, 986; *MT*, II, 399

25. Mirza Rustam	Irani	Oct. 1594	1595 (T)	1 yr.	Multan and several *parganas* of Baluchistan	Multan Baluchistan	*AN*, III, 993-4, 1011; *MT*, II, 399, 402; *TA*, II, 650; *MU*, II, 632-3; *AA*, I, 328-29; *ZK*, I, 99-101
26. Sayyid Bahauddin Bukhari	Indian Muslim	(1595)	–	–	Uchh	Multan	*AN*, III, 1021
27. Khan Azam Mirza Aziz Koka	Turani	1596	–	–	Multan (S)	Multan	*AN*, III, 1068; *ZK*, I, 80-99
28. Mir Abul Qasim Namakin	Irani	1598	Dec. 1598 (recalled to court)[139]	Few mths.	*Parganas*	Bhakkar	*AN*, III, 1021, 1117; *MU*, II, 509; *AA*, I, 525; *ZK*, I, 198-200
29. Mirza Ghazi Beg (s/o Jani Beg)	Turani	1600	1605	5 yrs.	Thatta (S)[140]	Thatta	*AN*, III, 1172, 1257; *MR*, II, 350; Tuzuk, I, 223; *MU*, II, 534-9; *AA*, I, 380-2; *ZK* (tr.), I, 139; *TU*, 231
30. Said Khan Chaghta	Turani	1602	1605	3 yrs.	Multan (S), Bhakkar (S)	Multan Bhakkar	*AN*, III, 1216, 1257; *AA*, I, 351; *MU*, II, 680; *TU*, 83

NOTES

1. As quoted in Irvine, *The Army of the Indian Moghuls*, p. 15.
2. For *alam* and *naqara*, see Abul Fazl, *Ain-i-Akbari*, 1: 52-3.
3. Abul Fazl, *Ain-i-Akbari* (Blochmann), 1: 410.
4. Abul Fazl, *Akbarnama*, 2: 162-3 [106-7].
5. Farid Bhakkari, *Zakhirat-ul-Khawanin*, 1: 17. According to Farid Bhakkari, 25 persons of lower rank were promoted to the *mansab* of 5000 by Bairam Khan. Cf. *Akbarnama*, 2: 163 [107]. The menial servants of Bairam Khan were promoted to the status of *khans* and *sultans*.
6. Abul Fazl, *Akbarnama*, 2: 162 [106-7]; Abul Fazl writes,

   To his own menial servants . . . he gave the titles of *Sultan* and *Khan* and presented them with . . . rich fiefs and productive territories, whilst he with total want of considerations made the *Khans*, the Princes, the officers, and the trusted servants of H.M. *Jinnat Ashiyani*, whose rank, claims and qualifications are known to everyone, to be in want of dry bread. Nay, he aimed at the life and honour of all of them, and he took no thought for old servants and domestics . . . and did not provide them, with even the smallest offices which might have been a means of livelihood to them.
7. Abul Fazl, *Ain-i-Akbari*, 1: 248; *Akbarnama*, 3: 1031 [671], 'An officer whose contingent comes up to his *mansab*, is put into the first class of his rank, if his contingent is one half and upward, he is put into the second class; the third class contains, those contingents which are still less'.
8. For a salary list of nobles, see Abul Fazl, *Ain-i-Akbari*, 1: 257-8.
9. The estimated income from land revenue of cultivable area was technically known as *jama*, *jamabandi*, *jama-i-raqmi*, *jama-i-qalmi*, *raqmi-i-qalmi*, *Akbarmana*, 2: 402, n. 3 [270]. Originally designed and calculated by Todar Mal on the basis of detailed measurement and old records of the local revenue officers such as *qanungo*. It was on the basis of this assessment of income that the revenues of *mahals* were assigned to *mansabdars* in lieu of their salaries under the Mughals. But as the entire land could not be cultivated, or part of it was damaged due to some calamity, the actual produce was always less than what had been originally ascertained, creating a gap between the two at every harvest. The actual produce was termed *hasil* or *hal-i-hasil*, the real rental realized by *jagirdars*. The *jama-i-raqmi* comprised the revenue figure derived from the previous regime and applied in the early years of Akbar's reign. As the expected income from land revenue was arbitrarily determined by the revenue officers, it could be easily inflated to meet the salary demands of *jagirdars*. The mode of assessment caused great confusion and distress in the rank of *jagirdars* who grew restive and complained. Muzaffar Khan, therefore, abolished this system under instruction from Akbar in 1576. Habib, *The Agrarian System*, pp. 178, 196-7, 240, 243, 261-2; Moreland, *The Agrarian System*, pp. 239-43. See also

Zahiruddin Malik, *Agrarian System in Medieval India*, Delhi: Rawat Publications, 2001, pp. 43-4; Srivastava, *Akbar the Great*, 2: 171-3.

10. Qaisar, 'Distribution of the revenue resources', in *The Mughal State*, ed. Muzaffar Alam and Sanjay Subrahmanyam, pp. 252-7. See for sanctioned pay schedule Shyamal Das, *Vir-Vinod*, 4 vols, Delhi: Motilal Banarsidass, 1966, 2: 428-31; W.H. Moreland, 'Description of Assignment Order', *Journal of Royal Asiatic Society*, 1936, pp. 641-2. However, a study has argued that the *jama-i-dahsala* could not all times and in all places exactly represent the actual receipts.
11. Shireen Moosvi, 'The Magnitude of the Land Revenue Demand and the Income of the Mughal Ruling Class Under Akbar', *Medieval India: A Miscellany IV*, pp. 96-7; Moreland, 'Description of Assignment Order', pp. 641-2.
12. Athar Ali, *The Mughal Nobility Under Aurangzeb*, p. 76.
13. Bayazid was obviously given a concession when Akbar offered him the *jagir* of Sunam with a *jama* of 29 lakh *dams* and the permission to keep any excess revenue for himself. Bayazid Bayat, *Tazkira-i-Humayun wa Akbar*, p. 363.
14. Abul Fazl, *Akbarnama*, 3: 692-3 [458-9].
15. Athar Ali, *The Mughal Nobility Under Aurangzeb*, p. 76.
16. There are numerous such references when officers were deputed to settle the *jama* of different *parganas*, *sarkars* and *subas*. See Abul Fazl, *Akbarnama*, 2: 260-1 [168-9], 402, n. 1 [270], 3: 91-3 [65-7], 166-7 [117-18], 688-90 [456-8], 830-2 [547-9], 907 [595]; *Tabaqat-i-Akbari*, 2: [275], [330]. For instance, according to Arif Qandhari, 'It was ordered in 1577-8, that Muzaffar Khan and "some clerks" accompanying him "should check (*muwazana numayad*) what was the amount of the hasil of the country of Gujarat and Mandu", and presumably on the basis of the figure so established, he was to assign *jagirs* in Gujarat'. See *Tarik-i-Akbari*, p. [210].
17. Bayazid Bayat, *Tazkira-i-Humayun wa Akbar*, pp. 363-4, 372-3.
18. Moreland, *The Agrarian System*, p. 94. It was Akbar's policy to keep the ports, mines, mints, etc., under the administrative charge of the centre. In 1593 Akbar did not assign the port of Lahari Bandar to Mirza Jani Beg, but declared it *khalisa*. The port cities being commercially significant and vulnerable to foreign aggression, particularly European, were kept under direct control of the centre by Akbar. Abul Fazl, *Akbarnama*, 3: 985-6 [641-2]; see also Sunita Zaidi, 'Problems of the Mughal Administration in Sindh, During the First Half of the Seventeenth Century', *Islamic Culture*, vol. LVII, no. 2, April 1983, pp. 150-60. In 1590 after the defeat of Qutlu, the famous temple of Jagannath at Puri and its environs was included into crown land and the other territories were returned to Nasir Khan (Qutlu's successor) as his *watan jagir*, see Abul Fazl, *Akbarnama*, 3: 880 [580-1]; *Maasir-ul-Umara*, 2: 52.

19. Abul Fazl, *Akbarnama*, 3:1026-31[669-71]; *Muntakhab-ut-Tawarikh*, 2: 416 [402].
20. Abul Fazl, *Akbarnama*, 3: 855 [565], 874-5[577-8].
21. Abul Fazl did not mention Muhibb Ali Khan Rohtasi in his list of grandees. The *Tabaqat* included him among the nobles of 4000 rank. See *Ain-i-Akbari*, 1: 466; *Tabaqat-i-Akbari*, 2: 664; *Tazkirat-ul-Umara*, p. 152.
22. For details of governor's appointment, transfer and dismissal in *sarkar* Bhakkar, see Mir Masum, *Tarikh-i-Masumi*, pp. 235-6, 242-51.
23. Abul Fazl, *Akbarnama*, 2: 486-7 [232].
24. After annexation, Sindh was given the status of a *suba* with five *sarkars* like the other *subas* of Lahore and Multan. In the *Ain-i-Akbari*, Thatta is not formally treated as a separate *suba*. It was deemed a *sarkar* of *suba* Multan, see Abul Fazl, *Ain-i-Akbari*, 2: 338-42. Cf. Irfan Habib, *Atlas of the Mughal Empire*, Delhi: Oxford University Press, 1982, Map 5A and notes, pp. 13-14. See Sunita Zaidi, 'Problems of the Mughal Administration in Sindh', p. 153.
25. For annexation of Sindh to Akbar's empire see Sunita Zaidi, 'Akbar's Annexation of Sindh—An Interpretation', in *Akbar and His India*, ed. Irfan Habib, pp. 25-32; Fatima Zehra Bilgrami, 'The Mughal Annexation of Sindh—A Diplomatic and Military History', in *Akbar and His India*, ed. Irfan Habib, pp. 33-54; Anita Paliwal, 'The Transition of Sindh to a Mughal Province—The Ghazi Beg Interlude, 1601-12', *Proceedings of the Indian History Congress*, 61st Session, Kolkata, 2000-1, pp. 303-6.
26. Abul Fazl, *Akbarnama*, 3: 979 [637-8]; *Maasir-ul-Umara*, 1: 743-8; *Ain-i-Akbari*, 1: 389-94.
27. Abul Fazl, *Akbarnama*, 3: 979 [637-8].
28. Ibid.
29. Abul Fazl, *Ain-i-Akbari*, 1: 391. Siwistan was not under the control of Mirza Jani Beg after 1592.
30. According to the author of the *Tarikh-i-Masumi*, Mirza Jani Beg died at Burhanpur in 1599 or 1600 from an attack of apoplexy or brain fever, see, *Tarikh-i-Masumi*, p. 257. But, according to Abul Fazl, he died because of excessive drink on 1 February 1601. See Abul Fazl, *Akbarnama*, 3: 1171-2 [782-3]; *Maasir-ul-Umara*, 1: 743-8.
31. Abul Baqi Nihawandi, *Maasir-i-Rahimi*, 2: 350. See also Amita Paliwal, 'The Transition of Sindh', pp. 303-6.
32. Chetan Singh, 'Centre and Periphery in the Mughal State', pp. 299-318. See also his *Region and Empire: Panjab in the Seventeenth Century*, Delhi: Oxford University Press, 1991, pp. 34-5.
33. For Sanjay Subrahmanyam's claim that the family members of Mirza Jani Beg held the *suba* till the middle of the seventeenth century see his paper, 'The Mughal State—Structure and Process? Reflections on Recent Western Historiography', *The Indian Economic and Social History Review*, vol. XXIX, no. 3, 1992, p. 310, n. 42.

34. He held it for the longest period of ten years.
35. As it appears Akbar policy to assign a *jagir* to the noble near the place of his posting.
36. Abul Fazl, *Akbarnama*, 3: 701 [464].
37. Ibid., 3: 1120 [749], 1144 [766].
38. Ibid., 3: 144 [103]; *Tarikh-i-Akbari*, 225 [194]; *Muntakhab-ut-Tawarikh*, 2: 185 [182-3].
39. Abul Fazl, *Akbarnama*, 3: 13 [8-9].
40. Ibid., 3: 8-9 [5-6]; *Medieval Gujarat*, p. 319.
41. The revenues of *watans* were always adjusted in the salary bills of the Rajput *mansabdars*. For Jodhpur, see Munhot Nainsi, *Marwar ra Pargana ri Vigat*, ed. Fateh Singh, Jodhpur: Rajasthan Oriental Research Institute, 1968, 1: 76-7, 83, 93; 2: 488-9.
42. Ahsan Raza Khan, *Chieftains in the Mughal Empire*, pp. 114, 208. For more details about Rajputs relations with Akbar and the *jagirs* they held under Akbar see, S. Inayat A. Zaidi, 'Akbar and the Rajput Principalities', in *Akbar and His India*, ed. Irfan Habib, pp. 15-24; Satish Chandra, 'Akbar's Rajput Policy and Its Evolution—Some Consideration', in *Akbar and His Age*, ed. Iqtidar Alam Khan, Delhi: Northern Book Centre, 1999, pp. 61-90; G.S.L. Devra, 'Raja, Mansab and *Jagir*—A Re-examination Mughal-Rajput Relations During the Reign of Akbar', in *Akbar and His Age*, ed. Iqtidar Alam Khan, pp. 70-81; Norman P. Ziegler, 'Some Notes on Rajput Loyalties During the Mughal Period', in *The Mughal State*, ed. Alam and Subrahmanyam, pp. 168-209.
43. Cf. Ahsan Raza Khan, *Chieftains in the Mughal Empire*, p. 207.
44. Abul Fazl, *Ain-i-Akbari*, 2: 273-282.
45. Saran, *The Provincial Government of the Mughals*, pp. 118-19.
46. Like the other *subas*, *suba* Agra was assigned to state employees in the form of *jagirs* by the emperor. Cf. K.K. Trivedi, *Agra: Economic and Political Profile of a Mughal Suba*, p. 119.
47. See Abul Fazl, *Ain-i-Akbari*, 2: 193-206; Trivedi, *Agra*, pp. 22-3.
48. Abul Fazl, *Ain-i-Akbari*, 2: 290-301.
49. For instance, during the revolt of Daud Khan, imperial officers were not in a position to collect revenues from their *jagirs*. Hence they preferred their salaries to be paid in cash instead of *jagirs*. Cf. *Maasir-ul-Umara*, 2: 289.
50. Moreland, *The Agrarian System*; Habib, *The Agrarian System*, p. 301; idem, 'The Social Distribution of Landed Property', p. 95; idem, 'The Eighteenth Century in Indian Economic History', in *The Eighteenth Century in India*, ed. Seema Alavi, p. 59; Athar Ali, *Mughal Nobility Under Aurangzeb*, p. 78; Noman Ahmad Siddiqi, *Land Revenue Administration*, pp. 110-11; Afzal Husain, 'Provincial Governors Under Akbar', *Proceedings of the Indian History Congress*, 33rd Session, Muzaffarpur, 1972, pp. 269-71. Frequent transfer of *jagirs* was also noted by European travellers, but their

observations cannot be generalized, see Hawkins, in *Early Travels in India*, p. 114; Jonnes De Laet, *Description of India and Fragment of Indian History*, pp. 94-5; Bernier, *Travels in the Mughal Empire*, pp. 226-7. For a slightly different version, see Mukhia, *The Mughal of India*, pp. 165-6.

51. I also agree with the subsequent research done by Satish Chandra that transfers of *jagirs* of large holders were not as frequent as previously believed. Cf. Satish Chandra, *Medieval India: Society, the Jagirdari Crisis and the Village*, p. 73. Nonetheless, he also did not clearly demarcate *jagir* and official post.
52. Abul Fazl, *Akbarnama*, 3: 280[198], 470-2, n. 3 [321-2], 475[324], 672[448], 779[511], 816-17[536-7]; *Tazkira-i-Humayun wa Akbar*, p. 302; *Muntakhab-ut-Tawarikh*, 2: 290[282]; *Tarikh-i-Akbari*, p. 258[222-4], (for more on this officer, see *Zakhirat-ul-Khawanin*, I: 215; *Maasir-ul-Umara*, 2: 226-8), he should not confounded with Muhibb Ali, the son of Mir Khalifa.
53. Iqtidar Alam Khan, 'Mughal Assignment System', p. 119.
54. Abul Fazl, *Akbarnama*, 2: 232[150]; *Tazkira-i-Humayun wa Akbar*, p. 310; *Muntakhab-ut-Tawarikh*, 2: 62[63]; *Tarikh-i-Akbari*, p. 142[106].
55. Abul Fazl, *Akbaarnama*, 3: 61-2[43], 356[247]; *Muntakhab-ut-Tawarikh*, 2: 138[134], 168[165]; *Tabaqat-i-Akbari*, 2: 367, 513 (for more on this officer see *Zakhirat-ul-Khawanin*, I: 190-3; *Maasir-ul-Umara*, 2:679-80).
56. Abul Fazl, *Akbarnama*, 3: 801[525], 878[579], 935[611], 999[650], 1060[711], 1120[749].
57. Ibid., 3: 358[248], 380[262], 493-4[336], 508[345], 790[518], 801[525]; *Muntakhab-ut-Tawarikh*, 2: 218[214], 376[364]; *Tabaqat-i-Akbari*, 2: 552 (on Bhagwan Dass, see *Zakhirat-ul-Khawanin*, I: 103; *Zakhirat-ul-Khawanin*, I: 404-5, on Man Singh, *Zakhirat-ul- Khawanin*, I: 103-11; *Maasir-ul-Umara*, 2: 48-57).
58. Abul Fazl, *Akbarnama*, 3: 801[525], 816[536], 872[576], 997-9[649-50], 1256[838]; *Muntakhab-ut-Tawarikh*, 2: 375[364]; *Tabaqat-i-Akbari*, 2: 622; Farishta, *Rise of Mohammedan Power in India*, 2: 161.
59. Abul Fazl, *Akbarnama*, 3: 459[314], 657[438], 878[579], 993[645], 1223[815]; *Muntakhab-ut-Tawarikh*, 2: 293[285]; *Tabaqat-i-Akbari*, 2: 538, 571 (for more on this officer, see *Zakhirat-ul- Khawanin*, I: 215; *Maasir-ul-Umara*, 2: 820-1).
60. Abul Fazl, *Akbarnama*, 2: 462[313], 485[330-1]; 3: 32[23-4]; *Muntakhab-ut-Tawarikh*, 2: 105[102], 110[106-07]; *Tabaqat-i-Akbari*, 2: 342, 351; *Tarikh-i-Akbari*, p. 268[233] (for more on this officer, see *Zakhirat-ul-Khawanin*, I: 210-11; *Maasir-ul-Umara*, 2: 745).
61. Bayazid Bayat, *Tazkira-i-Humayun wa Akbar*, p. 333; *Tarikh-i-Akbari*, p. 199[172]; *Akbarnama*, 3: 44[31], 59[42], 383[264], 681[453]; *Tabaqat-i-Akbari*, 2: 388, 404, 482; *Maasir-i-Rahimi*, 2:. 217 (for details about this officer see *Zakhirat-ul- Khawanin*, I: 172-6; *Maasir-ul-Umara*, 2: 534-6; see also *Ain-i-Akbari*, 1: 35, n. 2).
62. Abul Fazl, *Akbarnama*, 3: 990-1[644], 1069[717], 1120[749], 1216[810];

Muntakhab-ut-Tawarikh, 2: 401[388]; *Tabaqat-i-Akbari*, 2: 649 (for more on this officer, see *Zakhirat-ul- Khawanin*, I: 20-4; *Maasir-ul-Umara*, 2: 780-1).

63. For a detailed discussion, see Satish Chandra, 'Review of the Crisis of the *Jagirdari System*', in *The Mughal State*, ed. Alam and Subrahmanyam, pp. 357-8; see also Tapan Raychaudhuri, 'The Agrarian System of Mughal India', in *The Mughal State*, ed. Alam and Subrahmanyam, pp. 259-83.
64. Moosvi, *The Economy of the Mughal Empire*, p. 270.
65. Moreland, *The Agrarian System*, p. 93; Habib, 'The Social Distribution of Landed Property', pp. 95-8; Raychaudhuri and Habib, eds., *The Cambridge Economic History of India*, 1: 241; Moosvi, *The Economy of the Mughal Empire*, p. 197; Blake, 'The Patrimonial–Bureaucratic Empire', p. 295. For a similar study during Shahjahan's reign, see Qaisar, 'Distribution of the Revenue Resources of the Mughal Empire Among the Nobility', pp. 252-8.
66. H.K. Naqvi, *Urbanization and Urban Centres*, pp. 160-86.
67. Moreland, *The Agrarian System*, p. 94.
68. Abul Fazl, *Akbarnama*, 2: 25 [14]; *Muntakhab-ut-Tawarikh*, 2: 34 [40].
69. Bayazid Bayat, *Tazkira-i-Humayun wa Akbar*, p. 239.
70. Abul Fazl, *Akbarnama*, 2: 293-4 [264-5]; *Tazkira-i-Humayun wa Akbar*, pp. 239-40.
71. Abul Fazl, *Akbarnama*, 2: 436 [297-8]; *Muntakhab-ut-Tawarikh*, 2: 104 [101].
72. Abul Fazl, *Akbarnama*, 3: 97 [70]. An excellent historical survey of Mughal expansion in the province of Bengal is provided by Richard M. Eaton, *The Rise of Islam and Bengal Frontier, 1240-1760*, Delhi: Oxford University Press, 1994.
73. Abul Fazl, *Akbarnama*, 3: 164 [116].
74. Ibid., 2: 487 [332-3], 528-9 [363-4]; *Tabaqat-i-Akbari*, 2: 364.
75. Abul Fazl, *Akbarnama*, 3: 13-15 [9-11].
76. Ibid., 3: 1068 [716-17].
77. Ibid., 3: 1257 [839].
78. Abul Fazl, *Ain-i-Akbari*, 1:356.
79. Ibid., 1: 339.
80. Ibid., 1: 352-3.
81. Ibid., 1: 248.
82. Athar Ali, *The Mughal Nobility Under Aurangzeb*, p. 11.
83. For meaning of *khanazads/khanazadgi* see, Richards, *The Mughal Empire*, pp. 148-50; Streusand, *The Formation of the Mughal Empire*, pp. 146-8; Jos Gommans, *Mughal Warfare: Indian Frontier and High Roads to Empire, 1500-1700*, London: Routledge, 2002, pp. 57-8.
84. This follows the two classical studies on the subject of Mughal nobility: Satish Chandra, *Parties and Politics at the Mughal Court*, rpt, Delhi: People's Publishing House, 1979; Athar Ali, *Mughal Nobility Under Aurangzeb*. See also Athar Ali, *The Apparatus of Empire*.

85. For a more detailed analysis of the Turanis and Iranis in Mughal service, see Iqtidar Alam Khan, 'The Nobility Under Akbar and the Development of His Religious Policy, 1556-80', *Journal of the Royal Asiatic Society*, 1968, pp. 29-36; Afzal Husain, 'Growth of Irani Element in Akbar's Nobility', *Proceedings of the Indian History Congress*, 36th Session, Aligarh, 1975, pp. 167-79. See also A. Dadvar, *Iranians in Mughal Politics and Society, 1606-58*, Delhi: Gyan Publishing House, 1999.
86. For example, in or about 1613, Mirza Aziz Koka in a letter addressed to Emperor Jahangir, favoured Akbar for promoting the Turanis and Rajputs, accused Jahangir for promoting Indian Shaikhzadas and Khurasanis at the expense of the Turanis and Rajputs. See *Maktubat-i-Khan-i-Jahan Muzaffar Khan wa Gawalior Nama*, fol. 176-90. This collection contains Mirza Aziz Koka's letter to Jahangir.
87. Muhammad Abdur Rahim, 'The Position of the Afghans Under Akbar, 1526-1605', *Journal of the Pakistan Historical Society*, 1959, p. 126. For details of their role under the Mughals, see Muhammad Abdur Rahim, *The History of the Afghan in India, 1545-1631*, Karachi: Pakistan Publishing House, 1961; Rita Joshi, *The Afghan Nobility and the Mughals*, Delhi: Vikas, 1985; Iqtidar Alam Khan, 'Mughal Afghan Relation', *Proceedings of the Indian History Congress*, 24th Session, Delhi, 1961.
88. Niccolao Manucci, *Storia Do Mogor* or *Mogul India, 1653-1708*, tr. William Irvine, 4 vols, rpt, Delhi: Oriental Books, 1981, 2: 427.
89. For example, the Shaikhzadas of Nagaur. Akbar also established matrimonial ties with the Shaikhzadas of Delhi and Agra, see Badauni, *Muntakhab-ut-Tawarikh*, 2: 59-60[61-2]. See also Iqtidar Alam Khan, 'The Nobility Under Akbar', pp. 29-36.
90. Farid Bhakkari, *Zakhirat-ul-Khawanin*, 1: 104.
91. Iqtidar Alam Khan, 'The Nobility Under Akbar', p. 31.
92. Bayazid mentioned the allotment of this *jagir* to Bahadur Khan in AD 1561.
93. See also Ziegler, 'Some Notes on Rajput Loyalties', pp. 206-7.
94. Abul Fazl gives the impression as that the whole of Sirohi was given to Jagmal, but Nainsi, who gives a detailed account of the assignment of Sirohi to Jagmal makes it clear that he was given only half of Sirohi. *Munhot Nainsi ri Khyat*, I: 131-2.
95. Refaqat Ali Khan, *Kachhawahas Under Akbar and Jahangir*, Delhi: Kitab Publishing House, 1976, p. 168.
96. The Bikaner *watan* or Bikaner *dar-o-bast*, as it is called in the official records, consisted of the *parganas* of Bikaner, Pugal, Bikampur, Dadreva (*sarkar* Bikaner of *suba* Ajmer), Dronpur (*sarkar* Nagaur of *suba* Ajmer) and Sidhmukh and Bhadag (*sarkar* Hisar of *suba* Delhi). See for details, G.S.L. Devra, '*Raja*, *Mansab* and *Jagir*', pp. 70-80; see also S. Inayat A. Zaidi, 'Akbar and Rajput Principalities', pp. 15-24. Each ruler of Bikaner during Akbar's reign controlled the same area which was constituted as Bikaner *dar-o-bast*

in 1571. See for details *Raja Suraj Singh ri Vigat, Phootkar Vatan*, A.S.L.B., No. 206/2, pp. 90-1; see also Ziegler, 'Some Notes on Rajput Loyalties', pp. 168-210.

97. The Lucknow edition of the *Akbarnama* has Huna. See an elaborate note by Blochmann about sites mentioned by Abul Fazl, *Akbarnama*, 3: 478, n. 2. Whereas Nizamuddin Ahmad has Huba, see *Tabaqat-i-Akbari*, 2: 422, n. 1.
98. See the works cited in n. 96.
99. *Watan jagir*.
100. Ibid.
101. *Parganas* Satalmer and Pokhran were also assigned as *jagir* to Udai Singh (Mota Raja), but he could not bring them under his control, see Munhot Nainsi, *Marwar ra Pargana ri Vigat*, 1: 73, 76, 83; see also Ziegler, 'Some Notes on Rajput Loyalties', pp. 175, 177, 187.
102. His *jagirs* were valued at Rs. 3, 16, 175.
103. *Watan jagir*.
104. Ibid. See also V.S. Bhargava, *Marwar and the Mughal Emperor, 1526-1748*, Delhi: Munshiram Manoharlal, 1966, p. 64; *Vir Vinod*, 3: 818.
105. The strong resistance of the chief (*sardars*) of Bhatta forced Akbar to reassign it again to its ruler Bikramjit as his *watan jagir*.
106. *Watan jagir*.
107. In August 1574, Jaunpur and Banaras were included in the *khalisa-i-sharifa*. Munim Khan's *jagir* was transferred to Bihar. See Abul Fazl, *Akbarnama*, 3: 144 [103]; *Tarikh-i-Akbari*, p. 225 [194]; *Muntakhab-ut-Tawarkh*, 2: 185 [182].
108. Ahsan Raza Khan, *Chieftains in the Mughal Empire*, p. 106.
109. See Charles Stewart, *The History of Bengal*, Delhi: Oriental Publishers, 1971, pp. 162-3, 167.
110. Muhammad Sadiq Khan went to court without permission and was not admitted. Some time later when Shahbaz Khan went from Bihar to Bengal to take over charge from him, he again went to court and was appointed governor of Multan.
111. Sultan Khusrau was appointed nominal governor of Orissa and a portion of its revenue was assigned as his *jagir*. See Stewart, *The History of Bengal*, p. 187.
112. Man Singh was recalled to court and was appointed *ataliq* to Prince Sultan Khusrau.
113. Later, a *jagir* yielding a revenue of 5 to 6 lakh per annum was assigned to him in East Bengal. See *Ain-i-Akbari*, 1: 587.
114. In October-November 1580 Shaham Khan Jalair (*Akbarnama*, 3: 476) was sent against the Arab, who had been defeated by Shahbaz Khan and had oppressed the weak in Sarangpur area. On the basis of this reference, Iqtidar Alam Khan erroneously described him as the *jagirdar* of Sarangpur. Cf. Iqtidar Alam Khan, 'Mughal Assignment System', p. 118.

115. According to Abul Fazl and Badauni, it is Tabranda, while Nizamuddin calls it Tabarhindha. It is Bhatinda, see *Maasir-i-Rahimi*, 1: 674.
116. Sayyid Ahmad Khan Baraha was appointed to look after the *jagir* of Mirza Khan.
117. As he did not strictly follow the *dagh* regulation, his *jagir* was forfeited. His *jagir* in the province of Ahmedabad was incorporated into the *khalisa sharifa*. See *Tabaqat-i-Akbari*, 2: 239. Consequently, the Mirza was dismissed from service and placed in virtual confinement for nearly five years in his garden at Agra. See *Akbarnama*, 3: 208-9 [147]; *Muntakhab-ut-Tawarikh*, 2: 217-18 [214-15]; *Mirat-i-Ahmadi*, p. 113.
118. See also *Medieval Gujarat* based on Mohammed Ali Khan's *Mirat-i-Ahmadi*.
119. According to the *Tarikh-i-Akbari*, p. 240, n. 15, he died in AH 986/AD 1578, which is probably wrong. See *Akbarnama*, 3: 231; *Maasir-ul-Umara*, 2: 155.
120. Badauni says that the fort was placed under the charge of Qulij's sons.
121. Mirza Aziz Koka preferred Malwa and postponed his departure to Gujarat. Finally in the 35th regnal year he went to Ahmedabad. He considered this transfer to be equivalent to exile. For details of Mirza Aziz Koka's activities in Gujarat, see *Akbarnama*, 3: 876-7 [578], 948-9 [620], 961-7 [628-31]; *Mirat-i-Ahmadi*, 151-6.
122. He had not attended court for two years. Badauni, *Muntakhab-ut-tawarikh*, 386-7 [399-401], states that he had not appeared in court for the previous six years. According to the author of *Zakhirat-ul-Khawanin*, Mirza Aziz Koka had not attended the court for the previous ten years. *Zakhirat-ul-Khawanin*, 1: 96; see also *Mukatabat-i-Allami* (*Insha-i-Abul Fazl*), pp. 72-8.
123. According to Abul Fazl, he died in February 1601. See Abul Fazl, *Akbarnama*, 3: 1175.
124. He was appointed *ataliq* of Prince Murad in place of Ismail Quli Khan. As Prince Sultan was posted in *suba* Gujarat, his *jagir* was also transferred to Gujarat.
125. Badauni lists only *sarkars* Broach and Surat as his *jagir* and does not mention Baroda as part of his *jagir*.
126. After the death of Muhammad Sadiq Khan in 1597, he was appointed *ataliq* of Prince Sultan Murad and also assigned a *jagir* in Ahmedabad along with Prince Murad.
127. As an absentee governor, he was transferred to Bihar. Abul Fazl, *Akbarnama*, 3: [825]; *Mirat-i-Ahmadi*, p. 159.
128. He was appointed *vakil* in place of Pir Muhammad Khan by Bairam Khan.
129. The value of his *jagir* was two crore and fifty lakh.
130. In December 1589, Aziz Koka was transferred to Gujarat. He was not willing to go to Gujarat and represented against his posting, but his request was turned down and he was asked to proceed to Gujarat immediately.
131. He was appointed *ataliq* of Prince Sultan Murad and sent to Malwa along with the prince as *jagirdar*.

132. In addition to his *jagir* in Malwa, Ujjain and other *parganas* were allotted to Mirza Shahrukh in 1597 in the wake of his promotions. In 1602, Prince Sultan Daniyal resumed his *jagir* and later under the direction of Akbar, Daniyal's decision was disapproved and the *jagir* was again restored to Mirza Shahrukh. See Abul Fazl, *Akbarnama*, 3: 1069 [717], 1216 [810].
133. He was appointed *ataliq* of Mirza Shahrukh, who was posted in *suba* Malwa. Following his posting (*ataliq* of Shahrukh) in Malwa, Shahbaz's *jagir* was also transferred to Malwa.
134. Shahbaz Khan's *jagir* was confiscated as a punishment for his misbehaviour. Sadiq Khan was appointed *ataliq* of Mirza Shahrukh in place of Shahbaz Khan.
135. The value of his *jagir* was 50,00,000 *tankas*.
136. After some time it was restored to Mirza Jani Beg (the chief of Thatta).
137. According to the author of the *Tarikh-i-Masumi*, Mirza Jani Beg died at Burhanpur in AD 1599 or 1600 from an attack of apoplexy or brain fever; see *Tarikh-i-Masumi*, p. 257. Abul Fazl, however, asserts that he died of excessive drink in February 1601. See Abul Fazl, *Akbarnama*, 3: 1171-2 [782-3]; see also *Maasir-ul-Umara*, 1: 743-8.
138. *Watan jagir*, the whole of Thatta except Siwistan and Lahri Bandar was restored to Mirza Jani Beg. Thatta was previously assigned to Mirza Shahrukh.
139. As he treated the people of the area (*jagir*) harshly, he was on receipt of complaint called to court.
140. *Watan jagir.*

CHAPTER 4

Mughal Aristocracy

Apart from the politico-administrative institutions that constitute the basis of any empire, the symbols of royalty have always played an important role in creating and maintaining the image of the monarch. The Mughal Empire had also developed considerable symbology, which represented its outward pomp and show. Distinctions made on the basis of the honours granted have always been an important source of motivation for an aristocracy-based society. The ritual that, perhaps, best symbolized the personal loyalty of the subordinate to the emperor and the exchange of patronage for service was the exchange of gifts. The subordinate would present the emperor with a *nazr* or *peshkash*, and the emperor would reciprocate by presenting his servant with a *khilat*, bejewelled sword, saddle, or turban ornament, a fine horse, or a new office or title.

PRESENTS FROM THE NOBLES

The form of the *darbar* articulated the relationship between the emperor and his *mansabdars*. Court rituals and exchange of gifts occupied a pivotal place in Mughal politics and society. Streusand rightly observed that without the rituals which surround it, Mughal sovereignty did not exist.[1] The nature of the rituals propounded the nature of sovereignty. To begin with ordinary court routines, Abul Fazl and Thomas Roe describe the routines of Akbar and Jahangir. Akbar began his day by performing personal religious devotions, and then went to the *jharokha*, the famous small balcony from which he presented himself to the general public. Although Thomas Roe commented on Jahagir's court, his comments apply to Akbar's reign as well:

> This course is unchangeable, unless sickness or drink prevent yt; which must be known, for as all his subjects are slaves, so he in a kynd of reciprocal bondage, for he is tryed to observe these howres and customes so precisely

that if hee were unseene one day and noe sufficient reason rendred, the people would mutinie; two days noe reason can excuse, but that he must consent to open his doores and bee seene by some to satisfye others.[2]

The court rituals and exchange of gifts at the *darbar* and outside it enacted the formal ritual of authority and subordination. F.W. Bukler's comment on the relationship between sovereigns and officers is very apt in this context:

the king stands for a system of rule of which he is the incarnation, incorporating into his own body by means of symbolical acts, the person of those who share his rule. They are regarded as being parts of his body. . . and in their district or their sphere of activity they are the King themselves—not servants of the king but 'friends' or member of the king.[3]

As the definer of status and distributor of power, the emperor determined the nature and position of his subordinates.

Mansabdars presented two categories of gifts to the rulers: *nazr* and *peshkash*. The ruler also gave various types of gifts to the *mansabdars*. The term *nazr* (derived from Arabic *nadhr* or vow) implied an oath of allegiance that was customarily presented in person—as opposed to a *peshkash* or offering that could be sent to the emperor without the giver making a personal appearance. In this connection J.F. Richards writes:

During the great daily 'public' assemblies in the audience hall of the palace or camp, the Emperor and his officers enacted formal rituals of authority and subordination. Imperial officers called before the throne offered at a minimum several gold coins (*muhrs*) to the Emperor. After the sovei gn uttered formal verbal confirmation of promotions, new titles, postings, etc., he favoured the officer with a full or partial robe of honour, a horse or an elephant, jewelled weapons, money or other artefacts.[4]

Unfortunately, Indian scholars have not devoted sufficient attention to the exchange of gifts, whereas European and American scholars on South Asia have found it a fascinating topic for study.[5] Here one must disagree with Streusand that Abul Fazl did not focus much attention on the exchange of gifts.[6] Much information is available in the accounts of Abul Fazl and other chronicles of Akbar's reign as can be seen from Tables 4.1. and 4.2.[7]

The *nazr* was presented by nobles in cash on a special occasion when the *darbar* was held in jubilation of the occasion and the nobles arrived in court to make obeisance with *nazr*. The term *nazr* has a

Semitic root and literally means vow, but in the Mughal Empire, it referred to an expensive gift usually gold and silver coins, which were generally not in circulation. On most occasions, both princes and *mansabdars* presented 100 or 1,000 coins.

The presentation of coins or *nazr* probably represented the vow of loyalty. The practice of nobles offering presents to the emperor had become a part of the court etiquette.[8] In fact, it was a general custom all over Asia that 'the great are never approached with empty hand'.[9] The accounts of later European travellers are a testimony to this fact. In one such account Tavernier avers:

> Whoever it may be who desires to have audience of the king, they (the officials) ask before everything else, where the present is that he has to offer to him and they examine it to see if it is worthy of being offered to His Majesty. No one ever ventures to show himself with empty hands, and it is an honour obtained at no little cost.[10]

The *peshkash*, an annual offering in cash and kind, was made by the *mansabdars* in person or sent through their representatives. Apart from *mansabdars*, foreign ambassadors and subordinate rulers also presented a *peshkash* to the Mugal emperor.[11] *Peshkash* literally means (that which is) 'drawn forward', and is the most commonly used Persian term for a gift to a political superior signifying subordination. A *peshkash* see Table 4.1, generally consisted of precious articles of the territories and countries of the rulers, varying from precious diamonds and jewels to hunting animals, horses and war elephants. *Mansabdars* had to present a *peshkash* annually, but did not always do so and were not necessarily punished for this omission.[12] According to Athar Ali,

> There were certain occasions when the *peshkash* was expected from the nobles present at the Court. Such were the anniversaries of the Emperor's accession, the birth-anniversary of the Emperor, the *Nauroz* (Persian New Year's Day), the birth of prince or princes, the celebration of a victory and the Emperor's recovery from an illness. The nobles also offered *peshkash* whenever they wanted some particular favour from the Emperor. The *zamindars* offered *peshkash* at the time of their accession of their *gaddi* (throne) while the tributary princes offered an annual *peshkash*. The *peshkash* offered by the *zamindars* and tributary princes was different in nature from the *peshkash* of the ordinary nobles; it was a token of the recognition of the Emperor's supremacy, and also an assertion of the imperial rights in the appointment of a person to the *gaddi*.[13]

According to Niccolao Manucci, all the *amirs* were expected to offer presents to the emperor commensurate with their respective positions and ambitions.[14] Because of the emphasis in the chronicles on the word 'suitable', in relation to the payment of *peshkash* by the nobles and tributary rulers, it appears that the amount of *peshkash* was commensurate with the ranks of *mansabdars* and resources of the respective rulers. For instance, in 1594 Burhan-ul-Mulk Deccani's *peshkash* to the emperor consisted of 15 elephants, some fine clothing and a small quantity of gems. Referring to the amount of *peshkash* by Burhan-ul-Mulk, the author of the *Tabaqat-i-Akbari* categorically states that he did not send a suitable *peshkash*/tribute.[15] The value of the jewels presented to the emperor was always mentioned. Describing the amount of *peshkash* and the value of the jewel offered by Raja Ram Chand of Bhatta, the author of the *Tabaqat-i-Akbari* notes that he 'offered 120 elephants as *peshkash* and a ruby of the value of rupees 50 thousand'.[16] Unlike *nazr*, *peshkash* was not normally a cash gift and was sent to the ruler when the sender was not at court. The rulers of Bijapur, Golconda, Turan, etc., always sent their *peshkash* with their ambassadors to the Mughal court (see Table 4.1. for details). These ambassadors brought *peshkash* of their own, as did the emissaries of rulers not subordinate to the emperor.[17]

Princes and officers also offered *peshkash* when they had the honour of entertaining the sovereign at their residence.[18] The visit of the emperor to an *amir's* house was the highest honour which a noble could ever hope for. These visits of the emperor were considered a matter of extraordinary favour and fortune, and testified to the noble's prominence and influence. On such occasions the nobles organized large parties and presented lavish gifts to the emperor. Some nobles invited Akbar to their residence when he passed through the territory of their posting. On these occasions the nobles threw lavish feasts and the emperor would spend a couple of days at these feasts and he and the courtiers accompanying him would be entertained and offered gifts. In the 15th regnal year (1571), when Akbar arrived in Dipalpur he stayed for a few days with Khan Azam Mirza Aziz Koka. On the last day, lavish gifts were presented to him, such as Arab and Persian horses with saddles of silver, huge elephants with chains of gold and silver, housings of velvet and brocade, gold and silver, pearls and jewels, and invaluable rubies and garnets. Chairs of gold and silver, vases and vessels of gold and silver, luxurious dresses of Europe, Turkey and China and other precious gifts were presented. Similar presents were also offered to the young princes and the emperor's wives. All the ministers, dignitaries and attendants including every soldier of the army accompanying the emperor also received presents.[19] In 1572, Muzaffar Khan had the honour of entertaining the sovereign at his house. The *Tarikh-i-Akbari* of Arif Qandhari is the only chronicle that provides rich and poetic details of this visit and gifts transactions at the time.[20] Waxing eloquent about this visit and exchange of gifts, Arif Qandhari notes:[21]

> Every possible equipment for the grand celebration in all manners of festivities and enjoyment was affixed. The entire passage, measuring two thousand yards, from the royal palace up to his residence [Muzaffar Khan's] was decorated with various cloths such as *zarbaft*, Chinese silk, European velvet, *atlas* and *Kamkhab-i-Yazdi* for the emperor's steps. . . . All sides were beautifully equipped and were laced with every necessary commodities (of life). The uncountable number of quantities of gold and gems were scattered from all sides to grace the occasion.... From all sides, the edifice was canopied with brocade and velvet while silken-curtains and coloured pillars with the entire ground, covered with the golden cloth by the decorators (*farrashams*). A large tent, made of felt cloth outside and brocade and velvet inside, was fixed there. The floor of brocade, velvet and silk was further decorated with rugs from Khurasan and Iran, with incomparable refinement. The rooms inside were decorated with paintings in blue-colours. The palace which had attractive chambers on all sides its walls were polished white with lime so those were shining like mirror and one could see his envious reflection.
>
> The programme of the assembly of pleasure started. Male and female singers with their sweet and melodious voices started singing on the music of Sarod and other instruments which touched the height of the sky. Hearing the soul-stirring music of the party Venus itself came up to the roof of the sky and it observed this spectacular scene of the assembly in deep-wonderment.... The musicians played music like the songs of a nightingale. Reputed poets and prose writers composed the choicest poems and prose, which they recited and presented there.
>
> Burning frankincense and aloe-wood in gold and silver fire-places and the fragrant vapours rising out of them, were giving eternal life to the souls. Whatever requisite provisions and equipments required for making the assembly delightful and enjoyable had all been collected and its host was also fully adorned with entertainment of the guests.
>
> The assemblage of enjoyment was attractive like the faces of beauty. During the same time, reputed chefs prepared gourmet food, innumerable like stars in the sky. As a result of too many varieties of food and provision of all kinds

of drinks, appetite had itself vanished from the world. So many varieties of delicious dry fruits and sweets were prepared to serve that the grandeur of the garden of paradise was astonished.

The perfect and amicable arrangements impressed the emperor and he cast his affectionate eye on the Khan, conferred a white *khilat* (robe of special quality) with other honours on him. The emperor sat on the throne and all kinds of presents such as swords, studded-daggers, belts, jewelled aloe-burners, bowls placed before him in boats (trays) of gold and silver. The breeze full of ambar and musk was refreshing the souls of the angels even in skies.

Many other golden and silver articles, besides, chandeliers, plates and water-jugs of gold and silver were also presented. The finest pieces of cloth such as zarbaft of Rum, velvet of Europe, *kamkhab-i-Yazdi, atlas-i-Khatai* of Bukhara, studded *dupatta* and turbans, Deccani jewelled boxes, golden thread of Gujarat and the royal Muslin of Sunargaon were also presented to him. A horde of twenty-five elephants, who could run in the battlefield like fire and wind with their controlling crooks (ankush), frightening the eyes and throwing their trunks in anger like a polo ball . . . and looking like pythons who could pull down the sky with their trunks were also presented. The *mahavats* had decorated the trappings of their mountain like elephants with velvet and brocade of Europe, which were glittering like thunder and lightning.

A special (*khasa*) elephant, whose tusks covered with gold and decorated with precious rubies and gems, dressed with cornelian and precious pearls, was also presented.

Arabi horses, with lightning speed, Iraqi and Turkish horses, challenging the circling sky like clouds, in whose hoofs nails were fitted to walk slowly like the shadow of wall or to run fast to outrun their own shadow if they wish. The row of burden bearing camels with their high ridges like humps, with the speed of wind were also presented. For the blessed princes, who are the pearls of crown and throne, beautiful, angel like maid servants, diamond, ruby and *firuza* were presented. The princes appreciated all the presents. The Khan presented gifts to his near and dear ones along with his servants and attendants of the emperor.[22]

In 1582, Abdur Rahim Mirza Khan held a grand feast to celebrate his appointment as *ataliq* and he invited the emperor to grace the occasion by his presence. The latter could not refuse the request. Numerous officers participated in the function. The path from the fort up to his residence was strewn with flowers of gold and silver and near his residence rubies were scattered. At the entrance cloths of satin and velvet were spread on the ground to walk on. Within the compound a dais was erected at the cost of Rs. 1,25,000. When the emperor took his seat on it, Mirza Khan presented him precious jewels, expensive garments and sophisticated weapons of war. The emperor was so pleased with the celebration that he bestowed on Mirza Khan a drum, a *charquali*, a banner and all the insignia pertaining to a royal prince as a mark of favour which were never given to ordinary officers. When the emperor left, Mirza Khan donated the precious dais to the people gathered there. Even ordinary nobles took several things.[23]

Zain Khan Koka also entertained the emperor at his house. He covered a *chabutra* (terrace) with *tus* (goat hair) shawls which were very rare in those days and placed three tanks in front, one filled with water of Yazd, another coloured with saffron, and the third with argaja with over 1,000 dancing girls (*tawaif*) in the tanks. Streams of milk mixed with sugar flowed and rose water was sprinkled instead of water in the courtyard (to settle the dust). Filled baskets and vessels decorated with jewels were presented as *peshkash* along with noted elephants.[24] At the residence of Sharif Khan Atka, the emperor passed his time listening to vocal and instrumental music. Sharif Khan Atka presented him nine elephants and twenty-seven Iraqi and Arab horses and various fabrics as tribute.[25]

It is obvious from these instances that the Mughal rituals of welcoming and entertaining the emperor were on an epic scale, not just lavish. The splendour on such a scale was unheard of even in Europe. Such rituals and functions strengthened the bond between the sovereign and the aristocracy. It dazzled the subjects who participated either by being spectators or by rendering numerous services such as arranging and cooking on such a lavish scale.

Regarding the *peshkash* and gifts from the nobles to the emperor, both officers and princes frequently offered elephants or horses as *peshkash*, if they had access to them. For example, in 1561 Bahadur Khan and Sikandar Khan Uzbek presented elephants called Koh-para (a piece of a hill or mountain) and Saf-shikan (rank or line breaker) to Akbar.[26] Itimad Khan Gujarati gave a sea elephant as *peshkash* in 1567.[27] As mentioned earlier, Sharif Khan Atka presented nine elephants and twenty-seven Iraqi and Arab horses as *peshkash*.[28] In 1591, Khan Azam Mirza Aziz Koka sent choice elephants and thirty horses from Gujarat and Saadat Khan presented fifteen noted elephants in 1601.[29] In 1602, Prince Daniyal sent ten elephants and Prince Salim sent 977 elephants, of which only 350 were accepted by Akbar.[30] Qulij Khan sent 20 horses from Lahore in 1604-5.[31] Elephants and horses were also gifted by subordinate rulers. In 1577, the ruler of Golconda sent choice gifts including an elephant Fath Mubarak through his ambassador.[32] Qutlu Khan sent sixty choice elephants in 1584.[33]

The finest elephants and horses were presented as gifts. The question of offering ordinary gifts did not arise. As mentioned earlier, the court officials scrutinized whatever was offered by way of *nazr* or *peshkash.*

In addition to these, nobles occasionally brought curious gifts. For example, Abdur Rahim Khan-i-Khanan presented a horse which could fight with an elephant.[34] Zain Khan gifted a robe of black fox.[35] Nobles brought back rarities from other countries and presented them to the emperor. Sultan Khwaja who was appointed to the office of the command of the Haj brought back Arab horses and other rarities for the emperor.[36] An *Atlas* sent as a present by the Archbishop of Goa was graciously accepted by Akbar.[37]

Nobles made offerings is accordance with their rank. The emperor would accept either the entire or a part of the offerings. At times he only glanced at them and presented as having accepted the presents.[38] In 1577-8, Mihr Ali Sildoz had the honour of entertaining the emperor at his house. Only a few of his gifts were accepted by Akbar.[39] Zain Khan presented 170 elephants, but Akbar accepted only a few of them. In 1603, Prince Salim presented 12,000 *muhrs* and 977 elephants, of which only 350 elephants were accepted.[40] Presents offered by unfaithful officers were generally not accepted. The rebel Ibrahim Husain Mirza sent a present to the emperor in 1572, which was not accepted. Abul Fazl, the author of *Akbarnama*, and Ali Muhammad Khan, the author of *Mirat-i-Ahmadi*, argue that the emperor did not think that such a gift was given with a sincere intention.[41]

Whenever the emperor passed through the territories of nobles or neighbouring chiefs, etiquette demanded that princes, nobles and chiefs stood at the edge of their encampments to make a present to him. They offered gold *muhrs* or anything else befitting the occasion. When Akbar was at Lahore, the Raja of Kumaon came down the Shiwalik hills to pay his homage and brought rare presents including a yak and a musk deer among other things.[42] The failure to bring a present amounted to be a breach of etiquette.

The contemporary sources of Akbar's reign reveal that whenever presents were made to him (Akbar), he carefully calculated their intrinsic value. For example, in 1562, the ambassador of Shah Tahmasp

Safavi, the ruler of Persia, systematically arranged the presents before His Majesty (Akbar).[43] Also, in February 1584, Raja Ram Chand brought gifts for inspection.[44] In August-September 1589, the ambassador of Abdullah Khan, the ruler of Turan, brought gifts for assessment by the emperor,[45] and in 1593, 127 elephants sent by Man Singh were inspected by the emperor.[46]

Since the *mansabdars* were the emperor's employees, the booty they took during a campaign was his, not theirs. In practice, the emperor expected only a proportion of the booty to be sent to him as *peshkash* (to differentiate the other *peshkash*/presents from booty in Table 4.1 column 4 the word booty has been used to indicate that it was sent as *peshkash* to court). The booty which the officers brought had considered real value. Akbar and his successors had good use for gold, jewels and elephants, not to mention women of the harem. However, the economic or erotic value does not explain the importance of imperial jurisdiction over the booty. The transmission of booty to the court as *peshkash* stated and demonstrated the relationship between the ruler and the officer. The failure to send it meant a breach in the relationship.

In conclusion, the wealth of the nobles was derived from the posts conferred upon them by the emperor. A fair proportion of this wealth found its way back to the royal treasury. While it is true that *nazr* was usually a nominal amount, the *peshkash* must have imposed a real burden on the nobles. Sometimes the *peshkash* included gold coins or *muhrs* and various kinds of precious stones. According to Bernier, it was rather hard on the nobles to be expected to offer such costly presents. The motive and the rationale underlying these presents were manifold. Being ostentatious, nobles vied with one another in the choice of these presents. Offering a valuable present was, moreover, the easiest way to keep the emperor in good humour. Some of the *amirs* who may have been guilty of serious malpractices during the course of their career were anxious to avert their master's wrath, which may have been aroused by the insinuations of their enemies. Or, many of them wanted to ingratiate themselves with the emperor with a view to securing an increase in salary or an advancement in rank. They viewed these presents in the light of discreet investments and regarded the practice as a good business proposition. They were, therefore, generous with their pearls and diamonds on these occasions.[47]

Nevertheless, one may not be tempted to use gift exchange which embodies the central insights of Marcel Mauss's *The Gifts*: that every gift comes with obligations.[48] Presents should also be distinguished from bribes, as there was no secrecy about the former. They were recognized as part of the social etiquette prevalent at the time and were offered openly, even ostentatiously. They were an index to the position as well as the ambition of the person who offered them. Every *amir* kept a stock of gold *muhrs* (*asharfis*) and precious stones to be presented to the emperor on all solemn occasions.

TITLES AND DISTINCTIONS

Honorary distinctions have existed in all countries, and they have often served as an incentive to the subjects to put forth their best efforts. Apart from their official salaries derived from their *jagirs* or cash, the nobles frequently received rewards and distinctions from the emperor. Among the marks of honour bestowed by the Mughal emperor, the most important were title, robe of honour (*khilat*), standards, kettle-drums, flags, ensigns, etc., and presents such as swords, jewelled daggers, betel leaves, elephants, elephant gear, turbans, turban ornaments, horses, saddles and related accoutrements.

With regard to titles, the adoption and award of titles is an age-old tradition in history. The rulers themselves assumed such titles which expressed their divinity and superiority and awarded titles to their nobles which were an indication of their loyalty, faithfulness and meritorious services to the state on the battlefield or in administration or expressed their extraordinary proficiency in their work. These titles enhanced the status of the recipient in state and society. Under the Mughals, these appellations were so numerous and extensively conferred that often the original names of the persons on whom the titles were conferred were forgotten and the later historians learnt about these nobles only through their titles. In many cases these appellations were assumed to be the actual names of the nobles whereas they were just titles. Manucci, one of the later travellers observed that 'the king confers these names (by which the nobles were known) either as a mark of distinctions and of the esteem he holds them in by reason of their services or else from friendship and liking. These lords can acquire more wealth as well more titles'.[49]

The Mughal nobles were decorated with high sounding titles like *Amir Khan* (lord of riches), Zafar Khan (lord of victory), Sarbuland Khan (lord of exalted position), Saf-Shikan Khan (destroyer of the ranks of the enemy), Shujaat Khan (lord of bravery), Bahadur (bold), Jang (war), and Khan (lord). Distinguished titles included Amir-ul-Umara (the chief amir), Khan-i-Khanan (lord of lords), Khan-i-Azam (the great Khan), Khan Zaman (lord of the time), Khan-i-Muazzam (honoured lord), Khan-Jahan (lord of the world) and Khan-i-Alam (lord of the Universe), etc. While conferring a title on a Hindu the word Raja, Maharaja, Raiyan, Rao or Rana was added to the name of the person.[50]

The title ending with *Din* (faith) such as Zahir-ud-din (strength ever of the faith), Nasir-ud-din (defender of the faith) and Jalal-ud-din (glory of the faith), during the early years of Mughal rule in India, was reserved only for the emperors but in the later period such titles were conferred by the emperors on their nobles as well. Aurangzeb (1658-1707) was the first emperor to bestow the title of Ghazi-ud-din (warrior of the faith) on one of his generals, Mir Shahab-ud-din. Henceforth, it became a common practice.

A title once conferred by the emperor became the official name of the noble concerned. Some of the nobles were given more than one title. For example, a noble could be given one title at one point of time and another later. In 1560, Khwaja Muzaffar Ali who had already been conferred the title of Muzaffar Khan was given the title Darvesh Beg.[51] Tipur Das was given the titles of Rai Raiyan in 1601 and Raja Vikramaditya in 1605.[52]

The Mughals apparently inherited from the Sultans of Delhi the practice of bestowing titles upon their *amirs*. In Hindustan, wrote Babur, they gave permanent titles (Muqarrar-i-khitablar) to high favoured *amirs*, one such being Azam-i-Humayun (August Humayun), Khan-i-Jahan (lord of the world), and another Khan-i-Khanan (lord of lords).[53] The title of Azam Humayun was never conferred on any Mughal noble, but the other two titles were awarded to the highly favoured nobles.

The award of a title was an expression of imperial appreciation of the services of a noble. For instance, Shamsuddin Muhammad Khan Atka was given the title of Khan Azam at Sirhind in 1560 after he defeated Bairam Khan.[54] Abdur Rahim Mirza Khan earned the title of

Khan-i-Khanan after his victory over Muzaffar Shah III (Nanu) of Gujarat (pretender to the throne of the principality) who had occupied almost the entire province before he was defeated in battle on 25 January 1584.[55] A title could also be conferred on a noble when he was promoted so as to encourage him to do his work with greater vigour. In 1580, Aziz Koka was made Khan-i-Azam when he was deputed to lead an expedition to the eastern provinces.[56] Under the Mughal rulers, the title of Khan-i-Khanan was probably the highest that was conferred on any noble. According to some historians, this high sounding title can be traced back to the days of the decline of the Caliphate.[57] In Mughal India, the use of this title was known even during the reign of Babur. Babur had conferred the title of Khan-i-Khanan only on Dilwar Khan.[58] Humayun conferred this title on Mir Hindu Beg, who was entrusted with the government of Jaunpur. Throughout the Mughal period whenever this title was conferred upon any *amir*, it was generally accompanied by a large cash gift from the emperor for the maintenance of a matching position and dignity. Theoretically speaking, the title could be bestowed only on one *amir* at a time,[59] but the rule was not always strictly observed.

Under Akbar the title of Khan-i-Khanan was conferred on nobles whose services to the house were of the highest order. Bairam Khan who was credited with the restoration of the Mughal Empire in India and who had served the house most unflinchingly was the first recipient of this enviable title (d. 1561). In 1560, it was conferred upon Munim Khan, a very senior and influential noble (d. 1575).[60] The third recipient of this title was Abdur Rahim (d. 1627),[61] son of Bairam Khan, who received it at a comparatively young age. He justified the choice of the emperor in 1581 when he was selected to head the forces against Muzaffar Shah in view of the friction among senior nobles.[62] In the later period the title of Khan-i-Khanan was conferred on Asaf Khan (d. 1641) and Mir Jumla (d. 1663).

Great importance was attached to the title of Khan-i-Khanan. To what extent the nobles were enamoured by this title can be gauged, from the fact that Sultan Mahmud of Bhakkar (Sind) solicited the recommendation of Shah Tahmasp of Persia to secure this title. Since Munim Khan had already received the title Khan-i-Khanan, Sultan Mahmud could not achieve his object and moreover his offer was rejected on the grounds that the criterion was merit not recommendations.[63] While Abdur Rahim Khan-i-Khanan was facing problems in Gujarat, some of his nobles wanted him to wait for help from Qulij Khan of Malwa. Daulat Khan Lodi who had been transferred by Khan-i-Azam Aziz Koka to the service of Abdur Rahim Khan-i-Khanan, the latter was married to the sister of the former, suggested to Abdur Rahim that if he wanted to earn the title of Khan-i-Khanan, he should fight without waiting for a contingent.[64]

The awarding of titles was also used as a political device. During the initial years of Akbar's reign, a large number of nobles were awarded titles and dispatched to different parts of north India to extend the boundaries of the empire. Ali Quli Khan was not only given the title of Khan-i-Zaman, but also the *sarkar* of Sambhal and other *parganas* of the doab were assigned to him as *jagir*.[65] Abdullah Khan Uzbek received the title of Shujaat Khan and was allotted the *sarkar* of Kalpi.[66] Sikandar Khan received the title of Khan-i-Alam and Pir Muhammad was known as Nasir-ul-mulk.[67] The title was used either as a suffix or a prefix to the name. After earning the title, the nobles were addressed by the title. Whenever the emperor wanted to raise a commoner to the rank of an *amir*, he conferred upon him the title of Khan in the case of a Mohammadan and Rai or Raja in the case of a Hindu.

The title of Khan was a very common one and was bestowed upon several nobles by Akbar. Great care was exercised lest a person, who had not reached the requisite status, be given the title of Khan.[68] More than one title could also be conferred on nobles under Akbar. In 1572, Birbal (Mahesh Das) was given the title of Kavi-Rai (Prince of poets), because of his poetic genius[69] and, in view of his military prowess in Multan, he received the title of Birbal or Birbar (renowned warrior).[70] He was also conferred the titles of Sahib-us-Saif-o-Qalami[71] (master of sword and pen), Raja and Musahib-i-Danishwar (wise counsellor).[72] Man Singh was given the title of Farzand (son) for his loyalty to the emperor. He received the title of Mirza Raja[73] which was indicative of his high status. In November 1589, Man Singh was conferred the title of Raja after the death of his father Bhagwan Das.[74] It should be noted that there was a hereditary factor in the granting of titles during Akbar's reign. Sometimes, out of gratitude to a deceased noble, the emperor would confer his title upon his son or grandson. In 1604, Zahid received his father's title of Sadiq Khan.[75]

However, there were some instances when the nobles were reluctant to accept the title offered by the emperor, for example, Muhammad Niazi, Mirza Rustam Safavi and Abul Hasan Turbati. Muhammad Niazi refused to accept a title because he believed that there was no better name than Muhammad.[76] (For details of titles conferred upon nobles under Akbar see Table 4.2).

Regarding the gifts from the emperor to the *mansabdars*, it has been mentioned earlier that whenever any present was made to Akbar, he carefully calculated its intrinsic value. Those who presented the most valuable gifts generally received the highest rewards. According to Manucci, an observer of the later period, the king in his turn showered favours on his subjects by giving them elephants, horses, a set of robes and jewels.[77] He adds, the Mughal king bought through his governors and officials, pearls, horses and rare things to confer on princes and nobles. An *amir* could be given a present any time by the emperor, though the latter received presents only on special occasions.

The types of gifts given form a hierarchy parallel to that of rank. The basic gift of a *khilat* (robe of honour) transformed the *mansabdar* into an extension of the emperor. In Buckler's words:

> Robes of Honour are symbols of some idea of continuity or succession... that continuity rests on a physical basis, depending on the contact of the body of the recipient with the body of the donor through the medium of clothing . . . the donor includes the recipient within his own person through the medium of clothing.[78]

A robe of honour was made from an expensive fabric (silk, cotton, brocade or velvet, sometimes it was bejewelled); the core symbol was a cloak which was the outermost visible garment of courtly life. It was bestowed by the emperor along with other articles of clothing, such as a turban, a waist wrap, a shirt and shoes. Simplest robes consisting of a turban (*dastar*) including a long gown or a coat with a full skirt (*jama*), and a waist-scarf (*kamarband*) were given from the general wardrobe (*khilat-khanah*). More elaborate five- and six-piece outfits were from the storehouse for presents (*toshah-khanah*) and included a *sarpech* (bejewelled turban ornament), a band of the turban (*balaband*) and a tight short-sleeved jacket.[79] According to Tavernier, a seven-piece outfit included a cap, a long gown and a short jacket, two pairs of trousers (*salvar*), two pair of shirts (*kamiz*), two girdles, and a scarf.[80] The emperor's worn clothes (*malbus-i-khas*) and a robe from his personal wardrobe carried higher status than any other clothes which were given as an extraordinary act of favour or in recognition of some exceptional deed or service to the emperor.[81] In one case, Akbar took off his upper coat and put it on Bairam Khan's shoulders in view of his long and meritorious service.[82] Sir Thomas Roe, James I's ambassador to the court of Jahangir, also received one of Jahangir's own garments.[83]

According to F.W. Buckler, kings in the Middle East, both ancient and Muslim, bestowed the robes of honour. When the king gave these robes to his servants, he incorporated into his own body, by mean of certain symbolic acts, the persons of those who shared his rule. *Khilat* or *khila* in Arabic, Persian *sar-o pa or khilat* and *sir pau* in Marathi, the robe of honour, as it is customarily translated, conveys some idea of continuity or succession and that continuity rests on a physical basis, depending on contact with the body of the recipient with the body of the donor through the medium of clothing. In traditional Islamic society, the ceremonial exchange of an article of clothing known as *khilat* (plural *khila*) between a superior and an inferior was virtually ubiquitous. The practice was well established during the Abbasid period in Baghdad and involved the *Caliph* presenting a used article of his clothing to someone who thereby became, if he was not already, a dependent. Underlying the transfer of this piece of property was the notion that the article of clothing carried the *baraka* (essence) of its precious possessor and influenced the behaviour of the receiver. In the Sufi tradition, the presentation of the robe by a Shaikh to his followers remained one of the core ceremonies of legitimacy and loyalty for centuries. Within the Sufi tradition, there was a practice among Sufi teachers to give their own 'patched' robe (*khirqa, frock* and *muraqqa*) to their followers as a visible symbol of discipleship.[84] In some orders, the presentation of the robe literally passed the mantle of authority to a successor. In present narrative, however, most of the investiture anecdotes are secular, involving the emperor rather than the Shaikhs.

Notwithstanding the ceremony's centrality to Indian kingship, the *khilat* has received little scholarly attention. In the mid-1920s, F.W. Buckler undertook an imaginative exploration of the Mughal state by examining the role of the robe of honour,[85] but little has been written since. More recently, Stewart Gordon, Gavin R.G. Hambly and Gail Minault subjected the somewhat linear images sketched by Buckler to considerable and elegant nuancing. They recorded several agencies, objectives and nature for the grant of *khilat* in medieval India and other parts of the world.[86] Douglas E. Streusand and John F. Richards commented on the nature of the state while substantively touching upon the question of robes of honour.[87] Indian based scholars have largely neglected this important custom. Only Harbans Mukhia has in his *The Mughals of India* examined in brief the general importance of this custom. But his treatment is rather inadequate.[88]

As the definer of status and distributor of power, the ruler determined the nature and position of his subordinates. The ritual exchange of gifts at the Mughal *darbar* or camp embodied inter-personal relations. Mughal officers (*mansabdars*), as mentioned earlier, presented two categories of gifts to the ruler: *nazr* and *peshkash*. After the sovereign uttered a formal verbal confirmation of promotion, a new title, a piece of land and its revenue, a new posting, to lead a military campaign, etc., the sovereign favoured the officer with a full or partial robe of honour, horses, saddles and related accoutrements, flags, drums, elephants, elephant gear, turbans, turbans ornaments, bejewelled weapons, money and other artefacts. Of all the gifts the most coveted was the robe of honour. Most of the gifts for personal use thus bestowed could be construed to have some symbolic reference to the body and the person of the ruler, i.e. the ruler actually touched the robe of honour with either his hand or brushed it momentarily across his shoulder, owing to the very dense symbolic signification embedded in it. Distinction was however, made according to the position of the receiver.[89]

The *khilat* or *sar-o pa* comprised clothes from head to foot. The present of *sar-o pa*, the entire body wear, carried the impress of completeness, signified in the king's person, now being imparted to the recipient. Since the king's person symbolically expanded into the whole space of the empire, the recipient, too, was incorporated into the imperial presence and became a part and extension of it. Hence high prestige was attached to it.

The robes of honour ceremony encompassed a large geographical area, which at its maximum size stretched from Moorish Spain and West Africa to China.[90] In traditional Muslim society, the ceremonial exchange of an article of clothing (*khilat*) between a superior and an inferior was virtually ubiquitous. In the words of Clement Huart:

The gift of a robe of honour from the king's ward-robe was a very ancient custom. . . . Sapor II [Sassanian King of Persia] gave the Armenian general 'a royal garment, an ermine fur, a gold and silver pendant to attach to the eagle on his helmet, a diadem, breast ornaments, a tent, carpet and gold vessels. To reward the grand Mobed who brought him some good news, Ardashir I, filled his mouth with rubies, gold coins, pearls, and jewellery'.[91]

A well-known representation of Mahmud of Ghaznin (*c.* 999) depicts the invader of India proudly donning a silk robe of honour from the *Caliph* of Baghdad. Chronicles of his court describe Mahmud bestowing the robe to honour on his nobles. [92] The custom was common in the Delhi Sultanate as well as all the Deccan kingdoms and had spread into Hindu society. Elaborate robes were in use in Vijayanagar, specifically as a means of connecting the kingdom to the Islamicate world.[93] In the fifteenth century, a local Rajput chronicle records a father robing his sons as he sent them to seek their fortune.[94] Tens of thousands of honourific robes were used by the Mughal emperors, but the empire's rivals used them just as ubiquitously. The award of *khilat* became so popular with all classes of people that even the Sikh Guru Angad is credited with distributing two *khilats* to his followers every year.[95] An inventory of Shivaji's possessions prepared at the time of his death included thousands of his robes of honour.[96] Early European travellers to India had their portraits painted in the robes they received.[97] By the eighteenth century, this system of honour was as common in Tipu's Mysore as it was in Bengal.[98] By the nineteenth century, the ceremony had become a serious issue of legitimacy between the Mughal court and the emerging British colonial state. As the British gradually conquered north India in the early nineteenth century, they reduced the Mughal Empire to a shadow of its former self and the Mughal emperor to a mere pensioner. During the course of these events, the British East India Company made the transition from a subordinate to a ruler and the Mughal emperor from the ruler to a subordinate. This shift in power relations was symbolized by rituals of sovereignty, with the British initially offering signs of their submission, but later proving to be a prodigious present taker (*nazr*) and gift giver, *khilat* to the subordinate. Thus, the British demonstrated that the company, not the Mughal emperor, was the dominant force.

The practice of giving robes of honour was well established all across eastern Central Asia. The practice was fully developed at the court of Kublai Khan, as described by Marco Polo.[99] However, specific details of the robe ceremony varied considerably from kingdom to kingdom. The unifying factor was that high value was attached to a robe of honour, an elite attire suitable for courtly presence. A newly installed Hindu king in ancient India could not, it was believed, rule without 'aides' or 'ministers' and so he had to share royal authority—and royal wealth—among his followers or dependants. The king gave one of a variety of items to the man he appointed—a turban or headband (*patta*), an umbrella (*chatr*), a robe (*vastra*) or an ornament (*alamkara*) such as a necklace. The practice of bestowing such gifts did not become an important court ceremony in early medieval India, but they appear to have served much the same purpose. In the fourteenth century, Ibn-Battuta did not receive robes of honour from any of the Hindu rulers he visited on the west coast of India though he observed numerous instances of the robe ceremony in other parts of India.[100] He rightly concluded that India was beyond the edge of the known world of robes of honour. Stewart Gordon, too, did not find a single instance of the robing ceremony in India prior to the Muslim invasions.[101]

Robes were not, in any of the widely diverse cultural contexts, one of the core symbols of kingship. Under the Mughals, robes were only part of an elaborate transfer which often included nearly all the 'transactional' objects (such as bejewelled daggers, horses and saddles), plus some of the 'core symbols' of kingship (such as flag, standard and drums). The robing ceremony was associated with a specific kind of loyalty and legitimacy. The acceptance of a robe of honour was a precise recognition of the personal authority and largesse of the giver, and in return, recognition of the honoured position of the receiver, whether that position of king (as in the *caliph* to the early sultans of India), ambassador, official, successful general or creative poet.

The robe of honour was bestowed in the court of a ruler or one holding authority from the ruler, and some time dispatched to men stationed far from the capital. The robe presented was similar to those worn by nobles and the ruler in the court. The honoured person put on the robe either in the court or in a nearby dressing room. On the occasion of granting a robe of honour *Seir Mutakharin* describes the procedure thus:

The custom is that the man designed for that honour (*khilat*) passes into a neighbouring closet where a person prepared for that office hold over the man's turban, that which is bestowed upon him. He also assists in his putting on new clothes, that is *gown* and *sash*, over his *gown*; and in that condition, he proceeds to the presence, preceded by a principal mace-bearer, or *chobdar*, who proclaims his name and title aloud, with the reason of receiving that honour. This ceremony over, the man goes home, where he gets new clothes fitted to his body and he wears them for three days, or at least he wears the turban and the piece of jewel along with it.[102]

In the most direct way, by donning attire from the hand of the emperor in front of the court, the robe made the recipient part of the elite and suitable for continued appearance at court.

In the centuries before the Mughal conquest, robes of honour were in common usage in Muslim courts in both north India and the Deccan.[103] In the beginning of the sixteenth century, Babur's down-to-earth autobiography records very few instances of presentation or receipt of robes of honour. However, a close scrutiny of the events in the last decade of his life in India reveals that Babur gave and recorded substantial references to the robes of honour.[104] It is very interesting to note here that under Babur robes included transactional objects such as quiver, dagger and horses, but not core symbols of kingship such as standard or flags.[105] Well before the Mughal conquest, the robe ceremony had passed into the Rajput usage through intimate contact with the Muslim courts and thorough familiarity with the robing ceremony in the fourteenth century, if not before. During the early rule of the Mughals in India, Hindus fully understood the implication and significance of robes. One of the first robes of honour which Babur and Akbar gave was not to a Muslim, but to a Hindu. Babur bestowed it upon a Hindu in the Panjab who had helped him.[106] Akbar honoured Raja Bahar Mal Rajawat Kachhwaha (father of Bhagwan Das), his sons and relatives with robes, for taking amicable possession of the Narnaul fort from Haji Khan (a servant of Sher Khan) who had besieged it.[107] In western India, the robes of honour ceremony became a part of the kingly ritual in Gujarat in the sixteenth century. For example, Chingez Khan who succeeded Sultan Mahmud in Gujarat, daily gave away five or six dresses of honour from his private wardrobe, each single dress costing not less than Rs. 700 or Rs. 800 or Rs. 500.[108]

Other uses of the earlier robes of honour were transformed substantially in the subsequent reigns. For example, the practice of giving transactional objects and rewards to princes of the blood was so expanded that vast sums in cash, kingly symbols (*chatr*, flag, drums and standard) and jewels were transferred. Another transformation of the use of robes of honour was the sheer number of robes which were given. The *Humayunnama* mentions a feast organized by one of Humayun's principal wives during which 7,000 robes of honour were given. After his victory over Sultan Muhammad Lodi, 12,000 robes were given by Humayun; of which 2,000 were special.[109] The *Akbarnama* mentions 12,000 and 10,000 *khilats* carried to Mecca by the leaders of the caravan sponsored by the emperor.[110] The *Ain-i-Akbari* mentions that 1,000 full suits of costly fabric were made each season and 120 were available at all times.[111]

The practice of bestowing robes of honour was a daily routine in Akbar's court; he even had a small workshop for the production of robes in the outer fringe of his capital Fatehpur Sikri. The *khilat* was the epitome of transference. Robes of honour became fashionable along with the increasing opulence of the court. Robes of honour were no longer made of Chinese silk and furs of Central Asia, they were of brocades, velvets and gold thread silks typically found in Mughal paintings. There were subtle changes every few years in the size of the *sash*, or the number of ties, or the size of the chest opening, or a popular fabric.

During Akbar's reign, robes of honour became routinized. They were regularly bestowed on large numbers of nobles throughout the year. These were times of important life cycle ceremonies of the ruler and promotion into the *mansabdari* system and promotion within it. Akbar gave robes to Kamal Khan Gakkhar in 1559 when he defeated an Afghan tribe in Saranj (Malwa).[112] In 1560 after the defeat of Bairam Khan, a warm cloak (*daqu* dress) and a robe of victory (*fattahi*) were given to Shamsuddin Muhammad Khan Atka. In addition, he was presented kingly symbols like *naqara*, *alam* and *tumantuq*.[113] Munim Khan was given robes of honour and titles following his appointment as *vakil*.[114] After the successful military campaign of Malwa, Muqim Khan was honoured with a robe of honour.[115] Akin to the *mansabdari* system and many other features of Akbar's period, there was a movement to grade, quantify and monetarily evaluate each kind of robe of honour.

> All Articles which have been bought, woven to order, or received as tribute or presents, are carefully preserved; and according to the order in which they were preserved, they are again taken out for inspection, or given to be cut

and to be made up, or to be given away as presents. . . . Experienced people inquire continually into the prices of articles used both formerly and at present, as knowledge of the exact prices is conducive to the increase of the stock.[116]

Information about robes and their prices was so widespread at court that nobles understood the subtle degrees of favour of the emperor from the richness of the transactional objects. For example, the presentation of robes 'suitable to their rank' is a phrase which frequently occurs in the *Akbarnama*.[117]

The robe of honour rapidly became part of the etiquette associated with the acceptance of *farman* which mostly came with the robe of honour and transactional items. Unlike the earlier period, Akbar and his successors required a written contract (*farman*) of pay and perquisites for all those in the upper level of service. The *farman* and the robe of honour also came to 'stand in' for the emperor for men stationed far from the capital. The proper mode of receiving a *farman* (for example, augmenting one's appointment) was to don the accompanying robe of honour, place the *farman* on one's forehead, and perform *taslim*, i.e. bowing three times and moving the hand from the open palm against the forehead, to the back of the hand touching the ground.[118]

During the reign of Akbar, the granting of a robe of honour had been transformed from a strictly kingly privilege into one held by the commander in the field. Munim Khan presented a horse and a complete robe (*sar-o pa*) to Ali Quli Khan who had repaired a fort near Varanasi. Munim Khan also gave a sword with a jewelled belt and a robe of honour to Daud Khan of Bengal after his submission.[119] During Jahangir's reign, Mirza Nathan (a commander) also gave away robes of honour plus several other transactional objects such as a horse and a dagger.[120] By the time of the Balkh campaign (1640-7) during the reign of Shahjahan, the commander carried several thousand robes of honour, which he gave in the field when the campaign was successful.[121] Under Akbar, the robe of honour was transformed into an explicit symbol of submission, a role not observed in Babur's time. At Akbar's court, Afghans and rebel officers who proved loyal were pardoned with robes of honour.[122] A distinguished service of a military or non-military nature was not the only reason for the award of a *khilat*, even a message of condolence could be wrapped in it. For example, Akbar sent robes of honour with a condolence message to Raja Man Singh on the death of his son.[123] Jahangir sent *khilats* to the children of his father-in-law, Itmad-ud-Daula, 'to take them out of their mourning garments'.[124] *Khilats* were often used to win over political opponents or to convert adversaries into allies.

The other transactional items as well as some of the core symbols of kingship depended on and transmitted the status of the recipient. When Akbar appointed Sultan Murad governor of Malwa in 1591, he presented him a flag, a drum, an umbrella (*chatr*) and a whisk (*tugh*).[125] When Mirza Rustam Safavi, the grandson of Bahram Mirza, the brother of Shah Tahmasp, who was the governor of Zamin Dawar in Afghanistan, sought refuge with Akbar, the Mughal ruler sent him tents, screens, carpets and a bejewelled dagger in response to his request for sanctuary. When he appeared in court, Akbar gave him the rank of 5000, a substantial *jagir*, and later a flag and a drum. The gifts, which Akbar sent, were useful in the journey from Zamin Dawar to Lahore, especially in making the journey comfortable. In this way, the gifts indicated that Mirza Rustam would retain his high position in Mughal service.[126]

In 1599 when Akbar sent Abul Fazl to the Deccan, Shahbaz Khan against the Rana of Mewar, Mirza Shahrukh to Malwa and Mirza Rustam Safavi to Raisin, he gave each officer a robe of honour and a horse. They held different ranks and posts, and had already received various gifts indicating their status. The presentation of a horse and robe on their departure reinforced their connection to their master and stated that they were military—cavalry—servants.[127]

During the Mughal period, the symbols of kingship, which an emperor believed that he must possess in order to be an emperor, were at times bestowed on high ranking officers. For the Mughal emperor, these included coins minted in his name and the reading of his name at the Friday service. The symbols of kingship as listed in the late sixteenth-century *Ain-i-Akbari* were: throne, *chatr* (umbrella), *sayaban* or *aftabgir* (palm leaf sunshade), *kawkaba* (polished steel or golden ball carried on a long pole), *jhanda* (triangular flag), *naqara* (drums), *alam* (tall horsetail standard with metal finial), *tumantuq* (shorter yak tail standard), and *qur* (jewelled weapons).[128] The first four symbols were never bestowed on any officer under Akbar, except in very few cases the *chatr* was given to royal princes and towering nobles.[129] Under

Akbar, bestowed symbols frequently on nobles were *naqara*[130] and *alam*. Nobles were also allowed to play the *naqara* as a mark of special royal favour.[131] According to Abul Fazl and Badauni, occasionally high ranking nobles and princes were allowed to keep the kingly symbols: *naqara, alam, flag, chatr, tumantuq* and *qur* as a mark of royal favour.[132] When an *amir* ceased to enjoy the favour of the emperor, he could be called upon to surrender these at the order of the emperor.[133]

To sum up, the problems of kingship were never permanently or wholly solvable. Kings were constantly improvising—whether Mughal, Deccan, Sultanate, Maratha, Jat or Rajput. They were always experimenting with symbols and ceremonies, which would foster loyalty and their own legitimacy. The robe of honour ceremony was useful to kings in a variety of circumstances. The ceremony established a direct, personal link between the sovereign and the recipient. At best, the recipient was reminded of this link every time he wore the outfit, whether at court or on an assignment far away from the capital. He was also reminded that it was through the largesse of the king that he belonged to the elite group that wore valuable courtly textiles. Seeing the recipient, others were also reminded that loyalty to the emperor could bring such rewards to them. Their costumes indicated their nature and rank; receiving them from the king indicated that the king determined their status and political identity. The clothes made the man.

TABLE 4.1: PRESENTS OFFERED TO AKBAR

Sr. No.	*Names*	*Year(s)*	*Presents/Peshkash (Not Fully Defined)*	*Elephants*	*Horses*	*Other Items*	*Sources*
1	2	*3*	*4*	*5*	*6*	*7*	*8*
1.	Ambassador of Abdur-Rashid Khan (Ruler of Kashghar)	1556	Presents	–	–	–	*AN*, II, 36
2.	Sikandar Khan Afghan	1557	Presents	Elephants	–	–	*AN*, II, 91; *TA*, II, 223
3.	Munim Khan	1560	Rare and exquisite presents	–	–	–	*AN*, II, 188
4.	Ambassdor of Mirza Sulaiman (Ruler of Badakshan)	1560	Presents	–	–	–	*AN*, II, 188; *ZK*, I, 20-3
5.	Shamsuddin Muhamad Atka	1561	Presents	–	–	–	*AN*, II, 230
6.	Ali Quli Khan and Bahadur Khan	1561	Booty	Noted elephants such as Dilshankar, Pulta, Dalil, Sab-dilia and Jagmohan	–	–	*MT*, II, 44; *AN*, II, 229

(*contd.*)

1	*2*	*3*	*4*	*5*	*6*	*7*	*8*
7.	Adham Khan	1561	Booty elephants	Few	–	–	*AN*, II, 213-14; MU, I, 146
8.	Mirza Sharafuddin Husain	1562	Presents	–	–	–	*AN*, II, 243
9.	Ambassador of Shah Tahmasp Safavi (Ruler of Persia)	1562	–	–	–	Fiery Arab coursers, swift steeds from Iraq and Turkey, delicate cloths and wonderful curiosities	*AN*, II, 262; *TA*, II, 262-3; Farishita, II, 129
10.	Ram Chand (Raja of Bhatta)	1563	–	Elephants	–	Valuable jewels	*AN*, II, 280
11.	Khwaja Muin (Saint from Kashghar) (father of Mirza Sharafuddin Husain)	1563	–	–	–	Rare merchandise from Khita (China) and Kashghar	*AN*, II, 303
12.	Muhammad Qasim Khan Nishapuri and his Followers	1564	–	–	700 horses and mules	–	*AN*, II, 345
13.	Chingez Khan[134] (Sultan of Gujarat)	1564	*Peshkash*	–	–	–	*AN*, III, 351

14.	Ambassador of Miran Mubarak Shah (Ruler of Burhanpur)	1564	Presents	–	–	–	*AN*, III, 351; *MT*, II, 68; *TA*, II, 285
15.	Ambassador of Shah Tahmasp Safavi (Ruler of Persia)	1564	Presents	–	–	Rarities of Persia	*AN*, II, 358
16.	Khwaja Abdul Majid Asaf Khan	1565	–	Warlike elephants	Persian and Turkish horses	Rarities of Garaha	*AN*, II, 379; *TA*, II, 298
17.	Bahadur Khan and Sikandar Khan	1565	Presents	Elephants– Koh-para and Saf-shikan	–	Presents	*TA*, II, 309; *MT*, II, 84
18.	Ambassador of Raja Mukund Deo (Raja of Orissa)	1565	*Peshkash*	Noted elephants	—	–	*AN*, II, 382
19.	Ali Quli Khan	1565	–	Noted elephants such as Balsunder and Acapla (immovable)	–	–	*AN*, II, 388
20.	Muhammad Baqi Khan (s/o M. Isa Tarkhan, Ruler of Thatta)	1566-7	*Peshkash*	-	–	–	*AN*, III, 413
21.	Itimad Khan Gujrati	1567	*Peshkash*	Sea elephant	--	–	*AN*, II, 466

(contd.)

1	*2*	*3*	*4*	*5*	*6*	*7*	*8*
22.	Mahdi Qasim Khan	1569	Presents	–	Iraqi horses	–	*AN*, II, 491-2; *AA*, I, 373; MU, II, 505
23.	Chander Sain (s/o Raja Maldeo of Jodhpur)	1570	*Peshkash*	–	–	–	Farishta, II, 143
24.	Kalyanmal (Raja of Bikaner)	1570	*Peshkash*	–	–	–	Farishta, II, 143
25.	Khan Azam Mirza Aziz Koka	1571	–	Elephant with chains of gold and silver, juls[135] of velvet, gold brocade and goad (hooks)[136] of gold and silver	Arab and Iraqi horses with gold and silver saddles	Gems, pearls, emeralds, chairs and bedsteads, stools of gold and silver, utensils of gold and silver, fabrics of Firangi (Europe) and Rum (Consta-ntinople) and Khita (China) and Yezd[137]	*AN*, II, 528-9; *TA*, II, 364-5; Arif, 171; Farishta, II, 144; *MU*, I, 319-20

26.	Husain Quli Khan	1571	Presents	–	–	Gifts and dresses, five pieces of Pashmina, Zarbaft, Kamkhwab, atlas and velvet	*AN*, II, 529; *TA*, II, 366; Arif, 171 [133-4]
27.	Ambassador of Sultan Muhammad Khuda Banda (Ruler of Khurasan)	1572	Presents	–	Fast running Arab and Iraqi horses	Rarities of Persia	*AN*, III, 7-8; Arif, 191; Elliot, V, 342; *TA*, II, 373
28.	Amin Khan Ghori (Ruler of Junagarh)	1572	*Peshkash*	–	–	–	*AN*, III, 12; Elliot, 360-70
29.	Ludi Khan (Chieftain of Bihar)	1572-3	*Peshkash*	–	–	–	*AN*, III, 31
30.	Narain Das Rathore	1573	Presents	–	–	–	*AN*, III, 92
31.	Daud Afghan	1575	–	Noted elephants	–	Rarities of Bengal	*AN*, III, 185; *MT*, II, 199-200
32.	Mirza Sulaiman	1575	–	–	2 horses	-	*TA*, II, 475; *ZK*, I, 20-4
33.	Raja Todar Mal	1575	Booty	54 noted elephants[138]	–	Rarities of Bengal	*AN*, III, 222

(contd.)

1	*2*	*3*	*4*	*5*	*6*	*7*	*8*
34.	Husain Quli Khan	1575	Booty	54 elephants	–	Other things	Farishta, II, 153; *MU*, I, 649
35.	Ambassador of Ibrahim Qutb Shah (Ruler of Golconda)	1577	*Peshkash*	Elephant Fath Mubarak[139]	–	–	*AN*, III, 310
36.	Ambassador of Adil Khan (Ruler of Bijapur)	1577	*Peshkash*	Elephants	–	Rarities of Bijapur	*AN*, III, 296; *MT*, II, 257; *TA*, II, 503
37.	Ambassador of Abdullah Khan (Ruler of Turan)	1577	Presents	–	–	–	*AN*, III, 296; *MT*, II, 278; *TA*, II, 521-3
38.	Ambassador of Nizam-ul-Mulk (Ruler of Ahmadnagar)	1577	*Peshkash*	Elephants	–	Rarities of the Deccan	*AN*, III, 288
39.	Mirzada Ali Khan	1577	Booty	65 elephants[140]	–	–	*AN*, III, 277
40.	Raja Todar Mal and Itimad Khan Khwajasara	1577	Booty	304 elephants[141]	–	–	*AN*, III, 277; *MT*, II, 249; *TA*, II, 497
41.	Muzaffar Khan	1577	Presents[142]	30 elephants	–	Cloths, etc.	*AN*, III, 303; *MT*, II, 277; *TA*, II, 522n; Arif, 263

42.	Mihr Ali Sildoz	1578	Presents	–	–	–	*AN*, III, 328
43.	Raja Ali Khan (Ruler of Burhanpur)	1578	*Peshkash*	Renowned elephants	–	Various commodities	*TA*, II, 503
44.	Mal Gosain (Chieftain of Kuch-Bihar)	1578	*Peshkash*	54 elephants	–	Bengal rarities	*AN*, II, 349
45.	Raja Madhukar (Chief of Orcha)	1578	*Peshkash*	–	–	–	*AN*, III, 379
46.	Sultan Khwaja	1578-9	–	–	Horses of Arabian pedigree	Fabrics of Turkey and other European Countries (Rumi-wa-Firangi), Abyssian slaves and other rarities of Makkah[143]	*AN*, III, 382; *TA*, II, 516-17; *AA*, I, 466-7; *MU*, II, 895-6
47.	Masum Khan Kabuli	1579	–	39 elephants	–	–	*MT*, II, 277; *TA*, II, 522n
48.	Ambassador of Mirza Shahrukh (Ruler of Badakshan)	1579	–	–	Turki horses of Badakshi pedigree	Glittering rubies and strings of camels, both bulls and cow	*MT*, II, 276; *TA*, II, 520

(*contd.*)

1	*2*	*3*	*4*	*5*	*6*	*7*	*8*
49.	Isa Khan (Chieftain of Orissa)	1579-80	-	250 elephants	–	Gold vessels, aloe-wood, fine linen, cloth and Rs. 4 lakh	*MT*, II, 292
50.	Qutbuddin Khan Atka	1580	Presents	–	–	–	*AN*, III, 401
51.	Ambassador of Adil Khan (Ruler of Bijapur)	1581	*Peshkash*	Renowned elephants	–	–	*TA*, II, 519; *AN*, III, 388
52.	Muzaffar Khan	1581	Booty	171 elephants	–	Rarities of Bengal	*AN*, III, 439
53.	Birbar	1581	Presents	–	–	–	*AN*, III, 511
54.	Sharif Khan Atka	1581	–	9 elephants	27 Iraqi andArab horses	Various fabrics	*TA*, II, 539[144]
55.	Yusuf Khan (Ruler of Kashmir)	1581	*Peshkash*	–	–	–	*AN*, III, 550
56.	Ambassador of Nizam-ul-Mulk (Ruler of Ahmadnagar)	1583	*Peshkash*	–	–	–	*AN*, III, 597
57.	Qutlu Kararani	1584	–	60 elephants	–	Other gifts	*AN*, III, 653
58.	Raja Ram Chand (Raja of Bhatta)	1584	–	120 elephants	–	Ruby (worth Rs. 50,000)	*AN*, III, 637; *TA*, II, 595-6; *MT*, II, 345; MU, II, 583

59.	Raja of Sirohi	1585	*Peshkash*	–	–	–	*AN*, III, 710-11; *TA*, II, 583
60.	Yaqub (s/o Yusuf Khan, Ruler of Kashmir)	1585	*Peshkash*	–	–	Rarities of Kashmir	*AN*, III, 676
61.	Amin Khan Ghori	1585	*Peshkash*	Elephant Sherza	–	Other gifts	*AN*, III, 683
62.	Ambassador of Magh Ruler	1585-6	Presents	Elephants	–	–	*AN*, III, 722
63.	Ambassador of Raja Ali Khan (Ruler of Burhanpur)	1586	*Peshkash*	150 elephants	–	–	*TA*, II, 600; *AN*, III, 687
64.	Ambassador of Abdullah Khan (Ruler of Turan)	1586	–	–	Choice horses	Strong camels, swift mules, choice *postin* (dressing gowns) and other rarities	*AN*, III, 735; *TA*, II, 611
65.	Ambassador of Mirza Jani Beg (Ruler of Thatta)	1586	*Peshkash*	–	–	–	*AN*, III, 76
66.	Qulij Khan	1588	Presents	–	–	–	*MT*, II, 377
67.	Raja of Kumaon	1588	–	–	–	Yak, musk-deer and other things	*MT*, II, 377

(*contd.*)

1	*2*	*3*	*4*	*5*	*6*	*7*	*8*
68.	Ambassador of Mirza Jani Beg (Ruler of Thatta)	1588	Presents	–	–	–	*TA*, II, 621
		1589	Presents [145]	–	–	–	*TA*, II, 623
69.	Ambassador of Abdullah Khan (Ruler of Turan)	1589	Presents	–	–	–	*AN*, III, 857; *TA*, II, 627; Farishta, II, 161
70.	Medni Rai	1589	Presents	–	–	Deer and leopard (yuz)	*AN*, III, 881
71.	Ambassador of Shah Tahmasp (Ruler of Iran)	1589	Presents	–	–	–	*AN*, III, 820
72.	Raja Man Singh	1590	Booty	54 elephants	–	Other gifts	*AN*, III, 873, 901 (n. 3)
73.	Ambassador of Abdullah Khan (Ruler of Turan)	1590	Presents	–	–	–	*AN*, III, 885
74.	Rajas of Northern Hills[146]	1590	–	18 elephants	115 horses	205 hunting animals including hawks, falcons, etc., yaks (*qatas*) and other rarities	*AN*, III, 885
75.	Khan Azam Mirza Aziz Koka	1591	Presents	Choice elephant	–	Other rarities of Gujarat	*AN*, III, 889

76.	Ambassador of Mirza Jani Beg (Ruler of Thatta)	1591	*Peshkash*	–	–	–	*AN*, III, 889
77.	Ambassador of Shah Abbas (Ruler of Persia)	1591	Presents	–	–	–	*AN*, III, 893
78.	Raja Man Singh	1594	Booty	127 elephants[147]	-	Other articles	*AN*, III, 985; *TA*, II, 648; *MT*, II, 400
79.	Imad-ul-Mulk	1594	–	–	–	Royal falcon	*AN*, III, 1014
80.	Burhan-ul-Mulk (Ruler of Ahmadnagar)	1594	*Peshkash*[148]	–	–	–	*TA*, II, 650-1 (n. 3); *MT*, II, 403
81.	Isa Khan (Chieftain of Bengal)	1595	–	Elephant	–	Money and precious products	*MT*, II, 417; *AN*, III, 1031
82	Zain Khan Koka	1595	–	170 elephants[149]	–	–	*AN*, III, 1044
83.	Said Khan Chaghta	1595	Booty	100 elephants	–	Other articles	*AN*, III, 1031
84.	Mirza Muzaffar Husain	1595	–	–	100 Iraqi horses	Jewels	*AN*, III, 1030
85.	Ambassador of Abdullah Khan (Ruler of Turan)	1597	Presents	–	–	–	*AN*,III, 1103
86.	Prince Sultan Murad	1598	–	Few elephants	–	Swords, hawks and wrestlers	*AN*, III, 1098

(contd.)

1	*2*	*3*	*4*	*5*	*6*	*7*	*8*
87.	Wali Beg (s/o Payanda Khan)	1598	–	22 elephants	–	–	*AN*, III, 1115
88.	Ambassador of Shah Abbas (Ruler of Persia)	1598	–	–	101 Iraqi horses,[150] mares[151] (*qisraq*)	300 pieces of brocade,[152] 50 master-pieces of Ghias Naqshband, carpets,[153] choice coverlets (*takya namad*), splendid paincas, Turkish pavilions, embroidered mattresses, various seeds, nine goats (*murgaz*) whose fleeces yield wool (*suf*) and silk (*khara*), other rarities and 500 Turakmens in rich dresses	*AN*, III, 1113

89.	Ambassador of Shan Abbas (Ruler of Persia)	1599	Presents	–	Choice horses	–	*AN*, III, 1120
90.	Lala (s/o Birbar)	1599	–	16 elephants[154] (not present)	–	–	*AN*, III, 1122
91.	Bahadur Khan (Ruler of Khandesh)	1599	*Peshkash*	–	–	–	*AN*, III, 1146
92.	Abdur Rahim Mirza Khan (Khan-i-Khanan)	1599	Presents	–	Horse (which fought with an elephant)	–	*AN*, II, 1141
93.	Raja Man Singh	1599	Presents	–	–	50 valuable diamonds	*AN*, III, 1133
94.	Prince Sultan Daniyal	1599	Booty	206 elephants	–	–	*AN*, III, 1122
95.	Prince Sultan Daniyal	1601	Booty	–	–	Jewels	*AN*, III, 1178
96.	Saadat Khan (Chief of Fort Trimbak in Ahmadnagar)	1601	*Peshkash*	15 elephants	–	–	*AN*, III, 1184-5
97.	Prince Sultan Daniyal	1602	–	–	–	Diamond and a ruby[155]	*AN*, III, 1224
98.	Sarjeo (Chief of Canda, Central Province)	1602	*Peshkash*	14 elephants	–	–	*AN*, III, 1201
99.	Khan Azam Aziz Koka	1602	Booty	–	20 horses	–	*AN*, III, 1224
100.	Shah Beg Khan (Governor of Qandahar)	1602	Presents	–	–	–	*AN*, III, 1211

(contd.)

1	*2*	*3*	*4*	*5*	*6*	*7*	*8*
101.	Prince Sultan Daniyal	1602	Booty	10 elephants[156]	–	–	*AN*, III, 1213
102.	Qasim Khan (Ruler of Transoxiana)	1602	Presents	–	–	–	*AN*, III, 1223
103.	Prince Sultan Daniyal	1603	–	12 elephants	–	–	*AN*, III, 1229
104.	Prince Sultan Salim	1603	–	977 elephants (350 were accepted)	–	12,000 *muhrs*	*AN*, III, 1230
105.	Shaikh Abdur Rahman (s/o Abul Fazl); Abul Barkat (b/o Abul Fazl)	1603	–	3 elephants	–	7 strings of pearls and some ornamented vessels	*AN*, III, 1231
106.	Muhammad Quli	1603-4	–	–	12 swift horses	–	*AN*, III, 1235
107.	Prince Sultan Salim	1604	–	200 elephants	–	Diamond,[157] 209 *muhrs*	*AN*, III, 1247
108.	Ray Rayan Bikramjit	1604	–	2 elephants (*Iqbalnama* says 10)	–	–	*AN*, III, 1239
109.	Shaikh Farid Bakshi	1604-5	–	Elephant	–	5 valuable pearls, 4 rubies	*AN*, III, 1249

110.	Qutb-ul-Mulk (Ruler of Golconda)	1605	*Peshkash*	30 elephants with gold and silver equipments	–	Ornamented instruments	*AN*, III, 1256
111.	Qulij Khan	1605	–	–	20 horses	–	*AN*, III, 1256
112.	Hashim Khan	1605	–	4 elephants	–	–	*AN*, III, 1256
113.	Nuran Qulij Khan	1605	–	19 elephants	–	–	*AN*, III, 1256
114.	Jamaluddin Husain	1605	Presents	–	–	Jewels	*AN*, III, 1253
115.	Raja Man Singh	1605	Booty	Elephants	–	1,000 *muhrs* and Rs. 12,000	*AN*, III, 1256
116.	Mirza Ghazi Beg (s/o Mirza Jani Beg)	1605	*Peshkash*	–	–	–	*AN*, III, 1257
117.	Prince Sultan Salim	1605	–	Elephant	–	–	*AN*, III, 1252
118.	Prince Sultan Daniyal	1605	–	Elephant named Gajpati and two female elephants	–	–	*AN*, III, 1252

TABLE 4.2: AKBAR'S HONORIFIC INVESTITURE, AD 1556-1605

Sr. No.	*Names of Honouring Nobles*	*Honouring Years*	*Titles*	*Robes of Honour*	*Transactional Objects*	*Symbols of Kingship*	*Sources*
1	*2*	*3*	*4*	*5*	*6*	*7*	*8*
1.	Mir Ghiasuddin Ali	1556	Naqib Khan	–	–	–	*AN*, II, 35, 343; *TA*, II, 232; *MU*, II, 383
2.	Khwaja Sultan Ali	1556	Afzal Khan	–	–	–	*AN*, II, 48
3.	Bairam Khan	1556	Khan Baba, Khan-i-Khanan	–	–	–	*TA*, II, 216; Arif, 38
4.	Abdullah Khan Uzbek	1556	Shujaat Khan	–	–	–	*AN*, II, 71; AA, I, 401
5.	Sikandar Khan Uzbek	1556	Khan-i-Alam	–	–	–	*AN*, II, 71, 77; *MU*, I, 691
6.	Ali Quli Khan	1556	Khan-i-Zaman	–	–	–	*AN*, II, 71, 227; *TA*, II, 213; *MT*, II, 5
7.	Maulana Pir Muhammad	1556	Nasir-ul-Mulk	–	–	–	*AN*, II, 71; *MT*, II, 33; *TA*, II, 242
8.	Baharmal	Nov. 1556	–	Robes	–	–	*AN*, II, 70

9.	Bairam Khan	Sept. 1558	–	–	Elephant	*Alam*, drum, *tumantuq*	*AN*, II, 115
10.	Khwaja Aminuddin Mahmad	1558	Khwaja-i-Jahan	–	–	–	*AN*, II, 145; *TA*, II, 231, 355, 457
11.	Bahbal Khan	Jan. 1559	–	Robes	–	–	*AN*, II, 119
12.	Kamal Khan Gakkhar	Jan.-Feb. 1559	–	Robes	–	–	*AN*, II, 119
13.	Shamsuddin Muhammad Khan Atka	Apr. 1560	Azam Khan	–	–	*Alam*, drum, *tumantuq*	*AN*, II, 143
14.	Jan Muhammad Bahsudi	1560	Khan	–	–	–	*AN*, II, 184
15.	Mir Muhammad Khan	1560	Khan-i-Kalan	–	–	–	*AN*, II, 143; *AA*, I, 338-9
16.	Yuzsuf Muhammad Khan Atka	1560	Khan	–	–	–	*AN*, II, 185; *MU*, II, 1008
17.	Khwaja Muzzaffar Ali	1560	Muzaffar Khan, Darvesh Beg	–	–	–	*AN*, II, 159, 306; *TA*, II, 280; *MT*, II, 64; *MU*, II, 360
18.	Pir Muhammad Khan	Apr. 1560	–	–	–	*Alam*, drum, *tumantuq*	*AN*, II, 156; *MT*, II, 33; *TA*, II, 242; Arif, 80
19.	Khwaja Abdul Majid Harvi	Aug. 1560	Asaf Khan	–	–	*Alam*, drum,	*MT*, II, 38; *TA*, II, 246; *AN*, II, 169, 282; *MU*, I, 37

1	*2*	*3*	*4*	*5*	*6*	*7*	*8*
20.	Shamsuddin Muhammad Khan Atka	Sept. 1560	Khan Azam	*Daqu* dress, *fathahi*	–	–	*AN*, II, 174; *TA*, II, 257
21.	Munim Khan	Sept. 1560	Khan-i-Khan	Robes	Horse	–	*AN*, II, 174, 279; *TA*, II, 247
22.	Bairam Khan	Oct. 1560	–	*Malbus-i-khas*	Horse, Rs. 50,000 cash	–	*AN*, II, 181; *TA*, II, 249; Arif, 88; *MT*, II, 39
23.	Pir Muhammad Khan	May 1561	–	Robes	Horse	–	*TA*, II, 255
24.	Muhammad Ashghar (Mir Munshi)	Jun. 1561	Ashraf Khan	Elaborate robe	Studded sword	–	*AN*, II, 223; *TA*, II,255; Arif, 117-18
25.	Ali Quli Khan, Bahadur Khan	Aug. 1561	–	Elaborate robes	Jewelled waist dagger	–	*MT*, II, 44; *AN*, II, 229; *TA*, II, 257; MU, I, 351
26.	Sayyid Beg (Ambassador of Iran)	1562	–	Elaborate robes	Horse, 7 lakh *tankas* Curiosities of Hindustan	–	*TA*, II, 263; *MT*, II, 49
27.	Calma Khan	(1564)	Khan Aalam	–	–	–	*AN*, II, 343; *AA*, I, 411
28.	Muqim Khan (Shujaat Khan)	Aug. 1564	–	Robes	–	–	*AN*, II, 350; *MT*, II, 66; *TA*, II, 286; *MU*, II, 851

29.	Mulla Nuruddin Muhammad	Jan. 1566	Tarkhan	–	–	*Alam*, drum	*AN*, II, 292-3; *MU*, II, 461
30.	Husain KhanTukriya	–	–	–	–	Akbar's own crescent cimeter (sickle shaped emblem of Islam)	*MT*, II, 171
31.	Mirza Muhammad Hakim	Oct.-Nov. 1566	–	Robes	Special horse, saddle including bridle adorned with jewels	-	*AN*, II, 410; *MT*, II, 91
32.	Iskandar Mirza	1566-7	Ulugh Mirza	–	–	–	*AN*, II, 414
33.	Muhammad Sultan Mirza	1566-7	Shah Mirza	–	–	–	*AN*, II, 414
34.	Jumla Khan	(1567)	Khan-i-Alam	–	–	–	*TA*, II, 346
35.	Munim Khan	Feb.-Mar. 1567	–	Robes	–	–	*MT*, II, 104
36.	Khwaja Amina	(1568)	Khwaja Jahan	–	–	–	*MT*, II, 111
37.	Mahdi Qasim Khan	Feb. 1569	–	Robes	–	–	*AN*, II, 492
38.	Khwaja Husain (poet)	Nov.-Dec. 1569	–	Robes	Gifts, 2 lakh *tankas*	–	*TA*, II, 358
39.	Muhibb Ali Khan (s/o Mir Khalifa)	Mar. 1571	–	Robes	–	*Alam*, drum	*TA*, II, 367; *MT*, II, 138; *MU*, II, 222

1	2	3	4	5	6	7	8
40.	Birbar	1572	Kavi Rai	–	–	–	*MT*, II, 164; TA, II, 399; MU, I, 420
41.	Munim Khan	1572	–	Robes	Jewelled sword belt, horse with gilded saddle	–	*MT*, II, 138-9
42.	Sikander Khan Uzbek	1572	–	Robes	Jewelled sword belt, horse with gilded saddle	–	*MT*, II, 138-9
43.	Muzaffar Khan	Sept. 1572	–	White robes	–	–	Arif, 177
44.	Raja Bhagwan Das	Dec. 1572	–	–	–	*Alam*, drum	*TA*, II, 381; *AN*, III, 18-22; *MT*, II, 146-7; *MU*, I, 404
45.	Mirza Mirak	(1573)	Rizavi Khan	–	–	–	Arif, 194; *MU*, II, 76
46.	Khan Azam Mirza Aziz Koka, Mir Muhammad Khan, Fazil Muhammad Khan, Farrukh Khan, Qutubddin Muhammad Khan, Naurang Khan, Sharif Muhammad Khan, Baz Bahadur	Mar.-Apr. 1573	–	Robes	Arab horses with saddles and bridle of gold, sword and elephants	–	*AN*, III, 46-7; *TA*, II, 394; Arif, 200

47.	Mirza Ghiasuddin Ali	Nov. 1573	Asaf Khan	–	Special belt, ink stand with pen	–	Arif, 226; *TA*, II, 409, 421; *MT*, II, 322; *AN*, III, 90
48.	Muzaffar Khan	Nov. 1573	Jumat-ul-Mulk	Robes	–	–	*TA*, II, 424; Arif, 200
49.	Arab (s/o Hashim Khan)	1574	Niyabat Khan	–	–	–	*AN*, III, 134
50.	Shahrullah Khan	1574	Shahbaz Khan	–	–	–	*MT*, II, 174
51.	Ray Purkhottam	Jun. 1574	–	Robes	–	–	*AN*, III, 122
52.	Raja Todar Mal	Aug. 1574	–	–	Sword	*Alam*, drum	*AN*, III, 144; *MT*, II, 174
53.	Qazi Nizam Badakshi	Sept. 1574	Qazi Khan, Gazi Khan	Robes	Jewelled sword belt, dagger and Rs. 5,000	–	*TA*, II, 451-2; *MT*, II, 186; Arif, 226; *MU*, I, 584
54.	Husain Khan Tukriya	Dec. 1574	–	–	Arrow (from HM's quiver), shawl (from HM's ward-robe)	–	*MT*, II,187-8; *AN*, III, 154
55.	Daud Afghan	Apr. 1575	–	Luxurious robes	Sword and embroidered belt	–	*AN*, III, 185; *MT*, II, 199-200; Arif, 238
56.	Muzaffar Khan	Apr. 1575	–	Elaborate robes	Horse and trappings	–	Arif, 200; *MT*, II, 153

1	2	3	4	5	6	7	8
57.	Munim Khan	May 1575	–	Elaborate robes	*Farman*, jewelled sword belt, horse with saddle and bridle	–	*TA*, II, 469; *MT*, II, 200
58.	Husain Quli(Khan-i-Jahan)	Oct.-Nov. 1575	–	Robe (golden embroidery clock), *chaharqab* (special robe of the Sultan of Turan)	Gold jewels, ornamented belt and sword, horse with gilded saddle	–	*TA*, II, 480; *MT*, II, 222
59.	Daulat Khan Lodi	1575	–	Robes	Horses, shawl (HM's own shawl)	–	*ZK*, II, 69-70; *Tarikh-i-Khan Jahani*, II, 463; *MU*, I, 464-5; *MD*(H), III, 482-3
60.	Raja Man Singh, Ghazi Khan Badakshi, Khwaja Ghiasuddin Ali, Sayyid Ahmad, Sayyid Hashim Baraha, Jagannath, Sayyid Raju, Mihtar Khan, Madhu Singh Mujahid Beg, Khangar, Rai Lonkaran and others	Apr. 1576/ Jun. 1576	–	Valuable robes	Iraqi and Arab horses	–	*AN*, III, 237; TA, II, 485, 489; *MT*, II, 233; *MU*, II, 49

51.	Sayyid Abdullah Khan	Jul. 1576	–	Robes	Iraqi horses, gold	–	*TA*, II, 492
62.	Muzaffar Khan	1577	–	Robes (golden embroidery)	Saddle	–	Arif, 266
63.	Muhibb Ali Khan	Sept. 1577	–	Fabulous robes	–	–	*AN*, III, 304
64.	Shah Fakruddin Mashudi	(1578)	Naqib Khan (Niyabat Khan)	–	–	–	*AN*, III, 382; *TA*, II, 411; *MU*, II, 383
65.	Raja Bhagwan Das, Raja Jagannath, Raja Gopal, Jagmal Panwar and others }	Dec. 1578	–	Robes	Horses	–	*AN*, III, 380
66.	Qutbuddin Muhammad Khan Atka	1579	Beglar Begi	–	–	–	*AN*, III, 401; *MT*, II, 278
67.	Abdullah Sultan Puri	1579	Makhdum-ul-Mulk	–	–	–	*AN*, III, 395; *MU*, I, 95
68.	Humayun Farmuli (s/o Shah Farmuli)	1579	Humayun Quli Khan	–	–	–	*MT*, II, 291
69.	Masum Khan	1579	–	Robes (from HM's wardrobe)	*Farman*	–	*MT*, II, 274-6

(*contd.*)

1	*2*	*3*	*4*	*5*	*6*	*7*	*8*
70.	Muzaffar Khan, Rizvi Khan, Mir Adham, Rai Patara Das, Hakim Abul Fath, Mir Nijabat Khan, Mir Jamaluddin Husain Anju	Mar. 1579	–	Robes	Horses	–	*AN*, III, 386
71.	Mirza Aziz Koka	1580	Azam Khan	–	–	–	*AN*, III, 454; *TA*, II, 333; Arif, 186
72.	Itimad Khan Gujrati	1580	–	–	–	30 elephants, 100 horses	*AN*, III, 465
73.	Mehtar Sadat	(1580)	Peshrau Khan	–	–	–	*MT*, II, 285; *TA*, II, 526
74.	Mirza Aziz Koka, Sayyid Abdullah Khan, Qasim Khan, Mirza Ali Khan, Ishqi Khan, Mukhtar Beg, Yunam Beg, Sikandar Dakhni, Haidar Dost, Qadir Ali, Usta Zakariya, Qambar Sahari	Jun. 1580	–	Robes	Horses	–	*AN*, III, 454
75.	Itimad Khan Gujrati	Aug.1580	–	–	30 elephants, 101 horses	–	*AN*, III, 465
76.	Mir Ghayasuddin Ali of Qazwin	Jul. 1581	Naqib Khan	Elaborate robes	Special horse (*Khwasta*)	–	*AN*, III, 524

77.	Khan Azam Aziz Koka, Tarsun Khan, Shaham Khan, Shah Quli Khan Mahram, Shaikh Farid	Apr. 1582	–	Robes	Selected horses	–	*AN*, III, 567
78.	Mirza Khan Abdur Rahim, Zain Khan Koka, Ismail Quli Khan, Makhsus Khan, Muttalib Khan, Rai Surjan, S. Jamal Bakhtiyar, Shiroya Khan, Khizr Beg, Mir Abul Muzaffar, Mir Masum	Apr. 1583	–	Robes	Selected horses	–	*AN*, III, 591
79.	Mir Abu Turab, Khwaja Nizamuddin Ahmad, Khwaja Abul-Qasim, Muhammad Husain, S. Abul Muzaffar Beg, Muhammad Toqbai, Mir Muhibbullah, Mir Sharafuddin, Mir Salih, Mir Hashim, Shah Beg, Mir Masum Bhakkari, Zainuddin Kambu, Sayyid Jalal Bhakkari, Sayyid Abu Ishaq, Qambar Ishak Aqa, Pahlwan Ali Sistani	Jun. 1583	–	Robes	Horses	–	*AN*, III, 596-7

1	2	3	4	5	6	7	8
80.	Raja Ram Chand	Feb. 1584	–	–	101 horses	–	*AN*, III, 636-7
81.	Abdur Rahim Mirza Khan	Mar. 1584	Khan-i-Khan	Robes	Horse, jewelled belt	*Tumantuq*	*AN*, III, 643; *TA*, II, 578; *MT*, II, 346
82.	Nizamuddin Ahmad	Mar. 1584	–	Robes	Horse	–	*TA*, II, 578
83.	Faridun, Ali Muhammad Asp, Shah Beg, Gada Beg, Tash Beg Qucin, Takhta Beg, Qasim Parwana, Muzaffar Koka, Janish Bahdur, Tatar Beg, Ghaiur Beg, Ulugh Beg, Nur-Muhammad, Khwaja Khizr, Dost Muhammad Turnabi, Khaki Galaban, Qasim Koka, Khwaja Yaqut, Atam Bahadur, Khwasham Bahadur, Haidar Ali Arab, Qazi Izzatullah, Farrukh Beg	Dec. 1585	–	Robes	Horses, gold, rupees	–	*AN*, III, 714
84.	Janish Bahadur	1585	–	Robes	Horse, rupees	–	*MU*, I, 749
85.	Khwaja Fattullah Shirazi	1585-6	Azudullah	Robes	Horses, Rs. 5,000 cash	–	*AN*, III, 701; *TA*, II, 601; *MT*, II, 354; *MU*, I, 544

86.	Akbar's sons	1586	–	Own wardrobe's	–	Drums, *tumantuq*, royal insignia	*MT*, II, 353-4
87.	Mirza Shahrukh	1586	–	Royal robes	9 Iraqi horses, 5 elephants, camels, mules, slaves, Rs. 1 lakh	–	*TA*, II, 598; *MT*, II, 352; *MU*, II, 780
88.	Abdur Rahim Mirza Khan	1586	–	Robes	–	–	*TA*, II, 604
89.	Ambassador of Abdullah Khan (Ruler of Turan)	1587	–	–	Rs. 1.50 lakh, rare gifts	–	*TA*, II, 618-19; *MT*, II, 365-6
90.	Raja Man Singh	1589	Raja	Special robes	*Farman*, horse	–	*TA*, II, 630; *AN*, III, 236
91.	Raja of Radaur	May 1589	–	Special robes	101 horses	–	*AN*, III, 818
92.	Zain Khan Koka	Mar. 1591	–	–	–	*Naubat* (right to play drum)	*AN*, III, 889; *MU*, II, 1026
93.	Prince Sultan Murad	Sept. 1591	–	*Chaharqab* (gold threa-ded vest)	–	*Alam*, drum, *chatr*, *jhanda* (flag), *tumantuq*, musical band, emblems and insignia of nobility (Amarat)	*AN*, III, 911; *MT*, II, 391; *TA*, II, 634

1	*2*	*3*	*4*	*5*	*6*	*7*	*8*
94.	Bir Bandu (s/o Raja Ram Chand)	1592	Raja	–	–	–	*MU*, II, 583
95.	Shiroyah(s/o Sher Afghan)	1594	Khan	–	–	–	*AN*, III, 1000
96.	Khwaja Daulat Nazir	1594	Khan	–	–	–	*AN*, III, 999
97.	Qulij Khan	Aug. 1594	–	Robes horse	Special	–	*AN*, III, 1004
98.	Mirza Rustam	Sept. 1594	–	– carpet, jewelled dagger and belt	Tent, screen,	Drum, flag	*AN*, III, 992-4; *MT*, II, 402; *TA*, II, 650; *MU*, II, 633
99.	Mirza Aziz Koka	Sept. 1594	–	Robes	Horses, camels	–	*AN*, III, 1004
100.	Rai Patra Das	–	Raja Bikramjits Rai Raiyan	–	–	–	*AN*, III, 1249; *MU*, I, 411
101.	Shah Quli Khan Mahram	1597	–	–	–	*Alam*, drum	*MU*, II, 776
102.	Prince Sultan Daniyal, Qulij Khan, Ismail Quli, Mir Sharif Amuli }	Apr. 1597	–	Robes	Horses	–	*AN*, III, 1077
103.	Kalyar Bahadur	1598	Bahadur Khan	–	–	–	*AN*, III, 1108
104.	Mirza Shahrukh	Jan. 1599	–	–	–	*Alam*, drum	*AN*, III, 1120

105. Mirza Rustam	Jan. 1599	–	Robes	Horse	–	*AN*, III, 1120
106. Shahbaz Khan	Jan. 1599	–	Robes	Horse	–	*AN*, III, 1120
107. Abul Fazl	Jan. 1599	–	Robes	Horse, elephants	–	*AN*, III, 1120
108. Raja Man Singh	Nov. 1599	–	Robes	Horse	–	*AN*, III, 1142
109. Raja Pratap Singh	May. 1600	–	–	–	*Alam*, drum	*AN*, III, 1152
110. Mir Murtaza	Dec. 1600	–	–	–	*Alam*, drum	*AN*, III, 1166
111. Salbahan	1601	Raja	–	–	–	*AN*, III, 1223
112. Mirza Gazi Beg	Jan. 1601	–	Special robes	*Farman*	–	*AN*, III, 1172
113. Abul Fazl	Feb. 1601	–	Elaborate robe	Special horse	*Alam*, drum	*AN*, III, 1173
114. Sher Khwaja	Mar. 1601	–	–	–	*Alam*, drum	*AN*, III, 1177
115. Mirza Ali Beg Akbarshahi	Mar. 1601	–	–	–	*Alam*, drum	*AN*, III, 1177
116. Abul Fazl	May 1601	–	–	20 elephants, 20 guns (*hatnal*), 10 horses	–	*AN*, III, 1184
117. Abul Fazl	Feb. 1602	–	Robes	Horse, dagger, elephant (by Daniyal)	–	*AN*, III, 1201
118. Irij (s/o Khan Khanan)	1602	Bahadur	–	–	–	*AN*, III, 1223

1	*2*	*3*	*4*	*5*	*6*	*7*	*8*
119.	Husain Quli (s/o Qulij Khan)	1602	–	Robes	–	–	*AN*, III, 1222
120.	Qulij Khan	1602	–	–	Shawl	–	*AN*, III, 1222
121.	Taluk Chand	1602	–	–	Shawl	–	*AN*, III, 1222
122.	Prince Salim	1602	–	Robes	Special elephant, special horse	–	*AN*, III, 1223
123.	Mirza Shahrukh	1602	–	–	Horse	–	*AN*, III, 1216
124.	Khwaja Abdullah (Abdullah Firoz Jang)	1603	Safdar Khan	–	–	–	*AN*, III, 1235
125.	Mirza Shahrukh	Mar. 1603	–	–	Shawl	–	*AN*, III, 1229
126.	Raja Suraj Singh	Mar. 1603	Raja	–	–	Drum	*AN*, III, 1229; *MU*, I, 572
127.	Prince Salim	1603	–	Robes (HM's own turban)	Special elephant (on demand)	–	*AN*, III, 1230
128.	Abdur Rahim Mirza Khan	1603	–	–	Special shawl (*parm narm*)	–	*AN*, III, 1231
129.	Abu Nabi Bahadur Khan	1603	–	–	Jewelled waist dagger	–	*MU,* I, 351
130.	Prince Daniyal	Oct.1603	–	Robes (HM's own turban)	Special horse	–	*AN*, III, 1234

131. Zahid (s/o Sadiq Khan)	1604	Sadiq Khan	–	–	–	*AN*, III, 1239
132. Takhta Beg Kabuli	1604	Khan	–	–	–	*AN*, III, 1247
133. Mir Abu Turub (s/o Ashraf Khan)	1604	Ashraf Khan	–	–	–	*AN*, III, 1249
134. Muqim Khan	1604	Wazir Khan	–	–	–	*AN*, III, 1249
135. Prince Salim	Mar. 1604	–	Robes (black and white fox)	–	–	*AN*, III, 1238
136. Prince Daniyal	Mar. 1604	–	–	*Farman*, horse	–	*AN*, III, 1238
137. Raja Raj Singh	May. 1604	Raja	–	Horse, shawl	Drum	*AN*, III, 1239
138. Mirza Aziz Koka and others	Aug. 1604	–	–	Golden embroidered shawl to all servants of 5000-1000 rank, *dupatta* Gujarati shawl 900-500 rank, *kalabatan* shawls 400-100 rank, plain shawl below 100 rank, cloak to *Ahadis*	–	*AN*, III, 1245-6

1	*2*	*3*	*4*	*5*	*6*	*7*	*8*
139.	Asaf Khan	1604-5	–	–	–	*Alam*, drum	*AN*, III, 1249
140.	S. Farid Bakshi	1604-5	–	–	–	*Alam*, drum	*AN*, III, 1249
141.	S. Abdur Rahim	1604-5	–	–	Special shawl	–	*AN*, III, 1249
142.	Prince Khusrau	Aug. 1605	–	–	–	Drum, *tumantuq* (studded)	*AN*, III, 1257
143.	Mirza Gazi	Sept. 1605	–	–	Jewel	–	*AN*, III, 1239
144.	Abul Baqa Uzbek	Sept. 1605	–	–	Jewel	–	*AN*, III, 1239
145.	Abdi Khawaja	Sept. 1605	–	–	Jewel	–	*AN*, III, 1239

Note: Brace '}' indicates that each one of them honoured at identical occasion received similar items of gift given in the columns of the row.

NOTES

1. Douglas E. Streusand, *The Formation of the Mughal Empire*, Delhi: Oxford University Press, 1989, pp. 123-4.
2. Sir Thomas Roe, *The Embassy of Sir Thomas Roe to India, 1615-19*, ed. Sir William Foster, London: Humphery Milford, 1926; rpt. Delhi: Munshiram Manoharlal, 1990, pp. 86-7.
3. F.W. Buckler, 'The Oriental Despot', *Anglican Theological Review*, no. 10, 1927-28; in *Legitimacy and Symbols: The South Asian Writing of F.W. Buckler* ed. M.N. Pearson, Ann Arbor: University of Michigan, 1985, pp. 176-87.
4. J.F. Richards, 'The Formulation of Imperial Authority Under Akbar and Jahangir', in *Kingship and Authority in South Asia*, ed. John F. Richards, reproduced in *The Mughal State*, ed. Alam and Subrahmanyam, pp. 160-1.
5. Broader literatures relevant to this topic are: Bernard S. Cohn, 'The Mughal, Court Ritual and the Theory of Authority in the Sixteenth and Seventeenth Centuries'; Buckler, 'The Oriental Despot'; A.M. Hocart, *Kings and Councillors*, ed. Rodney Needham, Chicago: University of Chicago Press, 1970; Richards, 'The Formulation of Imperial Authority', 126-67; Streusand, *The Formation of the Mughal Empire*; Stewart Gordon, 'Robes of Honour: A "Transitional" Kingly Ceremony', in *The Indian Economic and Social History Review*, 33, no. 3, 1996, pp. 225-42; Gordon, ed., *Robes and Honour: The Medieval World of Investiture*, New York: Palgrave, 2001; idem, *Robes of Honour: Khilat in Pre-Colonial and Colonial India*, Delhi: Oxford University Press, 2003); Philip B. Wagoner, *Tidings of the King: A Translation and Ethnohistorical Analysis of Rayavacakamu*, Honolulu: University of Hawaii Press, 1993; idem, 'Sultan Among Hindu Kings: Dress, Titles and Islamicization of Hindu Culture at Vijayanagara', *The Journal of Asian Studies*, vol. 55, no. 4, November 1996, pp. 851-80; John R. McLane, *Land and Local Kingship in Eighteenth-Century Bengal*, Cambridge: Cambridge University Press, 1993; Arjun Appadurai, ed., *The Social Life of Things: Commodities in Cultural Perspective*, Cambridge: Cambridge University Press, 1986; Marcel Mauss, *The Gifts: Forms and Functions of Exchange in Archaic Societies*, tr. Ian Cunnison, New York: W.W. Norton 1967; Michael H. Fisher, 'The Resident in Court Ritual', *Modern Asian Studies*, vol. 24, no. 3, July 1990, pp. 419-58.
6. Both John F. Richards and Douglas E. Streusand found the reign of Shahjahan richer in sources for exchange of gifts in court than that of Akbar.
7. These tables assemble information pertaining to the exchange of gifts under Akbar, not only with the *mansabdars*, but also with foreign rulers and subordinate Indian rulers.
8. According to Badauni, 'Akbar issued a general order that every person from the highest to the lowest should bring him a present'. *Muntakhab-ut-Tawarikh*, 2:332 [322].
9. Bernier, *Travels in the Mughal Empire*, p. 61.

10. Travernier, *Travels in India*, 1: 140-1.
11. Monserrate, *The Commentary of Father Monserrate*, p. 207.
12. The author of the *Tabaqat-i-Akbari* states that all the rulers and governors of the Deccan sent tributes and presents to Akbar anually. Nizamuddin Ahmad, *Tabaqat-i-Akbari*, 2: 519.
13. Athar Ali, *The Mughal Nobility Under Aurangzeb*, p. 143.
14. Manucci, *Storia Do Mogor*, 2: 347-8.
15. Nizamuddin Ahmad, *Tabaqat-i-Akbari*, 2: 650-1. Abul Fazl, Badauni and translation in the Elliot V do not specify the *peshkash* offered by Burhan-ul-Mulk. See also Ahsan Raza Khan,*Chieftains in the Mughal Empire*, pp. 210-12.
16. Nizamuddin Ahmad, *Tabaqat-i-Akbari*, 2: 595-6 [391]. The text mentions *wa yak lal-i-abdar ki panjah hazar rupiya baha dasht dakhil-i-peshkash-i o bud.* See also *Muntakhab-ut-Tawarikh*, 2: 345 [335]; *Akbarnama*, 3: 636-7 [427]; *Maasir-ul-Umara*, 2: 583.
17. On the *peshkash* of the ambassadors, see Riazul Islam, *Indo-Persian Relations*, Tehran: Islamic Culture Foundation, 1970, p. 223; *Akbarnama*, 3: 296, 310, 735, 857, 885, 1103 [211, 221, 487, 566-7, 583, 739], gives a few instances of the submission of the ruler's *peshkash* (see Table 4.1 for more details).
18. Examples of officers entertaining Akbar in their houses include Munim Khan in 1560, vide *Akbarnama*, 2: 187-8 [123]; Muhammad Qasim Khan Nishapuri in 1564, vide *Akbarnama*, 2: 345 [224-5]; Farhat Khan and Shujjat Khan in 1567, vide *Akbarnama*, 2: 436-7 [298]; Bhagwan Das in 1569, vide *Akbarnama*, 2: 496 [339]; Husain Quli Khan in 1571, vide *Akbarnama*, 2: 529 [363-4]; *Tabaqat-i-Akbari*, 2: 366; Khan Azam Aziz Koka in 1571 and 1599, vide *Akbarnama*, 2: 528-9 [363-4]; *Tabaqat-i-Akbari*, 2: 364; *Akbarnama*, 3: 1120 [749]; Muzaffar Khan in 1572, vide *Akbarnama*, 2: 531 [365-6]; *Tarikh-i-Akbari*, 175-8 [138-44]; Sharif Khan Atka in 1581, vide *Tabaqat-i-Akbari*, 2: 538-9 [354]; Abdur Rahim Mirza Khan in 1582 and 1599, vide *Akbarnama*, 3: 583 [394], 1141 [763]; Zain Khan Koka in 1592, vide *Akbarnama*, 3: 937 [613], 1041 [698]; *Maasir-ul-Umara*, 2: 1027-8.
19. Abul Fazl, *Akbarnama*, 2: 528-9 [363-4]; *Tabaqat-i-Akbari*, 2: 364-5 [231-2]; *Tarikh-i-Akbari*, 171 [132-3]; Farishta, *Rise of Mohammadan Power in India*, 2: 144; *Maasir-ul-Umara*, 1: 319-20.
20. Abul Fazl only mentions the emperor's visit and does not refer to the exchange of gifts. Cf. Abul Fazl, *Akbarnama*, 2: 531 [365]. Neither contemporary nor near contemporary sources contain these details with the exception of Arif, who devotes seven pages to this visit and the exchange of gifts.
21. Qandhari, *Tarikh-i-Akbari*, 175-8 [138-44].
22. I have deleted Arif's *Bait*, *Nazm* and *Masnavi*.
23. Abul Fazl, *Akbarnama*, 3: 583 [393-4]; *Maasir-ul-Umara*, 2: 105.
24. Abul Fazl, *Akbarnama*, 3: 937 [613]; *Maasir-ul-Umara*, 2: 1027-8.
25. Nizamuddin Ahmad, *Tabaqat-i-Akbari*, 2: 538-9 [354].

26. Ibid., 2: 309; *Muntakhab-ut-Tawarikh*, 2: 84 [82].
27. It was an African elephant. This species has very long ears. See Abul Fazl, *Akbarnama*, 2: 491-2 [336].
28. Nizamuddin Ahmad, *Tabaqat-i-Akbari*, 2: 539.
29. Abul Fazl, *Akbarnama*, 3: 889, 1185 [586, 790-1].
30. Ibid., 3: 1213, 1230 [808, 819-20].
31. Ibid., 3: 1256 [838-9].
32. Ibid., 3: 310 [220-1]. The elephant named Fath Mubarak was renowned for his violence and even professional riders were afraid of mounting him. When the animal was brought before the emperor, he quickly tamed and mounted the elephent.
33. Abul Fazl, *Akbarnama*, 3: 653 [435].
34. Badauni, *Muntakhab-ut-Tawarikh*, 2: 353 [342].
35. Abul Fazl, *Akbarnama*, 3: 1238 [826].
36. Nizamuddin Ahmad, *Tabaqat-i-Akbari*, 2: 516 [341].
37. Monserrate, *The Commentary of Father Monserrate*, p. 28.
38. Jahangir, *Tuzuk-i-Jahangiri*, p. 23.
39. Abul Fazl, *Akbarnama*, 3: 328 [232].
40. Ibid., 3: 1230 [820].
41. *Medieval Gujarat*, p. 311; see also Abul Fazl, *Akbarnama*, 3: 12 [8].
42. Jahangir, *Tuzuk-i-Jahangiri*, p. 23.
43. Abul Fazl, *Akbarnama*, 2: 362 [170].
44. Ibid., 3: 636-7 [427].
45. Nizamuddin Ahmad, *Tabaqat-i-Akbari*, 2: 627.
46. Abul Fazl, *Akbarnama*, 3: 985. According to Nizamuddin Ahmad (*Tabaqat-i-Akbari*, 2: 648 [641]), 127 elephants and other articles were sent by Raja Man Singh.
47. Bernier, *Travels in the Mughal Empire*, p. 271.
48. For details, see Marcel Mauss, *The Gifts*.
49. Manucci, *Storia Do Mogor*, 2: 345.
50. R.K. Phul, *Armies of the Great Mughals*, Delhi: Oriental Publishers, 1978, pp. 198-9; Mubarak Ali, 'The Titles of the Mughal Nobility', in *Mughal India*, ed. Mohamad Taher, Delhi: Anmol Publishing House, 1997, 1: 89-96.
51. Abul Fazl, *Akbarnama*, 2: 159 [105].
52. Jahangir, *Tuzuk-i-Jahangiri*, p. 4; *Maasir-ul-Umara*, 1: 411.
53. Babur, *Baburnama*, p. 537.
54. Abul Fazl, *Akbarnama*, 2: 174-5 [114-15]. 'Shamsuddin Muhammad Khan Atka, who had done good service and returned victories, was entitled as *Azam Khan*'.
55. Badauni, *Muntakhab-ut-Tawarikh*, 2: 346 [336]; *Akbarnama*, 3: 643 [430-1].
56. Abul Fazl, *Akbarnama*, 3: 454 [308-9].
57. Amir Ali, *History of the Saracens*, London: Macmillan, 1921, p. 301.

58. Farishta, *Rise of Mohammadan Power in India*, 2: 25.
59. Abul Fazl, *Ain-i-Akbari*, 1: 250.
60. Abul Fazl, *Akbarnama*, 2: 174 [114].
61. Ibid., 3: 643 [442].
62. Badauni, *Muntakhab-ut-Tawarikh*, 2: 244-5 [237]; *Tuzuk-i-Jahangiri*, 1: 216; *Iqbalnama-i-Jahangir*, 2: 367.
63. Abul Fazl, *Akbarnama*, 2: 358 [237].
64. Farid Bhakkari, *Zakhirat-ul-Khawanin*, 1: 32; see also 2:71-2; *Maasir-ul-Umara*, 1: 693-4.
65. Abul Fazl, *Akbarnama*, 2: 71 [45].
66. Ibid.
67. Ibid.
68. Athar Ali, *The Mughal Nobility Under Aurangzeb*, p. 140; Onkar Nath Upadhya, *Hindu Nobility Under Akbar and Jahangir*, Agra: V.K. Publishers, 1992, p. 14.
69. Badauni, *Muntakhab-ut-Tawarikh*, 2: 164 [161].
70. Ibid., 2: 164-5 [161].
71. M.H. Azad, *Darbar-i-Akbari*, Lahore: Raifah-i-Am Press, 1939, p. 309.
72. Nizamuddin Ahmad, *Tabaqat-i-Akbari*, 2: 399.
73. Abul Fazl, *Akbarnama*, 3: 236 [166], it was the highest title conferred upon a Hindu by the Mughal emperor.
74. Ibid., 3: 863 [570], *Muntakhab-ut-Tawarikh*, 2: 384 [372]; *Tabaqat-i-Akbari*, 2: 597.
75. Abul Fazl, *Akbarnama*, 3: 1239 [826].
76. Abul Fazl, *Ain-i-Akbari*, 1: 540-1.
77. Manucci, *Storia Do Mogor*, 2: 349.
78. Cf. The early analysis of F.W. Buckler in which he argues that kings in the Middle East, both ancient and Muslim, employed the robe of honour. When the 'Eastern King' gave these dresses to his servants, 'he was incorporating into his own body, by means of certain symbolical acts, the persons of those who share his rule'. *Khilat* in Arabic and *saropa* in Persian, the robe of honour, as it is customarily translated, conveys 'some idea of continuity or succession' and 'that continuity rests on a physical basis, depending on contact with the body of the recipient with the body of the donor through the medium of clothing'. Buckler, 'The Oriental Despot', pp.176-87.
79. Irvine, *The Army of the Indian Moghuls*, p. 29; Streusand, *The Formation of the Mughal Empire*, pp. 141-2; Phul, *Armies of the Great Mughals*, pp. 200-4; Seid-Gholam Hossein Khan, *The Seir Mutakharin*, 4 vols, rpt, Delhi: Low Price Publications, 1990, 1: 15. Compare, for instance, distinct categories of robes in Ziauddin Barani, *Tarikh-i-Firozshahi*, ed. S.A. Khan, W.N. Lees and Kabiruddin, Calcutta: Asiatic Society of Bengal, 1860-2, pp. 271, 377; Ibn Battuta, *Travels in Asia and Africa, 1325-1354*, tr. H.A.R. Gibb, London: Routledge and Kegan Paul, 1929; rpt, Delhi: Oriental Publishers, 1986, pp. 149, 159, 212, 325.

80. Tavernier, *Travels in India*, 1: 132; see also Gavin R.G. Hambly, 'The Emperor's Clothes: Robing and Robes of Honour in Mughal India', in *Robes of Honour*, ed. Gordon, pp.38-9.
81. According to Manucci, 'sometimes the emperor would take off from his body his upper coat, and make the man put it on in the presence to signify that he loved him as he did his own person'. *Storia Do Mogor*, 2: 464.
82. Abul Fazl, *Akbarnama*, 2: 181[118]; *Tabaqat-i-Akbari*, 2: 249[149]; *Muntakhab-ut-Tawarikh*, 2: 39[43]; *Tarikh-i-Akbari*, p. 68[64].
83. Cf. Thomas Roe, 'a cloth of gould Cloak of his owne, once or twice worne, which hee caused to bee put on my back, and I made reverence . . . it is here reputed the highest of fauor to give a garment warne by the prince, or being new, once layed on his shouder'. In William Foster, ed., *The Embassy of Sir Thomas Roe to the Court of the Great Mogul*, 2: 334.
84. For an extensive discussion, see Jamal Elias, 'The Sufi Robe (*kirqa*) as a Vehicle of Spiritual Authority', in *Robes and Honour*, ed. Gordon, pp. 275-89. See also Gerhard Bowering, 'The *Aadab* Literature of Classical Sufism: Ansari's Code of Conduct', in *Moral Conduct and Authority: The Place of Adab in South Asian Islam,* ed. Barbara Daly Metcalf, Berkeley: University of California Press, 1984, pp. 72-87; Simon Digby, 'Tabarrukat and Succession Among the Great Chisti Shaikhs of the Delhi Sultanate', in *Delhi Through the Ages*, ed. R.E. Frykenberg, Delhi: Oxford University Press, 1986, pp. 63-103.
85. Buckler, 'The Oriental Despot', pp. 176-87; Tavernier, *Travels in India*, 1: 163.
86. Gordon, 'Robes of Honour', pp. 225-42; Hambly, 'The Emperor's Clothes', pp. 31-49; idem, 'From Baghdad to Bukhara, from Ghaznin to Delhi: The *Khilat* Ceremony in the Treatment of Kingly Pomp and Circumstances', in *Robes and Honour*, ed. Gordon; Gail Minault, 'The Emperor's Old Clothes: Robing and Sovereignty in Late Mughal and Early British India', in *Robes of Honour*, ed. Gordon, pp. 125-39.
87. Streusand, *The Formation of the Mughal Empire*, pp. 123-53; Richards, 'The Formulation of Imperial Authority', pp. 126-67.
88. Mukhia, *The Mughals of India*, pp. 15-16, 164-6.
89. The quality of the rewards was determined by the rank and status of the person upon whom they were conferred. In August 1604, on the day of 'Dusserah' gold-embroidered *shawls* were presented to all *mansabdars* of the rank of 5000 to 1000, *dopattu* Gujarati *shawls* were given to those of 900 to 500 rank, embroidered (*kalabatun*) *shawls* to the rank of 400-100 and plain *shawls* to the ranks below this. *Mandil* (perhaps mantle) were given to the *Ahadis*. See Abul Fazl, *Akbarnama*, 3: 1245-6[831-2].
90. Cf. Gordon, 'Robes of Honour', p. 226. See also Xinru Liu, *Silk and Religion: An Exploration of Material Life and the Thought of People, AD 500-1200*, Delhi: Oxford University Press, 1996; idem, 'Silk, Robes, and Relations Between Early Chinese Dynasties and Nomads Beyond the Great Wall', in

Robes and Honour, ed. Gordon; Antony Eastmond and Lynn Jones, 'Robing, Power, and Legitimacy in Armenia and Georgia', in *Robes and Honour*, ed. Gordon.

91. Clement Huart, *Ancient Persian and Iranian Civilization*, tr. R. Dobie, reissue, London: Routledge, 1972, p. 148.
92. 'Mahmud of Ghaznin donning a robe from the *Caliph*', Or. MS 20, fol., 121r. *Edinburgh University Library.* See Al-Utbi, *Tarikh-i-Yamini* and Abul Fazl Al Baihaki, *Tarikhu-s-Subuktigin.* Excerpts from both works are translated in *History of India as Told by Its Own Historians*, Elliot and Dowson, vol. II, rpt, Allahabad: Kitab Mahal, 1964, 2: 24, 74-5, 142-4.
93. For robes of honour ceremony in the Vijayanagar Empire, see Philip B. Wagoner, *Tidings of the King*, pp. 89, 140, 155, 158; idem, 'Sultan Among Hindu Kings', pp. 851-80.
94. Nainsi, *Marwar ra Pargana ri Vigat*, 2: 37.
95. See M.A. Macauliffe, *The Sikh Religion*, 6 vols, Oxford: Oxford University Press, 1909; rpt, Delhi: S. Chand & Co., 1963, 2: 40.
96. V.S. Vakaskar, ed., *Sabhasadaci Bahkar*, Poona, 1973; Bhimrao Kulkarni, ed., *Sabhasad Bakhar*, Pune: Anmol Prakashan, 1987. See examples of *Khilat* Ceremony in James Grant Duff, *History of the Marathas II*, ed. J.P. Guha, Delhi: Associated Publishing House, 1971, pp. 173-80; R.G. Pandey, *Mahadji Shinde and the Poona Durbar*, Delhi: Oriental Publishers, 1990; and V.G. Khobrekar, ed., *Record of Shivaji Period*, Bombay: Government Central Press, 1974, p. 130.
97. See, for example, the frontispiece of Tavernier, *Travels in India*, rpt, Delhi: Munshiram Manoharlal, 1995.
98. See John R. McLane, *Land and Local Kingship in Eighteenth-Century Bengal*, pp. 48-9, 106-15; Eaton, *The Rise of Islam and Bengal Frontier*, p.165.
99. Marco Polo, *The Book of Ser Marco Polo, The Venetian, Concerning the Kingdoms and the Marvels of the East*, tr. Henery Yule, New York: Barnes and Noble, 1969, cited in Gordon, 'Robes of Honour', *IESHR*, p. 227.
100. See, for example, Ibn Battuta, *Travels in Asia and Africa*, pp. 149, 159, 212, 262, 275, 325.
101. Gordon, 'Robes of Honour', pp. 226-31.
102. Seid-Gholam Hossein Khan, *The Seir Mutakharin*, 1: 43(fn.).
103. For example, Persian history of the Ghaznavids: *Tarikh-i-Yamini* of Al-Utbi and the *Tarikhu-s-Subuktigin* of Abul Fazl Al Baihaki describe Mahmud's receipt of a robe from the *caliph* of Baghdad in AD 999. Excerpts from both are translated in *History of India as Told by Its Own Historians*, Elliot and Dowson, for the presentation of robes of honour by Iltutmish and his receipt of robes from the *caliph* of Baghdad, see *Lubab-ul-Albad of Sadiduddin Muhammad Awfi*, excerpted in Iqtidar Husain Siddiqi, *Perso-Arabic Sources of Information on the Life and Conditions in the Sultanate of Delhi*, Delhi: Munshiram Manoharlal, 1992, pp. 8, 31; for robe ceremonies under Tughlaq, see *Masalik-ul-Abasar fi-Mamalik-ul-Amsar*, in *Perso-Arabic*

Sources of Information, pp. 118-19; for frequent references to robes of honour in fifteenth-century history, mainly relating to the Lodi kings, see *The Tarikh-i-Mubarakshahi of Yahiyabin Ahmad bin Abdulla Sirhindi*, tr. H. Beveridge, rpt, Delhi: Low Price Publications, 1990, p. 15.

104. See Babur, *Baburnama*, pp. 159-60, 612, 621-33, 650, 667, 685.
105. Ibid., pp. 159-60, 612, 621-33, 650, 667, 685.
106. Ibid., p. 393.
107. 'On one day when the robes of honour had been presented to the Raja and to his sons and other relatives', writes Abul Fazl, and they had been brought to the court to receive their conge. See, Abul Fazl, *Akbarnama*, 2: 70[45].
108. Badauni, *Muntakhab-ut-Tawarikh*, 2: 77[68].
109. Gulbadan Begam, *Humayunnama*, pp. 69, 114, 126; *Muntakhab-ut-Tawarikh*, I: 451; *Tabaqat-i-Akbari*, 2: 46.
110. Abul Fazl, *Akbarnama*, 3: 271[192], 306[217].
111. Ibid., *Ain-i-Akbari*, 1: 96.
112. Ibid., *Akbarnama*, 2: 119[78].
113. Ibid., 2: 143[95], 174[114].
114. Ibid., 2: 174[114]; *Tabaqat-i-Akbari*, 2: 274.
115. Abul Fazl, *Akbarnama*, 2: 350-1[229]; *Tabaqat-i-Akbari*, 2: 286; *Muntakhab-ut-Tawarikh*, 2: 66-7[67]; *Maasir-ul-Umara*, 2: 851.
116. Abul Fazl, *Ain-i-Akbari*, I: 94.
117. Ibid., *Akbarnama*, 2: 174[114]; 3: 714[474], 1245-6[831].
118. Ibid., *Ain-i-Akbari*, I: 168, 174. See, *Akbarnama*, 3: 1172[783].
119. Ibid., *Akbarnama*, 3: 185[130-1]; *Muntakhab-ut-Tawarikh*, 2: 199-200 [197-8]. See cover and jacket visual of Gordon, ed., *Robes of Honour*.
120. Mirza Nathan, *Baharistan-i-Ghayabi*, tr. M.I. Borah, 2 vols, Gauhati: Government of Assam, 1936, vol. I, p. 63. See also pp. 137, 230, 292, 576-80.
121. Inayat Khan, *Shahjahannama*, ed. W.E. Begley and Z.A. Desai, Delhi: Oxford University Press, 1990, p. 355.
122. See, for example, Abul Fazl, *Akbarnama*, 2: 119 [77], 229 [148], 492 [336]; *Muntakhab-ut-Tawarikh*, 2: 44 [49], 138-9 [135].
123. Abul Fazl, *Akbarnama*, 3: 1142 [784].
124. Cf. Mukhia, *The Mughals of India*, p. 165.
125. Abul Fazl, *Akbarnama*, 3: 911 [598].
126. Ibid., 3: 992-4 [644-6].
127. Ibid., 3: 1119-20 [749].
128. See, Abul Fazl, *Ain-i-Akbari*, 1: XXII, 52-3 and illustrations on plates VII-IX; See also Abdul Aziz, 'Thrones, Chair and Seats Used by Indian Mughals', *Journal of Indian History*, vol. 16, 1937, pp. 186-8; Irvine, *The Army of the Indian Moghuls*, pp. 30-5.
129. For example, see Abul Fazl, *Akbarnama*, 3: 911[598]; *Muntakhab-ut-Tawarikh*, 2: 391[378]; *Tabaqat-i-Akbari*, 2: 634.

130. The procedure of granting drums to a noble was rather amusing:

  That last mark of imperial favour is attended with the following ceremonial—two small nobuts or drums of silver, each about the size of a thirty two pounds shot, the aperature of which are covered with the parchment, are hung round the neck of a person on whom the honour is conferred and struck a few times, and he is thereby proclaimed as *Sahib-Nobut* and has drums made upon the proper scale which are beaten five times in the course of twenty-four hours. The beating of drums was a royal prerogative in the beginning of the Mughal period, but later on the nobles were also given this privilege.

  For details, see Abul Fazl, *Ain-i-Akbari*, I: XII, pp. 49, 53 and illustration on plate VIII; Irvine, *The Army of the Indian Moghuls*, p. 30.

131. Abul Fazl, *Akbarnama*, 3: 889[586]; *Maasir-ul-Umara*, 2: 1026.
132. Abul Fazl, *Akbarnama*, 2: 143[95], 156[104]; 3: 643[430], 911[598]; *Muntakhab-ut-Tawarikh*, 2: 21[28], 33[38-9], 171[168], 346[336], 391[378].
133. For example, see Badauni, *Muntakhab-ut-Tawarikh*, 2: 21[28], 33[39].
134. He was a slave of Sultan Mahmud Gujarati, who had become the ruler of Gujarat after the death of Sultan Mahmud.
135. *Juls*: ornamental cloths covering the backs and hanging over the sides of elephants.
136. Hooks for driving elephants.
137. These gifts were presented to Akbar, when the latter visited his residence in Dipalpur. In addition, Aziz Koka presented valuable gifts to the princes and women of the royal family.
138. He had captured these elephants in the battle of Tukaroi (Bengal).
139. See n. 32.
140. From the spoils of the eastern provinces.
141. These elephants were part of the spoils of Bengal. Badauni and Nizamuddin mention 500 elephants as opposed to 304 mentioned by Abul Fazl.
142. According to Badauni, he sent Rs. 5 lakh (Arif has 8 lakh) and other gifts to the emperor. It appears to me that as this money (5 lakh) was not a present from Muzaffar Khan, it was revenues due from Bengal to the central treasury. Since his appointment as governor of Bengal he had not sent any revenues to the central treasury, so he sent revenues along with other presents to the court. See also note by B. De, *Tabaqat-i-Akbari*, 2: 521-2n.
143. In 1576-7, he was made Mir Haj. On his return in 1578-9, he brought this much of mentioned gifts and offered them to the emperor.
144. These presents were offered to the emperor on the occasion of his visit to Sharif Khan Atka's house.
145. When Mirza Jani Beg's ambassador returned to Thatta, Akbar also sent his own ambassador Hakim-Ain-ul-Mulk with him to Thatta. When Hakim-Ain-ul-Mulk returned from Thatta in 1589, he presented Mirza Jani Beg's representation along with his *peshkash* to Akbar.

146. For a list of these *rajas* see Abul Fazl, *Akbarnama*, 884-5 [583].
147. Badauni and Nizamuddin mention 120 elephants.
148. Burhan-ul-Mulk did not send suitable *peshkash*/presents. His presents did not exceed 15 elephants, some tunics and headdresses of Deccan and small quantity of gems. This irked Akbar so much that he turned his attention to the conquest of Ahmadnagar. See Nizamuddin Ahmad, *Tabaqat-i-Akbari*, 2: 650-1n. Neither Abul Fazl nor Badauni specifiy the inappropriate tribute of Buhan-ul-Mulk.
149. Out of 170 elephants some were accepted. These were offered to the emperor during his visit to Zain Khan Koka's house.
150. Among them was a five-year old horse which was from the sea of Gilan (the Caspian). It had only two or three hairs on the mane and tail. However, it died on the way.
151. One of which was valued at Rs. 5,000.
152. All woven by noted weavers.
153. The cost in Persia was 300 *tumans* a pair.
154. He was advised by the emperor to bring some remarkable elephant from Bengal. Abul Fazl says that he presented 16 choice elephants.
155. A diamond weighing 27 *surkhs* (*rati*) and a ruby weighing 4 *misqals*. The *Iqbalnama* gives the weight of the diamond as 4 *misqals* and 5 *surkhs*.
156. Twenty elephants were captured in the battle against Malik Amber. Ten of these were sent to court and the remaining ten he kept with himself with the idea that he would present them whenever he would attend court.
157. Worth a lakh of rupees.

CHAPTER 5

Conclusion

The uncertainty of the early years of his reign probably made it clear to Akbar that he would have to found his kingdom on a sound administrative base. He inherited Delhi and some tracts of Panjab from Humayun. Delhi was lost shortly thereafter to Hemu, who subsequently posed a threat to Akbar's occupations in the Panjab. This caused panic in Akbar's camp and many nobles around him began to clamour for a return to Kabul to replenish their military power. However, Bairam Khan's bold decision to face the challenge rather than fall back changed the complexion of the situation. The resultant battle of Panipat saved the Mughals. Hemu was caught and executed; Delhi and Agra fell to Akbar.

During his half a century long reign from 1556 to 1605, Akbar's repeated victories enabled him to build a multiregional empire on the territories of defeated kingdoms. He and his advisers devised innovative and durable centralized institutions. The establishment of a firm system of governance required the efficient management of land revenue and its effective utilization under different heads. Out of the entire *jama* of the empire under Akbar, the share of *suyurghal* was at best a mere 3.4 per cent.[1] The major part of the *jama* was alienated in the form of territorial revenue assignments (*jagirs*) to *mansabdars*. The remainder belonged to the *khalisa*, where the revenue was collected directly for the imperial treasury. Even out of the *jama* of the *khalisa*, a portion must have been claimed by such *mansabdars* as were designated *naqdi*. The imperial establishment was financed mainly out of the balance of the *khalisa* revenues.

The references to *jagirs* in the available sources are not detailed and it is not possible to calculate the exact area of the *jagirs* allotted to the nobles nor the total area or revenue that was set aside under the head of *khalisa*. Limited evidence suggests that during Akbar's reign the *khalisa* constituted anything between 24 and 33 per cent of the total *jama*. The *jagirs* then would be between 67 and 76 per cent.

According to Shireen Moosvi, this would mean a modest estimate of 2,65,34,192 *dams* for payment of salaries, and an upper estimate of 1,30,69,079 *dams* for expense on the imperial establishment.[2] The actual expenses in the latter case were probably less because some of the nobles were also paid in cash from the *khalisa* revenues. This study indicates that the majority of *mansabdars* received their salaries in the form of land revenue assignment. Some modern scholars have argued that during the 19th to 24th regnal years the assignment system (*jagir*) was abandoned and the empire was put under direct administration (*khalisa*). Abul Fazl observes,

> In 1574-5 the provinces of the empire were divided into tracts, which produced a *kror* (ten million) of *tanka* (copper coin) in revenue. Each of these tracts had a collector, known as a *krori*, in charge of collecting the revenues. Simultaneously, all the land was made *khalisa. Jagirs* were eliminated.[3]

A fresh examination of the sources, however, supports the view that this change did not take place immediately; the administrative difficulties must have been formidable and this arrangement did not apply to Gujarat, Bihar and Bengal. Apparently, the conversion of *jagir* into *khalisa* began with the territory of Jaunpur, Varanasi and Chunar. How far the process went is uncertain, but many—if not most—*jagirs* were resumed. According to Afzal Husain, the correspondence of Hakim Abul Fath shows that at least the assignment of new *jagirs* had ceased because he states that Shahbaz Khan resumed this in 1581, confirming Badauni.[4] John F. Richards' analysis in this connection is worth quoting:

> The emperor resumed all *jagirs* or salary assignments for his officers in the north Indian provinces. All land now fell under the control of treasury, officials who would administer them directly. After five years of direct administration and experimentation, Akbar was able once again to place the land of north India with the *mansabdars*. The *jagir* system was reestablished with a more accurate base.[5]

Taking into account all the references to assignments, it may be said that the *jagirdari* system, as suggested by some scholars, was never completely abandoned.

The study of *jagirs* indicates that unless a *mansabdar* was a great noble or high in imperial favour, the assignment was in a distant and imperfectly subdued province. On the other hand, important and more settled areas like Jaunpur, Allahabad, Hisar-Firuza, Sirhind, Multan and Dipalpur were generally assigned to very important and high ranking nobles of the court. For example, in March 1557 Muhammad Quli Khan Barlas held Multan and at the end of the same year Multan was assigned to Bahadur Khan Uzbek. In 1560, Muhammad Qasim Nishapuri held Multan, but in 1563-4 Muhammad Quli Khan Barlas was again appointed the *jagirdar* of Multan. Multan was granted as *jagir* to Muhibb Ali Khan and Said Khan Chaghta in 1571 and 1573 respectively. Sialkot was the *jagir* of Sikandar Khan in 1556, but in 1580 it was assigned as *jagir* to Man Singh who later held the high rank of 7000 *zat*/6000 *sawar*. Dipalpur was also the *jagir* of influential nobles like Mirza Aziz Koka and Muhammad Sadiq Khan.

It appears that some of the more important places were frequently assigned to nobles who held a *mansab* rank higher than 4000. In 1595, Mirza Aziz Koka was the *jagirdar* of Multan and rose to the *mansab* rank of 7000 *zat*/6000 *sawar* in 1602 (see Tables 3.1-3.12). The case of Hisar-Firuza and Sirhind was somewhat different. The revenues of Hisar-Firuza and Sirhind were granted to royal princes. On some occasions they were also granted to Akbar's more important nobles. However, for the most part, the areas of Hisar-Firuza and Sirhind were under imperial control as part of *khalisa* land.

After its initial phase of development during the reigns of Babur and Humayun and the early years of Akbar, the Mughal nobility came to consist of certain well organized racial groups. The role of the nobility in the administration reveals that racial or religious considerations did not normally affect imperial decisions in making appointments to central or provincial posts. The chief considerations were individual potential and calibre. However, the significant point that emerges from Tables 3.1-3.12 and Appendix A is that the Turanis maintained their distinct position from the beginning till the end. On the basis of their share in the *jagirs*, it appears that they enjoyed about 41.27 per cent of the total revenues in the *jagirs*. According to Moreland, during the reign of Akbar just 70 per cent of the nobles—whose origin is known—were foreigners (Turanis and Iranis) whose families had either come to India with Humayun or had arrived at the court after the accession of Akbar.[6] The present study confirms this argument. In terms of *jagir* references, Turani and Irani families had about 67.63 per cent of share in the *jagirs*. Notably, one cannot ignore the sizeable number of Indian nobles. Though not in a majority, they formed an effective group within the ruling class during Akbar's reign.

In theory, the emperor appointed all the *mansabdars* personally. As general rule, individuals hoping for the grant of a *mansab* had to appear in person before him. Abul Fazl suggests that Akbar had the ability to evaluate the worth of an individual in a single glance.[7] The *Bakhshi* was assigned the duty of presenting before the emperor all aspirants. Leading nobles of the empire could also make recommendations for recruitment. Often governors of provinces and leaders of military expeditions recommended persons for appointment to the emperor. Their recommendations were generally accepted and *mansabs* were given to the persons they recommended. The tradition of conferring more favours upon selected nobles and their family members seems to have continued during Akbar's reign as well. A general policy was that if a *khanazad* served the emperor well, he could reach the same or even higher status than his relatives, for example, Khan Azam Mirza Aziz Koka, Raja Man Singh and Abdur Rahim Khan-i-Khanan. Yet, the promotion of non-*khanazads* to higher ranks and assignment to important *jagirs* cannot be overlooked.

When Akbar ascended the throne he had to contend with a serious crisis in the nobility. This made him conscious of the fact that for the consolidation of his empire a disciplined ruling class faithful only to the ruler was a necessity. Therefore, soon after taking over the reins of government he introduced administrative reforms that were aimed to curtail the power of different clans of nobles and to strengthen the central authority. The assignment of *jagirs* was done in such a way that no single clan of *jagirdars* could become dangerously influential in any particular area. From the data available it may be concluded that during the early years of Akbar's reign, the policy may have been to assign *jagirs* to members of a particular clan in the region administered by their leaders. In 1559, for instance, the entire Jalair clan was assigned *jagirs* in and around the *sarkars* of Lucknow and Awadh. In August 1560, Akbar awarded the Panjab to Shamsuddin Muhammad Atka and his brothers.[8] The Uzbeks were assigned *jagirs* in the Jaunpur region, Qaqshal in Kara-Manikpur and the Mirzas in Sambhal. The concentration of clans in particular regions was also facilitated by the tendency among influential superior nobles to procure *jagirs* for members of their own clans within the territory of their charges. Sometimes this was sought to be achieved even by violating or twisting the rules. Akbar later decided that the different ethnic and religious groups comprising the nobility should be balanced in a manner that their concentration in an area on ethnic grounds and family ties would not be possible. This would prevent them from forming a united block to oppose the emperor. Therefore, in 1567, there was a definite policy of not allowing the clans to remain concentrated in any particular region. Akbar declared it a state policy not to assign contiguous *jagirs* to members of the same family or clan group. In this connection Abul Fazl writes:

> Whenever a large body is gathered together of one mind and speech, and show much push and energy, it is proper to disperse them, firstly for their own good and secondly for the welfare of the community. Even if no improper act in consequence of the aggregation be seen or suspected such dispersion is the material of union, for security cannot be guaranteed where there is damage from the man-throwing wine of the world, and the weak-headed drinking of the cup of intoxication. Especially when strife-mongers and table bearers abound. Negligence is implanted in the human constitution.[9]

Another important reform, which aimed at eradicating tribal and clannish tendencies among the nobles, was the appointment of a junior member of the family at the head irrespective of his elders, who were also senior in service. The old Turanis in particular resented these measures because they affected them directly. These steps were strongly justified by Abul Fazl, the official historian of Akbar. These reforms had far-reaching effects. Akbar succeeded in breaking the strength of the important Turani factions, including the groups of clans. In their place he raised to high ranks younger elements from among both Turanis and Iranis. Further, he introduced in substantial numbers indigenous elements both Indian Muslim and Rajput chiefs.

Nevertheless, these racial or religious considerations should not be viewed as rigid, ascriptive categories indicating inbred loyalty or cohesion. The main concern of both the Mughal crown and the nobility was the stability of the empire with which their mutual interests were bound. There is hardly any example where this common interest was sacrificed by either of them for racial or religious causes. There was, therefore, diversity in unity, but this diversity was capable of producing tensions. Mirza Hakim had pinned his hopes on the tensions in 1581. He expected that the Iranis and Turanis in Akbar's force would go over to his side, while the Rajputs and Afghans would be slaughtered and the other Indians would be captured.[10] The Mirza's advisors did not know, adds Abul Fazl, the degree of loyalty of the Turanis and Iranis to Akbar, nor how brave the Rajputs and Shaikhzadas of India were.

Akbar's policy of *sulh-i-kul* was partly motivated by a desire to employ elements of diverse religious beliefs to prevent sectarian differences among them from interfering with their loyalty to the throne. On the basis of his liberal policy, some of his critics like Badauni, Sir Wolsley Haig, Edward Maclagan and V.A. Smith considered him to be pro-Hindu or anti-Muslim. The present study, however, shows that this was not the case as Akbar did not follow the advice of religious leaders in many matters. Akbar appears to have balanced different sections of the nobility. If Abdur Rahim Khan was awarded the title of Khan-i-Khanan, Raja Todar Mal was given the status of Mushrif-i-Diwan. If Raja Man Singh was granted the high *mansab* of 7000 *zat*/6000 *sawar*,[11] the same rank was granted to Khan-i-Azam Mirza Aziz Koka and Shahrukh Mirza.[12] It is logical to conclude that Akbar's attitude towards the nobility was not based on religious or racial considerations. He took into consideration the suitability of the person, the office and the political situation from time to time.

The main source of income of the pre-modern Indian state was land revenue. For this reason Akbar maintained a strict vigilance on the *jagirdars* and was particular about the welfare of the peasantry. To achieve this aim he adopted several measures. The government maintained a close and strict supervision over matters pertaining to revenue. Here, it should be reiterated (as discussed in Chapters 2 and 3) that the treatment of this question by eminent historians (from W.H. Moreland and Irfan Habib to Noman Ahmad Siddiqi) who critically discussed *jagirs*, transfer policy of *jagirs* and tenure of *jagirdars* in their *jagirs*, has been rather inadequate. Based primarily on observations made by European travellers, these scholars have held that *jagirs* were regularly transferred after short periods so that a particular assignment was seldom held by the same person for more than three or four years. They believed that Akbar decisively established this practice.

The point of departure in the present study is that at least during the reign of Akbar the transfer of *jagirs* of large holders was not as frequent as many scholars previously believed. As discussed in Chapter 3, there were several cases where the *jagirdars* with high *mansabs* remained undisturbed in their respective *jagirs* for as long as twelve or more years, before they were transferred. An officer could hold his assignment as long as he was competent and loyal, and if his services were not required elsewhere. The argument by these scholars that the assigned areas changed hands from time to time as a precautionary measure against assignees building a popular base within the confines of their *jagirs* seems untenable. Tracing the causes of the transfer of *jagirs* from different contemporary sources, this study seeks to make this point. To carry the argument further, available evidence indicates that during the reign of Akbar there was common *modus operandi* to assign *jagirs* to *mansabdars* either within or adjacent to the province of their postings. This is contrary to the view held by these scholars.

In theory, a noble's income and status depended entirely on the ruler's trust. In practice, once a man entered the imperial service, he could assume that he would keep his rank and have an appropriate *jagir* as long as he remained competent and loyal, treated the inhabitants of his *jagir* fairly, and came close to meeting the military obligations of his rank. Only obvious misconduct or disloyalty led to resumption of *jagirs*, fines, imprisonment, or execution. Disorders were firmly suppressed. For instance, in 1578 when the people of the Panjab complained against Shah Quli Mahram that he had failed to protect them against the oppressors, he was replaced by Said Khan.[13] Raja Man Singh was transferred from Kabul because of the oppressive behaviour of the Rajputs towards the people of the areas under his charge.[14]

Peace and order were successfully restored in the land with the help of an effective administrative system. Despite the despotic nature of the monarchy, the welfare of the subjects was not ignored. The nobles undoubtedly flourished more because of royal patronage. The ordinary peasant, however, had to be safeguarded against oppression of the powerful. That Akbar was aware of this is apparent from his numerous sayings in the writings of contemporary authors. For example, 'Tyranny is unlawful with everyone, especially in a sovereign who is the guardian of the world'.[15] A serious view was taken of the lapses committed by nobles. On 6 December 1598, while staying as a guest of Abul Said at Sirhind, Akbar found that his host had collected money by resorting to oppression. Akbar refused to stay with him and spent the night in an open field.[16] On 29 December 1598 Akbar ordered that Shaikh Sultan (*krori* of Thaneshwar) be hanged for oppression and corruption.[17]

Akbar did not overlook the necessity of periodically recognizing the good services of his nobles by rewarding them in various ways. *Mansabdars/jagirdars* also offered various types of presents to the emperor. In addition to *mansabdars*, foreign rulers (through their ambassadors) and subordinate rulers also presented *nazr* and *peshkash* to the emperor. In Chapter 4 it was argued that the transmission of gifts made the Mughal *mansabdars* symbolic extensions of the monarch. It strengthened the ties between the emperor and his officers. Their gifts demonstrated their position as his subordinates; the more valuable the gift the higher the rank of the giver. The emperor's gifts, most importantly robes of honour or *khilat*, transformed the officers into extensions of his body and provided the external marks of their status. A *mansabdar* with a low rank could be given only a robe of honour; a high officer or a prince serving as a provincial governor could be given a more elaborate robe, a bejewelled sword, a saddle, or a turban with a jewelled ornament, and a fine steed. Their costumes were indicative of their nature and rank; receiving them from the emperor denoted that the emperor determined their status and political identity. Buckler had argued that the gift of a robe by the Mughal emperor in a court ceremony symbolized the incorporation of the recipient into his person as his subordinate, to act in future as an extension of himself.[18]

The wealth of the nobles was derived from the posts conferred upon them by the emperor. It was discussed in Chapter 4 that a fair proportion of this wealth found its way back to the royal treasury. The nobles were bound by custom to offer suitable presents to the emperor on various occasions. Some of these presents were extremely costly and included of gold *muhrs* and a variety of precious stones. In addition to various rewards from the emperor, in the form of *mansabs*, promotions, large *jagirs*, titles and a variety of gifts, the emperor sometimes paid a casual visit to favoured and loyal nobles in the course of his travels. A visit by the emperor was perceived as an exceptional privilege and catapulted the favoured noble to a position of prominence and influence.[19] On these occasions, the nobles organized lavish feasts and gave valuable presents to the emperor. There were times when Akbar not only honoured his officers, but also showed personal concern for them. When Akbar forbade Bhagwan Das to enter the court in February 1586, the latter out of embarrassment stabbed himself with a dagger. Akbar took a personal interest in his treatment and appointed his best physicians to tend to him.[20] Sometimes Akbar went to the extent of risking his own life to save his officer's life. In 1584 during an elephant fight, the elephant Cacar, notorious for killing men, became violent and rushed toward Birbal and would have killed him had Akbar not ridden his horse between the elephant and Birbal. When the enraged animal rushed towards Birbal it was overcome by the majestic *durbash* (kind of spear with two horns and branches carried before the sovereign) and Birbal was saved. In October 1598, Pratap Singh attempted suicide by slitting his throat with a dagger and his condition was serious, Akbar appointed skilled surgeons to treat him and he recovered within no time.[21]

The power, wealth and *jagirs*, which the nobles enjoyed during their lifetime, were a temporary phenomenon. Most of the grandeur surrounding a noble's life ended with his death. The Mughal noble was only a servant of the state and the *jagir* held by him was on a service tenure. *A jagir* was only a form of payment for the services rendered by him and, therefore, when he died or was dismissed his service also came to an end and the state took over the *jagir*. As in the case of cash salary, it ceased with the termination of services of a noble. The sons of a noble, therefore, did not have a hereditary claim on the *jagir*. It was a mark of unusual favour for a Mughal emperor to permit an officer's sons to inherit a portion of his property. In principle, the state was fully justified in its action, though to the European travellers, familiar with the European system of hereditary landed aristocracy, the Mughal system by contrast appeared to be an act of despotism. These European travellers failed to understand the principles inherent in the *jagirdari* system. The Mughal law of escheat was applied so scrupulously that the entire personal property of the deceased noble was taken over by the state instantaneously at the time of his death. The reason was that the nobles while discharging their duties controlled huge funds of the state; besides, they were by and large in debt to the government having taken money in advance or enjoyed the revenue of their *jagir* without defrayal of their accounts with the state. Thus, when a noble died, his entire property was escheated (*zabt*) and the statement of the amount due from him (*mutalba*) was primed, and balanced with the escheated moveable property. As the *jagir* was not his property, the question of sharing it among his children did not arise. After the *mutalba*, the balance was shared among the heirs of the deceased. If the state claim was more than the worth of his property, the entire property was seized for realization of the dues. If there were no dues of the state his property was handed over to his heirs after identification.[22] This all was done at the discretion of the emperor and not necessarily according to the canon law of the Muslims or the Hindus. It is true that if a noble had died without heirs, the state was his only heir. Conforming to this practice, a prominent example was Munim Khan Khan-i-Khanan (d.1575). Badauni wrote, since he (Khan-i-Khanan Munim Khan) had no heir, the officials escheated all his wealth and gain to the crown which had been accumulated over many years.[23]

The entire structure of the Mughal Empire was based on the creation of a loyal and satisfied nobility which would support the emperor at all times. Akbar successfully achieved this through the creation of the *mansabdari/jagirdari* system. A closer look, however, reveals that the *mansabdari* system was based on the proper assignment of *jagirs*. The linkage between the *mansabs* and *jagirs* proved to be an effective weapon to control the nobility. In the ultimate analysis, the large majority of the *mansabdars* were *jagirdars* which formed the base of the Mughal administrative structure. Evidently, the crises/abuses in the *jagirdari* system of the seventeenth–eighteenth centuries which contributed towards the disintegration of the empire—the shortage of land for assignment as *jagir*, delay in the grant of *jagirs* to new entrants, cut-throat competition for *sair-hasil jagirs* (productive and easily manageable), later even for common *jagirs*, frequent transfers (as Hawkins and Bhimsen complain), decay of the practice of transfer, and *jagirs* becoming hereditary—had not set in during the reign of Akbar. It would, therefore, not be wrong to conclude that the stability of the Mughal Empire even in the later periods was based to a large extent on the essential principles of the *jagirdari* system. Akbar made a prodigious contribution to its evolution.

NOTES

1. Shireen Moosvi, *The Economy of the Mughal Empire*, p. 159.
2. Ibid., p. 197.
3. Abul Fazl, *Akbarnama*, 3: 166-7 [117-18].
4. Nizamuddin Ahmad, *Tabaqat-i-Akbari*, 2: 296; *Muntakhab-ut-Tawarikh*, 2: 192-4, 304-5 [189-91, 296]; *Tarikh-i-Akbari*, 231-2 [198]. See also Hakim Abul Fath Gilani, *Ruqat-i-Hakim Abul Fath*, pp. 26-7, 34, 37-8; Afzal Husain, 'The Letter of Hakim Abul Fath Gilani', pp. 189-93. Husain's research invalidates M.P. Singh, 'Akbar's Resumption of *Jagir*, 1575', *Proceedings of the Indian History Congress*, 28th Session, Mysore, 1966, pp. 208-11.
5. Richards, *The Mughal Empire*, pp. 84-6.
6. Moreland, *India at the Death of Akbar*, pp. 69-70.
7. Abul Fazl, *Ain-i-Akbari*, 1: 248.
8. Ibid., *Akbarnama*, 2: 126, 177 [82, 115-16].
9. Ibid., 2: 486-7 [332].
10. Ibid., 3: 538 [366].
11. Ibid., 3: 1257 [839].
12. Mutammad Khan, *Iqbalnama-i-Jahangiri*, pp. 506, 510.
13. Abul Fazl, *Akbarnama*, 3: 356-7 [247].
14. Ibid., 3: 790 [517-18].
15. Ibid., *Ain-i-Akbari*, 3: 451.
16. Ibid., *Akbarnama*, 3: 1116 [747].
17. Ibid., 3: 1118 [748].
18. F.W. Buckler, 'The Oriental Despot', in *Legitimacy and Symbols*, ed. M.N. Pearson, pp. 176-87.
19. Details of such visits by Akbar have been dealt with in my doctorate dissertation, which is not included, completely in this book, leaving the task for another occasion.
20. Abul Fazl, *Akbarnama*, 3: 745 [492]; A.L. Srivastava, *Akbar the Great*, 1: 325.
21. Abul Fazl, *Akbarnama*, 3: 774, 793 [508, 519].
22. Ali Muhammad Khan, *Mirat-i-Ahmadi*, tr. p. 238. For an extensive discussion on escheat, see Athar Ali, *Mughal Nobility Under Aurangzeb*, pp. 63-8.
23. Abdul Qadir Badauni, *Muntakhab-ut-Tawarikh*, 2: 221 [217].

APPENDIX A

RACIAL AND RELIGIOUS COMPOSITION OF *JAGIRDARS* UNDER AKBAR

Sr. No.	*Subas*	*No. of Jagir References*	*Princes*	*Turanis*	*Iranis*	*Rajputs/ Hindus*	*Indian Muslims*	*Afghans*	*Unknown*
1.	Agra	41	–	23	11	3	2	2	–
2.	Ajmer	51	1	13	10	20	5	–	2
3.	Allahabad	47	1	22	9	5	2	4	4
4.	Awadh	35	–	17	10	–	1	–	7
5.	Bengal	50	1	13	15	6	3	9	3
6.	Bihar	50	–	24	9	6	4	2	5
7.	Delhi	41	–	17	12	2	4	–	6
8.	Gujarat	48	1	16	13	1	10	6	1
9.	Kabul	36	–	24	9	1	1	–	1
10.	Lahore	54	–	21	12	11	3	1	6
11.	Malwa	67	1	23	26	5	5	1	6
12.	Multan	30	–	14	9	–	5	–	2
	Total	550	5 (0.90%)	227 (41.27%)	145 (26.36%)	60 (10.90%)	45 (8.18%)	25 (4.54%)	43 (7.81%)

APPENDIX B

RACIAL AND RELIGIOUS COMPOSITION OF NOBLES UNDER AKBAR

Period		*Total no. of Nobles*	*Turanis*	*Persians*	*Indian Muslims*	*Rajputs/ Hindus*	*Unspecified and Others*
1555		51	27 (52.94%)	16 (31.37%)	–	–	8 (15.68%)
1565-75	500 and above	96	38 (39.58%)	37 (38.54%)	9 (9.37%)	8 (8.33%)	4 (4.16%)
	Absolute numbers	176	67 (38.06%)	48 (27.27%)	25 (14.20%)	18 (10.22%)	18 (10.22%)
1580		272	66 (24.26%)	47 (17.27%)	44 (16.17%)	43 (15.80%)	72 (26.47%)
1575-95	1,000 and above	87	32 (36.78%)	24 (27.58%)	14 (16.09%)	14 (16.09)	3 (3.44%)
	500 and above	184	64 (34.78%)	47 (25.54%)	34 (18.47%)	30 (16.30%)	9 (4.89%)
At the time of Akbar's death	500 and above	95	30 (31.57%)	21 (22.10%)	8 (8.42%)	17 (17.89%)	19 (20%)

Sources: Iqtidar Alam Khan, 'The Nobility Under Akbar and Development of His Religious Policy, 1560-80', *Journal of the Royal Asiatic Society*, 1968, pp. 35-6; Afzal Husain, *The Nobility Under Akbar and Jahangir*, pp. 191, 196-8.

Glossary

abwab	in general cesses paid by the cultivator to the officials in addition to the land revenue
ahadis	cadre of high status cavalrymen employed directly by the Mughal emperor
amin	a revenue assessor; a collector
aimma/aima	revenue-free land granted by the Mughal government to learned and religious persons
amal-guzar	a revenue collector
amil	a revenue collector
arazi	measured area
banjar	wasteland, land left untilled for a long period
baraka	blessing, holiness, spiritual power inherent in a saint
bigha	a measure of land generally considered equal to 20 *biswas* or 4 *kanals*; also one-half of a *ghumaon*
biswa	1/20th of a *bigha*
chaknama	a document showing the size and boundaries of the measured land
charqab	a handsome robe of honour, a gold threaded vest (*turkish* style tunic)
chaudhuri	a semi-hereditary *pargana* level official, mainly concerned with revenue collection
crore	100 lakh, or 10 million
dagh	a brand on a horse for identification at inspection
dam	originally a copper coin, but a money of account under the Mughals; 40 *dams* were reckoned as equal to 1 rupee under Akbar; the ratio in actual practice varied from time to time
darbar	the royal audience; hall of audience; court
dastur-al-amal	the code of procedures

diwan	the head of revenue affairs
diwan-i-khalisa	the minister or officer-in-charge of the *khalisa-i-sharifa*
doab	the land between two rivers
farman	a document carrying an imperial order
faujdar	a commandant in-charge of law and order in an administrative division
gaz-i-ilahi	a measure of length introduced by Akbar
gumashta	agents of official; revenue collectors of *jagirdars*
hakim	a senior official; a governor
hasil	the revenue actually collected
huquq-i-diwani	fiscal claims of the government
inam	a *jagir* assigned as a 'reward' in excess of *mansab* pay claim
iqta	territorial revenue assignment; literary a synonym of *jagir*
iqtadar	literary a synonym of *jagirdar*
jagir	land revenue assignment, made for government service
jagirdar	a person holding a *jagir*
jama	standards estimate of net land revenue for the purpose of *jagir* assignment
jama-i-raqami	another term for *jama*
jihat	taxes on certain trades
karoh or *kos*	equal to about 2½ miles
khalisa-i-sharifa	territories and sources of revenues assigned to yield revenue for the imperial treasury
khanazads	'house born' or those whose ancestors had also served the empire
khasa-i-sharifa	the emperor's own establishment
khilat	a dress of honour, *vastra;* an article of costume presented by the ruling or superior authority to an inferior as an mark of distinction
khirqa	the patched frock worn by Sufis, often passed from a *pir* to his successor to symbolize the latter's legitimate succession
krori	a designation of the revenue collector in the *khalisa-i-sharifa*

lakh	100,000
madad-i-maash	a term most commonly used by the Mughals for land revenue alienated in favour of a religious personage or institution by the ruler
mahal	a revenue subdivision under Akbar, usually corresponding to *pargana*
makhdim	a Muslim religious scholar
mal-i-wajib	land revenue
mal-o-jihat	land revenue and taxes on certain trades, treated as a single head
mansab	literally an office, position or rank, indicating the status, obligations and remuneration of its holder in the official hierarchy during the Mughal Period
mansabdar	the holder of a *mansab*
mir-munshi	the chief draftsman of imperial letters, *farmans* and documents
muhr	a Mughal gold coin
mufti	a theologian deemed qualified to give opinion on questions of Muslim law
muhtarifa	taxes on artisans
muqaddum	a village headman
naqdi	officers who received their pay in cash
nazr	(Arabic *nadr* or vow) submission by an inferior of an offering of gold or silver coin to a superior; customarily presented in person
paibaqi	an area due for revenue assignment
pargana	the smallest Mughal administrative unit
parwana	a written order under the seal of a person in power
peshkash	tax; tribute; gift from a subordinate to one from whom an appointment is expected or received
qanungo	a middle level local revenue official
qasba	a town
qazi	a local judicial official
qismat	the division of produce; or of a village among different *jagirdars*
sair	market and transit dues
sanad	a written document or order conferring office of privileges

sarkar	a subdivision of a *suba*, usually comprising a group of contiguous *parganas*
sawar	a horseman, a numerical rank, indicating the size of the military contingent and the payment allowed for it
sayyid	a descendent of the Prophet Muhammad
shiqdar	a revenue collector; also used for a revenue official under a *jagirdar*
suba	a province or the largest administrative unit under the Mughals
subedar/subadar	a governor of a *suba* or province
suyurghal	a state grant for a lifetime or in perpetuity; same as *madad-i-maash*
taghaiyur	transfer of a *jagir*
talab	calling or sending for
tazkira	a collection of biographical accounts, compiled from both written and oral accounts
tuyul	revenue assignment; a synonym of *jagir*
tuyuldar	a synonym of *jagirdar*
wajh	a term for territorial revenue assignment under Akbar's predecessors and during his early years
wajhdar	a holder of *wajh*
watan-jagir	the hereditary principality of a chief (held in *jagir* permanently against the whole or part of a *mansab*)
yaddasht	memoranda
zamindar	a local level revenue collector, recognized but not appointed by the regime; usually head of the locally dominant lineage
zat	numerical rank (*mansab*) indicating status and personal pay

Bibliography

CONTEMPORARY AND NEAR CONTEMPORARY SOURCES

Abul Fazl, Allami iban Shaikh Mubarak Nagawari, *Akbarnama*, ed. Maulvi Agha Ahmad Ali and Maulvi Abdur Rahim, 3 vols, Calcutta: Asiatic Society of Bengal, 1873-87; rpt, Delhi: Kitab Publishing House, 1977, tr. Henry Beveridge, 3 vols, Calcutta: Asiatic Society of Bengal, 1897-1921; rpt, Delhi: Low Price Publications, 1998.

——, *Ain-i-Akbari*, ed. H. Blochmann, Calcutta: Asiatic Society of Bengal, 1867-77, 3 vols, vol. I, tr. H. Blochmann, revd. D.C. Phillott, vols. II and III, tr. H.S. Jarrett, revd. Sir Jadunath Sarkar, Calcutta: Asiatic Society of Bengal, 1927-49; rpt, Delhi: Low Price Publications, 1994.

Ahmad Yadgar, *Tarikh-i-Shahi*, ed. M. Hidayat Husain, Calcutta: Asiatic Society of Bengal, 1939.

Ahmad, Khwaja Nizamuddin, *Tabaqat-i-Akbari*, ed. Brajendranath De and Muhammad Hidayat Husain, 3 vols, Calcutta: Asiatic Society of Bengal, 1935, tr. Brajendranath De, Calcutta: Asiatic Society of Bengal, 1936.

Ali Muhammad Khan, *Mirat-i-Ahmadi*, ed. Sayyid Nawab Ali, 3 vols, Baroda: Gaekward Oriental Institute, 1927-35, tr. M.F. Lokhandawala, Baroda: Gaekward Oriental Institute, 1965.

Amin, Muhammad, *Anfaul-i-Akbar*, extracts translated in *The History of India as Told by Its Own Historians*, H.M. Elliot and D.J. Dowson, Allahabad: Kitab Mahal, 1964, vol. VI, pp. 244-50.

Babur, Zahiruddin Muhammad, *Baburnama*, Persian tr. Abdur Rahim Khan Khanan, English tr. Annette Susannah Beveridge, Delhi: Oriental Books, 1979.

Badauni, Abdul Qadir ibn Muluk Shah, *Muntakhab-ut-Tawarikh*, ed. Maulvi Ahmad Ali, Kabiruddin Ahmad and W.N. Lees, 3 vols, Calcutta: Asiatic Society of Bengal, 1868, vol. I, tr. E.S.A. Ranking, vol. II, tr. W.H. Lowe, vol. III, tr. T.W. Haig, Calcutta: Asiatic Society of Bengal, 1899-1925; rpt, Delhi: Idarah-i-Adabiyat-i-Delhi, 1973.

Bayazid Bayat, *Tazkira-i-Humayun wa Akbar*, ed. M. Hidayat Husain, Calcutta: Asiatic Society of Bengal, 1941.

Dughlat, Mirza Muhammad Haider, *Tarikh-i-Rashidi*, tr. E. Denison Ross, Delhi: Sagar Book House, 1974.

Elliot, H.M. and D.J. Dowson, *History of India as Told by Its Own Historians*, vols I-VII, Allahabad: Kitab Mahal, 1964.

Fani, Mohsin, *Dabistan-i-Mazahib*, lithograph, Lucknow: Newal Kishore Press, 1904.

Farishta, Muhammad Qasim Hindu Shah, *Tarikh-i-Farishta or Gulshan-i-Ibrahimi*, ed. J. Briggs, 2 vols, Lucknow: Newal Kishore Press, 1905, tr. J. Briggs, *History of the Rise of Mohammadan Power in India*, 4 vols, Calcutta: Asiatic Society of Bengal, 1908.

Gilani, Abul Fath, *Ruqqat-i-Abul Fath Gilani*, ed. Mohammad Bashir Ahmad, Lucknow: Newal Kishore Press, 1913; Lahore: Idarah-i-Tahqiqat-i-Pakistan, 1967-8.

Gulbadan Begam, *Humayunnama*, ed. and tr. Annette Susannah Beveridge, *The History of Humayun*, London: Royal Asiatic Society, 1902; rpt, Delhi: Oriental Books, 1983.

Husaini, Khwaja Kamgar, *Maasir-i-Jahangiri*, ed. Azra Alvi, Bombay: Asia Publishing House, 1978.

Jahangir, Nuruddin Muhammad, *Tuzuk-i-Jahangiri*, tr. Alexander Rogers and ed. Henry Beveridge, London: Royal Asiatic Society, 1909-14; rpt, Delhi: Munshiram Manoharlal, 1978.

Jauhar, Aftabachi, *Tazkirat-ul-Waqayat*, tr. Charles Stewart, Delhi: Idarah-i-Adabiyat-i-Delhi, 1972.

Khafi Khan, *Muntakhab-ul-Lubab*, ed. Maulvi Khabiruddin Ahmad, Gulam Qadir and T.W. Haig, 3 vols, Calcutta: Asiatic Society of Bengal, 1868.

Khan, Mutamad, *Iqbalnama-i-Jahangiri*, ed. Maulvi Abdul-Hayy and Maulvi Ahmad Ali Sahun, Calcutta: Asiatic Society of Bengal, 1865.

Khani, Muhammad Bihamad, *Tarikh-i-Muhmmadi*, tr. M. Zaki, Bombay: Asia Publishing House, 1972.

Khwandmir, *Qanun-i-Humayun*, tr. Beni Prasad, Calcutta: Asiatic Society of Bengal, 1940.

Lahori, Abdul Hamid, *Padshahnama*, ed. Kabiruddin Ahmad and Abdur Rahim, 2 vols, Calcutta: Asiatic Society of Bengal, 1867-8.

Maktubat-i-Khan-i-Jahan Muzaffar Khan wa Gawalior Nama, British Museum MS, Add. 16859 (contains a letter written by Mirza Aziz Koka to Jahangir).

Masum, Mir Muhammad, *Tarikh-i-Masumi*, ed. U.M. Daud-Pota, Pune: Bhandarkar Oriental Research Institute, 1938.

Mir Abu Turab Wali, *Tarikh-i-Gujarat*, with Introduction and Notes, ed. Sir E. Denison Ross, Calcutta: Asiatic Society of Bengal, 1909.

Nathan, Mirza, *Bahristan-i-Ghaybi*, ed. and tr. M.I. Borah, 2 vols, Guwahati: Government of Assam, 1936.

Niamatullah, Khwaja, *Tarikh-i-Khanjahani wa Makhzan-i-Afghani*, ed. Imam Al-Din, Dacca: Asiatic Society of Pakistan, 1962.

Nihawandi, Abdul Baqi, *Maasir-i-Rahimi*, ed. M. Hidayat Husain, 3 vols, Calcutta: Asiatic Society of Bengal, 1940.

Nisyani, Sayyid Tahir Muhammad, *Tarikh-i-Tahiri*, ed. Nabi Bakhsh Baloch, Hyderabad (Pakistan): Sindhi Adabi Board, 1964.

Nizami, Hasan, *Taj-ul-Maasir*, tr. Bhagwat Swroop, Delhi: Saud Ahmad Dehalvi, 1988.

Qandhari, Muhammad Arif, *Tarikh-i-Akbari*, ed. Sayyid Moinuddin Nadwi, Sayyid Azhar Ali and Imtiaz Ali Arshi, Rampur: Raza Library, 1962, tr. Tasneem Ahmad, Delhi: Pragati Publications, 1993.

Qazwani, Asad Beg, *Waqa'i-i Asad Beg (Nuksha-i-Ahwal-i-Asad Beg)*, London MS, Or.1996, 30 fols; Aligarh Muslim University, MS No. 270/40(4).

Salim, Ghulam Husain, *Riyazu-s-Salatin (A History of Bengal)*, tr. Abdus Salam, Delhi: Idarah-i-Adabiyat-i-Delhi, 1975.

Sarhindi, Shaikh Alahadad Faizi, *Akbarnama*, extracts translated in *The History of India as Told by Its Own Historians*, H.M. Elliot and D.S. Dowson, Allahabad: Kitab Mahal, 1964, vol. VI, pp. 116-46.

Sarwani, Abbas Khan, *Tarikh-i-Shershahi*, tr. B.P. Ambasathya, Patna: K.P. Jayaswal Research Institute, 1974.

TRANSLATED AND PUBLISHED DOCUMENTS

Ansari, M.A., ed., *Administrative Documents of Mughal India*, Delhi: B.R. Publications, 1984.

Dutta, K.K., ed., *Some Mughal Farmans, Sanads and Parwanas*, Patna: Bihar State Central Record Office, 1962.

Grewal, J.S and B.N. Goswamy, eds., *The Mughals and Jogis of Jakhbar*, Simla: Indian Institute of Advanced Study, 1967.

Habib, Irfan, 'Three Early *Farmans* of Akbar, in Favour of Ramdas, the Master Dyer', in *Akbar and His India*, ed. Irfan Habib, Delhi: Oxford University Press, 1997.

Husain, Iqbal, 'Calendar of Khairabad Documents, From 16th to 19th Century', *Islamic Culture*, 1979.

——, 'Akbar's *Farmans*—A Study in Diplomatic', in *Akbar and His India*, ed. Irfan Habib, Delhi: Oxford University Press, 1997.

Jafri, Sayyid Zaheer, 'A *Farman* of Akbar (1558) from the Period of the Regency', in *Akbar and His India*, ed. Irfan Habib, Delhi: Oxford University Press, 1997.

Jhaveri, K.M., *Imperial Farmans (1577-1805) Granted to the Ancestors of the Tikayat Maharaj*, translation and reproductions in English, Hindi and Gujarati with Notes, Bombay: Manilal Itcharam Desai (with News Printing Press), 1928.

'Miscellaneous Persian Documents from the Rajasthan Archives', Bikaner; Transcribed Copy No. 85, Aligarh: Department of History, Aligarh Muslim University.

Mukatabat-i-Allami (Insha-i-Abul Fazl), tr. Mansura Haidar, Delhi: Munshiram Manoharlal, 1998.

Petri, R.K., *Descriptive List of Miscellaneous Persian Documents (1633-1867)*, Delhi: National Archives of India, 1992.

Riazul Islam, *A Calendar of Documents on Indo-Persian Relations, 1500-1700*, 2 vols, Karachi: Institute of Central and West Asian Studies, University of Karachi, 1979-82.

Shakeb, Ziauddin-Ahmad, ed., *Mughal Archives: A Descriptive Catalogue of Documents Pertaining to the Reign of Shahjahan (1628-1658)*, Hyderabad: State Archives of Andhra Pradesh, 1977.

Srivastava, K.P., ed., *Mughal Farmans, 1540–1706*, Lucknow: State Archives of Uttar Pradesh, 1976.

Tirmizi, S.A.A., *Calendar of Acquired Documents*, Delhi: National Archives of India, 1983.

——, *Mughal Documents, 1526-1627*, vol. I, Delhi: Manohar, 1989.

——, *Mughal Documents, 1628-1659*, vol. II, Delhi: Manohar, 1995.

Yusuf Husain, ed., *Selected Documents of Shahjahan's Reign*, Hyderabad: Daftar-i-Diwani, 1950.

——, ed., *Selected Documents of Aurangzeb's Reign*, Hyderabad: Central Record Office, Government of Andhra Pradesh, 1959.

BIOGRAPHIES AND *TAZKIRAS*

Bhakkari, Shaikh Farid, *Zakhirat-ul-Khawanin*, ed. Syed Moin-ul-Haq, 3 vols, Karachi: Pakistan Historical Society, 1961, 1970 and 1974, vol. I in English tr. Z.A. Desai, Delhi: Idarah-i-Adabiyat-i-Delhi, 1993.

Blochmann, H., *Biographies in Ain-i-Akbari*, vol. I, rpt, Delhi: Low Price Publications, 1994.

Khan, Shah Nawaz and Abdul Hayy, *Maasir-ul-Umara*, ed. Maulvi Abdur Rahim and Ashraf Ali, 3 vols, Calcutta: Asiatic Society of Bengal, 1887-96, tr. Henry Beveridge, revd. and comp. Beni Prasad, 3 vols, Calcutta: Asiatic Society of Bengal, 1941-52; rpt, Patna: Janaki Prakashan, 1979; in Hindi *Mughal Darbar*, tr. Brij Ratan Das.

Ram, Kewal, *Tazkirat-ul-Umara*, tr. S.M. Azizuddin Husain, Delhi: Munshiram Manoharlal, 1985.

DICTIONARIES

Abdur Rashid Thattawi, *Farang-i-Rashidi, 1653-54*, ed. Abul Tahir Zulfiqar Ali Murshdabadi, Calcutta: Asiatic Society of Bengal, 1857.

Anand Ram Mukhlis, *Mirat-ul-Istilah, Encyclopedia Dictionary of Medieval India*, tr. Tasneem Ahmad, Delhi: Sundeep Publications, 1993.

'Bahar', Munshi Tek Chand, *Bahar-i-Ajam, 1739-40 A.D.*, Lithograph, Lucknow: Newal Kishore Press, 1916.

Muhammad Ghiyasuddin, *Ghiyas-ul-lughat*, Kanpur: Newal Kishore Press, 1878.

Platts, John, *A Dictionary of Urdu, Classical Hindi and English*, Delhi: Oriental Books, 1984.

Steingass, F., *Persian-English Dictionary*, rpt, Delhi: Munshiram Manoharlal, 1973.

TRAVELLERS' ACCOUNTS

Ansari, Mohammad Azhar, *European Travellers Under the Mughals, 1580-1627*, Delhi: Idarah-i-Adabiyat-i-Delhi, 1975.

Battuta, Ibn, *Travels in Asia and Africa, 1325-1354*, tr. H.A.R. Gibb, London: Routledge and Kegan Paul, 1929; rpt, Delhi: Oriental Books, 1986.

Bernier, Francois, *Travels in the Mughal Empire, 1656-68*, tr. Archibald Constable, revd. Vincent Smith, Delhi: Oriental Books, 1983.

De Laet, Joannes, *Description of India and Fragment of Indian History*, tr. J.S. Hoyland and annotated by S.N. Banerjee, *The Empire of the Great Mogol*, Bombay: Kitab Mahal, 1928.

Du Jarric, Pierre, *Account of the Jesuits' Mission at the Court of Akbar*, tr. C.H. Payne, *Akbar and the Jesuits*, New York: Harper & Brother, 1926; rpt, Delhi: Tulsi Publications, 1979.

Father A. Monserrate, *The Commentary of His Journey to the Court of Akbar*, trs. J.S. Hoyland and annotated by S.N. Banerjee, Delhi: Oxford University Press, 1922; rpt, Jalandhar: Asian Publications, 1993.

Foster, William, ed., *Early Travels in India, 1583-1619*, London: Humphrey Milford, 1921; rpt, Delhi: Munshiram Manoharlal, 1985.

Letters from the Mughal Court: The First Jesuit Mission to Akbar, 1580-83, tr. and ed. John Correia-A Fonso, Bombay: Gujarat Sahitya Prakashan, 1980.

Manrique, F.S., *Travels of Fary Sabastien Manrique, 1629-43*, tr. Eckford Luard, 2 vols, London: Hakluyat Society, 1927.

Manucci, Niccolao, *Storia Do Mogor or Mogul India, 1653-1708*, tr. William Irvine, 4 vols, rpt, Delhi: Oriental Books, 1981.

Mundy, Peter, *The Travels of Peter Mundy in Europe and Asia, 1608-1667*, ed. R.C. Temple, London: Hakluyat Society, 1914-24.

Polo, Marco, *The Book of Ser Marco Polo: The Venetian, Concerning the Kingdoms and the Marvels of the East*, tr. Henry Yule, New York: Barnes and Noble, 1969.

Roe, Sir Thomas, *The Embassy of Sir Thomas Roe to India, 1615-19*, ed. Sir William Foster, London: Humphrey Milford, 1926; rpt, Delhi: Munshiram Manoharlal, 1990.

Tavernier, Jean-Baptiste, *Travels in India, 1640-47*, tr. V. Ball, revd. William Crook, 2 vols, London: Humphrey Milford, 1925; rpt, Delhi: Oriental Books, 1977.

Wheeler J. Tolboys, ed., *Early Travels in India*, Delhi: Deep Publications, 1975.

BOOKS AND ARTICLES

Agrawal, C.M., *Akbar and His Hindu Officers: A Critical Study*, Jalandhar: ABS Publications, 1986.

Ahmad, Aziz, *Studies in Islamic Culture in the Indian Environment*, Oxford: Clarendon Press, 1964.

Alam, Muzaffar and Sanjay Subrahmanyam, eds., *The Mughal State, 1526-1750*, Delhi: Oxford University Press, 1998.

Alam, Muzaffar, *The Crisis of Empire in Mughal North India: Awadh and the Punjab, 1707-1748*, Delhi: Oxford University Press, 1986.

Alavi, Azra, *Socio-Religious Outlook of Abul Fazl*, Delhi: Idarah-i-Adabiyat-i-Delhi, 1983.

Alavi, Rafi Ahmad, 'New Light on Mughal Cavalry', in *Medieval India: A Miscellany II*, Bombay: Asia Publishing House, 1972.

Alavi, Seema, ed., *The Eighteenth Century in India*, Delhi: Oxford University Press, 2002.

Ali, Mubarak, 'The Titles of the Mughal Nobility', in *Mughal India* I, ed. Mohamed Taher, Delhi: Anmol Publishing House, 1997.

Ambasathya, B.P., *Contributions on Akbar and Parsees*, Patna: Janaki Prakashan, 1976.

——, *Some Non-Persian Sources of Medieval India*, Delhi: Idarah-i-Adabiyat-i-Delhi, 1979.

Ansari, Mohammad Azhar, *Chronicle of Akbar the Great: A Description of a Manuscript of the Akbarnama, Illustrated by the Court Painters*, Oxford: Oxford University Press, 1937.

——, 'Social Condition at the Court of Akbar and Its Influence on Society', in *Mughal India* I, ed. Mohamed Taher, Delhi: Anmol Publishing House, 1997.

Anwar, Firdos, *Nobility Under the Mughals, 1628-1658*, Delhi: Manohar, 2001.

Appadurai, Arjun, ed., *The Social Life of Things: Commodities in Cultural Perspective*, Cambridge: Cambridge University Press, 1986.

Ashraf, K.M., *Life and Conditions of the People of Hindustan, 1200-1550*, Delhi: Munshiram Manoharlal, 1970.

Athar Ali, M., 'Foundations of Akbar's Organisation of the Nobility—An Interpretation', *Medieval India Quarterly*, 1961.

——, *Mughal Nobility Under Aurangzeb*, Bombay: Asia Publishing House, 1966; revd edn, Delhi: Oxford University Press, 1997.

——, 'The Mughal Empire in History', Presidential Address to the Medieval Section, *Proceedings of the Indian History Congress*, no. 33, 1972.

——, 'The Passing of Empire: The Mughal Case', *Modern Asian Studies*, vol. 9, no. 3, 1975.

——, *The Apparatus of Empire: Awards of Ranks, Offices and Titles to the Mughal Nobility, 1574-1658*, Delhi: Oxford University Press, 1985.

——, 'The Mughal Polity—A Critique of "Revisionist" Approaches', *Proceedings of the Indian History Congress*, no. 52, 1991-2.

——, 'Political Structures of the Islamic Orient in the Sixteenth and Seventeenth Centuries', in *Medieval India I: Researches in the History of India, 1200-1750*, ed. Irfan Habib, Delhi: Oxford University Press, 1992.

——, 'Towards an Interpretation of the Mughal Empire', in *The State in India, 1000-1700*, ed. Hermann Kulke, Delhi: Oxford University Press, 1995.

Augustus, Frederick Count of Noer, *The Emperor Akbar*, tr. Annette Susannah Beveridge, Patna: Academica Asiatica, 1973.

Azad, M.H., *Darbar-i-Akbari* (in Urdu), Lahore: Rifah-i-Am Press, 1898, Hindi tr. Ram Chandar Verma, Varanasi: Kashi Nagri Pracharini Sabha, 1967-8.

Aziz, Abdul, 'Thrones, Chairs and Seats Used by the Indian Mughals', *Journal of Indian History*, vol. 16, 1937.

——, *Imperial Treasury of the Indian Mughal*, Delhi: Idarah-i-Adabiyat-i-Delhi, 1972.

——, *The Mansabdari System and the Mughal Army*, Delhi: Idarah-i-Adabiyat-i -Delhi, 1972.

Bagchi, A.K., 'The Mughal Economy: A Quantitative Study', *The Indian Historical Review*, vol. 13, nos. 1-2, 1986-7.

Banga, Indu, *Agrarian System of the Sikhs*, Delhi: Manohar, 1978.

Barnett, Richard B., *North India Between Empires: Awadh, the Mughals, and the British, 1720-1801*, Delhi: Manohar, 1987.

Bayly, C.A., *Rulers, Townsmen and Bazaars: North Indian Society in the Age of British Expansion, 1770-1870*, Cambridge: Cambridge University Press, 1983.

Beames, John, 'On the Geography of India in the Reign of Akbar', *Journal of the Asiatic Society of Bengal*, vol. 52, no. 1, 1984.

——, 'Notes on Akbar's *Subahs* with Reference to *Ain-i-Akbari*, Bengal and Orissa', *Journal of the Royal Asiatic Society*, 1996.

Bedi, P.S., *The Mughal Nobility Under Akbar*, Jalandhar: ABS Publications, 1985.

Berkemer, Georg et al., eds., *Explorations in the History of South Asia: Essays in Honour of Dietmar Rothermund*, Delhi: Manohar, 2003.

Bhadani, B.L., 'Revenue Estimation and Realization in the Mughal Empire', in *Mughal India* I, ed. Mohamed Taher, Delhi: Anmol Publishing House, 1997.

Bhargava, Visheshwar Sarup, *Mewar and the Mughal Emperors, 1526-1748*, Delhi: Munshiram Manoharlal, 1966.

Bhatt, Rajendar Shankar, *Mewar ke Maharana aur Shahinshah Akbar*, Jaipur: Saftik Sansthan, 1976.

Bilgrami, Rafat M., 'Some Mughal Revenue Grants to the Family and *Khanqah* of Sayyid Ashraf Jahangir', in *Medieval India: A Miscellany* II, Bombay: Asia Publishing House, 1972.

——, *Religious and Quasi-Religious Departments of the Mughal Period, 1556-1707*, Delhi: Munshiram Manoharlal, 1984.

Blake, Stephen P., *Shahjahanabad: The Sovereign City in Mughal India, 1639-1739*, Cambridge: Cambridge University Press, 1991.

——, 'The Patrimonial–Bureaucratic Empire of the Mughals', in *The State in India, 1000-1700*, ed. Hermann Kulke, Delhi: Oxford University Press, 1995.

Budhwar, Sunita, 'Assignment of *Jagirs* in Rajputana', *Proceedings of the Indian History Congress*, no. 35, 1975.

Burke, S.H., *Akbar the Great Mughal*, Delhi: Munshiram Manoharlal, 1989.

Burn, Sir Richard, ed., *The Cambridge History of India*, vol. 4: *The Mughal Period*, Cambridge: Cambridge University Press, 1937.

Chandra, Satish, *Parties and Politics at the Mughal Court*, Aligarh: Aligarh Muslim University, 1959; rpt, Delhi: People's Publishing House, 1979.

——, ed., *Medieval India: Society, the Jagirdari Crisis and the Village*, Delhi: Macmillan India, 1982.

——, ed., *Essays in Medieval Indian Economic History*, Delhi: Munshiram Manoharlal, 1987.

——, *Mughal Religious Policies: The Rajputs and the Deccan*, Delhi: Vikas, 1993.

Chatterjee, Partha and Anjan Ghosh, *History and the Present*, Delhi: Permanent Black, 2004.

Chaudhari, Neelam, *Social and Economic History of Mughal India*, Delhi: Discovery Publishing House, 1987.

Chitnis, K.N., *Socio-Economic History of Medieval India*, Delhi: Atlantic Publishers and Distributors, 1990.

Chopra, P.N., *Some Aspects of Social Life During the Mughal Age, 1520-1707*, Agra: Shiva Lal Agarwala, 1963.

——, *Life and Letters Under the Great Mughals*, Delhi: Asha Janak Publications, 1976.

——, *Society and Culture During the Mughal Age*, Delhi: Agam Publications, 1988.

Choudhury, M.L. Roy, 'Hindu Muslim Relation During the Mughal Period, 1556-1707 AD', *Proceedings of the Indian History Congress*, no. 9, 1946.

Cohn, Bernard S., 'Political Systems in Eighteenth Century India', *Journal of the American Oriental Society*, no. 82, 1962.

——, 'Structural Change in Indian Rural Society', in *Land Control and Social Structure in Indian History*, ed. Robert Eric Frykenberg, Delhi: Manohar, 1979.

——, *An Anthropologist Among the Historian and Other Essays*, Delhi: Oxford University Press, 1987.

Commissariat, M.S., *History of Gujarat*, 2 vols, Bombay: Orient Longman, 1938, 1957.

Dadvar, A., *Iranians in Mughal Politics and Society, 1606-58*, Delhi: Gyan Publishing House, 1999.

Day, U.N., *Medieval Malwa: A Political and Cultural History, 1401-1526*, Delhi: Munshiram Manoharlal, 1965.

——, *The Mughal Government, 1556-1707*, Delhi: Munshiram Manoharlal, 1994.

Desai, A.V., 'Population and Standard of Living in Akbar's Time', *The Indian Economic and Social History Review*, vol. 9, 1972.

——, 'Population and Standard of Living in Akbar's Time—A Second Look', *The Indian Economic and Social History Review*, vol. 15, no. 1, 1978.

Devra, G.S.L., *Rajsthan ki Prashasnik Vyavastha*, Bikaner: Dharti Prakashan, 1981.

——, '*Raja*, *Mansab* and *Jagir*—A Re-examination of Mughal–Rajput Relations During the Reign of Akbar', in *Akbar and His Age*, ed. Iqtidar Alam Khan, Delhi: Northern Book Centre, 1999.

Digby, Simon, *War Horse and Elephant in the Delhi Sultanate*, Oxford: Oxford University Press, 1971.

Duffy, Christopher, *Siege Warfare*, London: Routledge and Kegan Paul, 1979.

Eaton, Richard M., *The Rise of Islam and Bengal Frontier, 1204-1760*, Delhi: Oxford University Press, 1994.

Embree Ainslie T., 'Land Holding in India and British Institutions', in *Land Control and Social Structure in Indian History*, ed. Robert Eric Frykenberg, Delhi: Manohar, 1979.

Farooqi, Naimur Rehman, *Mughal-Ottoman Relations: A Study of Political and Diplomatic Relations Between Mughal India and the Ottoman Empire, 1556-1748*, Delhi: Idarah-i-Adabiyat-i-Delhi, 1989.

Farooque, Abdul Khair Muhammad, *Road and Communications in Mughal India*, Delhi: Idarah-i-Adabiyat-i-Delhi, 1977.

Fisher, Michael H., *A Clash of Cultures: Awadh, the British and the Mughals*, Delhi: Manohar, 1987.

Fox, Richard G., *Kin, Clan, Raja and Rule*, Berkeley: University of California Press, 1971.

Frykenberg, Robert Eric, ed., *Land Control and Social Structure in Indian History*, Delhi: Manohar, 1979.

Fukazawa, Hiroshi, *The Medieval Deccan: Peasants, Social System and States, Sixteenth to Eighteenth Centuries*, Delhi: Oxford University Press, 1991.

Gommans, Jos, *Mughal Warfare: Indian Frontier and High Roads to Empire, 1500-1700*, London: Routledge, 2002.

Gopal, Surendra, *Commerce and Crafts in Gujarat, 15th and 17th Centuries: A Study in the Impact of European Expansion on Precapitalistic Economy*, Calcutta: Asia Publishing House, 1975.

Gordon, Stewart, 'Robes of Honour: A "Transitional" Kingly Ceremony'. *The Indian Economic and Social History Review*, vol. 33, no. 3, 1996.

——, ed., *Robes and Honour: The Medieval World of Investiture*, New York: Palgrave, 2001.

——, ed., *Robes of Honour: Khil'at in Pre-Colonial and Colonial India*, Delhi: Oxford University Press, 2003.

Grewal, J.S., *Muslim Rule in India*, London: Oxford University Press, 1970.

——, *Medieval India: History and Historians*, Amritsar: Guru Nanak University Press, 1975.

Grover, B.R., 'Classification of Agrarian Land Under Akbar', *Proceedings of the Indian History Congress*, no. 23, 1960.

——, 'Nature of Land Rights in Mughal India', *The Indian Economic and Social History Review*, vol. 1, no. 1, 1963.

Gupta, S.P., 'Expansion of the Kachhwaha Territory in Mughal Times', *Proceedings of the Indian History Congress*, no. 24, 1961.

——, The *Agrarian System of Eastern Rajasthan, c. 1650-c. 1750*, Delhi: Manohar, 1986.

Habib, Irfan, *The Agrarian System of Mughal India*, Bombay: Asia Publishing House, 1963; revd. edn, Delhi: Oxford University Press, 1999.

——, 'The *Mansab* System, 1595-1637', *Proceedings of the Indian History Congress*, no. 29, 1967.

——, 'The System of Bills of Exchange (*Hundies*) in the Mughal Empire', *Proceedings of the Indian History Congress*, no. 33, 1972.

——, *An Atlas of the Mughal Empire: Political and Economic Maps with Detailed Notes, Bibliography and Index*, Delhi: Oxford University Press, 1982.

——,'*Mansab* Salary Scale Under Jahangir and Shahjahan', *Islamic Culture*, 1985.

——, ed., *Medieval India I: Researches in the History of India, 1200-1750*, Delhi: Oxford University Press, 1992.

——,'Agriculture and Agrarian Condition in South Gujarat, *c.* 1596', *Proceedings of the Indian History Congress*, no. 54, 1993.

——, *Essays in Indian History: Toward a Marxist Perception*, Delhi: Tulika, 1995.

——, ed., *Akbar and His India*, Delhi: Oxford University Press, 2000.

——, 'Classifying Pre-Colonial India', in *The Feudalism Debate*, ed. Harbans Mukhia, Delhi: Manohar, 2000.

——, *The Economic History of Medieval India: A Survey*, Delhi: Manohar, 2000.

——, 'The Eighteenth Century in Indian Economic History', in *The Eighteenth Century in India*, ed. Seema Alavi, Delhi: Oxford University Press, 2002.

Hasan, Ibn, *The Central Structure of the Mughal Empire*, Delhi: Munshiram Manoharlal, 1980.

Hasan, S. Nurul, 'New Light on the Relations of Early Mughal Rulers with Their Nobility', *Proceedings of the Indian History Congress*, no. 7, 1944.

——, *Thoughts on Agrarian Relations in Mughal India*, rpt, Delhi: People's Publishing House, 1984.

——,'*Zamindars* Under the Mughals', in *Land Control and Social Structure in Indian History*, ed. Robert Eric Frykenberg, Delhi: Manohar, 1979.

Heston, A.W., 'The Standard of Living in Akbar's Time—A Comment', *The Indian Economic and Social History Review*, vol. 14, no. 3, 1977.

Hodgson, Marshall G.S., *The Venture of Islam*, 3 vols, Chicago: University of Chicago Press, 1974.

Hossein Khan, Seid-Gholam, *The Seir Mutakharin*, 4 vols, rpt, Delhi: Low Price Publications, 1990.

Huart, Clement, *Ancient Persian and Iranian Civilization*, London: Routledge, 1972.

Husain, Afzal, 'Marriage Among Mughal Nobles as an Index of Status and Aristocratic Integration', *Proceedings of the Indian History Congress*, no. 33, 1972.

——, 'Provincial Governors Under Akbar, 1580-1605', *Medieval India: A Miscellany* II, Bombay: Asia Publishing House, 1972.

——, 'Growth of Irani Element in Akbar's Nobility', *Proceedings of the Indian History Congress*, no. 36, 1975.

——, 'An Unpublished Letter of Mirza Aziz Koka to Akbar', *Proceedings of the Indian History Congress*, no. 39, 1978.

——, 'Liberty and Restraint—A Study of Shiasim in the Mughal Nobility', *Proceedings of the Indian History Congress*, no. 41, 1980.

——, 'The Letter of Hakim Abul Fateh Gilani—An Unexplored Source for Akbar's Reign', *Proceedings of the Indian History Congress*, no. 44, 1983.

——, *The Nobility Under Akbar and Jahangir*, Delhi: Manohar, 1999.

Husain, Yusuf, *Glimpses of Medieval Indian Culture*, Bombay: Asia Publishing House, 1959.

Irvine, William, *The Army of the Indian Moghuls: Its Organisation and Administration*, Delhi: Eurasia, 1962.

Islam, Riazul, *Indo-Persian Relations: A Study of the Political and Diplomatic Relations between the Mughal Empire and Iran*, Teheran: Iranian Culture Foundation, 1970.

Islam, Zafarul, 'Nature of Landed Property in Mughal India', in *Mughal India* I, ed. Mohamed Taher, Delhi: Anmol Publishing House, 1997.

James, Bird, tr., *Medieval Gujarat: Its Political and Statistical History*, based on Mohammed Ali Khan's *Mirat-i-Ahmadi* transcribed in 1822 by Narsain Dass of the Kait tribe at Ahmedabad, Delhi: Indian Bibliographies Bureau, 1985.

Joshi, Rita, *The Afghan Nobility and the Mughals*, Delhi: Vikas Publishing House, 1985.

Kasturi, Malvika, *Embattled Identities: Rajput Lineage and the Colonial State in Nineteenth-Century North India*, Delhi: Oxford University Press, 2002.

Kaw, Mushtaq A., *The Agrarian System of Kashmir*, Srinagar: Aiman Publications, 2001.

Khan, Ahsan Raza, 'Babur's Settlement of His Conquests in Hindustan', *Proceedings of the Indian History Congress*, no. 29, 1967.

——, *Chieftains in the Mughal Empire During the Reign of Akbar*, Shimla: Indian Institute of Advanced Study, 1977.

Khan, Husain, 'The Mughal Nobility', in *Mughal India* I, ed. Mohamed Taher, Delhi: Anmol Publishing House, 1997.

Khan, Iqtidar Alam, 'The Formation of the Mughal Ruling Class—A Study of Akbar's Policies', *Proceedings of the Indian History Congress*, no. 18, 1955.

——, 'Mughal Afghan Relation, 1559-1574', *Proceedings of the Indian History Congress*, no. 24, 1961.

——, *Mirza Kamran—A Biographical Study*, Bombay: Asia Publishing House, 1964.

——, 'The Nobility Under Akbar and the Development of his Religious Policies, 1560-80', *Journal of the Royal Asiatic Society*, 1968.

——, 'Mughal Court Politics During Bairam Khan's Regency', in *Medieval India: A Miscellany* I, Bombay: Asia Publishing House, 1972.

——, 'The Turko-Mongol Theory of Kingships', in *Medieval India: A Miscellany* II, Bombay: Asia Publishing House, 1972.

——, *The Political Biography of a Mughal Noble: Munim Khan Khan-i-Khanan, 1497-1575*, Delhi: Orient Longman, 1973.

——, 'The Middle Classes in the Mughal Empire', Presidential Address to the Medieval Section, *Proceedings of the Indian History Congress*, no. 36, 1975.

——, 'The Mughal Assignment System During Akbar's Early Years, 1556-1575', in *Medieval India I: Researches in the History of India, 1200-1750*, ed. Irfan Habib, Delhi: Oxford University Press, 1992.

——, ed., *Akbar and His Age*, Delhi: Northern Book Centre, 1999.

——, *Gunpowder and Firearms: Warfare in Medieval India*, Delhi: Oxford University Press, 2004.

Khan, Kunwar Refaqat Ali, *The Kachhwahas Under Akbar and Jahangir*, Delhi: Kitab Publishing House, 1976.

Khan, M. Sadiq, 'A Study in Mughal Land Revenue System', *Islamic Culture*, 1938.

Khan, M.A., *The Court of the Great Mughals*, Delhi: Bachum, 1976.

Khosla, R.P., *Mughal Kingship and Nobility*, Delhi: Idarah-i-Adabiyat-i-Delhi, 1976.

Kolff, Dirk H.A., *Naukar, Rajput and Sepoy: The Ethnohistory of the Military Labour Market in Hindustan, 1450-1850*, Cambridge: Cambridge University Press, 1990.

Krishnamurthi, R., 'Akbar's Philosophy of Life', *The Indian Historical Quarterly*, no. 20, 1944.

——, 'Some Aspects of Akbar's Religion Position', *Proceedings of the Indian History Congress*, no. 23, 1960.

Kulke, Hermann, *Kings and Cults: State Formation and Legitimation in India and Southern Asia*, Delhi: Manohar, 1993.

——, ed., *The State in India, 1000-1700*, Delhi: Oxford University Press, 1995.

Lal, K.S., *The Mughal Harem*, Delhi: Aditya Prakashan, 1988.

Leonard, Karen, 'The "Great Firm" Theory of the Decline of the Mughal Empire', in The *Mughal State, 1526-1750*, ed. Muzaffar Alam and Sanjay Subrahmanyam, Delhi: Oxford University Press, 1998.

Ludden, David, *An Agrarian History of South Asia*, vol. IV.4 of *The New Cambridge History of India*, Delhi: Cambridge University Press, 1999.

Maclagan, Edward, *The Jesuit and the Great Mogul*, rpt, Delhi: Vintage Books, 1990.

Macauliffe, M.A., *The Sikh Religion*, rpt, Delhi: S. Chand & Co., 1963.

Majumdar, R.C., ed., *The History and Culture of the Indian People*, vol. II: *The Mughal Empire*, Bombay: Bharatiya Vidya Bhavan, 1951-74.

Malcolm, J., *A Memoir of Central India Including Malwa*, Delhi: Sagar Publications, 1970.

Malhotra, Yog Raj, *Babur's Nobility and Administration in India*, Jalandhar: ABS Publishers, 1996.

Malik, Zahiruddin, *Agrarian System in Medieval India*, Delhi: Rawat Publications, 2001.

Malleson, G.B., *Akbar and the Rise of Mughal Empire*, Ambala: Bhagi Publications, 1972.

Marshall, D.N. and V.D.D. Taraporevala, *Mughal Bibliography: Select Persian Sources for the Study of Mughals in India*, rpt, Delhi: Munshiram Manoharlal, 1991.

Mauss, Marcel, *The Gifts: Forms and Functions of Exchange in Archaic Societies*, tr. Ian Cunnison, New York: W.W. Norton, 1967.

McLane, Johan R., *Land and Local Kingship in Eighteenth-Century Bengal*, Cambridge: Cambridge University Press, 1993.

Menon, K.P., 'The Personality of Akbar', *Islamic Culture*, 1927.

Metcalf, Barbara Daly, ed., *Moral Conduct and Authority: The Place of Adab in South Asian Islam*, Berkeley: University of California Press, 1984.

Mishra, H.K., *Bureaucracy Under the Mughals, 1556-1707*, Delhi: Amar Prakashan, 1989.

Mohammed, Jigar, *Revenue Free Land Grants in Mughal India*, Delhi: Manohar, 2002.

Mohammed, K.M., 'The House of the Nobility in Mughal India', in *Mughal India* II, ed. Mohamed Taher, Delhi: Anmol Publishing House, 1997.

Moosvi, Shireen, '*Suyurghal* Statistic in the *Ain-i-Akbari*—An Analysis', *The Indian Historical Review*, vol. 2, no. 2, 1976.

——, 'Production, Consumption and Population in Akbar's Time', *The Indian Economic and Social History Review*, vol. 10, no. 2, 1973.

——, 'Note on Professor Alam Heston's Standard of Living in Akbar's Time', *The Indian Economic and Social History Review*, vol. 14, no. 3, 1977.

——, 'Evolution of *Mansab* System Under Akbar', *Journal of the Royal Asiatic Society*, 1981.

——, *The Economy of the Mughal Empire c. 1595: A Statistical Study*, Delhi: Oxford University Press, 1987.

——, *Episodes in the Life of Akbar: Contemporary Records and Reminiscences*, Delhi: National Book Trust, 1994.

Moreland, W.H., 'Description of Assignment Orders', *Journal of the Royal Asiatic Society*, 1917.

——, 'Value of Money at the Court of Akbar', *Journal of the Royal Asiatic Society*, 1918.

——, 'The Development of the Land Revenue System of the Moghul Empire', *Journal of the Royal Asiatic Society*, 1926.

——, *The Agrarian System of Moslem India: A Historical Essay with Appendices*, Cambridge: Cambridge University Press, 1929; rpt, Delhi: Oriental Books, 1968.

——, 'Rank (*Mansab*) in the Mogul State Service', in *The Mughal State, 1526-1750*, ed. Muzaffar Alam and Sanjay Subrahmanyam, Delhi: Oxford University Press, 1998.

——, *From Akbar to Aurangzeb: A Study in Indian Economic History*, rpt, Delhi: Low Price Publications, 1999.

——, *India at the Death of Akbar: An Economic Study*, rpt, Delhi: Low Price Publications, 1999.

Morris, Loretta, 'Land Revenue of Akbar', *Calcutta Review*, 1949.

Mukherjee, R.K., *Economic History of India, 1600-1800*, Allahabad: Kitab Mahal, 1967.

Mukherjee, Tarapada and Irfan Habib, 'Akbar and the Temples of Mathura and Its Environs', *Proceedings of the Indian History Congress*, no. 48, 1987.

——, 'Land Rights in the Reign of Akbar: The Evidence of the Sale-deeds of Vrindaban and Aritha', *Proceedings of the Indian History Congress*, no. 50, 1990.

Mukhia, Harbans, *Historians and Historiography During the Reign of Akbar*, Delhi: Vikas, 1976.

——, ed., *The Feudalism Debate*, Delhi: Manohar, 2000.

——, *The Mughals of India*, Oxford and Delhi: Blackwell Publishing, 2004-5.

Naik, Chhotubhai Ranchhodji, *Abdur Rahim Khan-i-Khanan and His Literary Circle*, Ahmedabad: Gujarat University, 1966.

Nainsi, Munhot, *Marwar ra Pargana ri Vigat*, ed. Fateh Singh, Jodhpur: Rajasthan Oriental Research Institute, 1968.

——, *Munhot Nainsi ri Khyat*, ed. Badri Prasad Sakaria, Jodhpur: Rajasthan Oriental Research Institute, 1960.

Naqvi, Hamida Khatoon, *Urbanization and Urban Centres Under the Great Mughals, 1556-1707*, Simla: Indian Institute of Advanced Study, 1972.

——, 'Incidents of Rebellions During the Reign of Emperor Akbar', *Medieval India: A Miscellany* II, Bombay: Asia Publishing House, 1972.

——, *History of Mughal Government and Administration*, Delhi: Kanishka Publishing House, 1990.

Nayeem, M.A., 'Mughal *Jagirdari* System', in *Mughal India* I, ed. Mohamed Taher, Delhi: Anmol Publishing House, 1997.

Nizami, Khaliq Ahmad, 'Naqshbandi Influence on Mughal Rulers and Politics', *Islamic Culture*, 1965.

——, *On History and Historians in Medieval India*, Delhi: Munshiram Manoharlal, 1983.

——, *State and Culture in Medieval India*, Delhi: Adam Publishers and Distributors, 1985.

——, *Akbar and Religion*, Delhi: Idarah-i-Adabiyat-i-Delhi, 1989.

Ojha, Gauri Shankar, *Rajputana ka Itihas*, Ajmer: Vedic Yantralaya, 1927-41.

Panikkar, K.N. et al., eds., *Making of the History: Essays Presented to Professor Irfan Habib*, Delhi: Tulika, 2000.

Pant, D., *Economic History of India Under the Mughals*, Delhi: Kanishka Publications, 1990.

Pearson, M.N., 'Political Participation in Mughal India', *The Indian Economic and Social History Review*, vol. 9, 1972.

——, ed., *Legitimacy and Symbols: The South Asian Writings of F.W. Buckler*, Ann Arbor: University of Michigan Press, 1985.

Perlin, Frank, 'State Formation Reconsidered', *Modern Asian Studies*, vol. 19, 1985.

Phul, Raj Kumar, *Armies of the Great Mughals*, Delhi: Oriental Publishers, 1978.

Prasad, R.N., *Raja Man Singh of Amber*, Calcutta: World Press, 1966.

Qaisar, A.J., 'Note on the Date of Institution of *Mansab* Under Akbar', *Proceedings of the Indian History Congress*, no. 24, 1961.

——, 'Distribution of the Revenue Resources of the Mughal Empire Among the Nobility', *Proceedings of the Indian History Congress*, no. 27, 1965.

——, *'Shahbaz Khan Kambu'*. *Medieval India: A Miscellany* I, Bombay: Asia Publishing House, 1972.

——, *The Indian Response to European Technology and Culture, 1498-1707*, Delhi: Oxford University Press, 2000.

Qureshi, Ishtiaq Husain, *Akbar: The Founder of the Mughal Empire*, Delhi: Idarah-i-Adabiyat-i-Delhi, 1987.

———, *The Administration of the Moghul Empire*, rpt, Delhi: Low Price Publications, 1990.

Radheshyam, 'Honours, Ranks and Titles Under Humayun to Shahjahan', *University of Allahabad Studies*, 1974.

Rahim, Muhammad Abdur, *History of the Afghan in India, 1545-1631*, Karachi: Pakistan Publishing House, 1961.

Rana, R.P., 'Agrarian Revolts in Northern India During the Late 17th and Early 18th Century', *The Indian Economic and Social History Review*, vol. 28, 1981.

Ray, B.C., *Orissa Under the Mughals*, Calcutta: Punthi Pustak, 1981.

Raychaudhuri, Tapan, *Bengal Under Akbar and Jahangir*, Delhi: Munshiram Manoharlal, 1969.

——, 'Agrarian System of Mughal India', in *The Mughal State, 1526-1750*, ed. Muzaffar Alam and Sanjay Subrahmanyam, Delhi: Oxford University Press, 1998.

Raychaudhuri, Tapan, and Irfan Habib, eds., *The Cambridge Economic History of India*, vol. I (*c. 1200-1757*), Cambridge: Cambridge University Press, 1982.

Raza, S.M., 'Procedures of *Jagir* Assignment from Akbar to Aurangzeb', Paper presented at the Indian History Congress, no. 36, 1975.

Reu, Bisheshwar Nath, *Mewar ka Itihas*, Jodhpur: Government Press, 1938.

Richards, J.F., *Mughal Administration in Golconda*, Oxford: Oxford University Press, 1975.

——, ed., *The Imperial Monetary System of Mughal India*, Delhi: Oxford University Press, 1987.

——, 'The Seventeenth Century Crisis in South Asia', *Modern Asian Studies*, vol. 24, no. 4, 1990.

——, 'The Formulation of Imperial Authority Under Akbar and Jahangir', in *The Mughal State, 1526-1750*, ed. Muzaffar Alam and Sanjay Subrahmanyam, Delhi: Oxford University Press, 1998.

——, *The Mughal Empire* (vol. 1.5 of the *New Cambridge History of India*), Cambridge: Cambridge University Press, 1993.

——, ed., *Kingship and Authority in South Asia*, Delhi: Oxford University Press, 1998.

——, Norms of Comportment Among Imperial Mughal Officers', in *Moral Conduct and Authority: The Place of Adab in South Asian Islam*, ed. Barbara Daly Metcalf, Berkeley: University of California Press, 1984.

Rizvi, Saiyid Athar Abbas, *Muslim Revivalist Movements in Northern India in the 16th and 17th Centuries*, Agra: Agra University, 1965.

——, *Religious and Intellectual History of the Muslims in Akbar's Reign with Special Reference to Abul Fazl*, Delhi: Munshiram Manoharlal, 1975.

——, 'The Empire and Bureaucracy: The Case of Mughal Empire', *Proceedings of the Indian History Congress*, no. 59, 1998.

Robert, Orme, *Historical Fragments of the Mogul Empire*, Delhi: Associated Publishing House, 1978.

Saran, Parmatma, *The Provincial Government of the Mughals*, rpt, Bombay: Asia Publishing House, 1973.

——, 'Socio-Religious Background at the Advent of Akbar: A New Approach', *Journal of Uttar Pradesh Historical Society*, no. 19, 1946.

Sarkar, Jagdish Narayan, *Mughal Economy Organisation and Working*, Calcutta: Naya Prakashan, 1987.

Sarkar, Sir Jadunath, *History of Aurangzeb*, 2nd edn, 5 vols combined into 4, Bombay: Orient Longman, 1974.

Savory, Roger, *Iran Under the Safavid*, Cambridge: Cambridge University Press, 1980.

Saxena, B.P., 'Ideals of Mughal Sovereigns', *Journal of Uttar Pradesh Historical Society*, 1941.

Schimmel, Annemarie, *Mystical Dimensions of Islam*, Chapel Hill, NC: University of North Carolina Press, 1975.

Schnepel, Burkhard, *The Jungle Kings: Ethnohistorical Aspects of Politics and Ritual in Orissa*, Delhi: Manohar, 2003.

Sharma, Dashrath, ed., *Dalpat Vilas*, Bikaner: Sardul Research Institute, 1956.

Sharma, G.N., *Mewar and the Mughal Emperor*, Agra: Shiva Lal Agarwala, 1954.

Sharma, Ram Sharan, 'The Organization of Public Service in Mughal Period, *1526-1707*', *Journal of Bihar and Orissa Research Society*, no. 23, 1937.

——, *Land Revenue in India*, Delhi: Motilal Banarsidass, 1971.

——, 'The Segmentary State and the Indian Experience', *The Indian Historical Review*, vol. 16, 1993.

Sharma, S.R., *The Religious Policy of the Mughal Emperors*, Agra: Shiva Lal Agarwala, 1972.

Shivram, Balkrishan, 'Some Notes on Mughal Assignment System', *Proceedings of the Punjab History Conference*, no. 36, 2004.

——, '*Padshah*, *Jagir*, and *Jagirdars*—A Re-examination of the Mughal *Jagirdari* System During the Reign of Akbar', *Proceedings of the Indian History Congress*, no. 65, 2004.

——, 'Legitimacy and Loyalty: The Mughal's "Robe of Honour"', *Proceedings of the Punjab History Conference*, no. 37, 2005.

——, 'Court Dress and Robing Ceremony in Mughal India', J.S. Grewal Award Essay, *Proceedings of the Indian History Congress*, no. 66, 2006.

——, 'From Court Dress to the Symbol of Authority: Robing and "Robes of Honour" in Pre-Colonial India', *Studies in Humanities and Social Science*, vol. 13, no. 2, IIAS, Winter, 2006.

——, 'Mughal Court Rituals: The Symbolism of Imperial Authority', Paper presented at the Indian History Congress, no. 67, 2007.

Shyamal Das, Kaviraj, *Vir Vinod*, 4 vols, Delhi: Motilal Banarsidass, 1966.

Siddiqi, Iqtidar Husain, '*Iqta* System Under the Lodis', *Proceedings of the Indian History Congress*, no. 24, 1961.

——, *Some Aspects of Afghan Despotism in India*, Aligarh: Three Men Publications, 1969.

——, *History of Shershah Sur*, Aligarh: P.C. Dwadash Shreni, 1971.

——, *Modern Writings on Islam in India*, Aligarh: International Book Traders, 1972.

——, *Mughal Relations with the Indian Ruling Elite*, Delhi: Munshiram Manoharlal, 1983.

——, *Perso-Arabic Sources of Information on the Life and Conditions in the Sultanate of Delhi*, Delhi: Munshiram Manoharlal, 1992.

——, *Sher Shah Sur and His Dynasty*, Jaipur: Publication Scheme, 1995.

——, *Medieval India: Essays in Intellectual Thought and Culture*, Delhi: Manohar, 2003.

Siddiqi, Noman Ahmad, *Land Revenue Administration Under the Mughals, 1700-1750*, Bombay: Asia Publishing House, 1970.

——, 'The *Faujdar* and *Faujdari* Under the Mughals', in *The Mughal State, 1526-1750*, ed. Muzaffar Alam and Sanjay Subrahmanyam, Delhi: Oxford University Press, 1998.

Singh, Chetan, 'Centre and Periphery in the Mughal State: The Case of the Seventeenth-Century Panjab', *Modern Asian Studies*, vol. 22, 1988.

——, *Region and Empire: Panjab in the Seventeenth Century*, Delhi: Oxford University Press, 1991.

Singh, Dilbag, 'Some Aspect of *Zamindari* and *Jagirdari* in Eastern Rajasthan', *Proceedings of the Indian History Congress*, no. 31, 1969.

——, *The State, Landlords and Peasants: Rajasthan in the Eighteenth Century*, Delhi: Manohar, 1990.

Singh, M.P., *Town, Market, Mint and Post in the Mughal Empire, 1556-1707*, Delhi: Adam Publishers and Distributors, 1985.

Singh, Mahender Pal, 'Akbar's Resumption of *Jagir*, 1575', *Proceedings of the Indian History Congress*, no. 28, 1966.

Singh, Raghuvir and Manohar Singh Ranawat, *Jodhpur Rajya ki Khyat*, Jaipur: Bhartiya Itihas Anusandhan Parishad (with Pansheel Prakashan), 1988.

Sinha, P.P., *Raja Birbal, Life and Time*, Patna: Janaki Prakashan, 1980.

Sinha, S.P., *Suba of Allahabad Under the Great Mughals*, Delhi: Jamia Millia Islamia, 1974.

Smith, Vincent A., *Akbar the Great Moghul, 1542-1605*, Delhi: S. Chand & Co., 1970.

Smith, W.C., 'The Mughal Empire and the Middle Classes', *Islamic Culture*, 1944.

——, 'Lower Class Uprising in the Mughal Empire', *Islamic Culture*, 1946.

Spear, Percival, *Twilight of the Mughals*, Delhi: Munshiram Manoharlal, 1991.

Srivastva, Ashirabadi Lal, 'Akbar and National Integration', *Journal of Indian History*, no. 40, 1962.

——, 'Some Misconceptions about Akbar the Great', *Journal of Indian History*, no. 42, 1964.

——, *Akbar the Great*, 3 vols, Agra: Shiva Lal Agarwala, 1972.

——, *Medieval Indian Culture*, Agra: Shiva Lal Agarwala, 1975.

Srivastava, M.P., *Social Life Under the Great Mughals, 1526-1700*, Allahabad: Chugh Publications, 1978.

Stein, Burton, *Peasant State and Society in Medieval South India*, Delhi: Oxford University Press, 1980.

——, 'The Segmentary State: Interim Reflections', in *The State in India, 1000-1700*, ed. Hermann Kulke, Delhi: Oxford University Press, 1995.

——, 'Politics, Peasant and the Deconstruction of Feudalism in Medieval India', in *The Feudalism Debate*, ed. Harbans Mukhia, Delhi: Manohar, 2000.

Stewart, Charles, *The History of Bengal: From the First Mohammadan Invasion until the Virtual Conquest of that Country by the English, A.D. 1757*, Delhi: Oriental Publisher, 1971.

Storey, C.A., *Persian Literature—A Bio-bibliographical Survey*, London: Royal Asiatic Society, 1937-39; rpt, Leiden: E.J. Brill, 1977.

Streusand, Douglas E., *The Formation of the Mughal Empire*, Delhi: Oxford University Press, 1989.

Subrahmanyam, Sanjay, 'Aspects of State Formation in South India and South-East Asia, 1550-1650', *The Indian Economic and Social History Review*, vol. 23, 1986.

——, 'The Mughal State-Structure or Process? Reflections on Recent Western Historiography', *The Indian Economic and Social History Review*, vol. 29, no. 3, 1992.

——, ed., *Money and the Market in India, 1100-1700*, Delhi: Oxford University Press, 1994.

Tara Chand, *Influence of Islam on Indian Culture*, Allahabad: Indian Press, 1946.

Tchitcherov, Alexander I., *Economic Structure in the Sixteenth-Eighteenth Centuries*, Delhi: Manohar, 1998.

Thomas, Edward, 'Revenue Resources of the Mughal Empire in India', rpt. in *The Chronicles of the Pathan Kings of Delhi*, Edward Thomas, Delhi: Munshiram Manoharlal, 1967.

Todd, James, *Annals and Antiquities of Rajasthan*, 2 vols, rpt, Delhi: K.M.N. Publishers, 1971.

Trimingham, J. Spencer, *The Sufi Orders in Islam*, New York: Oxford University Press, 1971.

Tripathi, R.P., *Rise and Fall of the Mughal Empire*, rpt, Allahabad: Central Book Depot, 1963.

——, *Some Aspects of Muslim Administration*, rpt, Allahabad: Central Book Depot, 1974.

Trivedi, K.K., 'Area Statistics of the *Suba* Agra in the *Ain-i-Akbari*', *Proceedings of the Indian History Congress*, no. 33, 1972.

——, 'Changes in Caste Composition of the *Zamindar* Class in Western Uttar Pradesh, 1595-1900', *Indian Historical Review*, vol. 2, no. 1, 1975.

——, 'The Share of *Mansabdars* in State Revenue-Resources: A Study of the Maintenance of Animals', *The Indian Economic and Social History Review*, vol. 24, no. 4, 1987.

——, *Agra: Economic and Political Profile of a Mughal Suba, 1580-1707*, Pune: Ravish Publishing, 1998.

Upadhya, Onkar Nath, *Hindu Nobility Under Akbar and Jahangir*, Agra: Y.K. Publishers, 1992.

Verma, Ramesh Chandra, *Foreign Policy of the Great Mughals,1526-1727*, Agra: Shiva Lal Agarwala, 1967.

Viladimirtsov, B.Y., *The Life of Genghis Khan*, tr. D.S. Mirsky, London: Benjamin Blom, 1935.

Wagoner, Philip B., *Tidings of the King: A Translation and Ethnohistorical Analysis of Rayavacakamu*, Honolulu: University of Hawaii Press, 1993.

——, 'Sultan Among Hindu Kings: Dress, Titles and Islamicization of Hindu Culture at Vijayanagara', *The Journal of Asian Studies*, vol. 55, no. 4, 1996.

Wheeler J. Talboys, *India Under the Muslim Rule: Political, Historical and Social Integration*, 2 vols, Delhi: Cosmo Publication, 1975.

Williams, L.F. Rushbrook, *An Empire Builders of the Sixteenth Century*, Delhi: S. Chand & Co., 1978.

Wilson, H.H., *A Glossary of Judicial and Revenue Terms*, Delhi: Munshiram Manoharlal, 1968.

Wink, Andre, 'Sovereignty and Universal Dominion in South Asia', *The Indian Economic and Social History Review*, vol. 21, 1984.

——, *Land and Sovereignty in India: Agrarian Society and Politics Under the Eighteenth Century Maratha*, Cambridge: Cambridge University Press, 1986.

Wittfogel, Karl, *Oriental Despotism: A Comparative Study of Total Power*, New Haven: Yale University Press, 1957.

Yadava, Narain Singh, *Hindu Nobility Under Akbar*, Delhi: University of Delhi, 1973.

Yasin, Mohammad, 'Akbar and Indian Nationalism', *Journal of Indian History*, 1960.

Yasin, Mohammad, *A Social History of Islamic India, 1605-1748*, Delhi: Munshiram Manoharlal, 1974.

Yezdi, Sharafudin Ali, *Political and Military Institutes of Tamerlane*, tr. Major Davy, Delhi: Idarah-i-Adabiyat-i-Delhi, 1972.

Zaidi, S. Inayat Ali, 'The Pattern of Matrimonial Ties between the Kachhwaha Clan and the Mughal Ruling Family', *Proceedings of the Indian History Congress*, no. 35, 1974.

——, 'The Origin of the Institution of *Watan Jagir*', *The Quarterly Review of Historical Studies*, no. 4, 1980-1.

——, 'Fads and Foibles: Perception of Administrative Traits of the Mughal State', *The Indian Historical Review*, vol. 29, nos. 1-2, 2002.

Zaidi, Sunita, 'The Mughals and the Rajput Chiefs', in *Mughal India* I, ed. Mohamed Taher, Delhi: Anmol Publishing House, 1997.

Zaman, M.K., *Mughal Artillery*, Delhi: Idarah-i Adabiyat-i-Delhi, 1983.

Zareen, Fauzia Abbaś, *Abdul Qadir Badauni—As a Man and Historiographer*, Delhi: Idarah-i-Adabiyat-i-Delhi, 1987.

Ziegler, Norman P., 'Some Notes on Rajput Loyalties During the Mughal Period', in *The Mughal Empire*, ed. Muzaffar Alam and Sanjay Subrahmanyam, Delhi: Oxford University Press, 1998.

Index